Chartered Institute for Securities & Investment Level 4 Investm

CW00953732

# STUDY TEXT

## Securities

Syllabus version 2

**In this December 2011 edition**

- A **user-friendly format** for easy navigation
- **Exam tips** to put you on the right track
- **Up-to-date material**, covering the **new syllabus** in full
- A **Test your Knowledge** quiz at the end of each chapter
- A full **Index**

APPROVED WORKBOOK

BPP LEARNING MEDIA

Published December 2011

ISBN 978 1 4453 7830 5

British Library Cataloguing-in-Publication Data
A catalogue record for this book
is available from the British Library

Published by

BPP Learning Media Ltd
BPP House, Aldine Place
London W12 8AA

www.bpp.com/learningmedia

Printed in Great Britain

Your learning materials, published by BPP Learning Media Ltd, are printed on paper sourced from sustainable, managed forests.

© BPP Learning Media Ltd

All our rights reserved. No part of this publication may be reproduced, stored in a retrieval system or transmitted, in any form or by any means, electronic, mechanical, photocopying, recording or otherwise, without the prior written permission of BPP Learning Media Ltd. The descriptions, examples and calculations shown in this publication are for educational purposes only. No liability can be accepted by BPP Learning Media Ltd for their use in any circumstances connected with actual trading activity or otherwise. Readers should seek specific advice for specific situations.

**A note about copyright**

Dear Customer

What does the little © mean and why does it matter?

Your market-leading BPP books, course materials and e-learning materials do not write and update themselves. People write them: on their own behalf or as employees of an organisation that invests in this activity. Copyright law protects their livelihoods. It does so by creating rights over the use of the content.

Breach of copyright is a form of theft – as well as being a criminal offence in some jurisdictions, it is potentially a serious breach of professional ethics.

With current technology, things might seem a bit hazy but, basically, without the express permission of BPP Learning Media:

- Photocopying our materials is a breach of copyright
- Scanning, ripcasting or conversion of our digital materials into different file formats, uploading them to facebook or e-mailing them to your friends is a breach of copyright

You can, of course, sell your books, in the form in which you have bought them – once you have finished with them (Is this fair to your fellow students? We update for a reason). But the e-products are sold on a single user license basis: we do not supply 'unlock' codes to people who have bought them secondhand.

And what about outside the UK? BPP Learning Media strives to make our materials available at prices students can afford by local printing arrangements, pricing policies and partnerships which are clearly listed on our website. A tiny minority ignore this and indulge in criminal activity by illegally photocopying our material or supporting organisations that do. If they act illegally and unethically in one area, can you really trust them?

# CONTENTS

# SECURITIES SYLLABUS

The Study Text references in the right-hand column below indicates the chapter and section in which each learning objective is covered. For example, learning objective 1.1.3 is covered in Chapter 1 Section 1.7.

| Syllabus Item | BPP Ref Chapter – Section |
|---|---|
| **1 Fixed Income Securities** | |
| **1.1 Characteristics of Sovereign and Government Bonds** | |
| 1.1.1 Understand the main issuers of government debt and the main investment characteristics, behaviours and risks of the major government bond classes:<br>– Supranationals<br>– Sovereign governments<br>– Public authorities: local government / municipalities<br>– Short, medium and long dated<br>– Dual dated<br>– Undated<br>– Floating rate<br>– Zero coupon | 1 – 1 |
| 1.1.2 Understand the relationship between interest rates and government bond prices:<br>– Yield<br>– Interest payable<br>– Accrued interest (clean and dirty prices)<br>– Effect of change in interest rates | 1 – 2 |
| 1.1.3 Understand the main investment characteristics, behaviours and risk of index-linked debt:<br>– Retail Price Index as a measure of inflation<br>– Process of Index Linking<br>– Indexing effects on price, interest and redemption<br>– Return during a period of zero inflation | 1– 1.7 |
| **1.2 Characteristics of Corporate Debt** | |
| 1.2.1 Understand the main issuers of corporate debt and the main investment characteristics, behaviours and risks of secured debt:<br>– Corporates<br>– Financial Institutions and special purpose vehicles<br>– Fixed and floating charges<br>– Debentures<br>– Types of asset backed securities<br>– Mortgage backed securities<br>– Securitization process | 1 – 7 |


BPP LEARNING MEDIA

| Syllabus Item | BPP Ref Chapter – Section |
|---|---|
| – Yield to maturity<br>– Roles of participants<br>1.2.2 Understand the main investment characteristics, behaviours and risks of the main types of unsecured debt:<br>– Income bonds<br>– Subordinated<br>– High yield<br>– Convertible bonds<br>– Rating | 1 – 7.3 |
| **1.3 Characteristics of Eurobonds**<br>1.3.1 Understand the main investment characteristics, behaviours and risks of Eurobonds:<br>– Types of issuer: sovereign, supranational and corporate<br>– Types of Eurobond: straight, FRN/ VRN, subordinated, asset backed, convertible<br>– International bank syndicate issuance<br>– Immobilization in depositories<br>– Continuous pure bearer instrument: implications for interest & capital repayment<br>– Taxation of interest and capital gains<br>– Accrued interest, ex-interest date | 1 – 7.6 |
| **1.4 Issuing Fixed Income Securities**<br>1.4.1 Understand the responsibilities and processes of the UK Debt Management Office in relation to the management and issue of UK Government debt:<br>– Gilts<br>– Treasury Bills<br>– Public Works Loan Board<br>– Primary market makers: Gilt Edged Market Makers (GEMMs)<br>– Intermediaries: Inter-Dealer Brokers (IDBs) | 1 – 8 |
| 1.4.2 Understand the main bond pricing benchmarks and how they are applied to new bond issues:<br>– Spread over government bond benchmark<br>– Spread over/under LIBOR<br>– Spread over/under swap | 1 – 7.5 |
| 1.4.3 Understand the purpose, structure and process of the main methods of origination, issuance and their implications for issuers and investors:<br>– Scheduled funding programmes and opportunistic issuance (e.g. MTN)<br>– Auction/tender<br>– Reverse inquiry (under MTN) | 1 – 9 |

| Syllabus Item | BPP Ref Chapter – Section |
|---|---|
| **1.5 Fixed income markets and trade execution** | |
| 1.5.1 Understand the role, structure and characteristics of government bond markets in the developed markets of UK, Germany, USA and Japan, and the emerging economies of Brazil, China, India and Russia (BRIC) including:<br>– Market environment: relative importance of Exchange vs. OTC trading<br>– Participants – primary dealers, broker dealers and inter-dealer brokers<br>– The impact of ratings and the concept of 'risk free'<br>– Currency, credit and inflation risks<br>– Inflation indexed bonds<br>– Access considerations<br>– Regulatory/ supervisory environment<br>– Relevant trade associations | 1 – 10 |
| 1.5.2 Understand the purpose and key features of the global strip market:<br>– Result of stripping a bond<br>– Number of securities possible from a strippable bond<br>– Zero coupon securities<br>– Access considerations | 1 – 1.8 |
| 1.5.3 Understand the role, structure and characteristics of global corporate bond markets:<br>– Decentralized dealer markets and dealer provision of liquidity<br>– Impact of default risk on prices<br>– Relationship between bond and equity markets<br>– Bond pools of liquidity versus centralized equity exchanges<br>– Access considerations<br>– Regulatory/ supervisory environment<br>– ICMA and other relevant trade associations | 1 – 10.6 |
| 1.5.4 Understand the key features of bond markets | 1 – 10.7 |
| 1.5.5 Understand the differences in yield, spread and price quotation methods, and the circumstances in which they are used | 1 – 7.5 |
| **1.6 Valuation of Fixed Income Securities** | |
| 1.6.1 Understand the purpose, influence and limitations of global credit rating agencies, debt seniority and ranking in cases of default/ bankruptcy:<br>– Senior<br>– Subordinated<br>– Mezzanine<br>– PIK (Payment in Kind) | 1 – 11 |

| Syllabus Item | BPP Ref Chapter – Section |
|---|---|
| 1.6.2 Analyse sovereign, government and corporate credit ratings from an investment perspective:<br>– Main rating agencies<br>– Country rating factors<br>– Debt instrument rating factors<br>– Investment & sub-investment grades<br>– Use of credit enhancements<br>– Impact of grading changes on price | 1 – 11 |
| 1.6.3 Analyse the factors that influence bond pricing:<br>– Yield to maturity<br>– Credit rating<br>– Impact of interest rates<br>– Market Liquidity | 1 – 2 |
| 1.6.4 Analyse fixed income securities using the following valuation measures, and understand the benefits and limitations of using them:<br>– Flat yield<br>– Nominal and real return<br>– Gross redemption yield (using internal rate of return)<br>– Net redemption yield<br>– Modified duration | 1 – 2 |
| 1.6.5 Analyse the specific features of bonds from an investment perspective:<br>– Coupon and payment date<br>– Maturity date<br>– Embedded put or call options<br>– Convertibility<br>– Exchangeable bonds | 1 – 7.3.7 |
| 1.6.6 Calculate and interpret:<br>– Simple interest income on corporate debt<br>– Conversion premiums on convertible bonds<br>– Flat yield<br>– Accrued interest (given details of the day count conventions) | 1 – 2, 1 – 7.3 |
| **2 Cash, Money Markets and the Foreign Exchange Market** | |
| **2.1 Cash Instruments and Markets** | |
| 2.1.1 Analyse the main investment characteristics, behaviours and risks of cash deposit accounts:<br>– Deposit taking institutions and credit risk assessment<br>– Term, notice, liquidity and access<br>– Fixed and variable rates of interest<br>– Inflation<br>– Statutory protection<br>– Foreign currency deposits | 2 – 2 |

| Syllabus Item | BPP Ref Chapter – Section |
|---|---|
| 2.1.2 Analyse the main investment characteristics, behaviours and risks of Treasury Bills:<br>– Purpose & method of issue<br>– Minimum denomination<br>– Normal life<br>– Zero coupon and redemption at par<br>– Redemption<br>– Market access, trading and settlement | 2 – 2.6 |
| 2.1.3 Analyse the main investment characteristics, behaviours and risks of Commercial Paper:<br>– Purpose & method of issue<br>– Maturity<br>– Discounted security<br>– Unsecured and secured<br>– Asset backed<br>– Credit rating<br>– Role of dealer<br>– Market access, trading and settlement | 2 – 2.7 |
| 2.1.4 Analyse the main investment characteristics, behaviours and risks of Repurchase Agreements:<br>– Purpose<br>– Sale and repurchase at agreed price, rate and date<br>– Reverse repo – purchase and resale at agreed price and date<br>– Documentation | 2 – 2.8 |
| 2.1.5 Analyse the main characteristics, risks and returns of money market funds<br>– Cash assets only<br>– Near cash assets<br>– Pricing, liquidity and fair value<br>– Market access, trading and settlement | 2 – 2.5 |
| 2.1.6 Analyse the factors to take into account when selecting between different types of cash deposits, accounts and money market funds | 2 – 2.5 |
| **2.2 Foreign Exchange Instruments and Markets** | |
| 2.2.1 Understand the role, structure and main characteristics of the foreign exchange market:<br>– OTC market<br>– Quotes, spreads and exchange rate information<br>– Market participants and access to markets<br>– Volume, volatility and liquidity<br>– Risk mitigation: rollovers and stop losses<br>– Regulatory/ supervisory environment | 2 – 3 |

| Syllabus Item | BPP Ref Chapter – Section |
|---|---|
| 2.2.2 Understand the determinants of spot foreign exchange prices:<br>– Currency demand – transactional and speculative<br>– Economic variables<br>– Cross- border trading of financial assets<br>– Interest rates<br>– Free and pegged rates | 2 – 3.2 |
| 2.2.3 Calculate forward foreign exchange rates using:<br>– Premiums and discounts<br>– Interest rate parity | 2 – 3.5 |
| 2.2.4 Analyse how foreign exchange contracts can be used to buy or sell currency relating to overseas investments, or to hedge non- domestic currency exposure:<br>– Spot contracts<br>– Forward contracts<br>– Currency futures<br>– Currency options | 2 – 3.8 |
| **3 Equities** | |
| **3.1 Characteristics of Equities** | |
| 3.1.1 Understand the main investment characteristics, behaviours and risks of different classes of equity:<br>– Ordinary cumulative, participating, redeemable and convertible preference shares, bearer and registered shares<br>– Voting rights, voting and non-voting shares<br>– Ranking for dividends<br>– Ranking in liquidation<br>– Tax treatment of capital gains and dividend income | 3 – 1 |
| 3.1.2 Understand the purpose, main investment characteristics, behaviours and risks of Depositary Receipts:<br>– American Depositary Receipts<br>– Global Depositary Receipts<br>– Beneficial ownership rights<br>– Unsponsored & sponsored programmes<br>– Transferability<br>– Dividend payments | 3 – 1.7 |
| **3.2 Issuing Equity Securities** | |
| 3.2.1 Understand the purpose, key features and differences between the following:<br>– Primary issues<br>– Secondary issues<br>– Issuing, listing & quotation<br>– Dual listings | 3 – 2 |

| Syllabus Item | | BPP Ref Chapter – Section |
|---|---|---|
| 3.2.2 | Understand the main regulatory, supervisory and trade body framework supporting UK financial markets:<br>– Companies Acts<br>– The Financial Services Authority (FSA) and UK Listing Authority (UKLA)<br>– HM Treasury<br>– The Panel on Takeovers and Mergers (POTEM)<br>– Exchange membership and rules<br>– Relevant trade associations and professional bodies | 3 – 3 |
| 3.2.3 | Understand the structure of the London Stock Exchange, the types of securities traded on its markets, and the criteria and processes for companies seeking admission:<br>– Main Market<br>– AIM<br>– PLUS markets<br>– Market participants<br>– Implications for investors | 3 – 2.2 |
| 3.2.4 | Understand the process of issuing securities in the UK without a prospectus:<br>– Principles of exemption established under the Prospectus Directive (PD)<br>– Purpose of the FSA Qualified Investor Register (QIR)<br>– Eligibility and registration criteria for Natural Persons and SMEs<br>– Terms of access for issuers seeking to use the Qualified Investor Register | 3 – 5 |
| 3.2.5 | Understand the purpose, structure and stages of an initial public offering (IPO) and the role of the origination team:<br>– Benefits for the issuer and investors<br>– Structure: base deal plus Greenshoe<br>– Stages of an IPO<br>– Underwritten versus best efforts<br>– Principles and process of price stabilisation | 3 – 6 |
| **3.3** | **Equity Markets and Trade Execution** | |
| 3.3.1 | Apply fundamental UK regulatory requirements with regard to trade execution and reporting:<br>– Best Execution<br>– Aggregation and allocation<br>– Prohibition of conflicts of interests and front running | 3 – 7 |

| Syllabus Item | BPP Ref Chapter – Section |
|---|---|
| 3.3.2 Understand the key features of the main trading venues:<br>– Regulated and Designated Investment Exchanges<br>– Recognised Overseas Investment Exchanges<br>– Structure and size of markets<br>– Whether quote or order driven<br>– Main types of order – limit, market, iceberg, named<br>– Liquidity and transparency<br>– Participants | 3 – 4.2, 3 – 7 |
| 3.3.3 Understand the key features of alternative trading venues:<br>– Multilateral Trading Facilities (MTFs)<br>– Systematic Internalisers<br>– Dark Pools | 3 – 7.7 |
| 3.3.4 Understand the concepts of trading cum, ex, special cum and special ex:<br>– The meaning of 'books closed', 'ex-div' and 'cum div', cum, special ex, special cum, and ex rights<br>– Effect of late registration | 3 – 10 |
| 3.3.5 Apply knowledge of key differences in the developed markets of UK, Germany, USA and Japan, and emerging markets of Brazil, China, India and Russia (BRIC), both on and off exchange:<br>– Regulatory and supervisory environment<br>– Structure and size of markets<br>– Liquidity and transparency<br>– Access and relative cost of trading | 3 – 9 |
| 3.3.6 Assess how the following factors influence equity markets and equity valuation:<br>– Trading volume and liquidity of domestic and international securities markets<br>– Relationship between cash and derivatives markets, and the effect of timed events<br>– Market consensus and analyst opinion<br>– Changes to key pricing determinants such as credit ratings and economic outlook | 3 – 11 |
| 3.3.7 Understand the purpose, construction, application and influence of indices on equity markets:<br>– Developed and emerging market regional & country sectors<br>– Market capitalization sub sectors<br>– Free float and full market capitalization indices<br>– Fair value adjusted indices | 3 – 11 |

| Syllabus Item | BPP Ref Chapter – Section |
|---|---|
| **3.4 Warrants and Contracts for Difference** | |
| 3.4.1 Analyse the main purposes, characteristics, behaviours and relative risk and return of warrants and covered warrants:<br>– Benefit to the issuing company<br>– Right to subscribe for capital<br>– Effect on price of maturity and the underlying security<br>– Exercise and expiry<br>– Calculation of the conversion premium on a warrant | 3 – 1.4 |
| 3.4.2 Analyse the key features of the main types of Contracts for Difference (CFDs), compared with other forms of direct and indirect investment:<br>– Types and availability of CFDs<br>– Differences in pricing, valuing and trading CFDs compared to direct investment<br>– CFD providers – market maker versus direct market access<br>– Tax efficiency<br>– Margin<br>– Market, liquidation & counterparty risks<br>– Size of CFD market and impact on total market activity | 3 – 1.8 |
| **4 Settlement, Safe Custody and Prime Brokerage** | |
| **4.1 Clearing, Settlement and Safe Custody** | |
| 4.1.1 Understand how fixed income, equity, money market and foreign exchange transactions are cleared and settled in the UK, Germany, USA and Japan:<br>– Principles of Delivery versus Payment (DVP) and Free Delivery<br>– Trade confirmation process<br>– Settlement periods<br>– International Central Securities Depositories (ICSD) - Euroclear & Clearstream International<br>– Exchanges | 4 – 1.1 |
| 4.1.2 Understand how settlement risk arises, its impact on trading and the investment process, and how it can be mitigated:<br>– Underlying risks: default, credit and liquidity<br>– Relative likelihood of settlement- based risks in developed and emerging markets<br>– Effect of DVP and Straight through Process (STP) automated systems<br>– Risk mitigation within markets and firms<br>– Continuous Linked Settlement | 4 – 2 |
| 4.1.3 Understand which transactions may be subject to or exempt from UK stamp duty/SDRT | 4 – 6 |

| Syllabus Item | BPP Ref Chapter – Section |
|---|---|
| 4.1.4 Understand the principles of safe custody, the roles of the different types of custodian, and how client assets are protected:<br>– Global<br>– Regional<br>– Local<br>– Sub custodians<br>– Clearing & settlement agents | 4 – 3 |
| 4.1.5 Understand the implications of registered title for certified and uncertified holdings:<br>– Registered title versus unregistered (bearer)<br>– Legal title<br>– Beneficial interest<br>– Right to participate in corporate actions | 4 – 4 |
| 4.1.6 Understand the function of nominees:<br>– Designated nominee accounts<br>– Pooled nominee accounts<br>– Corporate nominees<br>– Details in share register<br>– Legal ownership<br>– Effect on shareholder rights of using a nominee | 4 – 5 |
| **4.2 Prime brokerage and equity finance** | |
| 4.2.1 Understand the purpose, requirements and implications of securities lending:<br>– Benefits and risks for borrowers and lenders<br>– Function of market makers, intermediaries and custodians<br>– Effect on the lender's rights<br>– Effect on corporate action activity<br>– Collateral | 4 – 7 |
| 4.2.2 Understand the purpose and main types of Prime Broker equity finance services and their impact on securities markets:<br>– Securities lending and borrowing<br>– Leverage trade execution<br>– Cash management<br>– Core settlement<br>– Custody<br>– Rehypothecation<br>– Repurchase agreements<br>– Collateralized borrowing<br>– Tri-party repos<br>– Synthetic financing | 4 – 8 |

| Syllabus Item | BPP Ref Chapter – Section |
|---|---|
| **5 Securities Analysis** | |
| **5.1 Financial Statement Analysis** | |
| 5.1.1 Understand the purpose, structure and relevance to investors of balance sheets. | 5 – 1 |
| 5.1.2 Understand the purpose, structure and relevance to investors of income statements. | 5 – 1.4 |
| 5.1.3 Understand the purpose, structure and relevance to investors of cash flow statements. | 5 – 1.5 |
| 5.1.4 Analyse securities using the following financial ratios:<br>– Liquidity<br>– Asset turnover<br>– Gearing<br>– Profitability<br>– Dividend policy | 5 – 2.2 |
| 5.1.5 Analyse securities using the following profitability ratios:<br>– Net profit margin<br>– Equity multiplier<br>– Return on Capital Employed | 5 – 2.2 |
| 5.1.6 Analyse securities using the following investor ratios:<br>– Earnings per share<br>– Price / Earnings (both historic and prospective)<br>– Net dividend yield<br>– Net dividend / interest cover | 5 – 2.9 |
| 5.1.7 Understand the main advantages and challenges of performing financial analysis:<br>– Comparing companies in different countries and sectors<br>– Comparing different companies within the same sector<br>– Over-reliance on historical information<br>– Benefits and limitations of relying on third party research | 5 – 2.17 |
| **5.2 Accounting for Corporate Actions** | |
| 5.2.1 Understand the purpose and structure of corporate actions and their implications for investors:<br>– Stock capitalization or consolidation<br>– Stock and cash dividends<br>– Rights issues<br>– Open offers, offers for subscription and offers for sale<br>– Placings | 5 – 3 |
| 5.2.2 Calculate the theoretical effect on the issuer's share price of the following mandatory and optional corporate actions:<br>– Bonus/scrip<br>– Consolidation<br>– Rights issues | 5 – 3 |

| Syllabus Item | BPP Ref Chapter – Section |
|---|---|
| 5.2.3 Analyse the following in respect of corporate actions:<br>– Rationale offered by the company<br>– Understand the dilution effect on profitability and reported financials | 5 – 3 |
| **6 Collective Investments** | |
| **6.1 Characteristics of Collective Investment Funds and Companies** | |
| 6.1.1 Analyse the key features, accessibility, risks, tax treatment, charges, valuation and yield characteristics of open-ended investment companies (OEICs) / investment companies with variable capital (ICVCs). | 6 – 1 |
| 6.1.2 Analyse the key features, accessibility, risks, tax treatment, charges, valuation and yield characteristics of unit trusts. | 6 – 2 |
| 6.1.3 Analyse the key features, accessibility, risks, tax treatment, charges, valuation and yield characteristics of investment trusts. | 6 – 3 |
| 6.1.4 Analyse the key features, accessibility, risks, tax treatment, charges, valuation and yield characteristics of real estate investment trusts (REITs). | 6 –6 |
| **6.2 Exchange-Traded Funds** | |
| 6.2.1 Analyse the key features, accessibility, risks, tax treatment, charges, valuation and yield characteristics of the main types of Exchange Traded Funds (ETFs) | 6 – 7 |
| **6.3 Structured Products** | |
| 6.3.1 Analyse the key features, accessibility, risks, valuation and yield characteristics of the main types of retail structured products and investment notes, compared with other forms of direct and indirect investment:<br>– Structure<br>– Income and capital growth<br>– Investment risk and return<br>– Counterparty risk<br>– Expenses<br>– Capital protection<br>– Tax efficiency | 6 – 8 |
| **6.4 Analysis of Collective Investments** | |
| 6.4.1 Analyse the factors to take into account when selecting collective investments:<br>– Quality of firm, management team, product track record and administration<br>– Investment mandate – scope, controls, restrictions and review process<br>– Investment strategy<br>– Exposure, allocation, valuation and quality of holdings<br>– Prospects for capital growth and income<br>– Asset cover and redemption yield | 6 – 9 |

| Syllabus Item | BPP Ref Chapter – Section |
|---|---|
| – Track record compared with appropriate peer universe and market indices<br>– Location/ domicile/ Passporting arrangements<br>– Tax treatment<br>– Key man risk (KMR) and how this is managed by a firm<br>– Shareholder base<br>– Measures to prevent price exploitation by dominant investors<br>– Total expense and turnover ratios<br>– Liquidity, trading access and price stability | |
| **7 Portfolio Construction** | |
| **7.1 Market Information and Research** | |
| 7.1.1 Understand how to access and use regulatory, economic and financial communications:<br>– News services<br>– Government resources and statistics<br>– Broker research and distributor information<br>– Regulatory resources where relevant | 7 – 1 |
| 7.1.2 Understand the different types, uses and availability of research and reports:<br>– Fundamental analysis<br>– Technical analysis<br>– Fund analysis<br>– Fund rating agencies and screening software<br>– Broker and distributor reports<br>– Sector-specific reports | 7 – 1.5 |
| 7.1.3 Assess key factors that influence markets and sectors:<br>– Responses to change and uncertainty<br>– Volume, liquidity, and nature of trading activity in domestic and overseas markets<br>– Market abuse regime – enforcement and effectiveness<br>– Publication of announcements, research and ratings | 7 – 1.8 |
| 7.1.4 Assess the interactive relationship between the securities and derivatives markets, and the impact of related events on markets | 7 - 7 |
| 7.1.5 Assess the interactive relationship between different forms of fixed interest securities and the impact of related events on markets | 7 – 7.6 |
| **7.2 Portfolio Construction** | |
| 7.2.1 Understand the main types of portfolio risk and their implications for investors:<br>– Systemic risk<br>– Market risk – asset price volatility, currency, interest rates, commodity price volatility<br>– Investment horizon | 7 – 6 |

| Syllabus Item | | BPP Ref Chapter – Section |
|---|---|---|
| | – Liquidity, credit risk and default<br>– Counterparty risk | |
| 7.2.2 | Understand the core principles used to mitigate portfolio risk:<br>– Correlation<br>– Diversification<br>– Active and passive strategies<br>– Hedging and immunization | 7 – 6 |
| 7.2.3 | Understand the key approaches to investment allocation for bond, equity and balanced portfolios:<br>– Asset class<br>– Geographical area<br>– Currency<br>– Issuer<br>– Sector<br>– Maturity | 7 – 4 |
| 7.2.4 | Understand the main aims and investment characteristics of the main cash, bond and equity portfolio management strategies and styles:<br>– Indexing/ passive management<br>– Active/ market timing<br>– Passive-active combinations<br>– Growth versus Income<br>– Market capitalization<br>– Liability driven (LDI)<br>– Immunization<br>– Long, short and leveraged<br>– Issuer and sector-specific<br>– Contrarian<br>– Quantitative | 7 – 5 |
| 7.2.5 | Understand how portfolio risk and return are evaluated using the following measures:<br>– Holding period return<br>– Total return and its components<br>– Standard deviation<br>– Volatility<br>– Covariance and correlation<br>– Risk- adjusted returns<br>– Benchmarking | 7 – 6 |

| Syllabus Item | BPP Ref Chapter – Section |
|---|---|
| **8 Investment Selection and Administration** | |
| **8.1 Investment Selection** | |
| 8.1.1 Apply a range of essential information and factors to form the basis of appropriate financial planning and advice for clients:<br>– Financial needs, preferences and expectations<br>– Income and lifestyle – current and anticipated<br>– Attitude to risk<br>– Level of knowledge about investments<br>– Existing debts and investments | 8 – 1 |
| 8.1.2 Analyse and select strategies suitable for the client's aims and objectives in terms of:<br>– Investment horizon<br>– Current and future potential for capital protection, growth and yield<br>– Protection against inflation<br>– Risk tolerance<br>– Liquidity, trading and ongoing management<br>– Mandatory or voluntary investment restrictions<br>– Impact of tax<br>– Impact of fees and charges | 8 – 2 |
| 8.1.3 Analyse and select investments suitable for a particular portfolio strategy:<br>– Direct holdings, indirect holdings and combinations<br>– Role of derivatives<br>– Impact on client objectives and priorities<br>– Balance of investments | 8 – 3 |
| **8.2 Administration and Maintenance** | |
| 8.2.1 Apply key elements involved in managing a client portfolio:<br>– Systematic and compliant approach to client portfolio monitoring, review, reporting and management<br>– Selection of appropriate benchmarks to include market and specialist indices, total return and maximum drawdown<br>– Arrangements for client communication | 8 – 5 |
| 8.2.2 Apply measures to address changes that can affect a client portfolio:<br>– Client circumstances<br>– Financial environment<br>– New products and services available<br>– Administrative changes or difficulties<br>– Investment-related changes (e.g. credit rating, corporate actions)<br>– Portfolio rebalancing<br>– Benchmark review | 8 – 5.1.5 |

# 1 Fixed Income Securities

## INTRODUCTION

There are many different types of fixed income securities, including government and corporate bonds. Government bonds issued by the UK government are known as gilts and are issued to finance the government's expenditure over and above receipts from taxation.

Discounted cash flow techniques are central to identifying the value and interest rate risk of a bond.

To ensure that investors pay the correct amount of tax there is a system for calculating interest that has accrued within a bond's value.

Yield calculations identify expected returns from investing into bonds. The flat yield measures income return and the gross redemption yield measures the total return. Gross redemption yields for a particular issuers different maturity bonds may be plotted onto a graph to form a yield curve.

Corporate bonds may be secured or unsecured against the assets of the firm. Bonds which are unsecured will be required to offer a high return to investors to compensate them for the additional risk.

### CHAPTER CONTENTS

# CHAPTER LEARNING OBJECTIVES

## Fixed Income Securities

### 1.1 Characteristics of Sovereign and Government Bonds

**1.1.1** **Understand** the main issuers of government debt and the main investment characteristics, behaviours and risks of the major government bond classes:

- Supranationals
- Sovereign governments
- Public authorities: local government/municipalities
- Short, medium and long dated
- Dual dated
- Undated
- Floating rate
- Zero coupon

**1.1.2** **Understand** the relationship between interest rates and government bond prices:

- Yield
- Interest payable
- Accrued interest (clean and dirty prices)
- Effect of changes in interest rates

**1.1.3** **Understand** the main investment characteristics, behaviours and risks of index- linked debt:

- Retail Price Index as a measure of inflation
- Process of Index Linking
- Indexing effects on price, interest and redemption
- Return during a period of zero inflation

### 1.2 Characteristics of Corporate Debt

**1.2.1** **Understand** the main issuers of corporate debt and the main investment characteristics, behaviours and risks of secured debt:

- Corporates
- Financial institutions and special purpose vehicles
- Fixed and floating charges
- Debentures
- Types of asset backed securities
- Mortgage backed securities
- Securitization process
- Yield to maturity
- Roles of participants

**1.2.2** **Understand** the main investment characteristics, behaviours and risks of the main types of unsecured debt:

- Income bonds
- Subordinated
- High yield

- Convertible bonds
- Rating

## 1.3 Characteristics of Eurobonds

**1.3.1 Understand** the main investment characteristics, behaviours and risks of Eurobonds:

- Types of issuer: sovereign, supranational and corporate
- Types of Eurobond: straight, FRN/ VRN, subordinated, asset backed, convertible
- International bank syndicate issuance
- Immobilization in depositories
- Continuous pure bearer instrument: implications for interest & capital repayment
- Taxation of interest and capital gains
- Accrued interest, ex-interest date

## 1.4 Issuing Fixed Income Securities

**1.4.1 Understand** the responsibilities and processes of the UK Debt Management Office in relation to the management and issue of UK Government debt:

- Gilts
- Treasury Bills
- Public Works Loan Board
- Primary market makers: Gilt Edged Market Makers (GEMMs)
- Intermediaries: Inter-Dealer Brokers (IDBs)

**1.4.2 Understand** the main bond pricing benchmarks and how they are applied to new bond issues:

- Spread over government bond benchmark
- Spread over/under LIBOR
- Spread over/under swap

**1.4.3 Understand** the purpose, structure and process of the main methods of origination, issuance and their implications for issuers and investors:

- Scheduled funding programmes and opportunistic issuance (e.g. MTN)
- Auction/tender
- Reverse inquiry (under MTN)

## 1.5 Fixed Income Markets and Trade Execution

**1.5.1 Understand** the role, structure and characteristics of government bond markets in the developed markets of UK, Germany, USA and Japan, and the emerging economies of Brazil, China, India and Russia (BRIC) including:

- Market environment: relative importance of Exchange vs. OTC trading
- Participants – primary dealers, broker dealers and inter-dealer brokers
- The impact of ratings and the concept of 'risk free'
- Currency, credit and inflation risks
- Inflation indexed bonds
- Access considerations
- Regulatory/ supervisory environment
- Relevant trade associations

**1.5.2** **Understand** the purpose and key features of the global strip market

- Result of stripping a bond
- Number of securities possible from a strippable bond
- Zero coupon securities
- Access considerations

**1.5.3** **Understand** the role, structure and characteristics of global corporate bond markets:

- Decentralized dealer markets and dealer provision of liquidity
- Impact of default risk on prices
- Relationship between bond and equity markets
- Bond pools of liquidity versus centralized equity exchanges
- Access considerations
- Regulatory/ supervisory environment
- ICMA and other relevant trade associations

**1.5.4** **Understand** the key features of bond markets

**1.5.5** **Understand** the differences in yield, spread and price quotation methods, and the circumstances in which they are used

## 1.6 Valuation of Fixed Income Securities

**1.6.1** **Understand** the purpose, influence and limitations of global credit rating agencies, debt seniority and ranking in cases of default/ bankruptcy:

- Senior
- Subordinated
- Mezzanine
- PIK (Payment in Kind)

**1.6.2** **Analyse** sovereign, government and corporate credit ratings from an investment perspective:

- Main rating agencies
- Country rating factors
- Debt instrument rating factors
- Investment & sub-investment grades
- Use of credit enhancements
- Impact of grading changes on price

**1.6.3** **Analyse** the factors that influence bond pricing:

- Yield to maturity
- Credit rating
- Impact of interest rates
- Market Liquidity

**1.6.4** **Analyse** fixed income securities using the following valuation measures, and understand the benefits and limitations of using them:

- Flat yield
- Nominal and real return
- Gross redemption yield (using internal rate of return)
- Net redemption yield
- Modified duration

**1.6.5 Analyse** the specific features of bonds from an investment perspective:

- Coupon and payment date
- Maturity date
- Embedded put or call options
- Convertibility
- Exchangeable bonds

**1.6.6 Calculate** and interpret:

- Simple interest income on corporate debt
- Conversion premiums on convertible bonds
- Flat yield
- Accrued interest (given details of the day count conventions)

## Debt Instruments: Bonds

A bond may be defined as a negotiable debt instrument for a fixed principal amount issued by a borrower for a specific time, making a regular payment of interest/coupon to the holder until it is redeemed at maturity, when the principal amount is repaid. This is an example of a straight bond.

Bonds have emerged over the past few decades into being much more complex investments, and there are now a significant number of variations on the basic theme.

Whilst it is perhaps easy to be confused by the variety of 'bells and whistles' that have been introduced into the market in recent years, one should always bear in mind that the vast majority of issues are still straight bonds. The reason for this is that investors are wary of buying instruments they do not fully understand. If an issue is too complex, it will be difficult to market. The need to borrow means that bonds are issued by many different issuers including national governments, local authorities and supranational institutions such as the World Bank.

# 1 Sovereign and Government Bonds

**Learning objective**

**1.1.1** **Understand** the main issuers of government debt and the main investment characteristics, behaviour and risks of the major government bond classes: supranational, sovereign governments, public authorities: local government / municipalities, short, medium and long dated, dual dated, undated, floating rate, and zero coupon.

## 1.1 The PSNCR and UK government debt management

Governments, as a rule, spend more money in a year than they raise in revenue. As a consequence, they are obliged to borrow money to cover this deficit. This is generally known as the **Public Sector Net Cash Requirement (PSNCR)**.

(In the UK it is an agency of HM Treasury, the DMO, whose prime responsibility is to borrow money to finance the PSNCR. The **DMO** will borrow money in the short term through issuing **Treasury bills**, and in the long term through the issuance of **Government bonds** (Gilts in the UK).

## 1.2 Characteristic of UK Government bonds

A government bond is simply an **acknowledgement of debt**, issued by the government, with the promise to repay the debt at some date in the future. Over the life of the bond the holder receives interest, referred to as the **coupon**. On maturity the loan **(the principal)** is repaid.

**UK GILTS – cash market** www.ft.com/gilts

| Jan 16 | Price £ | Day's Chng | W'ks Chng | Int Yield | Red Yield | 52 Week High | 52 Week Low | Amnt £m | Last xd date | Interest due |
|---|---|---|---|---|---|---|---|---|---|---|
| **Shorts (Lives up to Five Years)** | | | | | | | | | | |
| **Tr 4pc '09** ........ | 100.39 | -0.03 | -0.08 | 3.98 | •0.98 | 100.85 | 99.02 | 18,141 | 27/02 | Se7 Mr7 |
| Tr 8pc '09 .......✦ | 104.74 | -0.09 | -0.21 | 7.64 | 0.98 | 106.22 | 102.93 | 393 | 17/09 | Mr25 Se25 |
| Tr 5.75pc '09 ...... | 104.32 | -0.09 | -0.18 | 5.51 | 0.82 | 104.98 | 100.39 | 15,596 | 27/11 | Je7 De7 |
| **Tr 4.75pc '10** ..... | 104.97 | -0.11 | -0.22 | 4.53 | 1.12 | 105.30 | 98.54 | 19,357 | 28/05 | De7 Je7 |
| Tr 6.25pc '10 ...... | 109.40 | -0.16 | -0.33 | 5.71 | 1.10 | 109.88 | 101.75 | 6,111 | 17/11 | My25 Nv25 |
| **Tr 4.25pc '11** ..... | 105.53 | -0.15 | -0.07 | 4.03 | 1.60 | 105.68 | 96.79 | 21,509 | 25/02 | Se7 Mr7 |
| Cn 9pc Ln '11 ..... | 117.74 | -0.23 | -0.21 | 7.64 | 1.67 | 118.03 | 109.49 | 6,650 | 4/07 | Ja12 Jy12 |
| Tr 7.75pc '12-15 ..✦ | 115.67 | -0.29 | -0.42 | 6.70 | 2.34 | 116.11 | 106.76 | 804 | 18/01 | Jy26 Ja26 |
| **Tr 5pc '12** ........ | 108.21 | -0.28 | -0.43 | 4.62 | 2.27 | 108.64 | 98.51 | 20,683 | 28/02 | Se7 Mr7 |
| Tr 5.25pc '12 ...... | 109.32 | -0.31 | -0.48 | 4.80 | 2.37 | 109.82 | 99.09 | 12,034 | 30/05 | De7 Je7 |
| Tr 9pc '12 .......✦ | 122.02 | -0.37 | -0.57 | 7.38 | 2.48 | 122.59 | 112.50 | 403 | 27/07 | Fe6 Au6 |
| **Tr 8pc '13** ........ | 123.63 | -0.48 | -0.66 | 6.47 | 2.61 | 124.43 | 111.41 | 7,619 | 19/09 | Mr27 Se27 |
| Tr 4.5pc '13 ...... | 107.76 | – | -0.40 | 4.18 | 2.51 | 108.27 | 95.97 | 18,549 | – | – |

In the UK, the market in government debt is referred to as the gilt-edged market. As you will see from the extract above, taken from the *Financial Times,* there are a wide variety of stocks available.

Let's take a typical issue, using arbitrary numbers, and examine the key features.

| TREASURY | 7.75% | 2012 – 15 | @ £126.45 |
|---|---|---|---|
| \| | \| | \| | \| |
| Name | Coupon | Maturity | Price |

The names of gilts are largely **irrelevant** since all gilt debt belongs to the government and ranks equally in credit risk.



BPP LEARNING MEDIA

### 1.2.1 Maturity

This is the date on which the government has agreed to repay the debt. In this case the government has issued debt with two dates, therefore reserving the right to redeem the debt between 2012, at the earliest, and 2015 at the latest. The decision on redemption will be taken with reference to the coupon. If the government is able to replace the borrowing at a cheaper rate they will redeem the stock on the earlier of the two dates. Gilt-edged stocks are classified with respect to their maturity dates. The official UK Debt Management Office definitions are

- **Shorts:** Gilts with less than **7 years** until redemption.
- **Mediums:** Gilts with between **7 and 15 years** until redemption.
- **Longs:** Gilts with **over 15 years** until redemption.

[*Note:* both the **London Stock Exchange** and *Financial Times* classify shorts as those with **up to 5 years** to run until redemption and mediums as those with **between 5 and 15 years** to run until redemption.]

Dual dated stocks, such as the example above, state two dates in between which they may be redeemed by the DMO. They are normally classified using the later of the two dates since this is the point on which redemption must take place. When interest rates are below the coupon rate, the government are likely to redeem the bonds at the earliest of the dates. If the current interest rate remains higher than the coupon rate then the government will redeem the bond as late as possible.

In the past, the government has been able to issue some bonds without giving a specific date on which redemption will take place. These **undated stocks** are all redeemable from a certain date. For example, the Treasury 3% '66 **Aft** has been redeemable since (**or after**) 1966, however, unlike double dated stocks there is no date by which the issue must be redeemed. Given that the **highest** coupon on these undated stocks is **4%** (the lowest is 2½%), it seems unlikely that they will ever be redeemed, as it is cheaper for the government to pay out a low coupon continuously.

**Zero coupon bonds**, as the name suggests, do not pay periodic coupon payments and as such will trade at below the par value of a bond. The UK government has not offered zero coupon bonds and market demand is satisfied by the use of STRIPS which allow dealers to sell the separate payments separately. (These are described later in more detail).

### 1.2.2 Coupon

The coupon is the **rate of interest** that will be paid **on the nominal outstanding amount** of the stock. In the UK, the convention is for this coupon to be paid on a **semi-annual basis** in equal instalments. However, there is an exception to this rule: **2½% Consolidated Stock which pays on a quarterly basis**. Gilts pay coupons **gross**, i.e. without any withholding tax being deducted. Investors are liable for income tax at the savings rate of 10%/20%/40%, depending on their marginal rate of income. However, an individual may **elect** for their own convenience to receive the coupon net of **20% withholding tax**. The cheque paying the coupon is referred to as the **warrant**.

## Example

Calculate the next coupon on £440 nominal value (NV) of Treasury 7% 2010, where the investor has made an election to receive the coupon net of withholding tax.

Coupon = Nominal value × Coupon × ½ × (1 – Tax rate)

= £440 × 0.07 × ½ × 0.80

= £12.32

### 1.2.3 Floating rate notes (FRNs)

With FRNs, the coupon is not fixed at the outset, but floats in line with market rates and is re-fixed on a regular basis. Every few months the market rate of interest is assessed, often using a measure such as the **LIBOR (London Inter-Bank Offered Rate) and adding to it a margin**. LIBOR represents the rate the largest banks are prepared to lend to each other and, therefore, provides a benchmark. The margin added reflects the additional risk the investor is taking in lending to a company.

With a fixed rate bond a change in interest rates will cause the price of the bond to change (so that the yield reflects the market rate of interest). With a FRN, however, the coupon will change in line with market interest rates. This will result in the value of the bond remaining **at/or around the par value**.

## Example

FRN issued at par, with an initial coupon of 8% gives a yield of

$$\frac{£8}{£100} \times 100 = 8\%$$

If market rates rise to 10%, what will be the impact on the price of the FRN?

## Solution

As rates rise, so will the coupon

$$\frac{£10}{£100} \times 100 = 10\%$$

Here, as interest rates rise, the coupon also rises, and the price remains constant. With a fixed coupon bond the price would have to fall.

In essence however, FRNs are simply bonds. The only important difference is that rather than paying a specified rate of interest, they pay a specified margin over a benchmark rate of interest which is re-examined on a regular basis. FRNs are normally long dated on issue.

## 1.3 US municipal bonds

US borrowing by state or local government is referred to as municipal, or 'muni' bonds. Munis are used to raise funds for US states, cities and specific local requirements such as education and sewage works. Two distinct forms of munis exist. 'Tax exempt' issues are offered, where individual states will issue bonds which are tax exempt (at both State and Federal level) for interest income for investors within their own state. 'Taxable' munis are less common, where the interest income is taxable by Federal taxation.

The Economic Recovery and Reinvestment Act in the US allowed for the creation of 'Build America Bonds' until 2011, which are taxable but offer Federal subsidies. They may be issued for any government purpose where tax exempt government bonds may be issued. The purpose of the act was to stimulate the US economy in light of the financial cuts in central government spending.

## 1.4 US government sponsored entities

A number of quasi-governmental institutions exist in the US markets, to fill gaps in the US financial markets. They are backed by the guarantee of the US government via the Fed and have been considered to be riskless. They may well trade at a slight premium to the equivalent US government securities principally due to lower liquidity.

The main Federal agencies are:

- Federal National Mortgage Association (Fannie Mae)
- Government National Mortgage Association (Ginnie Mae)
- Federal Home Loan Mortgage Corporation (Freddie Mac)
- Federal Home Loan Bank System (FMLB)
- Federal Farm Credit Bank (FFCB)

Prior to its 2004 privatisation, a further federal agency was the Student Loan Association (Sallie Mae), now the SLM Corporation.

The government sponsored entities were largely established in the 1930s as a part of the government programme of rebuilding the economy after the Wall Street Crash of 1929. The agencies were established with implied Federal guarantees that the national government would bail out the agencies in the event that default became a possibility. It was not until 2008 that this was made explicit as the markets became concerned that a number of these agencies might default.

## 1.5 UK local authority debt

The Local Government Group published a report 'Funding and Planning for Infrastructure' in which the suggestion was made that local authority bond issuance may prove to be an effective method of funding local infrastructure projects. They made the suggestion that the US model of municipal bonds which are tax free may be suitable. The report further discusses how local authority bonds were common prior to the 1980s when municipal spending limits were imposed by central government. The report makes mention of the £600 million Transport for London bond issuance aimed at upgrading the underground and financing 'Crossrail' as one of the few local authority issues in recent times. Issuances of local authority bonds have proved popular with investors when available.

Over the past decade, issuance in the market has dried up. Rather than allow the authorities to raise their own finance, the Local Authority Borrowing Requirements (LABR) has been subsumed into the PSNCR. The government has then made some of the finance raised through the PSNCR available via the Public Works Loan Board (PWLB). This constraint has now been relaxed and local authorities are allowed to borrow again in their own right.

The Private Finance Initiative (PFI) was launched by the government in order to encourage the use of private finance for major projects such as building bridges and hospitals. This aimed to encourage the local community to invest in projects that have a direct bearing on their environment and welfare. This may represent an additional drain on the banking sector or may alternatively act as the catalyst for the development of a non-government debt market. These bonds will not carry the formal backing of the government.

## 1.6 Supranational debt

Supranational bodies which represent the interest of many countries, also frequently fund their activities with bond offerings. World Bank Bonds are issued by the International Bank of Construction and Development. They may be attractive to investors due to their triple A rating or due to the fact that funds raised are used to fund development projects.

## 1.7 Index-linked stocks

Learning objective

**1.1.3 Understand** the main investment characteristics, behaviours and risks of index-linked debt: retail price index as a measure of inflation, process of index linking, indexing effects on price, interest and redemption, and return during a period of zero inflation.

One of the risks in investing in fixed rate bonds is that inflation will erode the value of the bond. In order to compensate for this, investors will expect a higher rate of interest, the nominal interest rate, which incorporates an inflation premium.

**Formula to learn**

| Nominal return = Real return + Inflation premium |
|---|

However, they still have a risk that, if inflation is higher than they expected, they may not have received a sufficiently high inflation premium when buying the bond.

To give investors protection against this, the government issues index-linked stocks, in addition to conventional and undated stocks. These are issues in which both the coupon and the capital redemption are linked to the rate of inflation. Thus, index-linked gilts are suitable for investors who wish to **protect themselves against inflation**.

### 1.7.1 UK index linked bonds

The principal sum (the capital upon redemption) and coupon are scaled up by the increase in the Inflation Index (in the UK the Retail Price Index (RPI)) from eight months prior to the date of issue, to eight months prior to the payment date. The reason for this is to ensure that investors are clear about their return during the six months prior to the payment of each coupon, so that accrued interest can be calculated.

Note: In 2005 the RPI lag was changed for any new issue of ILG to just three months before the coupon payment date. Existing ILGs issued prior to 2005 remain lagged by eight months.In a period of zero inflation, i.e. when there has been no increase in the RPI, the Real Return and Nominal Return will be the same.

## Example

A $4\frac{5}{8}\%$ index-linked stock is issued in September 1992, and pays a semi-annual coupon in March 2009.

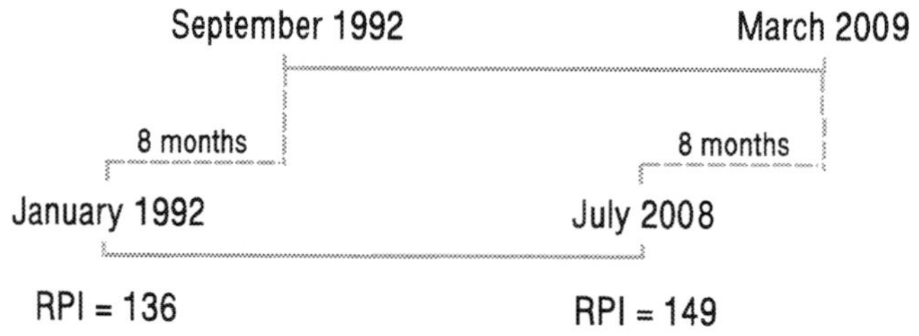


The bond has coupon payment dates in March and September. The March 2009 coupon will be half the annual coupon $\left(4\frac{5}{8}\% \div 2 = £2.31\right)$, uplifted by the RPI eight months prior to the coupon date (July 2008 = 149), compared with the RPI eight months prior to the issue date (January 1992 = 136).

$$£2.31 \times \frac{149}{136} = £2.53$$

Therefore, the March 2009 coupon will be £2.53, reflecting the inflationary uplift, i.e. 9.6% higher than £2.31.

If you look at the price of ILGs in the *Financial Times*, you will see that £100 NV trades considerably higher than £100. This is due to the capital being scaled up by changes in inflation.

## 1.8 Strips

earning objective

**1.5.2 Understand** the purpose and key features of the global strip market: Result of stripping a bond, Number of securities possible from a strippable bond, Zero coupon securities and access considerations.

STRIP stands for Separately Traded Registered Interest and Principal of Securities, and a strips market was introduced for UK gilts from late 1997. With the DMO currently announcing that there are two series of strippable gilts; the first paying coupons on 7 June/ 7 December, which became strippable in December 1997. The second series, paying coupons on 7 March/ 7 September, followed in April 2002. The DMO state further that they intend that future GILT issues will all be strippable. This market facilitates the trading of individual gilt cash flows rather than the whole bond. Thus, each coupon payment and the final redemption proceeds can be traded as if they were individual government-backed zero-coupon bonds. This is attractive to an investor who wishes to meet a specific liability with a government backed security, without the reinvestment risk that comes with a coupon bearing bond.

The DMO quote figures that in March 2010, 30 strippable gilts were in issue with a total amount outstanding of £655.6 billion, of these however only £2.3 billion nominal value were held in stripped form. The relatively slow growth of the market by users was explained by the DMO as being due to limitations placed upon pension fund trustees and the tax position of strip holders who are taxed each year on unrealised gains or losses.

The US has a similar and well developed market in STRIPs, which has operated since 1985. A number of other countries including Germany and Japan also operate such a system.

Given the requirement that gilts must be held in values to the nearest penny, when a gilt strip purchase is requested, the least size allowable must ensure that they are valued to a multiple of a penny (i.e. a value including half a penny would not be permitted). A further requirement is that gilts may only be stripped in increments of £10,000.

Gilt-edged market makers make a market in strips as a part of their general obligations. Consequently, strips seem no different from the existing bonds in issue, with the exception that strips are quoted on a yield basis. The only bodies who may 'strip' a bond are The Bank of England, The Treasury and GEMMs.

### 1.8.1 Taxation of strips

Because a strip does not pay income (i.e. coupons) it may be thought that the investment will not result in income tax payments, during its life. The tax system however will in fact tax the strip throughout its life. Where an individual holds a strip, it will be marked to market on an individual basis and gains will be taxed as income.

**Illustration of a STRIP**

Consider a strippable three year 8% coupon Gilt (paying semi-annual coupons), with a par value of $500,000:

6 semi-annual coupons

Semi-annual Coupon **$20,000**

Semi-annual Coupon **$20,000**

Semi-annual Coupon **$20,000**

Semi-annual Coupon **$20,000**

Semi-annual Coupon **$20,000**

Semi-annual Coupon **$20,000**

+

Principal Payment

Principal **$500,000**

## 2 Bond Prices and Interest Rates

**Learning objectives**

**1.1.2** **Understand** the relationship between interest rates and government bond prices: Yield, interest payable, accrued interest (clean and dirty prices) and effect of changes in interest rates.

**1.6.3** **Analyse** the factors that influence bond pricing: Yield to maturity, credit rating, impact of interest rates and market liquidity

**1.6.4** **Analyse** fixed income securities using the following valuation measures, and understand the benefits and limitations of using them: Flat yield, nominal and real return, gross redemption yield (using IRR), Net redemption yield, modified duration.

**1.6.6** **Calculate and interpret** flat yield, and interest income

## 2.1 Bond pricing

The price of a government bond is quoted in terms of the amount an investor must pay in order to obtain a nominal value of the stock (in the UK £100). Technically, an investor can buy as much of the bond as they require. The market simply adopts this as a convention for the quote.

Where the market price is greater than the nominal value, the bond is said to be priced **above par**. This happens if the bond pays an attractive coupon compared with today's interest rates. Where the market price is less than NV, the bond is said to be priced **below par**.

The market price of a bond is determined by looking at all future cash flows of the bond (always assume annual coupons) and working out today's value (present value) of these cash flows, i.e. stripping out the effect of interest rates. For example, if interest rates are 5%, then £100 today is worth £100 × 1.05 = £105 in one year's time and, therefore, £105 in one year is worth £105 ÷ 1.05 = £100 today.

This calculation for a bond may be expressed mathematically as follows.

Note in the exam the bond will have a life of no more than two years, so

**Formula to learn**

$$\text{Market price of a bond} = \frac{C_1}{1+r} + \frac{C_2 + R}{(1+r)^2}$$

where

$C_{1,2}$ = coupon in period 1 or 2 (assumed for the exam to be annual)

R = capital repaid at redemption (i.e. £100 nominal value)

r = yield to redemption (assumed to be market interest rates)

### Example

Calculate the price of a two-year 7% annual coupon bond where interest rates are 6% p.a.

| Period | **1** | **2** |
|---|---|---|
| Cash Flow | £7 | £107 |
| Present Value | £7 ÷ 1.06 = £6.60 | £107 ÷ $1.06^2$ = £95.23 |

Price of bond = £6.60 + £95.23

= £101.83

## 2.2 Factors influencing bond pricing

The market price of a bond will be affected by numerous factors some due to the issuer and some due to the market:

### 2.2.1 Issuer factors

- **Yield to the maturity** – the required yield to maturity in comparison to the rates offered by other benchmark bonds sets the price of the bond.
- **Seniority** – the risk associated with a bond depends largely on its seniority in respect to assets in the event of default and as risk and return are closely linked this will drive the price.

- **Structure** – As with seniority the structure of a bond will give rise to a particular level of risk and hence price.
- **Credit ratings** – are determined as an indication of the specific issue prospects and likelihood of the company defaulting.
- Bonds from respected issuers and where issues are large tend to be more liquid and hence result in lower yields and higher prices.

### 2.2.2 Market factors

- Liquid repo markets in a bond will mean that the price of a bond will change rapidly as interest rates vary.
- The market in bonds will generally be strongly linked to interest rates. As interest rates rise bond prices fall.
- An indication of the market's expectation of future interest rates may be derived from the derivatives market. It is possible to agree today the price of a ten year maturity bond in the derivatives market for up to one year in advance. If there is a significant difference between the prices expected in the futures market versus the cash market, the prices will be brought into line through a process of '**arbitrage**'.

## 2.3 Risk factors

An investor in a fixed income security is exposed to a number of different risks, and any complete assessment of a bond must include consideration of these factors. These risks include the following. In general the higher the level of risk, the lower will be the price in comparison to other equivalent bonds. (Note that prices falling will cause the yield to rise).

### 2.3.1 Interest rate risk

This is probably the most important risk because of the powerful relationship between interest rates and bond prices. Duration and modified duration (volatility) are the means of measuring this risk. Convexity is the measure that is used to explain the variation away from the predicted return. Discussion of this risk is covered in great detail later in this chapter.

### 2.3.2 Credit and default risk

Credit and default risk is the risk of the issuer defaulting on its obligations to pay coupons and repay the principal. The ratings by commercial rating companies can be used to help assess this risk.

### 2.3.3 Inflation risk

Inflation is a risk in fixed income investments as with higher levels of inflation the purchasing power of any income received will be reduced. High inflation is then a major risk for holders of fixed income securities.

Inflation risk is linked to interest rate risk, as interest rates tend to rise due to monetary policies and as such will compensate bondholders for inflation. Index linked bonds may protect investors against this risk, and as a consequence will offer lower yields.

### 2.3.4 Liquidity and marketability risk

This has to do with the ease with which an issue can be sold in the market. Smaller issues especially are subject to this risk. In certain markets, the volume of trading tends to concentrate into the 'benchmark' stocks, thereby rendering most other issues illiquid. Other bonds become subject to 'seasoning' as the initial liquidity dries up and the bonds are purchased by investors who wish to hold them to maturity.

#### 2.3.5 Issue specific risk

There may be factors specific to the issue, which tend to either increase or decrease the risk, e.g. issuer options such as the right to call for early redemption or possibly, holder options.

#### 2.3.6 Fiscal risk

Fiscal risk represents risk that withholding taxes will be increased. For foreign bonds, there would also be the risk of the imposition of capital controls locking your money into the market.

#### 2.3.7 Currency risk

For any investor purchasing overseas or international bonds, then there is obviously also the risk of currency movements.

## 3 The Yield Measure

The prices of bonds reflect the disparity between the coupons available and the additional risks undertaken by investors who buy in the longer dated (and therefore riskier) end of the market. The yield measure addresses these factors and produces one common valuation on which different stocks can be compared. Yields are stated as a percentage of the bond's market price.

There are three widely used bond yields: the **flat yield**; the **gross redemption yield**; and the **net redemption yield**.

### 3.1 The flat yield

#### Calculation

The simplest measure of the return used in the market is the flat (interest or running) yield. This measure looks at the annual cash return (coupon) generated by an investment as a percentage of the cash price. In simple terms, what is the regular annual return that you generate on the money that you invest?

**Formula to learn**

$$\text{Flat Yield} = \frac{\text{Annual coupon rate}}{\text{Market price}}$$

#### Example

We hold 10% Loan stock (annual coupon) redeemable at par in four years. The current market price is £97.25. Calculate the flat yield.

#### Solution

The flat yield for the above would be

$$\text{Flat yield} = \frac{£10.00}{£97.25} = 0.10283 \text{ or } 10.283\%$$

### 3.1.1 Uses of the flat yield measure

This measure assesses the **annual income return** only and is most appropriate when either

- We are dealing with **irredeemables**, which pay no return other than income into perpetuity; or
- Our priority is the short-term cash returns that the investment will generate.

### 3.1.2 Limitations of the flat yield measure

This measure, while of some use (particularly in the short term), has three important drawbacks for the investment markets.

- In addition to the coupon flows, bonds may have returns in the form of the redemption moneys. Where the bond has been purchased at a price away from par, this will give rise to potential gains and losses which are excluded from this calculation.
- The calculation completely ignores the timing of any cash flows and the time value of money.
- With some bonds (floating rate notes – FRNs), the return in any one period will vary with interest rates. If the coupon is not constant, then this measure is only of historic value unless the predicted return is used.

These limitations combine to make the flat yield of only marginal use.

## 3.2 Gross redemption yield (yield to maturity)

The gross redemption yield (GRY) is a measure of the **total return** an investor receives on a bond, before taking into account the effects of tax.

You will not be required to calculate the GRY of a bond in the exam, but candidates are required to show an understanding of what the figure represents, along with its uses and limitations.

In the example above, the flat yield of 6.6% only reflects the income we receive on our initial investment of £106.00. However, in analysing total return, we also need to take into account the fact that having invested £106.00 to buy the gilt at the outset, we receive £100.00 two years later on redemption, i.e. we make a £6.00 loss on the capital side. **Because we have purchased the bond above its par value of £100, the gross redemption yield will be lower than the flat yield.** Similarly, had we purchased the gilt for less than £100, we would have made a gain on redemption and found that the GRY was higher than the flat yield.

GRY = Flat yield + Gain on redemption (or – loss to redemption)

Bond trading above £100 ~ loss to redemption ~ GRY < FY

Bond trading below £100 ~ gain to redemption ~ GRY > FY

Whilst it may appear as though we simply need to make an adjustment to our flat yield calculation to take account of the gain or loss we make to redemption, in reality the calculation is more complex than this. This is because we also need to take into account the time value of money, the concept we met earlier when calculating the present value of a bond. In the example at the end of that section, we established the following.

If interest rates are 6%, the price of a two-year 7% coupon bond should be £101.83.

Having been told the interest rate, and the maturity and coupon of the bond, we are able to find our 'unknown', the price of the bond. If, instead, we knew the price, maturity and coupon of the bond, we could therefore use similar mathematical ideas to calculate a different 'unknown' – the interest rate. This interest rate is, in fact, the gross redemption yield, thus

If the price of a two-year 7% coupon bond is £101.83, its GRY is 6%.

{Note that you would not be required to calculate the GRY in the exam}

The best description of the gross redemption yield would be

**Exam tip**

> The rate of interest that if we use it to discount all future cash flows to today's present value and then sum them would give a value equal to the current bond price. This could also be described as the internal rate of return (IRR) of the bond.

Whilst the gross redemption yield is a commonly used measure of the return on a bond, it is not particularly useful to the average investor since it ignores the impact of taxation. The gross redemption yield is useful to **non-taxpayers** interested in the overall picture, such as **pension funds and charities**.

### 3.2.1 Calculating GRY

The gross redemption yield (GRY) resolves the issue of the redemption values and the time value of money by using discounted cash flow techniques.

The gross redemption yield is the internal rate of return (IRR) of

- The dirty price paid to buy the bond.
- The gross coupons received **to redemption**.
- The final redemption proceeds.

### 3.2.2 Mathematical formulation

This could be expressed mathematically as follows.

When GRY = r, then

$$\text{Price} = \sum \frac{C_t}{(1+r)^t} + \frac{R}{(1+r)^n}$$

Alternatively, this may be expressed as

$$\text{Price} = \frac{C_1}{1+r} + \frac{C_2}{(1+r)^2} + \frac{C_3}{(1+r)^3} + \cdots + \frac{C_n + R}{(1+r)^n}$$

It should be noted that these formulae **cannot** be algebraically solved (except in very rare circumstances) and must be found through trial and error.

### 3.2.3 Interpolation approach

Given that the mathematical equation can't be algebraically solved other approaches are adopted such as the 'interpolation approach'. Taking a simple example of a one year 10% bond to illustrate the case.

## Example 1

The one year bond is bought for £100 and redeemed one year later for £110 (£100 par plus the coupon). Calculate the return realised.

## Solution

Here we are making a £10 gain on a £100 investment, corresponding to a 10% return.

Clearly, with this very simple investment it was very easy to assess the return without recourse to DCF. However, if we were to discount this investment's cash flows at different rates we would find the following.

| Time | Cash Flow £ | Discount Factor (5%) | Present Value £ | Discount Factor (10%) | Present Value £ | Discount Factor (15%) | Present Value £ |
|---|---|---|---|---|---|---|---|
| 0 | (100.00) | 1 | (100.00) | 1 | (100.00) | 1 | (100.00) |
| 1 | 110.00 | $\frac{1}{1.05^1}$ | 104.76 | $\frac{1}{1.10^1}$ | 100.00 | $\frac{1}{1.15^1}$ | 95.65 |
| Net present values | | | £4.76 | | £0.00 | | (£4.35) |

What we can see here is that there is an inverse relationship between NPVs and required rates of return; as rates rise, NPVs fall. Appreciating this relationship is the key to understanding the examination approach to these questions.

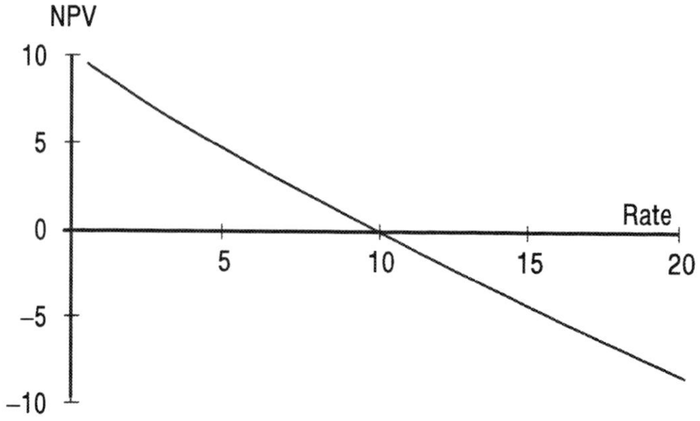


What we can also see in this example is that the GRY is 10% (the rate corresponding to a zero NPV), telling us that this investment is returning a GRY of 10.

### Assessment

An approximation to the GRY can be determined through a process called **interpolation**, though a trial and error approach is really the only way of finding the exact IRR. Through knowledge of the inverse relationship, however, the number of trials and errors can be minimised in a multiple choice exam where four alternative rates are offered.

### Steps

Calculate the NPV of the various cash flows using the second highest rate, which will give rise to three possibilities.

- If the NPV is zero, then the correct rate has been selected first time.
- If the NPV is positive, then the selected rate is too low and the IRR is a higher rate. Since the second highest rate was originally selected, the correct answer must be the highest rate offered.
- If the NPV is negative, then the selected rate was too high and the IRR is one of the two lower rates offered in the question. One of these two lower rates will need to be tried to determine which it is.

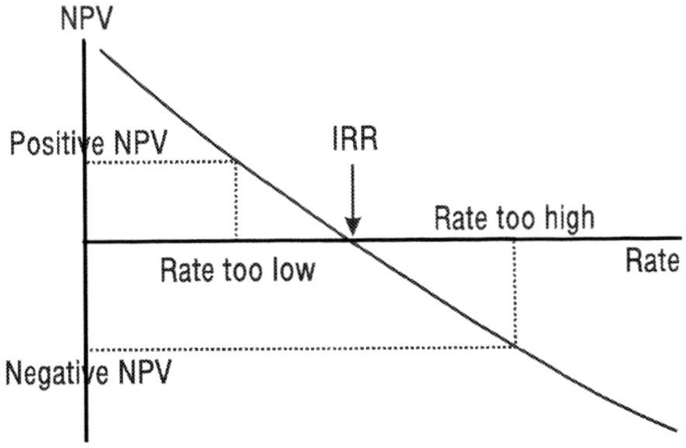


## Example 2

For a slightly more difficult example, consider a four year 7% annual coupon bond, currently trading at £97.83.

### Step 1

Try a discount rate of **7%** and calculate the Net Present Value:

$$NPV = -£97.83 + \frac{£7}{1.07} + \frac{£7}{1.07^2} + \frac{£7}{1.07^3} + \frac{£107}{1.07^4} = + £2.17$$

i.e. NPV is positive.

### Step 2

Try a discount rate of **8%** and calculate the Net Present Value:

$$NPV = -£97.83 + \frac{£7}{1.08} + \frac{£7}{1.08^2} + \frac{£7}{1.08^3} + \frac{£107}{1.08^4} = - £1.14$$

i.e. NPV is negative.

### Step 3

To interpolate the solution:

Begin with 7% as our starting point.

We are aiming for a NPV of zero, so we will find the difference between the NPV at 7% which is positive and the NPV at 8%, which is negative.

Difference between the two NPVs equals:

+£2.17 less -£1.14 = £3.31

To interpolate (i.e.to find the zero NPV) then find the proportion of the gap between 7% and 8% we must go from 7% to find the zero value

i.e. a distance represented by £2.17 out of a total of £3.31

GRY estimate = 7% + (+£2.17 / £3.31) × (8% - 7%) = 7.65%

## Estimate of GRY

The estimate of 7.65%, is only an approximation. To improve the estimate, we should continue making estimates to bring the two limits in from 7% - 8% and closer together, until one estimate is just negative and one is just positive.

### 3.2.4 Limitations of the GRY measure

As a measure of predicted return, the yield is limited, since it assumes that interest rates remain constant throughout the period and hence, that any coupon receipts may be reinvested at the same rate as the yield. If this is the case, then the GRY does represent the return achieved. If rates vary, however, the return achieved will differ from the GRY.

If the bond is not held to redemption, but sold at some earlier date, then the return achieved will be a function of the price of the bond (hence, interest rates) at the disposal date.

Even if the bond is held to redemption, the terminal value will differ, as the reinvested coupons will grow at a different rate, altering the ultimate return achieved.

## 3.3 The net redemption yield (NRY)

### 3.3.1 Calculation

The GRY measures the gross return before the effects of taxation. The net redemption yield (NRY) is the return that the investor can expect net of taxation.

The NRY is most appropriate for individual investors to help them assess their after-tax returns. As each individual has a different tax position, the NRY will obviously be different for different individuals. The market convention is to compute the NRY at assumed levels of personal tax such as 40%.

In the UK, the taxation treatment of the income and gain elements differs for individual investors. The coupon income is subject to income tax, however the capital gain (or loss) on gilts and sterling non-convertible debt is tax free.

The net redemption yield can, therefore, be calculated as the internal rate of return (IRR) of

- The dirty price paid to buy the bond.
- The **net** coupons received **to redemption** (net of the appropriate rate of tax).
- The final redemption proceeds.

### 3.3.2 Uses of the NRY measure

Since it is based on discounted cash flow techniques, as is the GRY, this measure overcomes the major deficiencies highlighted in relation to the flat yield and the GRY. It considers all cash returns and exactly when they occur and their tax implications for the investor.

The NRY therefore represents a realistic measure of the expected overall return to the investor at any point in time net of taxes.

### 3.3.3 Limitations of the NRY measure

The limitations of the NRY are as for the GRY, specifically it only represents the net return that will be achieved if interest rates to maturity remain constant throughout the holding period.

## 3.4 Gross equivalent yield or grossed-up NRY

### 3.4.1 Calculation

As we noted earlier, the tax status for individual investors holding gilts or sterling non-convertible debt is that coupons are taxed, but any capital gain is not. This may be contrasted with an investment in shares where both income and capital are subject to tax.

The Gross Equivalent Yield (GEY) calculates the gross return required from a fully taxed source of income in order to produce the same after-tax return as a particular bond.

The approach to the calculation is to measure the after-tax return that the bond is providing using the NRY calculation, which the fully taxed source of income will need to match, then gross this up for the appropriate tax rate to see what gross return is required from that source. The calculation is

**Formula to learn**

$$GEY = \frac{NRY}{1 - T_p}$$

where

$T_p$ = the personal tax rate upon which the NRY was calculated

## Example

We hold 10% Loan stock (annual coupon) redeemable at par in four years. The current market price is £97.25 based on a GRY of 10.8842% and an NRY of 6.8084% for a 40% taxpayer. Calculate the GEY.

## Solution

The flat yield for the above would be

$$GEY = \frac{6.8084}{0.60} = 11.3473\%$$

If the bond is valued below par it will generate a tax-free gain to maturity. Any fully taxed alternative would need to match this gain **after tax** and hence requires a higher return before tax. As a result the GEY will exceed the GRY.

Conversely, if the bond is valued above par, then the capital loss it will suffer to maturity would **not** attract tax relief, whereas it would on the fully taxed alternative. As a result, a much higher capital loss could be sustained on the fully taxed alternative whilst still having the same effect net of tax. The result is that the GEY will be lower than the GRY in this situation.

If a bond is valued at par, then the two measures will be identical as there will be no capital gain or loss, hence the tax treatment will be the same.

### 3.4.2 Uses

The use of this measure is to enable comparison of the returns of alternatives regardless of their tax treatment.

It does **not** represent the pre-tax return the bond will offer as that is given as accurately as can be by the GRY. Instead, it provides a benchmark for appraising alternatives that are fully taxed.

### 3.4.3 Limitations

Since it is based on the NRY, its limitations are as for that measure, specifically it only represents the gross return required from the alternative if interest rates to maturity remain constant throughout the holding period.

In addition, the calculation only caters for one tax rate, hence we must assume that this will also be constant over the period.

# 4 Gilt Settlement Values

## Introduction

The fact that capital gains on gilts are free of capital gains tax (whereas interest received is income taxable) historically led to tax avoidance, since investors ensured they always took profits on gilts by means of capital gains.

This was achieved by purchasing a gilt shortly after it went ex-dividend and then selling it cum dividend around six months later, just before the next interest payment date. The value of the gilt would rise due to the value of the accrued interest which was due to be paid in the near future. Any gain made on sale was effectively interest for the six months the gilt was held but was treated as a capital gain since it was received on sale of the gilt. This process was called 'bond washing'. UK gilts generally settle T + 1.

## 4.1 Clean and dirty pricing

In line with all international government bond markets, in 1986 the UK gilts market adopted a clean price method of quoting. **Clean pricing** means that the price quoted ignores the value of the **accrued interest**. In addition to the price quoted, any purchaser of a gilt must pay for the interest that has been accrued to date on that stock. The seller of the gilt will be liable to income tax on the interest received. This means that bond washing is not usually possible.

The total amount paid by the purchaser, being the clean price plus or minus any accrued interest adjustment, is referred to as the **dirty (or settlement) price**.

### 4.1.1 Purchasing cum div (cum dividend bargains)

For example, a gilt pays its coupon on 1 April and 1 October. The purchaser buys the gilt on 10 July whilst it is trading cum div. When the next payment date comes due, the purchaser receives the full six months coupon, even though he has not owned the bond for the entire period. Consequently, when the gilt is bought, the purchaser must compensate the initial holder for the interest which has been lost.

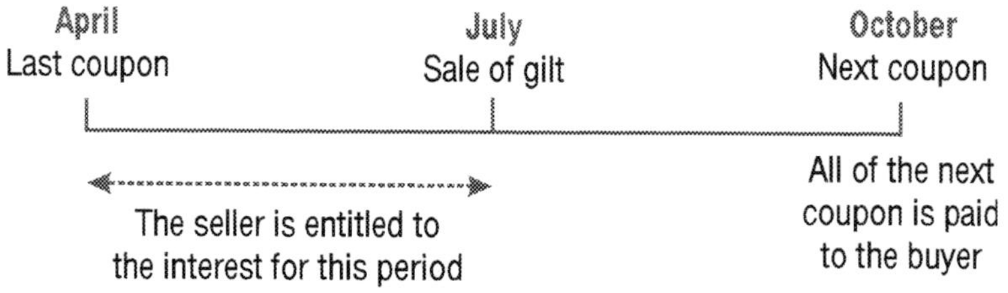


The purchaser therefore pays the clean price, plus the interest which has accrued from the **last coupon date up to the calendar day before the settlement date inclusive**. Settlement day is the first business day after the day of the trade (**T + 1**).

The formula used in the gilts market is

**Formula to learn**

| |
|---|
| Purchaser of a cum div stock pays: Clean price + Accrued interest |

Accrued interest is equal to the number of calendar days interest from the last coupon payment date until the calendar day before the settlement day (inclusive).

## Example

The last payment date is 1 April. On 10 July, an investor buys £10,000 nominal value of Treasury 8% @ £101.50. There are 183 days in the current dividend period. How much does the investor pay?

| | | (£) |
|---|---|---|
| (i) | The clean price<br>£10,000 @ £101.50 per £100 NV | 10,150.00 |
| (ii) | The accrued interest<br>$(£10{,}000 \times 8\% \times ½) = £400 \times \frac{101 \text{ days}}{183 \text{ days}}$ | 220.77 |
| | | 10,370.77 |

The number of calendar days for the accrued interest calculation is calculated as follows.

| | | |
|---|---|---|
| April | 30 | (includes 1 April) |
| May | 31 | |
| June | 30 | |
| July | 10 | (up to and including the day before settlement) |
| | 101 | |

### 4.1.2 Purchasing ex-div

If you purchase a gilt very close to the next coupon date, you will be too late to receive the next coupon. Gilt-edged stocks are marked ex-div **seven business days** prior to the payment day, in order to allow the Registrar and CREST enough time to ensure that the coupon is paid to the appropriate party. The exception to this is the **3½% War Loan** which has an ex-div period of **ten business days**. Any person buying the stock after it has been marked ex-div will not be entitled to the coupon. Consequently, the pricing of the stock reflects this.

## Example

An investor buys £20,000 nominal value 12% Exchequer @ £104.25 on 27 March. The next payment date is 1 April. There are 182 days in the current coupon period. How much does the investor pay?

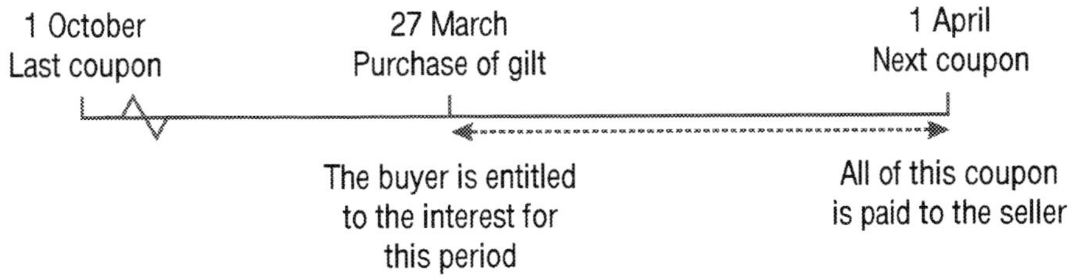


In this case, the purchaser of the bond will not receive any of the coupon directly from the DMO, even though he is holding the bond during part of the coupon period. This is because he has bought the gilt so close to the next coupon date that there is not time to update the register. Accordingly, he pays the clean price as determined by the market **less** the accrued interest that he is not going to receive.

**Formula to learn**

> Purchaser of an ex-div stock pays: Clean price – Accrued interest

Accrued interest is equal to the number of calendar days interest from the settlement day until the **calendar day** before the next coupon payment date (inclusive).

### Example

| | | (£) |
|---|---|---|
| (i) | The clean price<br>£20,000 @ £104.25 per £100 NV | 20,850.00 |
| (ii) | The accrued interest rebate<br>(£20,000 × 12% × ½) = £1,200 × 4 days/182 days | (26.37) |
| | | 20,823.63 |

In this example, the number of calendar days is worked out from the day of **settlement** (28 March) until the day **before coupon payment day** (31 March), i.e. four calendar days.

# 5 Volatility of Bonds

## 5.1 What causes bond prices to change?

**Changes in bond prices are primarily caused by changes in interest rates.** This can be illustrated by returning to our previous example of calculating the flat yield of a gilt (see below).

### Example

What is the flat yield of the 3½% War Loan trading @ £87.50?

$$\text{Flat yield} = \frac{£3.50}{£87.50} \times 100 = 4\%$$

For an investment of £87.50 the investor will receive £3.50 (gross) which is an effective return on their money of 4%.

If general interest rates were to rise to 5% then the holder of the bond would be receiving less than they could earn elsewhere. Consequently, they would sell their bond and invest the money with a bank or building society and earn 5%. This would create selling pressure in the bond market as all investors moved to sell bonds. In a market where there are more sellers than buyers the market price will invariably fall. As the market price falls the effect on the yield calculation will be to increase the yield. Prices will fall until the yield is equivalent to the general market rate of 5%. This will happen when the market price has fallen to £70.00.

$$\text{Flat yield} = \frac{£3.50}{£70.00} \times 100 = 5\%$$

The fundamental relationship for fixed interest bonds is as follows.

**Formula to learn**

| | |
|---|---|
| Interest rates rise | = Bond prices fall |
| Interest rates fall | = Bond prices rise |

In summary, because the coupon on the bond is fixed, if general interest rates fall, then having a fixed higher coupon is more attractive. If market rates rise then being locked into a lower fixed rate coupon is not as attractive.

## 5.2 The impact of volatility

Volatility refers to the risk that bond prices will either increase or decrease due to changes in interest rates. As we have seen, movements in bond prices are caused by movements in interest rates through the yield relationship. However, not all bonds respond to the same extent to a given change in interest rates and yields. Some bonds are more **sensitive** (i.e. the price moves more) than others. The basic maxim is that

Formula to learn

> Long-dated bonds are more sensitive than short-dated bonds
>
> Low-coupon bonds are more sensitive than high-coupon bonds

The logic behind this is that if interest rates rise then the holder of the shorter dated bond is only exposed to a lower return on the bond until redemption, when the money can be reinvested at the new higher return. In contrast, the holder of the longer dated bond does **not** have the prospect of forthcoming redemption to rely upon. They can only realise their money through selling the bond in the market.

In a similar fashion, the holder of the high-coupon bond is receiving his return on the bond more quickly and can, therefore, reinvest the coupons received at the new higher rate of return. The holder of the low-coupon bond has most of his money tied up until the bond's maturity, when a large capital gain is made. The only way he can exit from the bond position is by selling in the market (price risk).

As volatility is a source of risk, investors usually dislike it. However, if an investor is expecting interest rates to fall, and hence bond prices to rise, it may make sense for him to seek gilts with high levels of volatility, in order to expose himself to greater increases in the bond price.

## 5.3 Measurement of volatility

### 5.3.1 Macaulay's duration

This calculation gives each bond an overall risk weighting, which allows two bonds to be compared. In simple terms, it is a composite measure of the risk expressed in years.

Formula to learn

> Duration is the weighted average length of time to the receipt of a bond's benefits (coupon and redemption value), the weights being the present value of the benefits involved.

This concept can be shown diagrammatically.

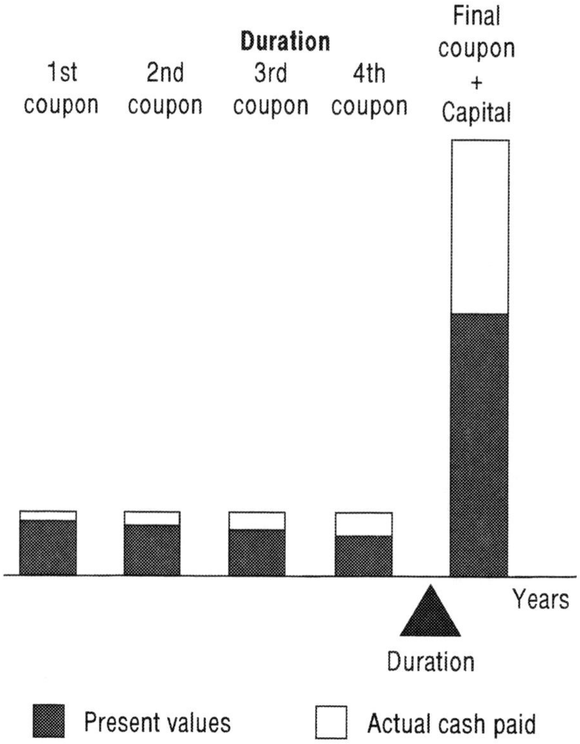


where the fulcrum or point of balance represents the duration of the bond.

### Calculation

Mathematically, duration can be expressed using the following formulae.

**Formula to learn**

$$\text{Macaulay's Duration (D)} = \frac{\sum(t \times PV_t)}{\text{Price}}$$

**or**

$$\text{Macaulay's Duration (D)} = \frac{(1 \times PV_1) + (2 \times PV_2) + (3 \times PV_3) + \cdots + (n \times PV_n)}{\text{Price}}$$

where

$PV_t$ = present value of cash flow in period t (discounted using the redemption yield)

n = number of periods to maturity

This may look difficult, but can be easily calculated in a normal DCF pricing table which simply adds one column next to the one used for valuation.

## Example

A bond pays an annual coupon of 9% and is redeemable at par in three years. Calculate the duration of the bond if interest rates are 8%.

## Solution

| Time | Cash Flow £ | DF (8%) | PV £ | t × PV £ |
|---|---|---|---|---|
| 1 | 9.00 | $\frac{1}{1.08}$ | 8.33 | 8.33 |
| 2 | 9.00 | $\frac{1}{1.08^2}$ | 7.72 | 15.44 |
| 3 | 109.00 (100.00 + 9.00) | $\frac{1}{1.08^3}$ | 86.53 | 259.59 |
| | | | £102.58 | £283.36 |

Using the above, the duration is

$$\text{Duration} = \frac{£283.36}{£102.58} = 2.7623 \text{ years}$$

Macaulay's duration can also be referred to as the **economic life of a bond**.

### 5.3.2 Properties of duration

The basic features of sensitivity to interest rate risk are all mirrored in the duration calculation.

- **Longer dated bonds** will have longer durations.
- **Lower coupon bonds** will have longer durations. The ultimate low-coupon bond is a zero-coupon bond where the duration will be the maturity.
- **Lower yields** will give higher durations. In this case, the present value of flows in the future will fall if the yield increases, moving the point of balance towards the present day, therefore shortening the duration.

The duration of a bond will shorten as the lifespan of the bond decays. However, the rate of their decay will not be the same. In our example above, a three-year bond has a duration of 2.7623 years. In one year's time, the bond will have a remaining life of two years, and a duration based on the same GRY of 1.9182 years. The lifespan has decayed by a full year, but the duration by only 0.8441 of a year.

## 5.4 Modified duration

Modified duration is a measure of bond volatility, which measures volatility due to both maturity and coupon levels. Modified duration may be described as the **percentage change in the price of a bond for a 1% change in the yield on that bond**.

In other words, if a bond has a modified duration of 3, we would see the bond price rise by 3% if the yield on the bond were to fall by 1%.

The change in price of the bond can be given by the following formula.

Formula to learn

$$\text{Modified duration} = \frac{\text{Macauly's duration}}{1 + \text{GRY}}$$

Thus from the previous example Modified duration $= \frac{2.7623}{1.08} = 2.5577$

**Formula to learn**

Change in price = -MD × Change in yield × Current price

Given bonds with varying modified durations, the bond with the highest modified duration will experience the biggest change in price and hence will be the most volatile bond.

Candidates will be given MD values in the exam, if needed for a calculation.

### Example

Calculate the new price of a bond with a modified duration of 6 when the current price is £104 and yields are expected to rise by 1%.

Change in price = –MD × Change in yield × Current price
= –6 × (+0.01) × £104
= –£6.24

New price = £104 – £6.24
= £97.76

## 5.5 Convexity

*Note: Convexity is no longer explicitly covered in the CISI syllabus, but we have included a discussion of convexity to give you a fuller understanding of the valuation process.*

Modified duration predicts a linear relationship between yields and prices. If the modified duration is 2, then if yields rise by 1%, the price will fall by 2%. If the rise in yields had been 3%, then the fall in price would have been 6%.

**The Price/Yield Relationship Predicted by the Modified Duration**

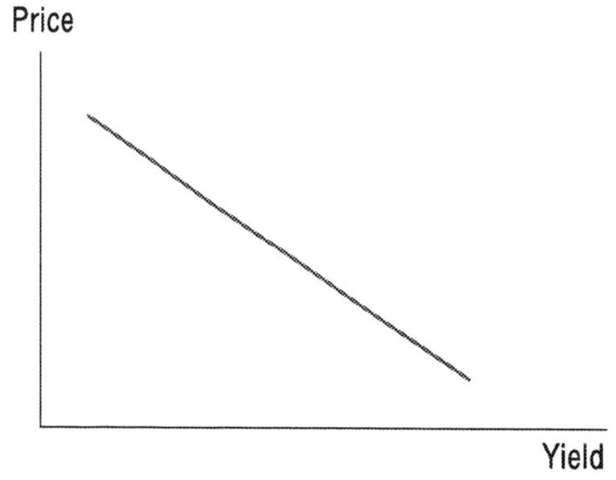


The slope of the line is the modified duration.

However, as the yield changes, then so will the duration and consequently, the modified duration. It is this which gives rise to the concept of convexity.

**The Impact of Changing Yields on the Modified Duration**

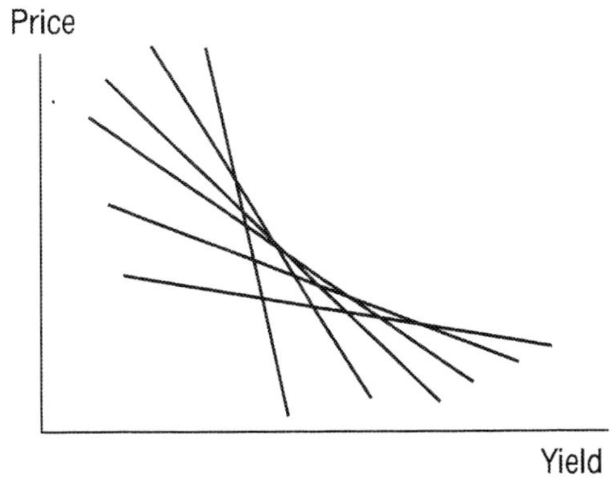


As the yield falls, the duration will increase and therefore, so will the modified duration. As modified duration increases, the line will steepen.

The actual relationship between the yield and price is given by the convex function that these individual linear relationships describe. We are after all aware that the relationship between bond prices and interest rates is not linear. The actual relationship between prices and yields is curved, with increases in yields resulting in prices falling, but at a reducing rate, as illustrated by the example at the start of this session.

The actual convex relationship and the linear one predicted by the modified duration formula are illustrated below.

**Convexity**

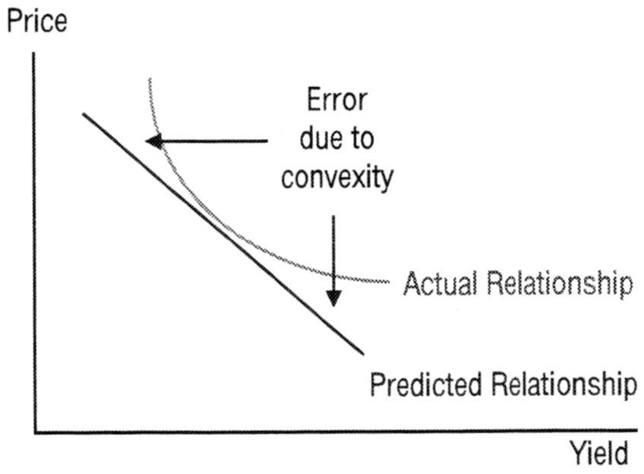


The impact of convexity will be that the modified duration will tend to **overstate the fall in a bond's price and understate the rise**. However, for relatively small movements in the yield, the modified duration will be a good estimate; the problem of convexity only becomes an issue with more substantial fluctuations in the yield.

### 5.5.1 Calculating convexity

The convexity calculation is somewhat complicated and may be derived via calculus:

$$\text{Convexity} = \frac{\sum t(t+1)\ \text{PVt}}{\text{Price}(1+\text{GRY})^2}$$

This rather unpleasant looking formula may be broken down and dealt with as illustrated below (using the same bond as used in the previous example):

| Time | Cash Flow £ | DF (8%) | PV £ | t × PV £ | t(t+1)PVt £ |
|---|---|---|---|---|---|
| 1 | 9.00 | $\frac{1}{1.08}$ | 8.33 | 8.33 | 16.66 |
| 2 | 9.00 | $\frac{1}{1.08^2}$ | 7.72 | 15.44 | 46.32 |
| 3 | 109.00 (100.00 + 9.00) | $\frac{1}{1.08^3}$ | 86.53 | 259.59 | 1,038.36 |
| | | | £102.58 | £283.36 | £1,101.34 |

Hence

$$\text{Convexity} = \frac{\sum t(t+1)\text{PVt}}{\text{Price}(1+\text{GRY})^2}$$

$$\text{Convexity} = \frac{1{,}101.34}{102.58 \times 1.08^2} = 9.2048$$

### 5.5.2 Use of convexity

The use of convexity is to:

- Give a more accurate assessment of the change in the price of a bond that will result from a given change in yields
- Indicate the risk of a bond fund immunisation strategy by comparing the convexity of the alternatives. Note, the relative convexity is unaffected by the consistent inclusion or exclusion of the ½ in the calculations.

### 5.5.3 Calculation of the proportionate change in price using both modified duration and convexity

Proportionate change in price = $-\text{MD} \times \text{DY} + 1/2\text{C} \times \text{DY}^2$

Where

MD = modified duration at the original GRY

C = convexity at the original GRY

$\Delta$Y = percentage change in GRY (expressed in decimal form)

Thus applying this relationship gives:

Proportionate change in price $= -\text{MD} \times \Delta\text{Y} + 1/2\text{C} \times \Delta\text{Y}^2$

$= -2.5577 \times (-0.005) + ½ \times 9.2048 \times (-0.005^2)$

$= 0.01290$ or 1.290%

## 5.6 Basis point value

The basis point value of a bond measures the dollar value of a change in interest rates of one hundredth of a percentage point (or in other words one basis point).

As with the use of the duration measure, a bond with a higher BPV will have greater sensitivity to changes in interest rates.

# 6 The Yield Curve

The yield curve is a graphical representation of the structure of interest rates, plotting the yield, offered by bonds, against maturity. This yield is the gross redemption yield, which assumes that all income has been reinvested.

## 6.1 Normal yield curve

**The Normal Yield Curve**

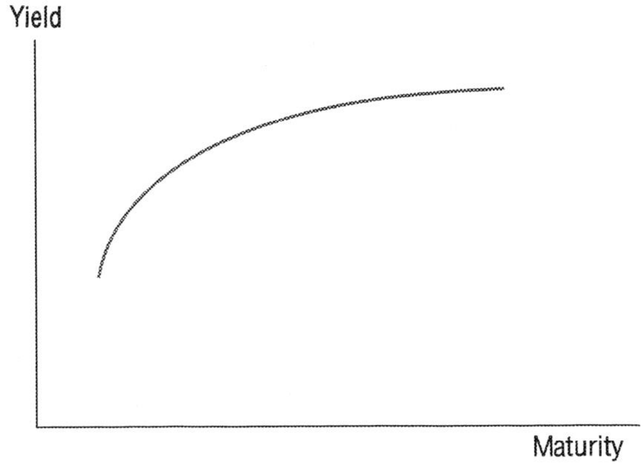


## 6.2 Liquidity preference

The theory states that if an investor's money is invested in longer term bonds, then he will require a greater return or risk premium to compensate for the lower level of liquidity that longer dated bonds have. There is also a higher level of credit risk, since there is a higher probability of default in the longer term. All these things combine to give an upward slope to the normal yield curve.

## 6.3 Expectations theory

Expectations theory states that the yield curve is a reflection of the market's expectation of future interest rates. If the market believes that the yield at the long end of the yield curve is likely to fall, then, in order to profit from the increase in bond prices that this will create, it will buy long-dated stocks. As a result, the demand for these stocks will rise and this demand pressure will force the bond price to rise. As a consequence, the yield will fall reflecting the expectation of a fall.

On the other hand, if the market believes that rates must rise, then the forces will work in the opposite direction and this will lead to a fall in the bond price and a rise in the yield.

## 6.4 Inverted yield curve

The expectations of the market can clearly be seen in an inverted yield curve.

**The Inverted Yield Curve**

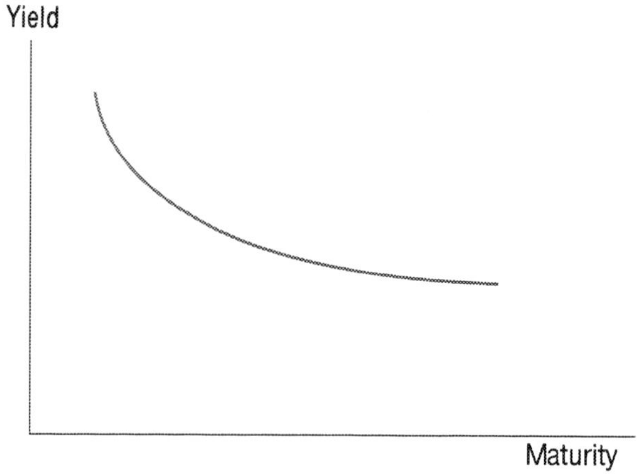


Here, the short-term rates are high but the market anticipates that this cannot last for long. The longer end of the market has anticipated this change by forcing yields down.

Another key element of the market's expectations will be the **expectation of inflation**. If the market believes that inflation will rise in the future, then the yields on the longer dated stocks must rise, in order to compensate investors for the fall in the real value of their money. The expectation of inflation is much more of a factor with the long end, rather than the short end of the yield curve.

### 6.5 Preferred habitat and market segmentation

Certain maturity ranges are appropriate for particular types of investors. In the UK, the short end of the market is dominated by the financial sector maintaining a proportion of their assets in liquid investments, whereas the long end of the yield curve is dominated by institutional investors, such as pension funds. In effect, this gives rise to two markets and may be reflected in a discontinuity or hump in the yield curve.

### 6.6 Supply-side factors

The availability of stocks in certain maturity ranges may lead to either an excess or shortage of stock and, consequently, an anomalous yield on some stocks.

## 7 Characteristics of Corporate Bonds

### Introduction

In much the same way that governments finance their deficits through the use of debt, companies who wish to spend more than they currently have available may also borrow money through the issuance of corporate bonds. Due to the increased risk of default, these bonds will yield more than government debt. Once again this illustrates one of the key maxims of investment – **greater risk requires greater reward**.

Corporate debt can take a wide variety of forms, and there are many different aspects to an issue which may need to be considered.

Trades in corporate bonds settle T + 3.

earning objective

**1.2.1 Understand** the main issuers of corporate debt and the main investment characteristics, behaviours and risks of secured debt: corporates, financial institutions & special purpose vehicles, fixed and floating charges, debentures, types of asset backed securities, mortgage backed securities, securitization process, yield to maturity and roles of participants.

Companies have the ability to issue debt which is secured against the company's assets. There are two types of legal charge that a company can issue over its assets.

## 7.1 A fixed charge security

A fixed charge security is a security given over a specific asset of the business. Where a particular asset has a fixed charge security over it, the company cannot dispose of the asset without the permission of the fixed charge holders. If the company defaults on the loan, the holder of the fixed charge has the right to remove the asset in question, dispose of it and use the proceeds to repay the debt to the bond holder. Any surplus on disposal must be returned to the company.

Bonds secured under a fixed charge are often referred to as **debentures or debenture stock**. The term stock means a loan which can be broken down into small units. With a straight debenture an investor can buy all of it, or none of it. With a debenture stock, as with a gilt-edged stock, the investor can buy as much, or as little, as desired.

## 7.2 A floating charge security

A floating charge security is secured against the assets in general rather than against specific assets. A floating charge has no effect until the company defaults on a loan. At this stage, the holder of a floating charge has the right to appoint a receiver to take over the running of the company. The receiver will then manage the company and any money generated will be used to repay the bondholder's debt.

Unlike a fixed charge, where the company loses the right to dispose of an asset covered by a fixed charge, the company has full rights over the assets of the business until there is an event of default. At that stage, and at that stage only, the charge crystallises.

Both fixed and floating charges must be **recorded with the Registrar of Companies**.

Fixed charges are legally superior to floating charges. This is demonstrated by looking at the order of pay-out on the liquidation of a company. The process of liquidation is one in which the company is wound up by a liquidator. The company is turned into its liquid asset – cash. Assets are sold, money is collected and then used to pay the creditors of the company in a legally specified order.

## 7.3 Unsecured debt

earning objectives

**1.2.2 Understand** the main investment characteristics, behaviours and risks of the main types of unsecured debt: Treasury bonds, income bonds, subordinated, high yield, convertible bonds and rating.

**1.6.6 Calculate and interpret** simple interest income on corporate debt, conversion premiums on convertible bonds.

While secured debt has specified assets held in the name of a specific bond issue, in the case of unsecured debt, this is not the case and as such the legal priority in the event of liquidation is of great importance when considering the possibility of recovering the money loaned.

### 7.3.1 Priority on liquidation of a company

The liquidator's task is to convert the company into cash as quickly and efficiently as possible. The order of pay-out, determined by the Insolvency Act, is as follows.

| Priority on liquidation | |
|---|---|
| 1. | The liquidator's fees |
| 2. | Fixed charge security holders |
| 3. | Preferential creditors (employees' wage arrears) |
| 4. | Floating charge security holders |
| 5. | Unsecured creditors |
| 6. | Subordinated creditors |
| 7. | Preference shareholders |
| 8. | Ordinary shareholders |

The liquidator will pay each category in full before moving on to the next. Since most liquidations are a result of insolvency, the likelihood is that there will be insufficient funds left to meet all debts. The order of liquidation is an attempt to reward those who have some form of security first, before moving on to the unsecured creditors.

When the liquidator runs out of money the category being dealt with at that stage will receive, on a pro rata basis, the proportion of their debt that can be covered by available funds.

For example, the unsecured creditors in a liquidation may receive only 14p in the pound. The important point to note is that shareholders receive their money last. As owners of the company they must take the risks, as well as reap the rewards. However, if the company is wound up and there is a surplus on liquidation, this surplus would be paid to the ordinary shareholders.

### 7.3.2 Treasury bonds

Government debt such as that issued by the US government in the form of Treasury Bonds ( which is backed by the credit and good faith of the US government). While however it is essentially unsecured in natures, investors do not require that specific assets are needed to secure the debt, the word of the government is considered enough.

While US bonds, UK gilts and those of many other developed economies carry very low credit risk, recently a number of countries have caused concerns for investors, with regard to their ability to repay their debts in light of widespread economic difficulties. A number of countries in the Eurozone including Greece and Ireland (who have both been downgraded by the credit rating agencies) are now considered to be a credit risk due to the increased risk that they fail to make repayments. The imbalance between the abilities of certain countries to fund their public spending and debt repayment against a worsening economic output means the risk of failure to pay when bonds mature has become a real concern to credit rating agencies. Countries such as the UK and US have a degree of advantage in this respect due to their control over their currency. While Eurozone countries are unable to issue currency, which is the preserve of the ECB, the UK and US retain control over their own currencies. This means that if necessary any debt could be paid with additional currency, although were too much to be created it would cause concern in the currency markets.

### 7.3.3 Income bonds

Income bonds are issued by companies and promise to pay interest only when the company has made sufficient profits to cover the payments. Investors will be remunerated for the additional risk caused the postponed payments by receiving higher interest payments. They have the lowest seniority of all issued bonds.

### 7.3.4 Subordinated bonds

It should be noted from the order of priority on liquidation that **subordinated** loan stock can be issued. A subordinated loan is one which on liquidation ranks below the unsecured creditors for payout. As such, subordinated creditors take on board a higher degree of risk and will obviously require a higher degree of return to compensate. One of the prime reasons for issuing subordinated stock in the past has been that it has a fairly beneficial impact on the capital adequacy calculation for any securities house or bank.

Finally, the value of a company is irrelevant if the stock itself has been guaranteed by another company. Often within groups of companies, one of the subsidiaries may borrow money from the market place. Its loan may have been guaranteed by the **parent** or **holding company** and is then referred to as **guarantee stock**. The value of this guarantee obviously depends upon the credit rating of the holding company and it would be classified as an **unsecured creditor**.

### 7.3.5 Permanent Interest Bearing Securities (PIBS)/Perpetual Subordinated Bonds

Permanent Interest Bearing Shares (PIBS) are a form of debt issued by mutual building societies. PIBS from demutualised building societies are known as perpetual subordinated bonds (PSB). Both are traded on the LSE. As the name suggests, they are perpetual issues with no date for redemption and carry a fixed (or floating) coupon, which are paid gross. Due to the PIBS holders ranking lowest of all creditors in the event of liquidation, the risk is relatively high. The coupons will therefore be quite high and will appeal to non taxpayers.

### 7.3.6 High yield bonds

A distinction may be drawn between high yield bonds and junk bonds. Both bonds offer investors high yield and trade primarily on their creditworthiness. Junk bonds status however tends to be a reflection of the poor quality of the issuer, while high yield bonds may reflect other factors such as the small size of the issuer or a lack of credit history. The key risk with a high yield bond is default risk. US studies have indicated that the default risk typically varies between 4% and 10%. The risk is highly correlated to the economic cycle. In addition it is important to look at the default rates by industry.

### 7.3.7 Convertible bonds

earning objective

**1.6.5** **Analyse** the specific features of bonds from an investment perspective: Coupon and payment date, Maturity date, Embedded put or call options, Convertibility and Exchangeability.

In addition to security, the issuers of a bond may attach various rights to the issue in order to encourage investors to buy in.

A **conversion right** gives the bondholder the right, at a specified date or dates in the future, to convert their bond into shares of the company. The rate of conversion will be fixed at the time of issue and represents an option to purchase the shares at a given price. Depending on the movement in the underlying share price this conversion right or option may be very valuable indeed. The trade-off in this sort of issue is that the coupon will often be much lower than the market would otherwise expect on a bond from that particular company.

The ranking on liquidation of convertible bonds will depend on the status of the underlying debt. However, the convertibles are rarely secured and it is fairly typical for the debt to be subordinated, meaning they rank lower on priority on liquidation than general creditors of the company.

The **conversion ratio** is the number of shares into which a fixed nominal value of bonds (in the UK, typically £100) can be converted. For example, if a given convertible could be redeemed for cash or for 50 ordinary shares per £100 nominal value, this bond would have a conversion ratio of 50.

One important measure often used in this market is to look at the **conversion premium** at which the bond is trading over the market price of the share.

## Example

X plc has issued convertible debt stock. The convertible right is that every £100 nominal of stock may, at a future date, be converted into 50 ordinary shares. At present, the bond is trading at £110 for £100 nominal and the market price of the share is £1.90.

Since the bond costs £110 and can in effect be converted into 50 shares, the equivalent purchase price per share is

£110 ÷ 50 = £2.20 per share

The current market price of the share is £1.90, therefore the convertible stock is being purchased at a premium of 30p over the current market price. This **conversion premium** may be expressed as a percentage of the current market price.

**Formula to learn**

$$\text{Conversion premium} = \frac{\text{Excess over current share price}}{\text{Current share price}} \times 100$$

(30p ÷ £1.90) × 100 = 15.79%

The investor must judge whether this premium is justifiable. Will the underlying share price move sufficiently over the life of the conversion right to generate a profit on conversion? The investor must also consider the coupon the bond is generating. Whilst this is likely to be low, it may be greater than the dividend on a share. If so it makes sense to hold the bond and then to convert, in the future, into the share itself.

The attraction of convertible bonds is that they offer a two-way bet. If the share price rises then the conversion right itself has value. If the share price falls, then at worst, the bondholder is left with a lower coupon bond (compared with a conventional corporate bond).

### 7.3.8 Exchangeable bonds

An exchangeable bond (known as an XB), is one which may be converted by the holder into shares of another company other than the issuer. It is common for the alternative company to be a subsidiary of the bond issuer.

The value of the exchangeable bond = Price of straight bond + Price of the option

### 7.3.9 Callable and putable bonds

#### Callable bonds

Callable bonds are where the issuer has the right to redeem the bonds at an agreed price prior to its maturity. This price may be above the normal redemption price and the extra price paid is referred to as the call premium.

The call provision is valuable to the issuer, but is a disadvantage to the investor, since the issuer will only exercise the call if it suits the issuer to do so. As a result, the price at which a callable bond can be issued will be lower than for a comparable straight bond, and the interest rate it will need to pay will consequently be higher.

A call provision will reduce the expected time to maturity of the bond, since there is a possibility that the bond will be retired early as a result of the call provision being exercised.

Call provisions will be exercised when the issuer can refinance the issue at a cheaper cost due to interest rates having fallen. For example, if a bond were issued when interest rates were 15% and interest rates have now fallen to 5%, the issuer could issue a new bond at the currently low i/r and use the proceeds to call back the higher coupon bond.

#### Putable bonds

This is where the investor has a **put option** on the bond, giving him the right to sell the bond back to the company at a specified price (the put price). The put price is typically around par, given that the bond was issued at par.

The benefit to the investor is that if interest rates rise after the bond is issued, they can sell the bond at a fixed price and reinvest the proceeds at a higher interest rate. As a result of the benefit to investors, putable bonds are issued at higher prices or lower coupons than comparable nonputable bonds.

### 7.3.10 Coupon

Most corporate bonds are issued with a fixed coupon rate. The coupon to be received is based upon the nominal value of the corporate bond held and the fixed coupon rate. This is calculated as for the previous coupon example for a gilt. There are, however, two major exceptions to this rule, namely floating rate notes (FRNs) and zero-coupon bonds.

## 7.4 Asset-backed securities (ABSs)

### 7.4.1 The securitisation process

The use of loans or mortgage payments to raise finance in the form of asset backed securities is referred to as the **securitisation process**. In order to issue asset backed securities, a company will set up a legal entity known as a special purpose vehicle (or SPV) which is a separate legal entity to the original company. Consider a situation where a company has issued loans to clients worth £50 million which will be repaid by the clients with regular payments in the future. The company sets up a special purpose vehicle (SPV) and sells the loans to the SPV in return for an immediate £50 million cash payment which is the finance that the company required. The SPV will in turn issue asset backed securities (ABS), backed by the loan payments which will be sold to investors to cover the £50 million that the SPV has paid the company.

Asset-backed securities (ABSs) are constructed by packaging together a group of securities and then issuing a new security whose purchaser has a claim against the cash flows generated by the original package. The process is known as **'securitisation'**. ABSs are securities that are backed by one or more particular asset(s), such as credit card debt, mortgages and other loans. They are 'backed' by assets because the cash flows from these underlying assets are the primary source of payments on the asset-backed securities.

When considering credit rating of asset backed securities, credit rating agencies will need to consider a number of factors:

The administration of the company which manages the securitised assets and collections of cash flows is of significant importance. The securitised assets themselves will require a high degree of analysis to consider the risk in the event of financial difficulties. This came to the fore recently when so called 'sub-prime' mortgages were used to secure mortgage backed securities. When the holders of a number of these mortgages defaulted, the MBSs themselves became a much higher default risk. The legal structure of the securities and its bankruptcy protection, and the mechanisms for cash flow payments will also be considered. Assessing these complex instruments is undoubtedly complex and has caused difficulties for the credit rating agencies who have been criticised for failing to accurately estimate their risk.

### 7.4.2 Mortgage-backed securities (MBSs)

Mortgage-backed securities (MBSs) are designed to give liquidity to the mortgage loan market by converting mortgage loans into tradable securities. The types of securities issued vary, being pass through securities or collateralised mortgage obligations (CMOs).

### 7.4.3 Mortgage pass through securities

Pass through certificates relate to a pool of mortgage loans. Payments under the bonds are financed through payments made on the underlying pool of mortgages to which the bonds relate. When mortgage borrowers make interest and capital repayments, these are passed through to the investor in the pass through certificates.

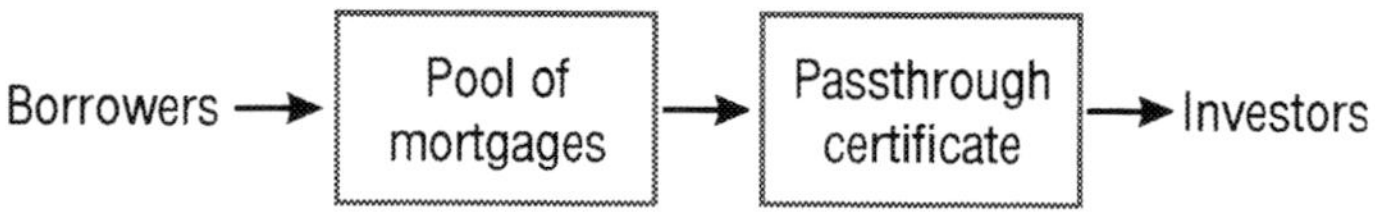


The interest payments passed through to the investors are lower than the interest payments made by the borrowers, reflecting servicing fees charged by the trustee of the pool.

One feature of pass throughs is that the **cash flows and final maturity are uncertain**, since any mortgage borrower forming part of the pool may decide to make a prepayment of the capital portion of the loan in advance of the planned schedule.

### 7.4.4 Collateralised mortgage obligations (CMOs)

CMOs are designed to redistribute the risk and return from a pool of mortgages to meet investors' needs. As a result, CMOs are not one form of security, as is the case with simple mortgage pass-through, but a range of different securities.

The original CMOs were fairly simple in structure and took the form of sequential pay tranches or bonds. The CMO is split into several tranches, identified as A, B, C, etc. Interest from the mortgages is paid to all tranches in proportion to their principal investment. However, principal repayments are first used to repay tranche A. When all of tranche A has been repaid, the next principal repayments are used to repay tranche B and so on.

Although the priority for repayment of principal is known, the timing of principal repayments is not.

The sequential order of repayment means that the first tranches will have average lives shorter than the underlying mortgage collateral while the later tranches will have average lives longer than the underlying collateral. These simple, sequential pay CMOs are sometimes referred to as plain vanilla CMOs.

An additional tranche, known as an accrual bond or Z bond, can also be created. The Z bond pays no interest in the early years. Instead, the interest is used to buy additional principal from the other tranches in a sequential pay CMO. The impact of a Z bond is to shorten the average life of the other tranches, while the Z bond has a very long average life.

A **collateralised bond obligation (CBO)** is where the ABS is typically backed by a pool of non-investment grade bonds (high yield bonds), emerging market bonds or corporate bank loans.

Where the pool is exclusively made up of bank loans, it is referred to as a **collateralised loan obligation (CLO)**.

### 7.4.5 Special purpose vehicle (SPV)

The use of a special purpose vehicle (SPV) enables a company to raise funds at a cheaper cost. If a company borrows money directly, it will need to pay a cost of funds based on its general credit quality. However, if it has a particular set of debtors, e.g. customers paying instalments on credit purchases, it can sell these assets to a SPV. These debtors are now separate from the general assets of the company. This means that if the company goes bankrupt, they should not be available to the creditors of the company. SPVs are sometimes called bankruptcy remote entities.

## 7.5 Spreads

arning objectives

**1.4.2 Understand** the main bond pricing benchmarks and how they are applied to new bond issues: Spread over government bond benchmark, Spread over/under LIBOR, Spread over/under swap

**1.5.6 Understand** the differences in yield, spread and price methods, and the circumstances in which they are used.

As stated earlier, to compensate the investor for the increased risk of lending to a corporate rather than the government, it will be normal for the yield on a corporate bond to be higher than for government debt of an equivalent maturity. The difference between the yields of different instruments is known as the **spread**. For a given maturity, there will be a particular government bond, the benchmark gilt, against which the yields on corporate bonds of the same maturity are measured. This will give the spread over the government benchmark.

For example, if a particular corporate bond with eight years to maturity is yielding 5.40%, and the eight year government benchmark bond is yielding 4.25%, the bond's spread over the government benchmark would be 1.15%. This could also be stated as 115 basis points, where **1 basis point = 0.01%**.

Spreads can also be measured against the benchmark rate of interbank interest known as LIBOR, or the interest rate swap quotes rates.

In the same example as above, if LIBOR was 4.75%, then the bond's spread over LIBOR would be 0.65%, or 65 basis points.

You may be asked in your exam to convert a spread over a benchmark yield into a spread over LIBOR, or *vice versa*.

## Example

A bond has a spread of 140 basis points over the benchmark yield of 4.75%. If LIBOR is 4.90%, what is the spread over LIBOR?

## Solution

Bond yield – 4.75% = 140 basis points = 1.40%

Bond yield = 4.75% + 1.40% = 6.15%

Spread over LIBOR = 6.15% – 4.90% = 1.25% = 125 basis points.

*Alternatively*

LIBOR spread over benchmark yield = 4.90% – 4.75% = 15 basis points

Bond's spread over LIBOR = 140 basis points – 15 basis points = 125 basis points.

Traders in bonds will consider the prevailing lending yields in the market. Appropriate yields for particular bonds will set the market price. The spreads over base rates such as LIBOR or government debt are then used to identify company specific factors.

## 7.6 Eurobonds

**Learning objective**

1.3.1 **Understand** the main investment characteristics, behaviours and risks of Eurobonds: Types of issuer; sovereign, supranational and corporate, Types of Eurobond; straight, FRN / VRN, subordinated, asset backed, convertible, international bank syndicate issuance, immobilization in depositaries, continuous pure bearer instrument; implications for interest and capital repayment, taxation of interest and capital gains, accrued interest and ex-interest date.

A Eurobond is a debt instrument issued by a borrower (typically a government or a large company) outside of the country in whose currency it is denominated. For example, a US dollar Eurobond could be issued anywhere in the world except for the US. As such, a better name for it might be an 'international bond'. Eurobonds frequently carry no security, other than the name and credit rating of the issuer.

Another important feature of bonds issued in this market is that for the most part they are issued in **bearer form**, with no formal register of ownership held by the company. These bearer documents are immobilised at central depositories, such as Euroclear and Clearstream, which provide clearing and stocklending facilities.

Most Eurobonds are issued in **bullet form**, redeemed at one specified date in the future. However, a number of issues have alternative redemption patterns. Some bonds are redeemed over a number of years with a proportion of the issue being redeemed each year. Whilst Eurobonds are not issued in registered form, each will have an identifying number. A **drawing** of numbers is made every year from the pool of bonds in issue, the numbers drawn are published, and the bonds are called in and redeemed. This redemption process is known as a drawing on a Eurobond.

As with other bonds, a variety of options are available on the issuance of Eurobonds.

- **Floating rate notes** (FRNs) – Given that the primary risk associated with holding a bond is interest rate risk (interest rate rises will cause bond prices to fall), Eurobonds may be issued with coupons that adjust in line with interest rates to maintain the capital value at around par. The question is, as the bonds are issued internationally, which interest rate? The London Inter Bank Offered Rate (LIBOR) is most commonly used, with the most common alternative rate being Euro Interbank Offered Rates collected as an average of the rates quoted by the largest European banks.
- **Subordinated** – Subordinated Eurobond issuances will have the lowest seniority and hence the greatest risk.

- **Asset backed** – The Eurobond will be backed by a particular asset or some form of collateral.
- **Convertible bonds** – Similar in nature to the convertible bonds discussed elsewhere in this chapter, they offer the option of converting the bond into shares of the issuing company.

Since Eurobonds are international in nature, and are not issued under the auspices of any domestic economy and are therefore not governed by any domestic withholding tax legislation, all coupons are paid gross of tax. This will serve to make Eurobonds tax efficient investments, since the investor receives the gross coupon. Obviously, in each domestic tax regime the Eurobond interest is taxed in accordance with normal rules. The alternative is that the investor receives their coupon net of withholding tax and is then able to reclaim it if they are a non-taxpayer. At present there is some debate within the European Union as to the imposition of withholding taxes.

The Eurobond market is in effect an international market in debt. Companies issuing debt in the Eurobond market have their securities traded all around the world and are not limited to one domestic market place.

There is no formal market place for Eurobond trading. The market is telephone driven and the Eurobond houses are based in London. The market is regulated by the **International Capital Markets Association** (ICMA), formerly known as the International Securities Markets Association (ISMA), which operates rules regulating the conduct of dealers in the market place. ICMA also monitors pricing through its **TRAX price reporting system**. Trades must be reported into TRAX within **30 minutes**. Whilst the market operates on a telephone basis, price quotes are available through screen-based systems such as Reuters and Telerate.

Settlement is conducted for the market by two independent clearing houses, **Euroclear and Clearstream**. These clearing houses immobilise the actual Eurobonds in their vaults and then operate electronic record of ownership. The clearing houses exchange information about deals relating to holdings in the other's vault via an electronic information system known as **The Bridge**.

Settlement in the Eurobond market is based on a **three-business day** settlement system (T + 3). Once again, the important feature about the records maintained by the two clearing houses is that they are not normally available to any governmental authority, thereby preserving the bearer nature of the documents.

When Eurobonds are traded, accrued interest is calculated along similar principles to those for government debt discussed earlier. However, rather than the 'actual/actual' day count used for UK bonds, the conventions used for Eurobonds is a '30/360' day count, where the days in each month are rounded to 30, giving 360 days in the year.

**Eurobonds prices are quoted as clean prices.** In the Euromarkets, there is no problem with ex-div dates since given the efficiency of the systems there is no need to set an ex-div date in advance. Therefore, there is **no ex-div period** for Eurobonds.

The methods of Eurobond issuance are identical to those of corporate bond issues in the domestic markets, with international. Banks making up the syndicate to facilitate the issuance in different markets (See below)

# 8 UK Government Bond Issuance

Learning objective

**1.4.1 Understand** the responsibilities and processes of the UK Debt Management Office (DMO) in relation to the management and issue of UK Government debt: Gilts, Treasury Bills, Public Works Loan Board, Primary market makers: Gilt edged Market Makers (GEMMS) and Intermediaries: Inter-dealer brokers (IDBs).

## 8.1 Government bonds

Government bonds are issued to provide the Government with funds when required with a number of approaches used.

Over the past few years in the UK, the Debt Management Office DMO has gradually introduced a structured issuance timetable by running auctions at the end of each month. The DMO envisages that each auction will be for at least £2bn nominal and will tend to be issued into one of the existing benchmark stocks, known as a 'tranche'. The dates of each auction are made available at the outset of the year. Prior to the beginning of each calendar quarter, the DMO will announce the maturity range for each of the auctions taking place in that quarter. The maturities to be issued will have been discussed with market participants in order to establish the most appropriate mix of stocks.

This removes some of the flexibility that the DMO has enjoyed in the past but creates a more certain environment in the market. The overall level of supply is relatively fixed and the market is aware of when stock will be issued. However, these reforms fall some way short of a complete overhaul of the issuance system. In many markets, such as the US, there is no flexibility whatsoever with regard to issuance timetable or maturity of stocks to be issued, since these have been fixed well in advance.

Indeed unlike most other government bond markets, the DMO still possesses the ability to issue stock directly into the secondary market via the creation of tap stocks. These taps will be used to support the market's liquidity rather than exploit timing advantages.

The process of bond auctions as the method of issuing bonds means that the successful bidder will pay the price that they bid, which means that bidders run the risk of overpaying.

Running alongside each competitive auction are non-competitive bids where investors can apply for up to **£500,000 of nominal value for conventional gilts** and **£250,000 for index-linked gilts**. Applicants through non-competitive bids will receive the gilts they applied for at a weighted average of accepted prices in the auction. The smaller investors can participate in the primary market for gilts, whilst avoiding the necessity of determining an appropriate price.

## 8.2 Treasury Bill issuance

Treasury bills (T-bill) represent a promise to repay (**a promissory note**) a set sum of money by the Treasury (via the Debt Management Office) at a specified date in the future, normally not longer than **91 calendar days (three months)**. Usually, the minimum block size for trading would be **£25,000** though prices are stated per £100 of principal.

T-bills are issued by way of a **weekly tender** when bids are made on a **yield basis** to three decimal places and by 11:00 London time. The bills then trade at a discount to their face value. The Bank's T-bill issues are not part of the government's funding programme per se, but are much more an instrument of monetary policy. Where members of the public wish to participate in the tenders, they must do so via one of a number of possible Treasury Bill primary participants (a role played by many of the large banks), and must purchase a minimum of **£500,000** nominal value of bills. Treasury Bill tenders are also open to DMO Cash Management Counterparties and a small number of wholesale market participants. The tender results in a single price being fixed for all bidders, unlike the auction which results in each successful bidder paying the price bid.

### 8.2.1 Published prices

The General Collateral (GC) repo rate (adjusted by a spread reflecting recent Treasury bill tender results and supply and demand factors) is used to calculate the DMO published CREST reference prices for UK Treasury Bills. This reference price is published by the DMO at the end of each business day. The DMO makes clear that these prices are indicative mid prices which are for the purpose of CREST valuation of collateral transfers, and not offers by the DMO to buy or sell at this price.

### 8.2.2 Participants in the government bond market

All member firms of stock exchanges such as the LSE are broker-dealers. Broker-dealers have **dual capacity**. This means they can act as agents on behalf of the customer and as principals dealing directly with the customer.

Some broker-dealers can elect to take on board a higher level of responsibility and become primary dealers or **market makers**. Primary dealers are the focus of market activity, and their obligation is to ensure that there is always a **two-way price** in the securities in which they are market makers.

In the international context, the UK is unusual in adopting this **quote-driven system**. The majority of the world's stock markets operate on the basis of order-driven systems. In these markets, the brokers bring the whole order to the market and see whether any other broker will take it.

## 8.3 UK gilt-edged market makers (GEMMs)

The Gilt-Edged Market Makers (GEMMs) are the focus of the market place in the UK. Their role is to ensure that two-way quotes exist at all times for all gilts. Market makers are allowed to enter the market by the Debt Management Office, an Executive Agency of HM Treasury. They must decide to make a market in either all conventional gilts (a conventional GEMM) or all index-linked gilts (IG GEMM), or both.

Once accepted as a gilt-edged market maker, the firm is obliged to make a market in either **all conventional gilts** or **all index-linked gilts** at a size deemed appropriate by the Debt Management Office.

A firm has the obligation to make firm prices to **all member firms** of the LSE (except other market makers and IDBs) and also **to clients known directly to them**. In line with the requirements for pre-trade transparency, GEMMs should make their quotes available to the market place through appropriate price networks.

There are onerous restrictions placed on what gilt-edged market makers may do and with whom they are able to deal. To counter these disadvantages, the gilt-edged market makers have a **direct relationship with the Debt Management Office** which keeps them informed of its intentions with regard to the market. The Debt Management Office also acts as a source of borrowing for GEMMs, in that it buys back certain gilts from the market in much the same way as the Bank of England acts as the lender of last resort to the money markets.

In addition, GEMMs have exclusive access to Inter-Dealer Brokers (IDBs) with regard to gilts.

### 8.3.1 Gilt inter-dealer brokers

The Gilt Inter-Dealer Brokers (IDBs) act as an escape valve for GEMMs. If a GEMM were to build up a large position in a particular stock and then decide to unwind it, it might be difficult to achieve without revealing to the rest of the market that he was long or short of a stock. This is obviously a dangerous position and would discourage gilt-edged market makers from taking substantial positions. The IDBs provide an anonymous dealing service, allowing GEMMs to unwind positions.

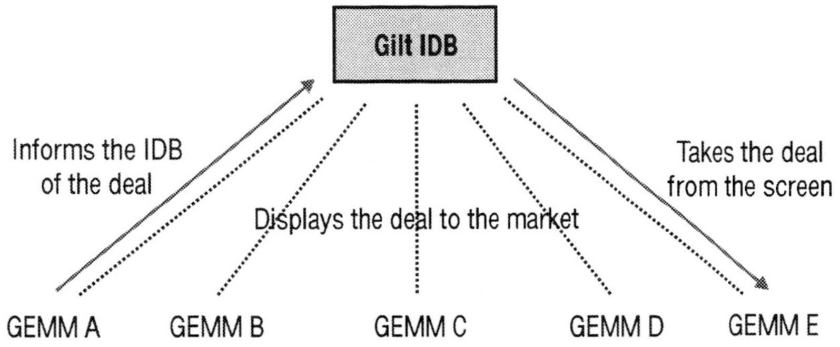

For example, market maker A is long of £50m of stock and wishes to unwind this position. Market maker A then contacts one of the IDBs and states the type, amount and price of the stock that is for sale. This information is then entered on to the IDB screen (the IDBs have screens in all of the market makers' offices) and once the price is on the screen, other market makers may call into the IDB to deal. Dealing takes place at the price quoted on the screen. Even once the deal is struck, the IDB will not reveal the name of the other market maker.

In effect, two trades are made. Market maker A sells to the IDB, the IDB then sells to the incoming market maker E. It should be noted, however, that the IDB does not take the position on its books – it undertakes **two matched principal to principal trades**. The IDBs make their money by charging commission to market makers who hit, lift or take the price from the screen. A very small percentage of the transaction value is paid in commission since the IDBs take no risk dealing with solvent market makers and the transaction sizes are substantial.

It is important to remember that the **gilt** prices available on the IDB screens are for market makers only, and this information may not be passed on by market makers to the rest of the market, i.e. the GEMMs have 'exclusive' access to the IDB screen. There are intermediaries who can arrange matched principal to principal trades between any user called wholesale dealer brokers.

To further facilitate the gilt market, the DMO offers a 'Standing Repo Facility' which allows GEMMs or DMO counterparties to enter into reverse repo arrangements with the DMO. The repo will generally be for next day settlement but may be rolled forward for up to two weeks.

## 9 Corporate Bonds Issuance

**Learning objective**

**1.4.3** **Understand** the purpose, structure and process of the main methods of origination, issuance and their implications for issuers and investors: scheduled funding programmes and opportunistic issuance (e.g. MTN) auction/tender and reverse inquiry (under MTN).

In the domestic market, the most common form of issuance is via a placing. In the Euromarkets, a more structured approach is required in order to cope with the size of the issues involved.

**New Issues in the Corporate Bond Market**

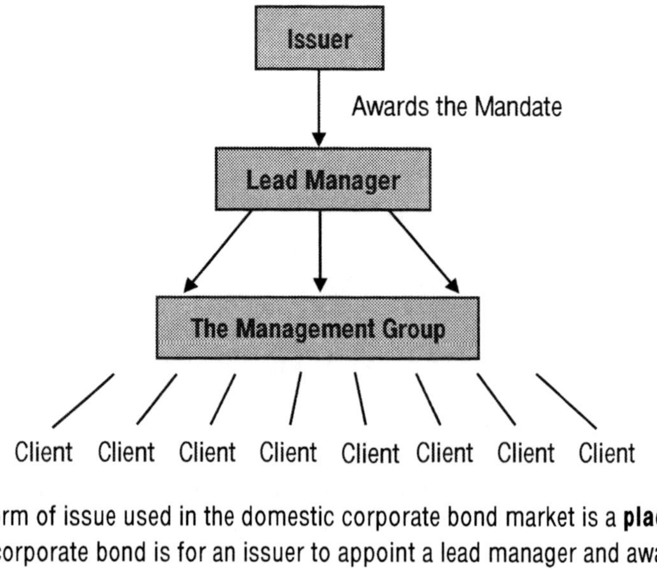


The most common form of issue used in the domestic corporate bond market is a **placing**. A traditional method of issuing a corporate bond is for an issuer to appoint a lead manager and award them the mandate. The mandate gives the lead manager the power and responsibility to issue the bond on the issuer's behalf.

A **bought deal** is where the lead manager agrees detailed terms with the issuer, including the coupon and the maturity. In normal issues, the lead manager has the ability to amend the terms of the issue as market conditions dictate.

The lead manager may then create a management group of other issuing houses. Each house receives a portion of the deal and places it with its client base. Alternatively, the lead manager may elect to run the entire book alone, and omit the other members of the management group.

There are a number of variations on this method of issue. Under a **fixed price re-offer**, the members of the management group are prohibited from selling the bonds in the secondary market at below the issue price until the syndicate has been broken. The syndicate will break when the lead manager believes the bulk of the issue has been placed.

The traditional programmes of bond issuance were somewhat cumbersome because of the requirement to register each in turn with the relevant regulator. To get around this, companies would often chose to make arrangements with banks to enable them to borrow money on a scheduled basis. i.e. a scheduled funding programme.

A recent development of this process is the 'shelf registration'. These programs allow a single registration with a regulator (originally in the US with the SEC) allowing a series of bond issues over a period of time up to two years at any 'opportunistic' time when market rates are favourable.

In the UK a firm listed on the official list wishing to obtain shelf registration, would approach UKLA (the FSA) with a 'shelf document' following UKLA approval, the documents will then be published on the UKLA website on an annual basis. The document contains similar material to that of the listings documents. As the firm then choses to list further securities over the course of the next year they need only publish and circulate a short 'issue note'.

In the US the medium-term note (MTN) has been widely used with this process, with maturities of between two and ten years. On occasion inquiries might be made to dealers in MTNs from clients wanting a particular bond. These 'reverse enquiries' may lead to the issuer issuing bonds on demand. The market in MTNs took off in 1982, when the SEC introduced rule 415, which enabled issuers to offer medium term notes in a fashion similar to that of the issuance of commercial paper.

### 9.1 MTN market

MTN issuers will use service of dealers to offer the MTNs, The dealers will advertise a range of yields available for varying maturities up to the ten year maximum. Investors will approach dealers who will then deal with the issuing firm to obtain the MTNs. The dealers also support a secondary market in the MTNs. Where the specific MTN wanted by an investor is not quoted, they may well place a 'request with a dealer who then approaches the firm. This is referred to as a 'reverse inquiry'. MTNs are credit rated like corporate bonds.

## 10 International Government Bond Markets

earning objective

1.5.1 **Understand** the role, structure and characteristics of government bond markets in the developed markets of UK, Germany, USA and Japan, and the emerging economies of Brazil, China, India and Russia (BRIC) including: Market environment: relative importance of Exchange vs. OTC trading, Participants – primary dealers, broker dealers and inter-dealer brokers, The impact of ratings and the concept of 'risk free', Currency, credit and inflation risks, Inflation indexed bonds, Access considerations, Regulatory/ supervisory environment and Relevant trade associations.

## 10.1 UK - The Debt Management Office (DMO)

The Debt Management Office (DMO), as an Executive Agency of HM Treasury, is the lead regulator in the gilts market. Its objective is to ensure that the gilts market remains solvent, liquid and, above all, fair. The reason for this commitment is that the DMO is obliged to issue, on the Government's behalf, gilts to fund the Public Sector Net Cash Requirement (PSNCR). In order to do this, the DMO must have access to the markets. It is the DMO which allows participants to enter the gilts market and thereafter monitors their capital adequacy on a daily basis.

## 10.2 US – The US Treasury

The US government bond market is the largest in the world having expanded rapidly in the 1980s. this size is evident in both the quantity of issuance in the primary market and volumes of activity in the secondary market.

The market is not dissimilar in structure from the UK gilt market. This is due to the UK reforms that have been designed to bring the two markets into line. Indeed, the general direction of all government bond markets has been towards greater 'fungibility' or similarity, with the US being seen as the role model.

### 10.2.1 The Fed

The key player in the market is the Federal Reserve (the 'Fed'). As the US central bank, the Fed, through open market operations, manipulates liquidity to control US monetary policy. The Fed is largely independent; the only political involvement comes in the appointment of the board. To this extent, many argue that the Fed is less independent than the Bundesabnk. However, in many ways this possibility of political influence is more apparent than actual. For if a President were to try to 'rig' the Fed, then it is likely that the markets would react unfavourably and the benefits of credibility would be eroded very quickly.

The Fed's own publications summarise the objectives of the Board of Governors and the 12 Federal Reserve banks as being the following.

- Conducting the nation's monetary policy by influencing money and credit conditions in the economy in pursuit of full employment and stable prices. However, the clear focus of policy is towards the latter of these two objectives in the belief that price stability is a prerequisite for higher levels of employment.
- Supervising and regulating banking institutions to ensure the safety and soundness of the nation's banking and financial system and to protect the credit rights of consumers.
- Maintaining the stability of the financial system and containing the systemic risk that may arise in financial markets.
- Providing certain financial services to the US government, the public, financial institutions, and foreign official institutions, including playing a major role in operating the nation's payments system.

### 10.2.2 Types of issue of US government bonds

- **Treasury bills (T-Bills)** – These have a maturity of three months to one year and are issued at a discount to face value.
- **Treasury notes (T-notes) –** These are coupon securities and are issued with initial maturities of between two and ten years.
- **Treasury bonds (T-bonds) –** These are again coupon securities and are issued with an initial life of over ten years.

- **Treasury Inflation Protected Securities (TIPS) –** In 1997, the US government issued treasury inflation protected securities or index-linked bonds for the first time. In part, this was seen as an unusual decision by the markets, who initially viewed it as a worrying sign with regard to the government's commitment to low inflation, it actually reinforces it by ensuring that if inflation does take off, government finance cost will likewise rise in nominal terms. On TIPS, the principle value is adjusted for changes in the CPI to reflect inflation and the coupon is a fixed rate payable on this adjusted value.

## 10.3 Japan

The Japanese government bond market is the second largest in the world. The market has basically grown from nothing in the early 1960s to its current size. From that point on, the government has consistently borrowed money initially to finance investment in the nation's infrastructure.

However, more recently the poor economic conditions within Japan have led to a need to borrow in order to finance fiscal injections into the economy.

The Japanese bond market is dominated by government bonds. This domination is not in terms of volume, where Japanese Government Bonds (JGBs) account for only half of the market, but in the secondary market where they account for the majority of the secondary market trading.

Initially the market was dominated by domestic investors, however, due both to size of issuance and the growing importance of the Yen, the market has attracted increasing numbers of overseas investors. To aid this internationalisation of the market the government has introduced a number of liberalising measures, though it is still impossible to settle and deliver JGBs outside Japan.

The Japanese market has in the past been regarded as one of the least developed and most 'investor unfriendly' markets amongst the major government bond markets. The Bank of Japan was until recently one of the least independent of all the central banks. However, steps have been taken in order to bring the markets into line with the other major markets. These steps have included a greater level of say for the BoJ in the establishment of policy.

It is still the case that many international investors regard the Japanese market as a hostile environment and therefore tend to avoid it. Only 5% of JGBs are owned by non-Japanese citizens.

There are three main types of instrument issued:

- **Treasury bills –** issued with three and six month maturities, these are discount securities issued via public auction twice a month. The market is not active and external investors only have limited access.
- **Medium Term Notes –** These are two year maturity notes that are issued via an auction every two months.
- **Government bonds –** These are conventional debt securities predominantly with a maturity of ten years. The government does issue 'super longs' that have a maturity of 20 years. The Ministry of Finance has also placed a number of 30-year zero coupon bonds in the past.

## 10.4 Government Bond Markets Summary

| | Japan (JGB) | US T-Bond | Brazil | Russia | German Bund | Eurobonds | UK Corporates | Indian | China | UK Gilt |
|---|---|---|---|---|---|---|---|---|---|---|
| Coupon Frequency | Semi-annual | Semi-annual | Annual | Semi-annual | Annual | Annual | Annual | Semi-annual | Annual | Semi-annual |
| Settlement | 3 business days | Same/ Next day | 3 business days | 3 business days | 3 business days | 3 business days | 3 business days | 3 business days | 3 business days | Same/ Next day |
| Registered or bearer | R or B | R | R | B | B | B | R | B | B | R |
| Normal life | 10 years, some super longs with life of 40 years | Life of over 10 years | Varied | Varied | Mostly 10 years | Varied | | Mostly 10 years | Varied | Varied |
| Withholding tax | 25%, but bilateral agreement reduces to 10% | None | None | None | None | None | 20% | None | None | None or 20% if elected |
| Medium-term debt | – | T-Note life of 2 to 10 years | | | BOBLs with lives of up to 5 years and Schatz with lives of 2 to 6 years | – | – | 5 years | | – |
| Settlement agencies | Japanese Government Bond Clearing Corporation (JGBCC) | Federal Reserve | | | Euroclear and Clearstream | Euroclear and Clearstream | CREST | Negotiated Deal Settlement | | CREST, Clearstream Euroclear and Bank of New York |
| Accrued interest convention | $\frac{\text{Actual}}{365}$ | $\frac{\text{Actual}}{\text{Actual}}$ | $\frac{\text{Actual}}{\text{Actual}}$ | $\frac{\text{Actual}}{\text{Actual}}$ | $\frac{\text{Actual}}{\text{Actual}}$ | $\frac{\text{Actual}}{\text{Actual}}$ | $\frac{\text{Actual}}{\text{Actual}}$ | $\frac{\text{Actual}}{\text{Actual}}$ | $\frac{\text{Actual}}{\text{Actual}}$ | $\frac{\text{Actual}}{\text{Actual}}$ |

## 10.5 The corporate bond market

In much the same way that governments finance their deficits through the use of debt finance, companies who wish to spend more than they currently have available may also borrow money through the issuance of bonds. Due to the increased risk of default, these bonds will yield more than Government debt. Once again this illustrates one of the key maxims of investment – **greater risk requires greater reward**.

Corporate debt can take a wide variety of forms, and there are many different aspects to an issue which might need to be considered.

## 10.6 The global corporate bond market

**Learning objective**

**1.5.3 Understand** the role, structure and characteristics of global corporate bond markets: Decentralized dealer markets and dealer provision of liquidity, Impact of default risk on prices, Relationship between bond and equity markets, Bond pools of liquidity versus centralized equity exchanges, Access considerations, Regulatory/ supervisory environment, ICMA and other relevant trade associations.

The market in fixed interest debt issued by companies in the UK is relatively small. The limited interest reflects in part the risk attached, but perhaps more importantly, the UK investment market's obsession with shares. Another reason why the market in corporate bonds is less active than the market in gilts is its fragmentation. There are a large number of issues, but unlike the gilts market which has an equally large number of issues, each issue can have very different characteristics. A major risk is the credit risk of default by the issuer.

The UK market in corporate bonds is again focused both around the activities of market makers on the LSE and also a decentralised market where dealers appointed by the issuer provide liquidity in the market by acting as agent between principles. These trades on the decentralised market are not completed on a formal exchange but provide potential investors with buy and sell prices offered by other investors.

With the on exchange trades, the firms that wish to be market makers in the stocks apply to the LSE for permission to deal. Unlike the market making obligation in the gilts market, here market makers are only obliged to quote firm prices (in a marketable quantity determined by the LSE) to **broker-dealers** and not to customers known to them or fellow market makers. The Mandatory Quote Period is 08:00 to 16:30 for UK bonds.

Where a firm which is not registered as a market maker in a security and either

- Effects a principal transaction; or
- Conducts an agency cross

with, or on behalf of, a customer, then the firm must take all reasonable steps to ensure that the transaction price is better than the best price available in the market in that size.

Corporate bonds settle **three business days** after the day of trade (T + 3).

### 10.6.1 Regulation of issuers

If a company wishes to issue its securities to the public it must conform to some basic rules and procedures. Initially, all securities issues are governed by the Public Offers of Securities Regulations (POSRs). However, if a borrower wishes to attract a high level of interest in their issue then they may elect to face the more onerous set of exchange regulations known as the Listing Rules. These rules are administered by the UK Listing Authority (a role of the Financial Services Authority ).Issues in excess of £20 million are reported to the British Merchant Bankers Association (BMBA) who operate an unofficial queuing system that aims to ensure that two large issues do not hit the market at the same time. The Bank of England does however insist that the lead manager is effective for each issue and this requires them to be organised And managed in the UK or from a country outside with reciprocal agreements with UK brokers.

### 10.6.2 Regulatory environment of trading

The London Stock Exchange acts as a recognised investment exchange and is required to follow the FSA rules. Any security listing on the LSE must have satisfied the listing rules as laid out in the Rule Book. The admission and trading rules are set out by the LSE while the full listing rules are the responsibility of the UKLA (a role of the FSA).

Where a firm wishes to act as an agent or principal in the trading of bonds they will be required to authorised by the FSA before carrying out the activity. Any breach of FSA rules will then risk the firm being subjected to serious penalties. The individuals who work for the firm in particular FSA specified roles such as customer roles or managing positions will be required to be approved by the FSA and as such subject to FSA control, and potential punishment such as fines or prohibition orders.

### 10.6.3 The International Capital Markets Association (ICMA)

The ICMA is a body formed to regulate the practise of issuing new securities into the Eurobond market. It does so through a rule book that provides recommendations on the way in which issues should be structured and how the timetable of issuance should be dealt with. Trading of Eurobonds once issued, generally takes place between ICMA dealers who will quote two way prices on request. The market in Eurobonds is relatively illiquid however, with the majority of Eurobonds being held to maturity.

## 10.7 Global electronic bond markets

| Learning objectives | 1.5.4 **Understand** the key features of the bond markets |
|---|---|

Bonds which have a high liquidity tend to trade on electronic systems, such as Bloomberg, as opposed to voice trading via telephone. Government bonds and certain corporate bonds are of a sufficient liquidity for these electronic systems. It is generally possible to find bond futures and options trading on regulated exchanges, giving them a higher level of liquidity.

Where bonds are of a lower liquidity such as high yield bonds the procedure is often to employ an RFQ (request for quote) to the dealer who will generally be the issuing bank.

Over-the-counter deals between dealers are also employed where bonds are of low liquidity or the size of the transaction is unusually large. In addition to the exchange trading mentioned previously, the following terms may be used to describe the different participants and methods of trading.

### 10.7.1 Electronic markets

- Inter-dealer (also known as business-to-business or B2B). Examples include Electronic Training Platforms (ETPs) such as MTS and Brokertec.
- Customer to dealer (also known as business-to-customer or B2C). Example ETPs include Tradeweb, BondVision, proprietary Single Dealer Platform (SDP). Where dealers are providing bond investors with liquidity.

Bond trading is carried out around international markets and as such should allow 24 hour access to the market. The dealers who are prepared to make a market in the bonds will find this attractive due to the bid – offer spread from which they can profit.

#### 10.7.1.1 The London Stock Exchange's Electronic Order Book for Retail Bonds (ORB)

In 2010, the London Stock Exchange launched the ORB to offer trading in bonds for the private investor. A number of gilts and 'retail size' UK corporate bonds are available in trading denominations of £1,000 or similar.

The LSE describes the functioning of the ORB factsheet on the LSE website:

- dedicated market makers will quote two-way prices in a range of retail bonds throughout the trading day and all other registered member participants will also be able to enter orders into the book

- new market model means private investors will be able to see prices on-screen and trade in bonds in a similar way as they currently do for shares
- settlement of order book trades can be instructed automatically by our X-TRM post-trade router via direct input into CREST
- functionality available for trade data on electronic executions will be fed into X-TRM which will calculate the accrued interest payable and instruct settlement in CREST on behalf of the counterparties'

The LSE factsheet further states:

'This new trading service for bonds will be made available as two new segments on our TradElect platform:

- UKGT – 'UK Gilts'
- UKCP – 'UK Corporates'

It will offer an electronic order-driven model similar to SETS with continuous two-way pricing provided by market makers (submitted as named executable quotes) and where other market participants are able to enter market orders and limit orders. The trading day will start with an initial opening auction phase running from 8.00 to 8.45 followed by continuous trading until market close at 16.30.'

### 10.7.2 The over-the-counter market (OTC)

Over the counter trades tend to be bonds which have low liquidity and frequently the issuing company may be so small that they will not be listed on an exchange.

- Inter-dealer voice trading. This could include making a direct call to a dealer at another bank, or going to a voice broker to deal with another bank
- Customer-to-dealer voice trading. A traditional stockbroker dealing with a customer over the phone.

In both cases dealing is done away from the exchange and without the participation of a market maker.

## 10.8 OTC swaps

Alongside the exponential growth of exchange traded derivatives over the past decade, there has been a similar, if less visible, growth in over the counter 'OTC' products in particular the market in swaps.

Certain aspects of the exchange traded derivatives market have proved irksome for users, such as the limited availability of products, the fixed delivery dates, standardised contract sizes, limited exercise prices and expiry dates and the strictures of exchange margining rules have all lead to make the bespoke OTC markets especially attractive.

As the world's derivatives exchanges have become busier, they have also become more competitive. The profit margins for all exchange members , from brokers to principal traders, have thus been squeezed. Investment banks have seen more sophisticated and more opaque OTC market as providing an opportunity to maximise profits from their derivative skills. Over time, it can be expected that the OTC market will itself become crowded, but it should be borne in mind that as OTC market contracts are undertaken on a bilateral basis, rather than via a clearing house, only institutions with good credit ratings can hope to be large players.

Swaps are agreements under which counterparties agree to swap specific cash flows. For example, in the interest rate swap, the counterparties agree to exchange future interest payments. Historically, these arrangements were first developed as corporate to corporate deals with any financial intermediary simply acting as a broker. Now the financial intermediaries act as market makers. Swaps are executed where no counterparty exists as yet, holding one side of the deal on their own account (warehousing one leg) until a counterparty can be found. In this way, they face the true risk of an intermediary. The market makers build a book of transactions that offset each other overall, if not on a deal-by deal basis.

To minimise the credit risk of OTC derivatives contracts, participants normally take a lengthy due diligence investigation of their counterparty to avoid contracts which are likely to default.

There is also a growing use of central counterparty clearing services provided by clearing houses, which accepts certain OTC trades as intermediary, protected by a margining service. There is a move by regulators to encourage such margining.

Counterparties to an OTC product are at risk if either the paperwork does not operate as envisaged in the case of a default, or if one party is acting in a capacity which is not authorised.

The International Swaps & Derivatives Association (ISA) has produced a standard master agreement to cover most bilateral OTC transactions.

According to the bank for international settlements, there was $615 trillion outstanding notional value of OTC derivatives in the second half of 2009. In this relatively unregulated market there is international concern regarding the combined counterparty risk. Another factor in this market is the difficulty in valuing these positions. Whilst exchange traded contracts are marked to market against authoritative settlement prices, many OTC positions are valued by the issuing bank. This may not provide the objectivity required by many trustees and custodians.

# 11 Credit and Default Risk

**Learning objectives**

**1.6.1** **Understand** the purpose, influence and limitations of global credit rating agencies, debt seniority and ranking in cases of default/ bankruptcy: Senior, Subordinated, Mezzanine and PIK (Payment in Kind).

**1.6.2** **Analyse** sovereign, government and corporate credit ratings from an investment perspective: Main rating agencies, Country rating factors, Debt instrument rating factors, Investment & sub-investment grades, Use of credit enhancements and Impact of grading changes on price.

## 11.1 Credit risk

Corporate bonds are exposed to a greater degree of credit risk than gilts. Credit risk covers the risk that the issuer will default on his obligations to pay interest and capital, and is measured by the rating agencies.

## 11.2 Rating agencies

The credit risk of bonds is assessed by the various rating agencies, such as Moody's and Standard & Poor's. They will ascribe bonds with a credit rating. Should they decide to downgrade this rating, the return investors' demand will increase (the discount rate), causing the price to fall. Alternatively, a rating upgrade will reduce the required return of investors causing the price to rise.

## 11.3 Credit ratings

The purpose of credit ratings is credit risk evaluation, i.e. identifying the probability of default by an issuer. It is not a recommendation to take investment actions, since it does not take into account factors such as price and the preferred investment characteristics of the investor. Ratings are usually assigned to individual issues and hence do not serve as a general purpose of rating the issuer.

Credit ratings are calculated from financial history and current assets and liabilities. Rating agencies focus on various accounting ratios such as interest cover, in order to identify the probability of the subject being able to pay back the loan.

It is conventional for issuers in the Euromarkets to have a credit rating. Whilst this does not in itself make the company any more secure, it will mean that potential investors have a clearer perception of quality. Credit ratings are sub-categorised between prime/investment grade and junk/non-investment grade, and we need to be aware of the cut-off points between these gradings.

Government bonds often achieve the highest credit ratings from the ratings agencies, and (in late 2010) governments including US, UK, France and Germany have been given the top credit ratings by Moody's, Standard and Poor's and Fitch Ratings. Other governments however such as those of Ireland, Japan and Greece are rated lower due to the higher perceived risk of default. A lower credit rating is likely to result in the bonds value falling, and thus the yield and hence the respective government's cost of issuing debt will rise.

| Standard & Poor's | Moody's | Fitch Ratings | Meaning |
|---|---|---|---|
| | Investment Grade (Prime) | | |
| AAA | Aaa | AAA | Highest quality (prime) |
| AA+ | Aa1 | AA+ | |
| AA | Aa2 | AA | High quality |
| AA– | Aa3 | AA– | |
| A+ | A1 | A+ | |
| A | A2 | A | Strong quality |
| A– | A3 | A– | |
| BBB+ | Baa1 | BBB+ | |
| BBB | Baa2 | BBB | Adequate quality |
| **BBB–** | **Baa3** | **BBB–** | |
| | Non-Investment Grade (Non-Prime or Junk) | | |
| **BB+** | **Ba1** | **BB+** | Capacity to pay uncertain |
| BB | Ba2 | BB | |
| BB- | Ba3 | BB- | |
| B+ | B1 | B+ | |
| B | B2 | B | High risk |
| B- | B3 | B- | |
| CCC+<br>CCC<br>CCC- | Caa1<br>Caa2<br>Caa3 | CCC | Vulnerable to default |
| CC | Ca | CCC | |
| C | C | CCC | |
| D | | DDD | Already in default |

## 11.4 Credit analysis

The objective of credit analysis is to assess the ability of a borrower to service and repay its loan obligations. In evaluating credit risk there are three key issues to be borne in mind.

- How probable is it that a default will take place?
- How severe will the loss be if there is a default?
- When will any default take place (near term/far term)?

It is the answers to these three questions that allow rating agencies to fully appraise the credit risk of the bond.

A number of general factors that will be considered in undertaking such an assessment. These will include

- **Economic cyclicality** – The responsiveness of an industry to cyclical factors should be considered. Industries may closely track GDP growth (e.g. retailers). Alternatively, they may be defensive stocks with relatively slow growth (e.g. utilities).
- **Growth** – A company's growth should be compared to the growth trend of its own industry and any differences should be analysed and explained.
- **Competition** – Increasing competition will reduce prices and increase costs, increasing credit risk.
- **Sources of supply** – Companies with guaranteed stable, low-cost sources of supply will be favourably placed compared to companies without such sources. For example, paper companies need a readily available cheap source of wood pulp, i.e. forest lands.
- **Regulation** – Regulation itself is not a credit problem, however, the credit analyst will need to look at regulation and see whether it is resulting in excessive costs for the industry, highly restricted prices and restrictions on the company making good business decisions.
- **Labour** – More labour-intensive industries will give greater cause for concern than less labour-intensive industries. A heavily unionised industry that is highly militant is going to increase credit risks. The historical occurrence of strikes, the likelihood of future strikes, the relative power of the unions and related factors should be considered.
- **Financial analysis** – Obviously one key source of information in determining the viability of a company will be the financial statements. The key issues considered will be the level of assets, liabilities, profits and cash flow generation, all of which are discussed in detail later in this Study Text. The key ratios that will be considered (also covered later in this Study Text) will be
  - Debt to equity
  - Interest cover
  - Asset cover
  - Current ratio
  - Quick ratio

## 11.5 Credit enhancement

Whilst the general considerations shown above impact upon the credit rating of the organisation, certain measures can be taken to enhance the credit rating.

**Internal enhancements** come in numerous forms. Asset backed securities may be over collateralised so that the underlying assets which provide the cash flow (such as mortgages) are in excess of the face value of the bond. This allows for the possible default of a proportion of the loans without the bond itself defaulting. A related concept is that of excess spread, where the interest from underlying assets is greater than the interest required to be paid out by the bond. The difference between the two rates are referred to as the 'excess spread'. Reserve accounts up to pre specified amounts may be created to cover any losses which might be suffered due to defaults of any underlying assets.

**External enhancements** such as letters of credit may be provided by third parties to guarantee payment up to a pre-arranged level to cover losses, where the underlying assets fail to make sufficient payments. This is generally provided in return for a payment, generally to an investment bank. The credit risk of these very banks however has led to doubts about the value of such an arrangement. Surety bonds may also be employed to make payments in the event of the assets defaulting. Again however this also relies upon the credit rating of the organisation offering the surety bond.

## 11.6 Credit analysis factors of specific issues

### 11.6.1 Country rating factors

In analysing sovereign credits we are usually reviewing the best credits in the market. This is particularly true when governments are raising debt in their own currency, since the short term, they will be able to print additional money supply in order to meet their obligations.

However, where governments begin to borrow in other currencies and when the economic fundamentals are not as strong, then the credit begins to weaken.

### 11.6.2 Company v Country analysis

The object of country credit analysis is to assess the ability and willingness of the company to service its debt obligations on a timely basis. Differences between company and country may be summarised as follows:

- Countries can't be forced to make debt payments, meaning that willingness to pay is an important feature.
- Data on countries will come from different sources from company data. Company data includes, amongst others, annual reports, whereas country data includes newspapers, research documents etc.
- Due diligence on a country is costly and difficult when compared to a company.
- Subjective factors are more important when analysing countries, such as interpreting political and economic developments.

A number of political and economic risk factors play a part in the willingness and ability of a country to service its debt. These include the system of government and decision making, including its ideological beliefs. The domestic and regional stability is also important. Indications of the level of economic risk include the diversification of the economy and the level of economic resources such as oil possessed by the country.

Historically developed governments raising finance in their own currency have been awarded AAA ratings, due to the ability to access the tax system to raise revenue and the ability to 'print' money in the short term.

Where government have their credit rating lowered as with the recent instances of Greece and Ireland, the cost of borrowing increases for the country in question.

## 11.7 Corporate debt analysis

### 11.7.1 Senior corporate debt

As previously described, senior debt is repaid earlier in the event that the company faces liquidation. The net assets of the company will need evaluation by looking at the estimated liquidation value of assets on the balance sheet.

### 11.7.2 Subordinated corporate debt

Subordinated creditors take on board a higher degree of risk and require a higher degree of return to compensate.

The value of a company is irrelevant if the stock itself has been guaranteed by another company.

### 11.7.3 Mezzanine debt

Mezzanine debt is senior only to common stock. It will be structured either as subordinated debt or as preferred shares.

### 11.7.4 PIK (Payment in Kind)

With PIKs, the issuer has the option to pay interest in cash or by issuing additional securities in lieu of cash for a specified period of time. When additional securities are issued, the interest due is effectively being rolled up into the principal sum outstanding.

The benefit of PIKs, which are a form of zero coupon bond, for the issuer is that they give financial flexibility. Debt such as this will sit below all other forms of debt and may be referred to as a form of 'mezzanine debt'.

# Chapter Roundup

## Characteristics

- A bond is a negotiable debt instrument for a fixed principal amount issued by a borrower for a specific period of time and typically making a regular payment of interest.
- The interest payment is known as the coupon and it is based on the nominal value of the bond. The nominal value also refers to how much capital shall be paid on maturity.
- Bonds may be issued by governments and companies. Bonds issued by the UK government are known as **Gilts**.
- Index linked gilt coupons and redemption proceeds are linked to the RPI with either a 3 month (post September 2005) or 8 month (pre September 205) lag.
- The DMO has responsibility for issuing gilts at regular gilt auctions to finance the PSNCR.
- Gilt-edged market makers (GEMMs) have an obligation to create a liquid market in gilts during the mandatory quote period.
- Corporate bonds may be issued with a wide variety of different structures and different levels of security and payment benefits. Secondary trading is limited but is primarily off exchange.
- Dealing costs are
  - Bid-offer spread.
  - Brokers commission for retail investors.

## Pricing

- Bond pricing is based on the principals of discounted cash flow.
- Market convention for gilts
  - Quoted yield = 2× semi-annual yield.
  - Quoted price = clean price.
- Clean and dirty pricing conventions are designed to ensure investors pay the correct amount of tax on their accrued interest.
  - Cum div

    $$\text{Dirty price} = \text{Clean price} + \text{Periods coupon} \times \frac{\text{Days}}{\text{Days in period}}$$

  - Ex div

    $$\text{Dirty price} = \text{Clean price} - \text{Periods coupon} \times \frac{\text{Days}}{\text{Days in period}}$$

## Yields

- The flat yield represents the income return to an investor. The gross redemption yield represents the total return to an investor, on the assumption the investment will be held to maturity.
  - $\text{Flat yield} = \dfrac{\text{Annual coupon}}{\text{Market price}}$
  - GRY = Calculated using trial and error

- NRY = IRR if after tax returns (NB: only coupon taxed)

- $GEY = \frac{NRY}{1-T_p}$

- Relationships

| Bond Value | Relationship |
|---|---|
| Above Par (loss to redemption) | Flat Yield > GRY > GEY |
| At Par | Flat Yield = GRY = GEY |
| Below Par (gain to redemption) | Flat Yield < GRY < GEY |

- Yield curves represent the gross redemption yield on bonds issued by a particular issuer.
- The normal yield curve is upward sloping though an inverted yield curve if markets expect interest rates will fall.
- A spot rate is the rate of interest from now to a given future date.
- A forward rate is the rate of interest from one future date to another.

## Risk

- Macaulay's duration measures the sensitivity of a bond to changes in interest rates and is measured in **years**.

  - Macaulay duration (D) = $\frac{\sum(t \times PV_t)}{Price}$

- Modified duration indicates the percentage change in a bond's price given a 1% change in yields.

  - Modified Duration/Volatility = $-\frac{\text{Macaulay duration}}{1+GRY}$

- Forecasting price changes

  - $\%\Delta P = -MD \times \Delta Y$
    $\Delta P = -MD \times \Delta Y \times P$

- Convexity is a measure of the curvature in the true relationship between prices and yields.
- Rating agencies provide credit ratings on individual bonds based on the credit quality of the bond and its overall risk of default.

# TEST YOUR KNOWLEDGE

*Check your knowledge of the chapter here, without referring back to the text.*

1. Define a callable bond.

2. What inflation rate are index-linked gilts tied into?

3. What is an FRN?

   A Fixed Rate Note
   B Fixed Rate Notification
   C Floating Rate Note
   D Floating Rate Notification

4. Calculate the price of a two-year annual 6% coupon bond with a discount rate of 5.5% and a nominal value of £100.

5. An 8% Treasury is redeemable in four years. Calculate its price if rates are 7%

6. 8% Treasury stock was quoted at 97.3125 on Friday 10 November. Interest payment dates are 15 May and 15 November. Calculate the following as on 10 November.

   (a) Flat yield per annum.
   (b) Price paid for £100 nominal.

7. Conversion 10¼% stock was quoted at £104.91 on Tuesday 23 February. Interest payment dates are 22 May and 22 November.

   (a) What was the flat yield on 23 February?
   (b) What would a purchaser on 23 February pay for £100 nominal?

8. Exchequer 13½% stock was quoted at 117.875 on Friday 16 September. Interest payment dates are 22 March and 22 September.

   *Calculate*

   (a) The flat yield on 16 September.

   (b) You buy £1,000 nominal on Friday 16 September, how much would you pay excluding transaction costs?

9. You buy £10,000 nominal of 3½% War Loan on Tuesday 2 September cum div and pay £3,915.10 excluding transaction costs. Interest payment dates are 1 June and 1 December.

   *Calculate*

   (a) The quoted price per £100 nominal on 2 September.
   (b) The flat yield on 2 September.

10. A bond is bought for £92.40 with six full years to maturity and paying a 4% annual coupon. What is its GRY

A 5.37%
B 5.52%
C 5.74%
D 5.91%

11. A £100 bond is priced at £105.47 with an 8% coupon payable at the end of each of the next twelve years, and is then redeemable at par. What is its yield to maturity?

A 7.00%
B 7.10%
C 7.20%
D 7.30%

12. A bond has three years before being redeemed at par at maturity and pays a 6% coupon at the end of each of the three years. Spot interest rates (payable at the end of each year) are 8% in the first year, 7% in the second year and 6% in the third year. Calculate the price of this bond.

13. A bond with a life of two years will pay a 5% coupon at the end of each of the two years. The bond will be redeemed at par. If spot rates are 6% in the first year and 7% in the second year (payable at the end of each year), what is the price of this bond?

14. List the different risks of investing in a bond.

15. A bond pays an annual coupon of 6% and has three years to redemption. If it is yielding 7%, what is its duration?

18. If a bond has three years to redemption and pays a 7% annual coupon, with interest rates at 10%, what is the duration of the bond?

17. If the coupon rate on a bond increases, what will be the impact on its duration?

18. A 10% bond is redeemable in exactly three years and pays interest annually. Calculate the duration if its yield is 9%

19. A bond has three years to redemption at par and pays an 8% coupon at the end of each of the three years. If its yield is 7.5%, what is the duration of this bond?

20. A bond is priced at £103.47 and has a modified duration of 4.64. If yields rise by ½%, what will the new price of the bond be?

# TEST YOUR KNOWLEDGE: ANSWERS

1. A bond where the issuer has the right to redeem the bond early.

   **(See Section 1.6.9)**

2. Retail Price Index

   **(See Section 1.4.3)**

3. C

   **(See Section 1.6.6)**

4. £100.93

   $$\frac{6}{1.055}+\frac{106}{1.055^2}=5.69+95.24=100.93$$

   **(See Section 2.2)**

5. **Price**

| Time | Cash Flow (£) | DF (7%) | PV (£) |
|---|---|---|---|
| 1–4 | 8 | $\frac{1}{0.07}\left(1-\frac{1}{1.07^4}\right)=3.387$ | 27.10 |
| 4 | 100 | $\frac{1}{1.07^4}$ | 76.29 |
| | | | 103.39 |

   **(See Section 2.2)**

6. (a) Flat yield = $\frac{\text{Annual coupon}}{\text{Market (clean) price}}=\frac{8.00}{97.3125}$ = 0.08221 or 8.221%

   (b) With the deal date of Friday 10 November, settlement is Monday 13 November, hence the accrued interest days equals 13 November to 14 November inclusive, i.e. two days. The coupon period runs from 15 May to 14 November, a period of 184 days.

| | (£) |
|---|---|
| Quoted clean price | 97.3125 |
| Less: Accrued interest $\frac{2}{184}\times 4$ | (0.0435) |
| Price paid per £100 nominal | 97.2690 |

   **(See Sections 2.3 and 3.1)**

7. (a) Flat yield = $\frac{\text{Annual coupon}}{\text{Market (clean) price}} = \frac{10.25}{104.91} = 0.0977$ or 9.77%

(b) Accrued interest is from 22 November (last coupon date) to 23 February (day before settlement day) inclusive, i.e.

| | | Accrued | Coupon |
|---|---|---|---|
| Days | November | 9 | 9 |
| | December | 31 | 31 |
| | January | 31 | 31 |
| | February | 23 | 28 |
| | March | | 31 |
| | April | | 30 |
| | May | | 21 |
| Dirty price paid | | 94 | 181 |

| | (£) |
|---|---|
| Quoted clean price | 104.91 |
| Add: accrued interest $\frac{94}{181} \times 5.125$ | 2.66 |
| Dirty price paid | 107.57 |

A purchaser on 23 February would pay £107.57 for £100 nominal.

**(See Sections 2.3 and 3.1)**

8. (a) Flat yield = $\frac{\text{Annual coupon}}{\text{Market (clean) price}} = \frac{13.50}{117.875} = 0.1145$ or 11.45%.

(b) Settlement will take place on Monday 19 September, hence the accrued interest is calculated from 19 September to 21 September inclusive, i.e. three days. The coupon period runs from 22 March to 21 September, a period of 184 days.

| | (£) |
|---|---|
| Quoted clean price | 117.875 |
| Less: Accrued interest $\frac{3}{184} \times 6.75$ | (0.110) |
| Price paid per £100 nominal | 117.765 |

The price paid on 16 September for £1,000 nominal equals 10 × £117.765 equals £1,177.65

**(See Sections 2.3 and 3.1)**

9. (a) Accrued interest is for the period 1 June (last coupon date) to 2 September (day before settlement date) inclusive, hence

| | Accrued | Coupon |
|---|---|---|
| June | 30 | 30 |
| July | 31 | 31 |
| August | 31 | 31 |
| September | 2 | 30 |
| October | | 31 |
| November | | 30 |
| | 94 | 183 |

Accrued interest equals $\frac{94}{183} \times 1.75 = £0.899$

| | (£) |
|---|---|
| Price paid (dirty price) per £100 nominal = £3,915.10 ÷ 100 | 39.151 |
| Less: Accrued interest | (0.899) |
| Quoted (clean) price | 38.252 |

(b) Flat yield = $\frac{\text{Annual coupon}}{\text{Market (clean) price}} = \frac{3.50}{38.252} = 0.0915$ or 9.15%

**(See Sections 2.3 and 3.1)**

10. Through trial and error

| Time | Cash Flow (£) | DF (5.52%) | PV (£) |
|---|---|---|---|
| 0 | (92.40) | 1 | (92.40) |
| 1–6 | 4.00 | $\frac{1}{0.0552}\left(1-\frac{1}{1.0552^6}\right)$ | 19.96 |
| 6 | 100.00 | $\frac{1}{1.0552^6}$ | 72.44 |
| | | | 0.00 |

**(See Section 3.3)**

11. Through trial and error

| Time | Cash Flow (£) | DF (7.3%) | PV (£) |
|---|---|---|---|
| 0 | (105.47) | 1 | (105.47) |
| 1–12 | 8.00 | $\frac{1}{0.073}\left(1-\frac{1}{1.073^{12}}\right)$ | 62.54 |
| 12 | 100.00 | $\frac{1}{1.073^{12}}$ | 42.93 |
| | | | 0.00 |

**(See Section 3.3)**

12.

| Time | Cash Flow (£) | DF | PV (£) |
|---|---|---|---|
| 1 | 6 | $\frac{1}{1.08}$ | 5.56 |
| 2 | 6 | $\frac{1}{1.07^2}$ | 5.24 |
| 3 | 106 | $\frac{1}{1.06^3}$ | 89.00 |
| | | | 99.80 |

**(See Section 4.4)**

13.

| Time | Cash Flow (£) | DF | PV (£) |
|---|---|---|---|
| 1 | 5 | $\frac{1}{1.06}$ | 4.72 |
| 2 | 105 | $\frac{1}{1.07^2}$ | 91.71 |
| | | | 96.43 |

**(See Section 4.4)**

14. Interest rate risk, credit/default risk, inflation risk, liquidity risk, issue specific risk, fiscal risk and currency risk.

**(See Section 5.1)**

15.

| Time | Cash Flow £ | DF (7%) | PV £ | tPV £ |
|---|---|---|---|---|
| 1 | 6 | $\frac{1}{1.07}$ | 5.61 | 5.61 |
| 2 | 6 | $\frac{1}{1.07^2}$ | 5.24 | 10.48 |
| 3 | 106 | $\frac{1}{1.07^3}$ | 86.53 | 259.59 |
| | | | 97.38 | 275.68 |

$$\text{Duration} = \frac{275.68}{97.38} = 2.83 \text{ years}$$

**(See Section 5.2.3)**

18.

| Time | Cash Flow £ | DF (10%) | PV £ | tPV £ |
|---|---|---|---|---|
| 1 | 7.00 | $\frac{1}{1.10}$ | 6.36 | 6.39 |
| 2 | 7.00 | $\frac{1}{1.10^2}$ | 5.79 | 11.58 |
| 3 | 107.00 | $\frac{1}{1.10^3}$ | 80.39 | 241.17 |
| | | | 92.54 | 259.11 |

$$\text{Duration} = \frac{259.11}{92.54} = 2.80 \text{ years}$$

**(See Section 5.2.3)**

17. Low-coupon bonds are more sensitive to interest rates than higher coupon bonds and therefore have higher durations. If the coupon increases the duration decreases.

**(See Section 5.2.3)**

18.

| Time | Cash Flow (£) | DF (9 %) | PV (£) | tPV (£) |
|---|---|---|---|---|
| 1 | 10 | $\frac{1}{1.09}$ | 9.17 | 9.17 |
| 2 | 10 | $\frac{1}{1.09^2}$ | 8.42 | 18.84 |
| 3 | 110 | $\frac{1}{1.09^3}$ | 84.94 | 254.82 |
| | | | 102.53 | 280.83 |

$$\text{Duration} = \frac{280.83}{102.53} = 2.74 \text{ years}$$

**(See Section 5.2.3)**

19.

| Time | Cash Flow (£) | DF (7.5%) | PV (£) | tPV (£) |
|---|---|---|---|---|
| 1 | 8.00 | $\frac{1}{1.075}$ | 7.44 | 7.44 |
| 2 | 8.00 | $\frac{1}{1.075^2}$ | 6.92 | 13.84 |
| 3 | 108.00 | $\frac{1}{1.075^3}$ | 86.94 | 260.82 |
| | | | 101.30 | 282.10 |

$$\text{Duration} = \frac{282.10}{101.30} = 2.78 \text{ years}$$

**(See Section 5.2.3)**

20. Proportionate change in price = MD × $\Delta$Y = –4.64 × 0.005 = –0.0232 or –2.32%

This is a negative figure, hence prices will fall by 2.32% or £2.40 (£103.47 × 2.32%) to £101.07 (£103.47 – £2.40).

**(See Section 5.2.4)**

# 2 Cash, Money Markets and the Foreign Exchange Market

## INTRODUCTION

Money market investments are those with a maturity of less than 12 months. This includes investments such as T-bills, commercial paper and certificates of deposit.

The money markets are a predominantly institutional market for investors looking to make investments for short periods of time, retail investors primarily using cash deposits for the same purpose. Cash deposits and money market investments are both stable in price and have little in the way of credit risk.

Currencies are traded in both a spot market for immediate currency trades, and a forward market which allows for agreements to buy and sell currencies in the future.

Forward rates are computed by banks and based on interest rate differentials. These interest rate differentials may then be applied to the spot rate to compute the forward rate.

### CHAPTER CONTENTS



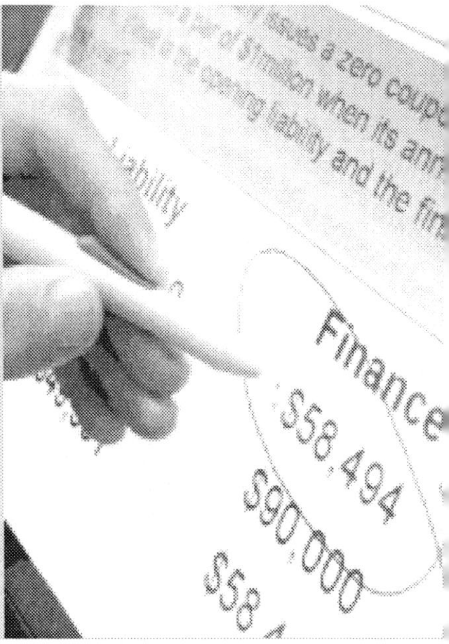

# Chapter Learning Objectives

## Cash, Money Markets and the Foreign Exchange Market

### 2.1 Cash Instruments and Markets

**2.1.1** **Analyse** the main investment characteristics, behaviours and risks of cash deposit accounts:

- Deposit taking institutions and credit risk assessment
- Term, notice, liquidity and access
- Fixed and variable rates of interest
- Inflation
- Statutory protection
- Foreign currency deposits

**2.1.2** **Analyse** the main investment characteristics, behaviours and risks of Treasury Bills:

- Purpose & method of issue
- Minimum denomination
- Normal life
- Zero coupon and redemption at par
- Redemption
- Market access, trading and settlement

**2.1.3** **Analyse** the main investment characteristics, behaviours and risks of Commercial Paper:

- Purpose & method of issue
- Maturity
- Discounted security
- Unsecured and secured
- Asset backed
- Credit rating
- Role of dealer
- Market access, trading and settlement

**2.1.4** **Analyse** the main investment characteristics, behaviours and risks of Repurchase Agreements:

- Purpose
- Sale and repurchase at agreed price, rate and date
- Reverse repo – purchase and resale at agreed price and date
- Documentation

**2.1.5** **Analyse** the main characteristics, risks and returns of money market funds

- Cash assets only
- Near cash assets
- Pricing, liquidity and fair value
- Market access, trading and settlement

**2.1.6** **Analyse** the factors to take into account when selecting between different types of cash deposits, accounts and money market funds

### 2.2 Foreign Exchange Instruments and Markets

**2.2.1 Understand** the role, structure and main characteristics of the foreign exchange market:

- OTC market
- Quotes, spreads and exchange rate information
- Market participants and access to markets
- Volume, volatility and liquidity
- Risk mitigation: rollovers and stop losses
- Regulatory/ supervisory environment

**2.2.2 Understand** the determinants of spot foreign exchange prices:

- Currency demand – transactional and speculative
- Economic variables
- Cross- border trading of financial assets
- Interest rates
- Free and pegged rates

**2.2.3 Calculate** forward foreign exchange rates using:

- Premiums and discounts
- Interest rate parity

**2.2.4 Analyse** how foreign exchange contracts can be used to buy or sell currency relating to overseas investments, or to hedge non- domestic currency exposure:

- Spot contracts
- Forward contracts
- Currency Futures
- Currency Options

# 1 An Overview of the Money Markets

The money markets are the focus for trading in short-dated (conventionally with maturities of under one year) interest-bearing products and hedging instruments. The market itself is a complex intermeshed structure with a wide variety of instruments and is generally used by **wholesale investors**.

The London money market is a complex market where banks balance their liquidity requirements and the Bank of England attempts to control the interest rate.

**The London Money Market**

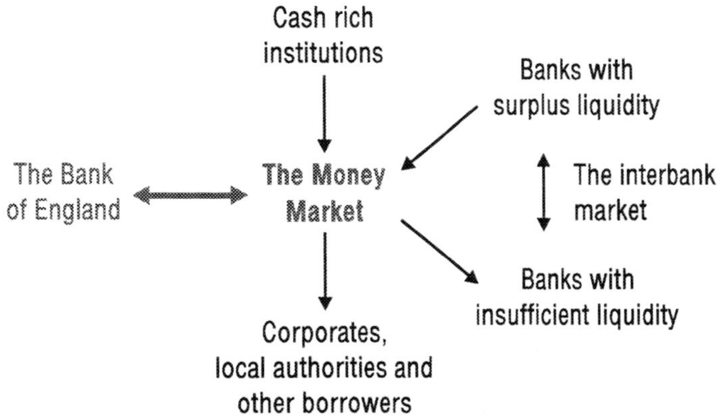

The Bank of England is a key player in the market. The Bank's role is focused on the implementation of policy rather than the raising of finance (which is the responsibility of the Debt Management Office of the Treasury). It is through the money markets that the Monetary Policy Committee is able to dictate the direction of interest rates and monetary policy.

The Bank of England's final role in the market is as the **'Lender of the Last Resort'**, whereby the Bank ensures that the market will not fail to meet its obligations. As the credit crisis Of 2008/09 showed, this is not a blank cheque to the industry. The Bank will, however, step in where there is a 'systemic' risk to the market.

The principal users of the market are the banks. Banks make their money by taking in deposits from individuals and lending them out at a higher rate to borrowers. In doing so, the bank always has to ensure that they have enough liquid assets to meet the demands by their investors for cash. The bank will achieve this by carrying a proportion of the money invested in the form of cash and will also put other money on deposit at very short notice. The remainder of their liquidity will be held in the form of short-term investments such as gilts that are easily convertible into cash.

Banks can also manage their liquidity via the interbank markets. Those banks with surplus funds can earn a return by passing them to banks short of funds. The average rate at which funds can be raised is **LIBOR (London Interbank Offered Rate)** and the average rate earned on deposits is **LIBID (London Interbank Bid Rate)**. Secured lending and borrowing also takes place via the repo market, which is discussed later.

Other participants include cash-rich institutions that use the money markets as a safe channel to earn returns on their liquid assets. Larger corporates may use the money markets as a source of short-term flexible finance and in order to hedge interest rate risk.
The money market is thus aimed at wholesale clients to gain access to liquidity; retail clients also play a part in the market in their use of retail cash instruments.

# 2 Cash Instruments and Markets

**Learning objective**

**2.1.1 Analyse** the main differences characteristics, behaviours and risks of cash deposit accounts: deposit taking institutions and credit risk assessment, term notice, liquidity and access, fixed and variable rates of interest, inflation, statutory protection, foreign currency deposits

A cash investment is an arrangement that promises to pay a rate of interest and to return the initial investment intact. Cash investments can be divided into two distinct types, namely savings/deposit accounts and money markets. The principal characteristics of savings/deposit accounts can be summarised as follows:

- The capital is not exposed to investment risk and there is no potential for capital growth
- The return is in the form of interest payments
- The capital is returned on demand or at the end of the stated term

## 2.1 Principal deposit-takers

The principal UK deposit-takers are:

- Banks
- Building societies

Supervision of the prudential soundness of these banks and building societies in the UK is the responsibility of the Financial Services Authority. UK authorised deposit taking institutions are regulated by the Financial Services and Markets Act 2000.

### 2.1.1 Banks

Banks are listed public limited companies, owned by their shareholders. The rights of account holders are limited to the terms and conditions of the account.

### 2.1.2 Building societies

A **building society** is a mutual organisation, owned by its members. The members are the investment account holders and borrowers. Members of the Society have voting rights. Some former building societies have 'demutualised' and turned themselves into banks, while others have been bought by banks. On **demutualisation** or acquisition of the Society, members may be entitled to a 'windfall' payment reflecting a share of the reserves of the organisation that have been built up over its life. However, most of the remaining building societies now require new account holders to waive their rights to such windfall payments, often by signing over the entitlement to charity. This is intended to prevent people opening accounts speculatively in the hope of gaining a windfall.

## 2.2 Bank and building society accounts

### 2.2.1 Current and savings account

**Current accounts** are bank accounts for day-to-day cash management. Current accounts offer instant access (see below) and offer the following facilities:

- Pay and receive cheques
- Pay and receive automated bank transfers (standing orders, direct debits and direct credits)
- Make cash withdrawals with a cash card
- Internet and telephone banking
- Overdraft facilities

The interest rate earned on cash deposits has, historically, been low and the rate charged on overdrafts has been quite high. Historically, **savings accounts** did not offer such facilities and tended to require notice of withdrawal (see below) but did offer higher rates on cash deposits. Now the distinction between current and savings accounts is becoming more blurred with some current accounts offering quite high deposit rates and some savings accounts offering many of the above facilities together with instant access. The overall rate earned on a deposit/savings account can be reduced by the effect of extension dates. Many accounts default to an extension rate once the initial agreed deposit period is over. The extension rate tends to be considerably lower than the market rate.

### 2.2.2 Instant access accounts

As the name implies, an **instant access account** allows the investor immediate access to funds. The investor will want to keep some funds available on instant access at minimum risk, for emergency purposes. Some accounts give instant access **subject to restrictions**. For example, an account might allow only two withdrawals per year.

### 2.2.3 Notice accounts

With a **notice account**, the investor must give, for example, 30, 60 or 90 days' notice of withdrawal otherwise he will lose interest. There may be a higher rate of interest available to compensate for the requirement to give notice. However, the investor should be careful to weigh the advantage of any higher rate offered against the disadvantage of the loss of liquidity and the costs of penalties if the money needs to be withdrawn earlier than planned.

Interest paid monthly will generally be slightly lower than on an instant or notice account which pays interest annually because of the increased frequency of payment of interest. When interest is credited month after month, the interest itself will begin to earn interest as soon as it is credited. Thus the frequency of the compounding of interest is an important consideration when evaluating different savings accounts.

### 2.2.4 Regular savings

Some accounts allow for **regular savings** to be made each month, possibly with some access to funds without penalty.

### 2.2.5 Cash ISAs

Individual Savings Accounts (ISAs) allow a tax free deposit of up to £5,100 per tax year for any UK resident tax purposes over 16. Due to the nature of the cash deposits, the benefit of cash ISAs is effectively an exemption to income tax.

There is no minimum investment level or notice period other than any imposed by the provider. The current £5,100 annual subscription limit for a cash ISA refers to the amount of money paid in. If a withdrawal is made, subsequent payments into the ISA must still not exceed the £5,100 limit overall.

A large number of deposit taking institutions also provide cash ISAs and various financial institutions provide ISAs, which may, or may not, include a cash component.

### 2.2.6 Time deposits accounts or 'bonds'

**Time deposits** or **term accounts** offer investors terms that involve tying up the deposit for a fixed period, often at **fixed rates**. The period may range from seven days to several years, and there may be a fairly high minimum for such

arrangements. Time deposits may be offered as '**bonds**'. (Note that this is a different, and potentially confusing, use of the term 'bond', compared with the use of the same word for the asset class of gilts and other fixed interest securities. With time deposit 'bonds', there is no fluctuation in capital values, as there is with fixed interest securities.) The bond offer may be open for a specified period, or the deposit-taker may reserve the right to withdraw the offer at any time. The bond could run for a fixed term: one, two, three, four or five years, with severely restricted access subject to a penalty, or no access at all. Interest may be **tiered.** For example, a five-year 'step-up bond' might offer a gross rate of interest of 3.0% in year one, 3.25% in year two, 3.50% in year three, rising to 4.0% in year four and a final 4.5% in year five.

### 2.2.7 Foreign currency accounts

Some UK banks offer accounts denominated in foreign currencies, such as the euro and the US dollar. Foreign currency accounts can be useful to someone with income or expenses in the foreign currency. With such an account the investor faces the additional risk of exchange rate fluctuation.

### 2.2.8 Offshore deposit accounts

Accounts at overseas branches of UK banks and building societies are open to UK residents and expatriates. The deposits can be held in **sterling** or **other currencies**, for example euros or US dollars. UK residents seeking an offshore deposit account will generally use a bank or building society in Jersey, Guernsey or the Isle of Man. The range of accounts available may be designed for the needs of international clients particularly, including multicurrency accounts, although onshore accounts might be found to be more varied and more flexible for some individuals. The client can select an instant access, notice or fixed rate, fixed term account. The sterling interest rates offered generally reflect UK interest rates. The investor in an offshore deposit account will normally be able to conduct transactions by internet, post or bank credit transfer. The **interest risk** for an offshore deposit held in sterling is the same as for one held onshore, for a variable rate account, interest rates may change. If the deposit is held in foreign currency, there is the additional risk of changes in exchange rates. Investors should be aware that a high interest rate in a currency probably reflects the fact that the currency is weak and that the exchange rate is liable to deteriorate, wiping out any interest rate benefit. The other risk to consider is that of the security of the institution. Deposits might be held with a fully owned subsidiary of a major UK bank or building society. If the investment is in Jersey or Guernsey, there is no Depositor Protection Scheme. If the investment is deposited in the Isle of Man, a compensation scheme is available which, like the UK Financial Services Compensation Scheme, secures 100% of the first £50,000 invested. Gibraltar has a Deposit Protection Scheme providing compensation of 90% of total deposits up to a maximum of £18,000 (or 20,000 euros if greater). When investing in offshore accounts investors should therefore consider

- Interest rates available in comparison to sterling
- The strength of the currency and the likelihood for a currency appreciation or depreciation
- The volatility of the currency, an additional risk for the investor that requires compensation
- Potential volatility of overseas interest rates when rates have not been fixed
- Financial security of the deposit taker
- Any statutory protection available

### 2.2.9 Private banks

High net worth individuals may make use of private banks who offer their clients a range of tailored services not normally offered by 'high street banks'. Lines of credit, wealth management and tax planning are examples of services offered. Charges for such accounts may well be higher than those of retail banks.

## 2.3 The risks of holding cash investments

As we have seen banks or building societies, even large ones, can go bust. Indeed, if it had not been for the intervention of the UK Government, Northern Rock would have gone into liquidation. Therefore in order to assess the risk associated with placing deposits with a financial institution the following factors must be considered:

- Creditworthiness of the bank or building society
- Extent of any compensation payable will depend on the bank protection schemes which as we have already seen, in the UK, is limited to £50,000 (rising to £85,000 from 31 December 2010)

It should also be noted that inflation is a key risk of cash deposits, given that a high inflation rate will eat into the spending power of any fixed sum.

The creditworthiness of a bank or building society is assessed by looking at:

- Tier one capital ratio which is used to assess the bank's capital adequacy
- Credit ratings which are issued by credit rating agencies such as Standard & Poors to assess the default risk associated with bonds issued. These ratings provide an indication of the bank's stability and its ability to repay debts
- CD rates which indicate the cost of insuring a bank against default by using a credit default swap

## 2.4 Statutory protection

With a deposit investment, the **capital** is secure in that the original capital is returned when the deposit is withdrawn, or the account matures, subject to any penalties which will have been made explicit in the terms and conditions of the account. Some degree of **capital risk** does however exist for the depositor. This is because there is a chance that the deposit-taking institution fails, default risk, and therefore defaults and does not repay depositors' capital. This happened with the Bank of Credit and Commerce International, which collapsed in 1991. If a UK deposit-taker fails, the depositor will have recourse to the **Financial Services Compensation Scheme (FSCS),** which is administered by the Financial Services Authority (FSA).

### 2.4.1 Financial Services Compensation Scheme limits

The FSCS will pay compensation following default by a bank or building society of 100% of the first £50,000 deposited per depositor in each separately authorised institution. These FSCS compensation limits:

- Apply only to UK sterling deposits held at a UK branch of the deposit-taker
- Apply to each depositor with an institution, and not to each individual account with the institution
- Apply separately to each joint account holder: therefore, two joint account holders could each receive up to £50,000*, for a joint account in which £100,000 was deposited The **ceiling on compensation** available through the FSCS leads some investors to consider **spreading** their capital among a number of banks and building societies in order to reduce the overall risk.

The benefit of spreading the risk in this way should be weighed against the possible disadvantage of less interest being earned because of the investor missing out on higher rates offered for larger deposits.

* This will increase to £85,000 from 31/12/2010

### 2.4.2 EU Deposit Guarantee Schemes Directive

Under the EU Deposit Guarantee Schemes Directive, all member States of the EEA are required to establish a deposit guarantee scheme which gives a minimum level of protection for depositors of €20,000 per eligible depositor in the event of a bank failure. A bank established in another EEA State should be a member of that State's compensation scheme, which is designed to protect depositors in that EEA country, and those with accounts at branches in other EEA countries.

## 2.5 Money market funds

**Learning objective**

**2.1.5** **Analyse** the main characteristics, risks and returns of money market funds, cash assets only, near cash assets, pricing, liquidity and fair value, market access and trading and settlement.

**2.1.6** **Analyse** the factors to take into account when selecting between different types of cash deposits and accounts and money market funds.

A money market fund is one which invests at least 95% of its assets in money market instruments, i.e. cash and near cash such as bank deposits, certificates of deposit, very short-term fixed interest securities or floating rate notes. Money market funds represent an alternative to a savings account and offer a home for the cash element of a portfolio or a safe home for funds when markets are volatile.

### 2.5.1 Risk and returns associated with money market funds

Returns on a money market fund will depend upon the composition of the underlying portfolio and the charges levied by the fund, although they should typically reflect LIBOR, the short term inter bank lending rate of return. Typically, annual charges are very low and the initial charges are close to zero. Money market funds carry the same risks as other cash investments. That is to say:

- Credit risk which depends on the types of instrument in which the fund invests and the credit rating of the issuing institutions. It should be noted however, that a money market fund can diversify against the risk of a single institution going bust as it will invest in a range of instruments from many providers

- Inflation risk
- Interest risk
- Currency risk if the fund is invested in foreign currencies

### 2.5.2 Assessment of money market funds

Assessment of money market funds requires consideration of the:

- Type of security the fund invests in
- Duration and maturity structure of the fund
- Diversification of the fund
- Procedures used to establish and monitor the credit quality of the underlying instruments

One may divide cash or near cash deposits into three categories:

- Short term tactical cash, which can be held invested as high interest accounts with highly rated banks, or in high rated short term investments such as UK treasury bills.
- Longer Term strategic cash and near cash instruments. These will tend to invest only in Treasury bills and other highly rated commercial paper borrowed by highly rated companies. US 'munis' may also form a part of such a fund.
- Enhanced cash funds invest in the above mentioned instruments but also in more risky investments such as longer maturity government debt, lower rated commercial paper, or asset backed securities. Their higher risk will aim for higher returns.

Investors in money market funds may invest in funds taking a number of structural forms, similar to those of other collective investment vehicles such as OEICs or unit trusts.

### 2.5.3 Money market accounts

Some banks offer the facility to make **money market** deposits for periods ranging from overnight to five years. A bank can offer interest at a rate that is personal to the investor, based on current money market rates (i.e. comparable to LIBOR). One bank offers money market deposits either for a fixed term with fixed interest, or on a notice basis with variable interest, making the account responsive to changes in interest rates. Deposits may be 'rolled over' on maturity to reinvest money if not required. A **call** account will allow the investor to access their money by the following day. This is close to the terms of an instant access account. The principle of a fixed interest rate for a specified period is the same as for term deposits, but the use of the term 'money market deposit' usually implies that a tailored arrangement is made to meet a particular investor's needs. Money market deposits can be appropriate for investors with larger sums to invest – for example, proceeds from a house sale pending a later house purchase. There may be a **minimum investment** of £25,000 - £50,000 or more. The commissions charged will vary from bank to bank.

### 2.5.4 Institutional Money Market Funds

Large institutions will frequently 'sweep' surplus funds to a money market fund overnight or while not required. This aims to achieve some return on funds while they might otherwise be earning no return, with low risk and high liquidity. (Retail Money market funds on the other hand are offered primarily to individuals, by many providers with varied terms. The initial investment is generally high – possibly around £50,000).

## 2.6 Treasury Bills

**Learning objective**

**2.1.2** **Analyse** the main investment characteristics, behaviours and risks of Treasury Bills, purpose & method of issue, minimum denomination, normal life, zero coupon and redemption at par, redemption, market access and trading and settlement.

A Treasury bill is a short-term instrument issued by a government and is also known as a **T-bill**. The purpose is to raise short-term finance for the government. This is an **obligation** to repay a set amount of money, normally in **91 calendar days' time** and, as with all bills, is issued at a **discount** to its face value. For example, the DMO might issue a three-month £1m Treasury bill to the market at a discount – investors might be prepared to pay £985,000 now in order to receive £1m in three months' time.

Note: Maturities can also be 28, 182 and 364 days.

As the T-bills are for such a short maturity, there is no point in paying a coupon. The investor's reward comes from the gain on selling the bill for more than the purchase price or from receiving the par value (nominal or face value) on redemption by the DMO.

Usually, the minimum block size for trading would be **£25,000** though prices are stated per £100 of principal.

T-bills are issued by way of a **weekly auction** when bids are made on a **yield basis** and then trade at a discount to their face value. The Bank's T-bill issues are not part of the government's funding programme per se, but are much more an instrument of monetary policy.

The principal measures used to evaluate T-bills are as follows.

**Formula to learn**

$$\text{Discount rate} = \frac{100 - \text{Discounted value}}{100} \times \frac{365}{\text{Days}}$$

**Formula to learn**

$$\text{Interest rate or yield} = \frac{100 - \text{Discounted value}}{\text{Discounted value}} \times \frac{365}{\text{Days}}$$

### Example

91-day T-bill issued at £98.

**Discount rate**

$$\frac{£100 - £98}{£100} \times \frac{365}{91} = 0.0802 \text{ or } 8.02\%$$

**Interest rate or yield**

$$\frac{£100 - £98}{£98} \times \frac{365}{91} = 0.0818 \text{ or } 8.18\%$$

Local authorities may also raise short term finance by using **local authority bills** that have characteristics very similar to Treasury bills.

It is conventional for bills to **trade on the discount rate**, i.e. it is the discount rate that is quoted rather than the price or yield, and this requires the holder to convert to the yield in order to compare with other investments.

## 2.7 Commercial paper

earning objective

**2.1.3 Analyse** the main investment characteristics, behaviours and risks of Commercial paper, purpose & method of issue , maturity, discounted security, unsecured and secured, asset backed, credit rating, role of dealer, market access and trading and settlement.

Commercial paper (CP) is a short-term debt instrument issued by a company with a maturity normally of 12 months or less. When a company wishes to borrow using commercial paper, a common method is to set up a commercial paper programme for a fixed number of years and select a bank or banks to act as dealers. The programme will be for a fixed amount (e.g. £500m). This amount is not for immediate borrowing but rather a maximum amount up to which the company will borrow then repay as and when required. If they wish to borrow £20m for three months then the bank will contact potential lenders to get the money if possible although the banks do not guarantee to find lenders. It is hoped that borrowing from lenders directly will lower the cost of borrowing.

CP will pay **no interest**, instead trading at a discount to nominal value. The discount will reflect credit risk and time to maturity.

Commercial paper is normally unsecured and will, therefore, either be issued by companies with very high credit ratings or guaranteed by a bank.

Commercial paper is generally unsecured, but issues are sometimes securitised in the form of asset backed commercial paper. The company can sell receivables to an investment bank who will then issue asset backed commercial paper to investors backed by the cash flows from the receivables. The fact that the commercial paper is asset backed should make borrowing cheaper for the issuing firm.

## 2.8 The government bond repo market

earning objective

**2.1.4 Analyse** the main investment characteristics, behaviours and risks of Repurchase agreements, purpose, sale and repurchase at agreed price and date and documentation

A bond repo is a **sale and repurchase agreement at an agreed price**. The basis of the transaction is that the holder of a bond is able to sell his holding of a particular bond in order to raise cash. Simultaneous to the sale, the holder enters into an agreement to repurchase the bond at a date in the future, at the same price plus interest. The biggest repo market in the UK involves UK Government bonds (known as gilts). The standard documentation for a repo is produced by the **International Capital Markets Association (ICMA)** or **The Bond Market Association (TBMA)**.

## Example

### Leg one

A quantity of £200,000 worth of bonds is sold for £180,000. The size of this haircut will depend on the securities subject to the repo and the duration of the loan. The repo rate will be set at this point, let us say 3% for a 90-day repo.

Note: The lender of the cash (£180,000) is only prepared to do this if the collateral value (£200,000) is greater than the loan. This is because the collateral's value can fluctuate. The lender of the cash wants the protection that the buffer/haircut affords.

### Leg two

The bonds are repurchased for £180,000 plus interest. The interest is worked out on a simple basis using the following formula.

$$\text{Interest} = \text{Principal amount} \times \text{Repo rate} \times \frac{\text{Days}}{365}$$

$$£180,000 \times 0.03 \times \frac{90}{365} = £1,331.51$$

Therefore, the sum due on repayment is £181,331.51. The original lender will receive the bonds provided as collateral in return for the repayment.

This repo transaction represents an effective way for the firm to finance its holding of the bond. The initial position taken would otherwise represent a cash drain on the business. The repo allows the holder to raise cheap cash on the back of the bond. The cash raised in this fashion can then be used to take additional positions, thereby gearing up the initial capital of the investor allowing larger positions to be entered into.

The end result is, in effect, a secured loan where one party borrows money on the surety of the gilts that they own. In UK terms, given the security of the loan the rates will be below LIBOR.

The other side of the repo is the **reverse repo** which may allow participants in the market to go short of stock. With a reverse repo an investor buys gilts now for cash. Simultaneously he enters into an agreement to sell the bond back in the future.

As a result of the reverse repo the investor is able to borrow stock now, which can be used to settle short trades. Eventually the investor will be obliged to unwind his short position and complete the repo by buying stock in the market and selling the stock back to the original owner with whom he entered into the repo.

It is worth noting that the vast majority of reverses will not be driven by the desire to short the underlying market, but rather represents a method of making collateralised, and therefore secure, short-term deposits of surplus cash.

Most contracts are short term, often overnight, and many have no set redemption date. The first leg of a repo transaction will normally **settle on the same day it is agreed (T + 0)**. Contracts with no set redemption date simply roll over at the end of each day unless either party cancels the deal. These are referred to as **open repos**. Contracts which have fixed maturities in excess of overnight are referred to as **term repos**.

### 2.8.1 Repo risks

It is the essential purpose of a repo agreement that the money lent is secured against collateral paid, i.e. the bonds sold represent the collateral, which is generally of a high quality such as gilts.

It is however possible that during the period of a repo, the value of the collateral might deteriorate. It is common for a haircut to be taken which means that money lent in the agreement will be less than the initial market value of the bonds. This reduction in value or 'haircut' allows for a fall in value over the term. It is also possible that additional collateral or variation margin may be required to cover any falls in bond value during the term of the repo agreement.

### 2.8.2 Risks and credit ratings of money market instruments

The credit risk of money market instruments occurs because of the generally unsecured nature of most instruments such as commercial paper, although some may have credit enhancement. Commercial paper is very often rolled over to continue the debt beyond its life. This involves the issuer issuing further commercial paper and there is a risk of this new issue being made. This represents 'rollover risk' for the investor.

The table below represents the credit ratings offered by the three major credit rating agencies for commercial paper.

| | Credit rating agencies | | |
|---|---|---|---|
| | Moody's | S&P | Fitch |
| Highest quality | P-1 | A-1* | F1* |
| Satisfactory | P-2 | A-2 | F2 |
| Adequate | P-3 | A-3 | F3 |
| Speculative | N-P | B / C | F4 |
| In default | N-P | D | F5 |

*S&P offers its highest rating as A1+ and Fitch as F1+

### 2.8.3 Settlement of money market instruments

In September 2003, money market instruments were introduced into CREST, part of Euroclear. The existing CREST settlement system for gilts and equities was to be integrated, to allow for the settlement of **money market instruments (MMIs)**. Previously, the issue, transfer and settlement of certain MMIs was carried out through the Central Moneymarkets Office (CMO). The CMO ceased operations in October 2003.

Money market instruments are traditionally short-term transferable securities, with maturities of up to one year. They include securities such as Treasury bills (T-bills), Certificates of Deposit (CDs), local authority bills, bank bills and Commercial Paper (CP). MMIs are also traditionally **bearer** instruments.

The electronic settlement system of CREST required the creation of an **'eligible debt security' (EDS)**, which is the dematerialised equivalent of the MMI. These EDSs are the same, in economic terms, as the underlying MMI. However, an EDS may only be held and transferred in the dematerialised form within CREST. These EDSs are registered securities, which are settled using CREST settlement functionality, with the registration details maintained by CREST. There are no such materialised EDSs. However, banks may still issue certificated MMIs outside of CREST.

## 3 Foreign Exchange

earning objective

**2.2.1** **Understand** the role, structure and main characteristics of the foreign exchange market, OTC market, quotes, spreads and exchange rate information, market participants and access to the markets, volume, volatility and liquidity, risk mitigation, rollovers and losses, regulatory / supervisory and environment

### 3.1 Overview of the foreign exchange markets

Foreign exchange trading, or FOREX as it is commonly known, is the dealing by professional players of the currencies of various countries. London is the biggest centre in the world for FOREX trading, with over $600bn traded per day. Although some FOREX is required for overseas trade, the majority is for speculative purposes, where FOREX traders seek to exploit a particular view on interest rate differentials or exchange rate movements.

**There is no formal market place for FOREX trades**. In London it is purely over-the-counter (OTC) with settlement of T + 2. Prices are advertised on screens and deals are conducted over telephones. The major players are investment banks and specialist currency brokers. This is not a market place where the private investor gets directly involved – his currency needs are met through specialist money organisations, who themselves have accessed the currency markets through their own specialist broker.

## 3.2 Spot transactions

The **spot market** is the market for **immediate** currency trades. These trades will **settle in two business days (T + 2)**. This may exclude public holidays in the countries of the two parties to the trade and also in the country of the currency. (For example, a German bank dealing in the sterling market with an American bank must take into account public holidays in Germany, the US and the UK.) On occasion however, investors choose to 'rollover' their open positions or, in other words, extend an unsettled position so as to extend a speculative market position for longer. This in effect requires a position to be closed and another position to be immediately opened.

The underlying users of the spot market are widespread, but the common factor between them will be the relatively large sums involved. The spot currency market would not be used by, for example, holiday makers exchanging small amounts, but would potentially be used by the *Bureaux de Change* themselves with much larger amounts to buy and sell. Other examples of market users would include a fund manager who receives cash from a sale of securities in one currency, but needs to settle a purchase in another, or a global business that regularly undertakes transactions in several different currencies.

The risks for participants in the spot currency market include, firstly, the risk of counterparty default and, secondly, the constant fluctuation of exchange rates (leading to decreases or increases in, say, the sterling value of an amount held in euros, until a transaction has been agreed). The former has been significantly reduced by continuous linked settlement (CLS), and the latter can be removed by use of the forward currency market. Both of these areas are discussed later in this chapter.

The market has no formal market place and trading takes place via telephones, with prices being quoted on screen services. The spot market quotes **bid offer** prices in the form of a **spread**, normally based against the US dollar (USD) as the fixed currency. The main exceptions to this are GBP/USD (known as **cable**) and the EUR/USD, where the variable USD is quoted against the fixed sterling or fixed euro unit.

### GBP/USD spot rate

| USD 2.0275 | USD 2.0385 |
|---|---|
| The buyer's rate | The seller's rate |
| GBP 1 will get USD 2.0275 | USD 2.0385 will get GBP 1 |

To help you remember which is the correct to use, it may be useful to remember that the **bank will always give you the worst of the two rates.**

## Example: Calculating spot settlement amounts

GBP/USD Spot Rate **USD 2.0275 – USD 2.0385**

To convert GBP 100 into USD GBP 100 × **USD 2.0275** = USD 202.75

To convert USD 100 into GBP $\frac{\text{USD 100}}{\textbf{USD 2.0385}}$ = GBP 49.06

### 3.2.1 Characteristics of the foreign exchange market

The Bank for International Settlements the (BIS) provides a triennial report on the foreign exchange markets.

The bank provides detailed information on its website regarding the FX market.

The headline figures from the BIS April 2010 survey are the following:

**Turnover on the Global foreign exchange market**

- Global foreign exchange market turnover was 20% higher in April 2010 than in April 2007, with average daily turnover of $4.0 trillion compared to $3.3 trillion.
- The increase was driven by the 48% growth in turnover of spot transactions, which represent 37% of foreign exchange market turnover. Spot turnover rose to $1.5 trillion in April 2010 from $1.0 trillion in April 2007.
- The increase in turnover of other foreign exchange instruments was more modest at 7%, with average daily turnover of $2.5 trillion in April 2010. Turnover in outright forwards and currency swaps grew strongly. Turnover in foreign exchange swaps was flat relative to the previous survey, while trading in currency options decreased.
- As regards counterparties, the higher global foreign exchange market turnover is associated with the increased trading activity of "other financial institutions" - a category that includes non-reporting banks, hedge funds, pension funds, mutual funds, insurance companies and central banks, among others. Turnover by this category grew by 42%, increasing to $1.9 trillion in April 2010 from $1.3 trillion in April 2007. For the first time, activity of reporting dealers with other financial institutions surpassed inter-dealer transactions (i.e. transactions between reporting dealers).
- Foreign exchange market activity became more global, with cross-border transactions representing 65% of trading activity in April 2010, while local transactions account for 35%.
- The percentage share of the US dollar has continued its slow decline witnessed since the April 2001 survey, while the euro and the Japanese yen gained relative to April 2007. Among the 10 most actively traded currencies, the Australian and Canadian dollars both increased market share, while the pound sterling and the Swiss franc lost ground. The market share of emerging market currencies increased, with the biggest gains for the Turkish lira and the Korean won.
- The relative ranking of foreign exchange trading centres has changed slightly from the previous survey. Banks located in the United Kingdom accounted for 36.7%, against 34.6% in 2007, of all foreign exchange market turnover, followed by the United States (18%), Japan (6%), Singapore (5%), Switzerland (5%), Hong Kong SAR (5%) and Australia (4%).

The market in FX is often highly volatile, with economic data reports rapidly having an effect on investor's views of the market.

### 3.2.2 Regulation in the Foreign Exchange Market

#### Commodity Futures Trading Commission

##### US markets

The **Commodity Futures Trading Commission (CFTC)** regulates all on-exchange derivatives trading, with the exception of those areas covered by the SEC. It also has responsibilities for regulation of the Foreign exchange market

Like the SEC, it is a government agency and is responsible for

- Regulating US futures and options exchanges (except the CBOE).
- Overseeing the activities of the National Futures Association (NFA).

The **NFA** acts as the self-regulatory organisation for futures firms using delegated powers from the CFTC. This includes the **screening and registration of all firms and individuals who want to conduct futures and forex-related business with the public.** They also run an **arbitration scheme,** similar to the Financial Ombudsman Scheme in the UK, to help resolve disputes between clients and NFA member firms.

#### UK

The UK market is largely regulated by the FSA. A significant role in market good practice however arises from 'The London Foreign Exchange Joint Standing Committee (FXJSC)', which describes its role on its website:

'The London Foreign Exchange Joint Standing Committee (FX JSC) was established in 1973 under the auspices of the Bank of England, in the main part as a forum for banks and brokers to discuss broad market issues and the focus of the Committee's regular work remains issues of common concern to the different participants in the foreign exchange market.'

'One of the main responsibilities of the Committee is to maintain the Non-Investment Products Code. This is a voluntary code of good market practice which covers bullion, wholesale deposits as well as the FX market. It is maintained in conjunction with the Sterling Money Markets Liaison Group, the London Bullion Market Association, and certain trade associations'

### 3.2.3 Foreign exchange spot rates

**Learning objective**

2.2.2 **Understand** the determinants of spot foreign exchange prices: currency demand-transactional and speculative, economic variables, cross border trading of financial assets, interest rates and free and pegged rates.

In order to be able to make informed decisions on currency exposure and overseas investment, it is important to appreciate the factors affecting exchange rates and the likely future direction of exchange rates.

## 3.3 Shorter term factors affecting exchange rates

### 3.3.1 Interest rates

In the short term, high interest rates will attract 'hot money' from around the world seeking high yields into a currency. This will create demand for the currency and increase the exchange rate. Investors borrowing in one currency to deposit into another are referred to as engaging in carry trades.

### 3.3.2 Balance of payments

If the UK has a balance of payments surplus, then it is exporting goods with a higher value than it is importing. In order to pay for these goods, overseas customers will need to purchase sterling. Demand for sterling will increase, meaning that the currency will strengthen. Alternatively, as is unfortunately more likely to be the case, if the UK has a balance of payments deficit, then UK companies will need to sell sterling to buy overseas currencies to fund their purchases. This will cause sterling to weaken.

### 3.3.3 Economic growth

Economic growth will stimulate demand for a currency both through capital flows into the country, due to attractive investment opportunities, and current account flows, due to increased supply and demand for the country's traded goods and services. Alternatively, a credit boom, which causes demand for overseas goods and services, will cause the currency to weaken.

### 3.3.4 Fiscal and monetary policies

Taxation and public spending policies have a direct impact on economic growth. Government borrowing plans will impact on interest rates, as will monetary policy, which aims to reduce or increase money supply through changes in interest rates.

### 3.3.5 Natural resources

The discovery or existence of valuable natural resources, such as oil, can cause a currency to strengthen dramatically.

### 3.3.6 Currency block membership

Some currencies are pegged to the US dollar, such as certain middle Eastern currencies. Such formal or informal relationships should be noted, since they will have a key impact on the exchange rate.

### 3.3.7 Political events

Central bank intervention can affect exchange rates, although experience has shown that it is sometimes the speculators who win the day rather than the central authorities. On top of this, events such as elections, public opinion polls, government ministers' statements and press releases can all affect the exchange rate.

### 3.3.8 Speculators

Rapid changes in exchange rates may result from speculation in the FX markets, on 16$^{th}$ September 1992, currency speculators short sold around ten billion dollars in value of sterling and in doing so drove down the value of the pound. (The impact of this on the UK was severe enough to drive it out of the Exchange Rate Mechanism (The ERM).

### 3.3.9 Currencies regarded as 'Safe havens'

The US dollar has frequently in the past been regarded as a 'safe haven' for cash in difficult economic conditions. Investors prefer to hold a currency which they feel is safe. Other 'safe' currencies have included the Swiss franc and the Yen.

## 3.4 Longer term factors affecting spot rates

### 3.4.1 Inflation

In the shorter-term, the exchange rate is determined by supply and demand factors and, to a greater or lesser extent, market sentiment. Longer-term exchange rates are determined by **purchasing power parity**, which is a relationship between economies and the levels of **inflation** they suffer. Purchasing power parity is best explained by way of a small example.

If a basket of goods costs £100 in London and the same basket of goods costs €200 in Paris, this predicts the exchange rate between the two countries will be £1 = €2. However, if the two economies suffer differing rates of inflation then, over time, the exchange rate will alter.

If, after a number of years, the basket of goods costs £115 in London, due to the impact of inflation on UK prices, and yet remains at €200 in Paris, this would suggest that the exchange rate between the two currencies is now £1 = €1.74 – a decline in the value of sterling. This theory of exchange rate behaviour can also be referred to as **The Law of One Price**.

Short-term supply and demand features may well mask this overall trend, but purchasing power parity gives an underlying theme to the foreign exchange markets. If one economy consistently has an inflation rate in excess of its competitors, then its currency will deteriorate against its trading partners.

### 3.4.2 Trade imbalances

Recent decades have seen large imbalances in the trade in goods and services between various trading partners. The export of Chinese goods to the US in far greater volumes than the trade in the opposite direction has lead to Capital account movements of US government securities in the opposite direction.

### 3.4.3 Exchange rate management

#### Free floating exchange rates

The majority of currencies in the world at this time might be described to exist within free floating exchange rates with one another. These currencies including the dollar against most currencies may be subject at times from interventions from central banks, who control factors such as the interest rate. Maintaining a low interest rate nay be considered as keeping a currency weak against it's trading partners to attract more export activities and enhance stimulating an economy.

#### Managed Floating exchange rates

Where more extreme activities are applied by a central bank, the term 'managed floating may be applied. An example would be those members of the ERM where countries including the UK pound were required to be kept within restricted exchange rates to other currencies. The ERM involved many countries who went on to join the EU, and it was the actions of currency speculation as described above which drove the UK out of the ERM and possibly lead to the decision to stay outside the Euro currency.

#### Pegged exchange rates

Fixed exchange rates where exchange rates are not allowed to float at all but instead are rigidly managed are less common than they once were. Before the current era of world trade it was easier for governments to peg their currency to that of a key trading partner.

The 'gold standard' where countries fixed their currencies in terms of a certain amount of gold, was probably the most significant attempt to maintain fixed exchange rates. To maintain their currency a country would buy or sell gold at a fixed rate. The 'Bretton Woods agreement' which ran from 1946 to 1971, allowed other governments to sell gold to the US treasury at $35 per ounce. The breaking of the gold standard has led to what is known as 'fiat money' where the value of a currency is driven by factors of supply and demand for the goods and services of the issuing country.

## 3.5 Forward transactions

| Learning objective | **2.2.3 Calculate** forward foreign exchange rates using; premiums and discounts and interest rate parity. |
|---|---|

#### Definition

The forward market is a market in currencies at an agreed date in the future.

It enables you to agree a rate today (the forward rate) at which the currencies will be exchanged on an agreed future date. The benefit of this is **certainty** – although you may not need the foreign currency until three months' time, you can fix the price at today's forward exchange rate.

Many users of the forward market will, in principle, be no different from the spot market participants discussed earlier. The key is that it enables users to remove the risk of exchange rate fluctuations before the agreed settlement date. For example, a UK company expecting to receive a large payment in US dollars from a customer in a month's time may be concerned that the dollar will weaken between now and the date the payment is received, causing a reduction in the company's sterling profits. Entering into a one-month forward agreement today to sell the dollars will eliminate this risk by fixing the amount of sterling that will be receivable on exchange. The downside is that, were the dollar to strengthen against sterling over the next month, the company would not make any additional profit from the exchange movement.

### 3.5.1 Calculating forward rates

Forward rates are quoted as premiums (pm) or discounts (dis) to the spot rate.

## Example: Calculating forward rates

GBP/USD Spot Rate USD 2.0275 – USD 2.0385

One-month forward 0.37c – 0.35c pm (37-35 pips)

Three-month forward 1.00c – 0.97c pm

What is the one-month forward rate?

**NB:** In the above example the three-month forward premium could be described as 100-97 **pips**.

## Solution

It is **important to remember** that these premiums or discounts are quoted in cents, whereas the spot rate is quoted in dollars.

To obtain the forward rate the **premium is subtracted** from the spot rate or the **discount is added** to the spot rate. (To aid memory, consider that the premium or discount describes where the spot rate is relative to the forward rate.)

Based on the above figures, the one-month forward rate is

| | |
|---|---|
| | USD 2.0275 – USD 2.0385 |
| Less premium | (USD 0.0037 – USD 0.0035) |
| | USD 2.0238 – USD 2.0350 |

## Example: Calculating forward settlement amounts

Using the above example.

GBP/USD one-month forward rate **USD 2.0238 – USD 2.0350**

To convert GBP 100 into USD GBP 100 × **USD 2.0238** = USD 202.38

To convert USD 100 into GBP $\frac{\text{USD 100}}{\text{USD 2.0350}}$ = GBP 49.14

### Calculation of forward rates

One important factor to remember about this market is that it does not reflect an expectation of what the spot rate will be in three, six or nine months' time. It is simply a mathematical result of the difference in interest rates in the two countries.

## Example

In the example below, three-month sterling interest rates were 10%, meaning the interest rate for the three-month period is 2.5% (10% × 3/12). Three-month dollar rates were 6%, meaning the interest rate for the three-month period is 1.5% (6% × 3/12).

| **Now spot rate** | | | | **Three months' time forward rate** |
|---|---|---|---|---|
| £1,000 | → | @ 3-month £ rates at 2.5% | → | £1,025 |
| ↓ | | | | ↓ |
| @ $1.4275 | | | | Therefore @ $1.4135 |
| ↓ | | | | ↑ |
| $1,427.50 | → | @ 3-month $ rates at 1.5% | → | $1,448.91 |

The forward rate is simply calculated on the basis that the money is invested at the current rate of interest in the two countries. At the end of the period, the relationship between the value of the two deposits gives the forward rate.

$$\frac{\$1,448.91}{£1,025} = \$1.4135$$

If this relationship were not the case, then it would be possible to make an arbitrage profit by borrowing in one currency, converting it at today's spot rate into the other currency and placing this on deposit for, say, three months. At the same time, a forward contract could be taken out to reverse the original spot transaction, locking in a profit.

## 3.6 Interest rate parity formula

The link between exchange rates and interest rates can be worked through using first principles as above. Alternatively, the link can be summarised by the **interest rate parity** formula, which says that

**Formula to learn**

$$\text{Forward rate} = \frac{1+r_v}{1+r_f} \times \text{Spot rate}$$

Where:

$r_v$ = interest rate in country with variable currency for the relevant period.
$r_f$ = interest rate in country with fixed currency for the relevant period.

## Example (continued)

$$\text{Forward rate} = \frac{1.015}{1.025} \times \$1.4275 = \$1.4135$$

It is worth noting the specific way in which $r_v$ and $r_f$ are calculated. They should be based on the number of days in the period. For example, if dollar interest rates for a three-month (91-day) period are 8%, the relevant value for $r_v$ is (8% × 91/360) 2.02%. If sterling interest rates for a three-month (91-day) period are 10%, then the relevant value for $r_f$ is (10% × 91/365) 2.49%.

The use of a **360-day year for dollar** interest rates and a **365-day year for sterling** is market convention. When banks work out the yield they wish to pay or receive, they take this into account in their quote.

## 3.7 Cross rates

In some cases, it is not possible to find a quote for two currencies against one another. For example, an investor holding sterling wishing to buy Turkish lira will be unable to find a market place in which the two currencies are traded against each other.

However, the investor will find a US dollar/sterling market and a US dollar/lira market. In such a case, the investor can use sterling to buy US dollars and, subsequently, use the US dollars to buy lira.

When the rate at which the overseas currency is bought or sold is calculated in this manner, it is referred to as the **cross rate**.

Where there is a market between two currencies, the actual rates available in that market should be consistent with the cross rates. This rate can be calculated by going via the dollar. If the two rates are significantly different, this may identify an **arbitrage opportunity**.

## 3.8 Using foreign exchange derivatives

Learning objective

2.2.4 **Analyse** how foreign exchange contracts can be used to buy or sell currency relating to overseas investments, or to hedge non-domestic currency exposure: spot contracts, forward contracts, currency futures and currency options.

Currency forwards are very widespread instruments in the financial industry. Like spot currency transactions, for major exchange rates other than sterling, a forward exchange rate is quoted as the number of units of that currency that are equivalent to one dollar.

### 3.8.1 Currency futures

Surprisingly there are no currency futures (exchange traded contracts) traded on the London exchanges. This is because the banks themselves provide a market place in these products. When derivative products are not traded on an exchange they are traded OTC (as with currency forwards) which allow the contract size and delivery dates to be mutually agreed at the time of trade. Despite London's lack of exchange traded currency products, there are two US exchanges that do trade them, the Chicago Mercantile Exchange (CME) and the Philadelphia Stock Exchange (PHLX).

The quotation of all the US currency products is in American terms.

If you buy a currency future (going long the future), you must enter into an obligation to buy the foreign currency, e.g. sterling or Yen and thus sell US dollars. If you believe that the foreign currency will strengthen then a speculator would take this position.

If you sell a currency future, you enter into an agreement to sell the foreign currency and thus buy US dollars. A speculator believing that the foreign currency is to weaken against the dollar would sell the future (i.e. go short).

### 3.8.2 Currency options

Currency options allow the right but not the obligation to buy or sell a currency again against the dollar, so a £ call gives the right to buy sterling for dollars at an agreed exchange rate for an agreed period of time.

Those who engage in business activities overseas which will result in the receipt or payment of a foreign currency in the future can use derivative products to hedge the foreign exchange risk. For example, a company which will receive euros in three months' time might use a euro forward which fixes the exchange rate today for the exchange in three months.

### 3.8.3 Currency swaps

As described in chapter 7 section 4.5, currency swaps involve the exchange on a principal value of one currency with an equivalent value of another currency. Over the course of the swap period, payments are made in the respective currencies in line with the fixed or variable interest rates agreed at the outset of the swap.

### 3.8.4 Synthetic agreement for forward exchange (SAFE)

'SAFE' agreements are effectively similar in nature to currency swaps with the important difference that the principle value of the currencies are not exchanged. At the start of the swap. Instead interest payments are made on what are notional values of each currency and at the end of the SAFE agreement a sum is exchanged based upon the different values of each currency at that time. SAFE agreements are essentially a Contracts for Difference CFDs.

# Chapter Roundup

## Cash deposits

- Bank deposit offering low returns and having low volatility.
- FSCS pays 100% of the first £50,000 of money deposited per person per separately authorised deposit taker.

## Money markets

- Markets for trading shot-term liquidity primarily used by banks and institutional investors.
- Bank of England influences interest rates via the money markets through its weekly treasury bill auctions.
- Interest rates
  - Base rate = Rate set by Bank of England.
  - LIBOR = London interbank offered rate.
  - LIBID – London Inter-bank bid rate.
- The Bank of England acts as lender of last resort to the money markets.

## Money market instruments

- The money market is where banks, companies and institutional investors trade investments of a short maturity.
- Money market investments include Treasury bills, local authority bills, Bills of Exchange (Banks bills and eligible bills), Commercial Paper and Certificates of Deposit.
- Short term credit ratings are provided by rating agencies.
- Treasury bills are issued by the DMO and may be described by their discount rate or their interest rate/yield. They normally have a maximum term of 91 days and a minimum block size of £25,000. They trade on a yield basis (the yield is quoted)

  $$\text{Discount rate} = \frac{100 - \text{Discounted value}}{100} \times \frac{365}{\text{Days}}$$

  $$\text{Interest rate or yield} = \frac{100 - \text{Discounted value}}{\text{Discounted value}} \times \frac{365}{\text{Days}}$$

- Bill of exchange is an acknowledgeable of an obligation to pay a specified sum at a given maturity date. If it is accepted by a bank it becomes a bank bill and is tradeable, if the bank is on the list of eligible banks it becomes an eligible bill.
- Commercial paper is the corporate equivalent of a treasury bill. It is unsecured, has a maturity <12 months and is unsecured.
- CDs are securitised bank deposits that pay a regular coupon. They have maturities up to five years and trade on a yield basis (the yield is quoted). The minimum denomination is usually £100,000 going up in steps of £10,000 above this level.
- Repo = sale and repurchase agreement that is effectively a securitised loan. A bond is 'sold' but it is agreed to be 'repurchased' later, the price difference being the interest on the loan.

  $$\text{Interest} = \text{Principal amount} \times \text{Repo rate} \times \frac{\text{Days}}{365}$$

- FRNs pay coupons linked to LIBOR.
- Settlement of most money market investments takes place on CREST if they have been dematerialised as EDSs.

### Currency markets

- There is no formal market place for foreign currency, trading takes place by phone.
- The spot market is the market for immediate currency trades, settlement is T + 2 business days.
- Direct quote = number of units of local currency per single unit of foreign currency.
- Indirect quote = number of units of foreign currency per single unit of local currency.
- American terms = number of dollars per single unit of the second currency.
- European terms = number of units of the second currency per single dollar.
- If a currency strengthens it can buy more units of the second currency.
- If a currency weakens it can buy fewer units of the second currency.
- A forward currency transaction is an agreement to buy or to sell a currency at a future date at a price agreed today.

### Exchange rates

- Exchange rates are quoted with a bid-offer spread.
- Forward rates are quoted at a premium or discount to the spot rate.
- Forward rates are computed on the basis of interest rate parity.
- Forward rate $= \frac{1+r_V}{1+r_F} \times$ Spot rate

  or

  Spot rate x $(1+r_v)$ = Forward rate x $(1=r_F)$
- Longer-term exchange rates are determined by purchasing power parity which is the relationship between economies and the level of inflation they suffer.
- Future rate = $\frac{1+i_V}{1+i_F} \times$ Spot rate

  or

  Spot rate x $(1+i_v)$ = Forward rate x $(1+i_F)$

# Test Your Knowledge

*Check your knowledge of the chapter here, without referring back to the text.*

1. What is the cover provided for cash deposits under the Financial Services Compensation Scheme?

2. What is the primary risk for a cash deposit?

3. What roles does the Bank of England have in the money markets?

4. What are the interest rates at which banks borrow and lend between each other?

5. What is an eligible debt security?

6. Who issues Treasury bills?

7. What is the discount rate and the interest yield on a Treasury bill that is priced at £99.30 and has 32 days to maturity?

8. What is an eligible bill?

9. What are the normal characteristics of commercial paper?

10. What is the highest short-term credit rating obtainable from Moody's?

11. How do CDs trade?

12. A repo is a sale and repurchase agreement at an agreed price. *True or False?*

13. What is the settlement period for spot currency trades?

14. Where a forward rate is quoted at a premium to the spot rate, the premium should be

    A Deducted from the variable spot quote
    B Added to the variable spot quote
    C Deducted from the fixed spot quote
    D Added to the fixed spot quote

15. What factors drive short-term movements in exchange rates?

16. What factors drive long-term movements in exchange rates?

# Test Your Knowledge: Answers

1. 100% at the first £50,000 of money deposit per person per separately authorised deposit taker

   **(See Section 2.1.2)**

2. That the deposit taker will become insolvent when the deposit exceeds the FSCS limit

   **(See Section 2.1.2)**

3. The Bank of England

   – Sets interest rates
   – Acts as lender of last resort

   **(See Section 3.1)**

4. LIBOR and LIBID

   **(See Section 3.1)**

5. A dematerialised money market deposit

   **(See Section 2.2)**

6. The DMO

   **(See Section 2.2)**

7. Discount rate = $\frac{100.00 - 99.30}{100.00} \times \frac{365}{32} = 0.0798$ or 7.98%

   Yield = $\frac{100.00 - 99.30}{99.30} \times \frac{365}{32} = 0.0804$ or 8.04%

   **(See Section 3.2)**

8. A bill of exchange that has been accepted by an eligible bank

   **(See Section 3.3)**

9. Unsecured, maturity < 12 months, trade at a discount

   **(See Section 3.4)**

10. P – 1

    **(See Section 3.3.1)**

11. CDs trade on a yield basis

    **(See Section 3.5)**

12. True

    **(See Section 3.6)**

13. T + 2

    **(See Section 2.1)**

14. A

    **(See Section 2.2)**

15. Interest rates, economic growth, balance of payments, fiscal and monetary policy, natural resources, currency block membership, political events.

    **(See Section 3.1)**

16. Inflation and purchasing power parity.

    **(See Section 3.2)**

# 3 Equities

## INTRODUCTION

Equities offer a form of long-term financing to companies. There are various different types of shares that a company may issue, the most common being referred to as ordinary shares.

There is an active primary market in the UK and other countries. This enables companies to issue new shares to investors. Furthermore, the Exchanges such as the London Stock Exchange (LSE) and the New York Stock Exchange (NYSE) offers a developed secondary market to allow investors to sell and buy shares.

### CHAPTER CONTENTS

# Chapter Learning Objectives

## Equities

### 3.1 Characteristics of Equities

**3.1.1 Understand** the main investment characteristics, behaviours and risks of different classes of equity:

- Ordinary, cumulative, participating, redeemable and convertible preference shares, bearer and registered shares
- Voting rights, voting and non-voting shares
- Ranking for dividends
- Ranking in liquidation
- Tax treatment of capital gains and dividend income

**3.1.2 Understand** the purpose, main investment characteristics, behaviours and risks of Depositary Receipts:

- American Depositary Receipts
- Global Depositary Receipts
- Beneficial ownership rights

- Unsponsored and sponsored programmes
- Unsponsored and sponsored programmes
- Transferability
- Dividend payments

### 3.2 Issuing Equity Securities

**3.2.1 Understand** the purpose, key features and differences between the following:

- Primary issues
- Secondary issues
- Issuing, listing and quotation
- Dual listings

**3.2.2 Understand** the main regulatory, supervisory and trade body framework supporting UK financial markets:

- Companies Acts
- The Financial Services Authority (FSA) and UK Listing Authority (UKLA)
- HM Treasury
- The Panel on Takeovers and Mergers (POTAM)
- Exchange membership and rules
- Relevant trade associations and professional bodies

**3.2.3** **Understand** the structure of the London Stock Exchange, the types of securities traded on its markets, and the criteria and processes for companies seeking admission:

- Main market
- AIM
- PLUS markets
- Market participants
- Implications for investors

**3.2.4** **Understand** the process of issuing securities in the UK without a prospectus:

- Principles of exemption established under the Prospectus Directive (PD)
- Purpose of the FSA Qualified Investor Register (QIR)
- Eligibility and registration criteria for Natural Persons and SMEs
- Terms of access for issuers seeking to use the Qualified Investor Register

**3.2.5** **Understand** the purpose, structure and stages of an initial public offering (IPO) and the role of the origination team:

- Benefits for the issuer and investors
- Structure: base deal plus green shoe
- Stages of an IPO
- Underwritten versus best efforts
- Principles and process of price stabilisation

## 3.3 Equity Markets and Trade Execution

**3.3.1** **Apply** fundamental UK regulatory requirements with regard to trade execution and reporting:

- Best execution
- Aggregation and allocation
- Prohibition of conflicts of interests and front running

**3.3.2** **Understand** the key features of the main trading venues:

- Regulated and Designated Investment Exchanges
- Recognised Overseas Investment Exchanges
- Structure and size of markets
- Whether quote or order driven
- Main types of order – limit, market, iceberg, named
- Liquidity and transparency
- Participants

**3.3.3** **Understand** the key features of alternative trading venues:

- Multilateral Trading Facilities (MTFs)
- Systematic Internalisers
- Dark Pools

**3.3.4** **Understand** the concepts of trading cum, ex, special cum and special ex:

- The meaning of 'books closed', 'ex-div' and 'cum div', cum, special ex, special cum, and ex rights
- Effect of late registration

**3.3.5** **Apply** knowledge of key differences in the developed markets of UK, Germany, USA and Japan, and emerging markets of Brazil, China, India and Russia (BRIC), both on and off exchange:

- Regulatory and supervisory environment
- Structure and size of markets
- Liquidity and transparency
- Access and relative cost of trading

**3.3.6 Assess** how the following factors influence equity markets and equity valuation:

- Trading volume and liquidity of domestic and international securities markets
- Relationship between cash and derivatives markets, and the effect of timed events
- Market consensus and analyst opinion
- Changes to key pricing determinants such as credit ratings and economic outlook

**3.3.8 Understand** the purpose, construction, application and influence of indices on equity markets:

- Developed and emerging market regional and country sectors
- Market capitalization sub sectors
- Free float and full market capitalization indices
- Fair value adjusted indices

### 3.4 Warrants and Contracts for Difference

**3.4.1 Analyse** the main purposes, characteristics, behaviours and relative risk and return of warrants and covered warrants:

- Benefit to the issuing company
- Right to subscribe for capital
- Effect on price of maturity and the underlying security
- Exercise and expiry
- Calculation of the conversion premium on a warrant

**3.4.2 Analyse** the key features of the main types of Contracts for Difference (CFDs), compared with other forms of direct and indirect investment:

- Types and availability of CFDs
- Differences in pricing, valuing and trading CFDs compared to direct investment
- CFD providers – market maker versus direct market access
- Tax efficiency
- Margin
- Market, liquidation and counterparty risks
- Size of CFD market and impact on total market activity

# 1 The Nature of a Share

**Learning objective**

**3.1.1 Understand** the main investment characteristics, behaviours and risks of different classes of equity: Ordinary, bearer and registered shares, voting rights, voting and non-voting shares, cumulative, participating, redeemable and convertible preference shares, ranking for dividends, ranking in liquidation and tax treatment of capital gains and dividend income.

The shareholders of a company are the **owners** of the company. Historically businesses were so small that one individual could finance the whole enterprise. As businesses became larger it was difficult for one individual to provide sufficient finance for the operation. Companies allow a large number of individuals to pool their capital into one organisation, therefore facilitating the formation of larger companies.

Each owner (shareholder) contributes capital and, in return, receives shares (i.e. share of ownership). The more an individual contributes, the greater the allotment of shares. As the owners, the shareholders take the greatest risks. If the company performs badly they will lose their money. However, they normally have only a **limited liability**; limited to the amount that they agreed to contribute.

This is known as the share's **nominal value**. Normally, this amount (and normally a premium in excess of it) will have been paid in full when the share was first issued. However, occasionally this is not the case and only a portion of the nominal value has been paid up (for public companies, this portion must be at least a quarter of the share's nominal value). Shares of this kind are known as **partly paid shares**. Companies can require the holders of partly paid shares to pay up all or part of the remainder at a future date by making a **call** on the company's shares.

On the other hand, if the company prospers then the shareholders will reap the rewards. Debt, such as a corporate bond, will only ever receive its interest, or coupon payments and the capital repayment upon maturity. In contrast, shares do not normally have a fixed return and participate fully in the remaining profits of the business. These profits may be distributed by way of a dividend or can be retained within the operation in order to increase the potential for future profit.

## 1.1 Equity shares

Ordinary shares are often referred to as equity shares. Here, the term equity means that they have an equal right to share in the profits of the company. For example, if a company has 10,000 Ordinary shares, each share is entitled to $\frac{1}{10,000}$ of the profits made during any period.

### 1.1.1 The normal characteristics

The right of Ordinary shares are detailed in the company's constitutional documents and in particular, the **Articles of Association**. However, it is normal for Ordinary shares to possess a **vote**. This means that the holder of any Ordinary shares may attend and vote at any.meetings held by the company. Whilst the day-to-day control and management of the company is dealt with by the directors and managers, the shareholders must retain the right to decide upon the most important issues that affect the business.

As discussed above, the shareholders also have an equal right to share in any **dividends** that are distributed by the company. However, a dividends distribution is **not guaranteed**. If profits for the year are low the company will be unlikely to pay a dividend, although 'uncovered dividends', paid from previous years' profits may be paid.

### 1.1.2 Special types of Ordinary shares

#### 'A' class Ordinary shares and 'B' class Ordinary shares

Where a company wishes to issues a number of types of share with different rights and privileges, then they will be issued as different classes. The rights which may potentially differ include:

- Whether dividends will be received ('A' class shares frequently have no voting rights).
- The nature or absence of voting rights.

It may well be that class 'A' shares offer superior rights to class 'B' shares although this need not be the case. A company may indeed offer any number of different classes of share such as class 'C' or class 'D' as there is no statutory limit to the number of classes.

### 1.1.3 Bearer shares

The majority of shares issued by UK companies are registered securities. This means that the names of the legal owners of the shares appear on a register (a legal document maintained by the company's registrar) and share certificates, if issued, are only *prima facie* evidence of ownership. When such shares are transferred between owners it is, therefore, necessary for the registrar to be informed and the register to be updated. This process is covered in the chapter on settlement later in this Study Book.

However, if permitted by its own Articles of Association, a company may issue certificates in bearer form (also known as warrants, though not to be confused with those mentioned later in this chapter) representing ownership of fully paid shares. No register is maintained of the holders of such bearer shares, thus legal ownership is transferred by delivery of the certificates themselves. The main advantage of these shares is that no stamp duty will be payable when they are transferred, although stamp duty is payable on the original issue of the shares at a rate of 1½% (three times the normal amount). Bearer shares are rare in the UK.

## 1.2 Preference shares

As mentioned above, Ordinary shares carry the full risks and rewards of ownership. Another type of share which a company can issue is a preference share. These take on debt-like characteristics and offer only limited risks and returns.

### 1.2.1 The normal characteristics

A preference share is preferred in two basic forms.

1. The preference share **dividend must be paid out before any ordinary dividend can be paid**. It is conventional for preference shares to be **cumulative** and if the dividend is not paid in any one year, the arrears and the current year's dividend must be paid before any ordinary dividend can be paid in the future. The assumption is that preference shares are cumulative unless stated otherwise.
2. The second way that they have preference over ordinary shares is in the order of pay-out in the event of a winding-up. Preference shares **will be paid prior to Ordinary shares**. On liquidation of the company, the preference shareholders will only ever receive up to the **nominal value** of the shares. This is not the case for ordinary or equity shares. Equity shares would receive anything that remains after all other investors have been paid.

In order to receive these benefits, preference shareholders must relinquish a number of rights normally attached to shares.

Firstly, the dividend on preference shares is **normally a fixed dividend**, expressed as a percentage of the nominal value. For example, 7% £1 preference shares: these shares would pay a dividend each year of 7p per share. The quoted rate on a preference share is net of tax at 10%.

Secondly, it is conventional for preference shares to carry **no voting rights**. However, most company constitutions contain a clause which states that if the dividend on a cumulative preference share has not been paid for **five years**, preference shareholders will receive the right to attend and vote at general meetings of the company. It should be remembered that, as with all dividends, the payment is at the discretion of the directors and no shareholder may sue for an unpaid dividend.

### 1.2.2 Preference shares as investments

As we can see, preference shares offer the rewards one would normally see attached to a debt instrument – a fixed return with no voting rights. However, they carry greater risk since they are nearer the bottom of the liquidation priority table in the event of a winding-up.

There are, however, a number of special features that can be added to preference shares to enhance their appeal and make them attractive potential investments for individuals.

### 1.2.3 Special types of preference shares

Some preference shares can be specified as **participating shares**. A participating share has a right, when profits reach certain levels, to take a share of those profits as opposed to simply receiving a fixed return. This participation right **may** also apply to the proceeds on a winding-up (liquidation).

Preference shares may also be issued **with conversion rights**. These rights will allow the preference shares to be converted into Ordinary shares at specified rates in the future. As such, the preference share in this instance is more like a convertible debt instrument than a share.

Convertible preference shares may be used for debt restructuring where outstanding debts are sometimes waived in return for issued convertible preference shares. Similarly convertible shares may be offered to the shareholders of the offeree company to delay increased share ownership in the combined company and hence dilution.

Finally, preference shares may be given **specified redemption dates**. For the most part, shares are not seen to be redeemable but preference shares sometimes carry a redemption date, making them seem once again more like debt than shares. One particular type of redeemable preference share is a **zero coupon preference share**. To compensate for a lack of income, these shares will provide capital gains and **often carry voting rights**.

As with convertible bonds, a conversion ratio will fix the number of ordinary shares which the security can be converted into. The conversion ratio may be used to calculate the conversion premium or discount.

$$\text{Conversion prem. or disc.} = \left( \frac{\text{Conversion} \times \text{Market Price of Convertible Shares} - 1}{\text{Market Price of Ordinary Shares}} \right) \times 100$$

## Example

Van Berg industry has issued 8% convertible preference shares which can be converted into ordinary shares at a rate of 6 preference shares for each 1 ordinary share. The current market value of the preference shares is $1.40 and the ordinary shares issued by Van Berg are trading at $6.80.

$$\text{Conversion premium or discount} = \left( \frac{6 \times \$1.40 - 1}{\$6.80} \right) \times 100 = 8.8\% \text{ premium}$$

It is most likely that the preference shares will trade at a premium due to the excess paid for the flexibility offered by the option to convert. The preference shares offer lower risk than ordinary shares with the advantage that should the company shares rise in value they may be converted.

## 1.3 The UK and dividend tax credit

When a shareholder receives a dividend, it is paid out of company profits on which they have already paid (or are due to pay) corporation tax. The tax credit allows for this and is available to the shareholder to offset against any Income Tax that may be due on their 'dividend income'.

### 1.3.1 Working out tax credits

The dividend received by the shareholder represents 90 per cent of the gross 'dividend income'. **Dividends on UK shares are received net of a 10% tax credit**. This means a dividend of £90 has a £10 tax credit, giving gross income of £100 to include in the income tax computation. The tax credit can be deducted in computing tax payable but it cannot be repaid. Higher rate taxpayers pay tax at 32½% on their gross dividends and can deduct the 10% tax credit. This is the same as taxing the net dividend at 25%. For example, a higher rate taxpayer receiving a net dividend of £9,000 will pay tax of £2,250, which is £3,250 (£10,000 @ 32½%) less £1,000 (£10,000 @ 10%). This is the same as taking 25% × £9,000. Dividend income above the higher rate (£150,000 of income 2010/11) is taxed at 42.5%.

The current UK rate of capital gains tax for gains when selling shares is 28% from June 2010.

## 1.4 Warrants

**Learning objective**

**3.4.1** **Analyse** the main purposes, characteristics, behaviours and relative risk and return of warrants and covered warrants: benefit to the issuing company, right to subscribe for capital, effect on price of maturity and the underlying security, exercise and expiry and calculation of the conversion premium on a warrant.

If you own an equity warrant, it gives you the **right, but not the obligation**, to buy a **new** share in a company at a fixed price on or before a stated expiry date.

For example, a particular warrant may give you the right to buy two new shares in XYZ plc for a price of 80p each, expiring in 2010.

An investor who owns this warrant has the potential to gain considerably if the value of XYZ plc rises significantly. By 2010, XYZ plc shares may be worth much more than 80p each, but the holder of the warrant will be able to buy two new shares from the company for 80p, whatever their market value. This is known as **exercising** the warrant. In this event, the investor will effectively realise a gain of however much the total value of the two shares exceeds the total purchase price of 160p (for two shares at 80p each). If this gain represents more than the investor paid for the warrant in the first place, then they will have made a net profit.

On the other hand, if the share price goes down, the investor will not be exposed to increasing losses, since they have no obligation to buy the shares. If the share price is at or below 80p, the warrant will simply not be exercised. All the investor will have lost overall, then, will be whatever they paid initially to buy the warrant itself.

However, when warrants are first issued by companies, there is often no specific price paid by the investor for the warrant. This is because they are often 'given away' as an extra incentive for investors to subscribe to a debt issue. This is known as issuing bonds with warrants attached and the benefit to the issuing company is that their debt is more attractive as it gives the investor the chance to benefit if the company's share price rises.

In many ways this is similar to a company issuing a convertible bond in that it gives to an investor in a debt instrument the added benefit of equity upside. However, where debt is issued with warrants (as opposed to issuing convertible debt) the holder of the bond may split the warrant off and trade both aspects of the security separately.

### 1.4.1 Warrant pricing

Once warrants have been issued (whether or not initially attached to a bond) they can be traded between investors, and therefore have a market price. The price for which warrants can be purchased consists of two elements, known as **time value** and **intrinsic value**. The intrinsic value is sometimes also known as the formula value, whereas the time value is often known as the premium.

## Example

Let's consider the same XYZ plc warrant that we mentioned above but imagine that it now has a market price of 50p.

| | |
|---|---|
| **Warrant Terms** | Each warrant gives the right to buy two new shares |
| **Exercise Price** | 80p |
| **Share Price** | 90p |
| **Warrant Price** | 50p |

The formula value (or intrinsic value) represents the gain that would be realised if the warrant were to be exercised now, i.e. if the investor bought two shares worth 90p each for the exercise price of 80p each.

Formula value = (Share price – Exercise price) × No. of new shares

= (90p – 80p) × 2

= **20p**

Any additional payment for the warrant, prior to expiry, will represent the time value or premium. In this case, investors are prepared to pay an extra 30p (50p – 20p) of time value for the chance that they might make more profit in the future.

It should be remembered that warrants are highly geared investments and carry with them a higher degree of risk than, for example, shares.

Although someone buying the above warrant could lose no more than the 50p they have paid for it, they will lose this 50p (which represents 100% of their investment) if the share price falls to and remains at 80p or below at expiry. If the investor instead bought the two new shares above (for a total of 180p), the shares would need to become worthless for 100% of the investment to be lost.

### 1.4.2 Conversion premium of a warrant

If following the purchase of a warrant, the exercise price is paid to purchase the underlying shares; the overall price to get these shares tends to be higher than if the shares had been purchased immediately without the use of the warrant. This fact leads to the calculation of the conversion premium.

Conversion premium/discount = (Warrant price + Exercise price) – Share price

For example: the premium on a warrant is 45p and exercise price is 375p. The warrant is exercised when the share price is 410p;

Conversion premium = (45p + 375p) – 410p

= 10p

## 1.5 Covered warrants

Technically a warrant, as described above, can only be issued by the company itself, since it gives the investor the right to buy new shares in the company. Covered warrants, however, are instruments issued by securities houses. These are warrants over the shares of another company, either giving the investor the right to buy the shares at a fixed price (a **call warrant**) or the right to sell the shares at a fixed price (a **put warrant**). The former will leave the investor in a similar position to that of owning a conventional warrant, whereas the latter will enable the investor to gain from falls in the value of the underlying security. This is therefore a useful way to hedge exposure to an underlying share. In order to cover its position, the securities house may own shares in the relevant company, or warrants on the company's shares.

In practice, most covered warrants are **cash settled**. This means that, on exercise, the investor does not make or take delivery of the underlying shares, but simply receives a cash amount representing the gain which would have been realised on exercise of the warrant. Covered warrants are priced using a calculation of their 'fair value'. If this is the case, since no shares are actually being bought or sold, there will be **no stamp duty** payable on trading or exercise of the warrant.

## 1.6 Comparison table

| | Warrants | Covered Warrants |
|---|---|---|
| **Issuer** | The company to whom the underlying shares relate | Third party, e.g. investment bank, who also acts as a 'market maker' |
| **Maturity** | Long dated | Average life of six to 12 months (some up to five years) |
| **Trading** | London Stock Exchange | London Stock Exchange |
| **Types** | Right to buy | Right to buy or sell |
| **Stamp Duty** | Yes | No |
| **Exercise** | Physical shares | Usually cash settled (though some are physically settled) |

## 1.7 Depository receipts

**Learning objective**

**3.1.2 Understand** the purpose, main investment characteristics, behaviours and risks of Depositary Receipts: American Depositary Receipts; Global Depositary Receipts; Beneficial ownership rights, unsponsored & sponsored programmes, unsponsored and sponsored programmes transferability.

**American Depository Receipts** (ADRs) are a common form of trading of overseas shares in the US. The purpose is to encourage US investors to buy overseas company shares. The shares are lodged with an American bank, which then issues a receipt for the shares (ADR). This receipt is in **bearer** form and **denominated in US dollars**. ADRs are listed and trade on the New York Stock Exchange, NASDQ and the American Stock Exchange. A number of ADRs trade on the London Stock Exchange.

It is possible to trade ADRs in what is known as '**pre-release form**'. Here, the holding bank releases the receipt to the dealer prior to the deposit of shares in its vaults. The dealer may then sell the ADR in the market, however, the **cash** raised through this trade must then be lodged with a holding bank **as collateral** for the deal. This situation may exist for a maximum of **three months**, at the end of which the broker must purchase shares in the cash market. The broker must then deposit the shares with the holding bank, which then releases the collateral.

In line with the domestic American markets, settlement for ADRs takes place three business days after the trade **(T + 3)**.

The ADR holder has all the transferability of the American form document with **no stamp duty**, other than a **one-off fee, payable by the creator upon creation of 1½%**. Dividends are received by the bank which holds the shares. They are then converted into dollars and paid to the ADR holder. The holder of the ADR has the **right to vote**, just like ordinary shareholders, except that their vote will be exercised, on their behalf, by the depositary bank.

The company issuing the underlying shares will very often initiate the ADR scheme themselves contacting the issuing banks and 'sponsoring' the issue. Sponsored issues may be structured in one of three levels, Level 1 issues will trade over the counter (OTC) and require minimum regulatory restrictions. Level 2 programs will require additional SEC compliance and may be exchange listed, which gives them greater investor exposure. Level 3 offerings allow public offerings to be made in the US via an ADR offering, this requires the highest level of regulation.

Unsponsored issues will trade over the counter and are a form of Level 1 issue.

The issue process takes the following general form:

- The issuing company will approach a 'depositary' bank and agrees terms regarding the size and nature of the issue
- The issuing company then issues the shares to the depositary bank
- The depositary bank then creates and sells the ADRs to US investors
- The revenue raised is then paid to the issuing company

### 1.7.1 Transfer to underlying shares

The investor can convert ADRs to underlying shares by returning the certificates to the issuing house with instructions (usually via a broker) to cancel the ADRs. The issuing house will then instruct the custodian bank to deliver the relevant number of underlying shares to the investor. ADRs may well represent more than one underlying share.

### 1.7.2 GDRs – Global Depository Receipts

**Global Depositary Receipts** in their nature are very similar to ADRs. Where ADRs are aimed at the US investor, GDRs provide international investors the opportunity to invest in companies in overseas markets.

An example would be the GDRs that trade on the International Order Book of the London Stock Exchange, e.g. Samsung.

## 1.8 Contracts for difference (CFDs)

**Learning objective**

**3.4.2 Analyse** the key features of the main types of Contracts for Difference (CFDs), compared with other forms of direct and indirect investment: Types and availability of CFDs, differences in pricing, valuing and trading CFDs compared to direct investment, CFD providers – market maker versus direct market access, tax efficiency, margin, market, liquidation & counterparty risks and size of CFD market and impact on total market activity.

Together with futures and options, **Contracts For Difference (CFDs)** come under the FSA's definition of '**derivatives**'. CFDs are a relatively new type of contract and are offered by many companies which also offer **spread betting**. CFDs can often be purchased through the internet. CFDs are different from traditional **cash-traded** instruments (such as equities, bonds, commodities and currencies) in that they do not confer ownership of the underlying asset. Investors can take positions on the price of a great number of different instruments. Many of the companies offering CFDs offer contracts in thousands of UK, US, European and Far Eastern shares. The price of the CFD tracks the price of the underlying asset, and so the holder of a CFD benefits, or loses, from the **price movement** in the stock, bond, currency, commodity or index etc. But the CFD holder does not take ownership of the underlying asset.

CFDs are **margin-traded**, meaning that the investor does not have to deposit the full value of the underlying asset with the CFD provider, instead the investor must deposit margin of around 5% - 20% of the value of the underlying value. Thus, an investor or fund manager can use CFDs to buy exposure to market movements using only a fraction of the capital they would require in the cash market. The investor then has a geared position relative to the capital deposited. CFDs allow the investor to benefit from downward movements in a share or other price if they choose. This has the effect of adopting a position of '**short selling**' the stock. This flexibility, and the possibility of **margin trading**, means that CFDs can be used flexibly either for hedging or speculation. CFD positions would require Initial margin plus possible variation margin payments based upon marking to market of the position.

When a company offering CFDs sells a contract, it may seek to 'hedge' its own liability to pay out for price movements in the stock concerned by buying a matching quantity of the stock in the market. However, if the company has customers adopting long and short positions, these will in effect cancel each other out, and so the degree to which the company has to hedge will be reduced. The costs of CFDs comprise a cost built into the **spread** of the CFD price, together with a daily **funding charge which is required to keep the position open**. The daily charge relates to the borrowing cost of maintaining the market position.

Given that the trade in CFDs does not result in the purchase of the underlying share, the transaction will not require the payment of stamp duty. This lack of stamp duty and the ability to leverage gains have led to growing attraction of the CFD market to investors.

Investors in Contracts For Difference are required to pay capital gains tax on profits, with losses being potentially carried forward to reduce future CGT.

### 1.8.1 Contract for Difference Risk

The CFD market in the UK has grown rapidly in recent years, by some estimates it now accounts for around 50% of UK equity trading. For the investor however, as with all investments, the risks associated with the investment must be considered:

**Market risk** – the leverage effect of trading on margin increases the risks of market movements. Investors can take out stop loss positions to minimise the liability of a long position, or a stop limit if the position is short.

**Counterparty risk** – CFD brokers are exposed to risk if the counterparty fails to meet margin payments when they make losses. This puts the brokers at risk of financial failure.

**Liquidation risk** – The markets underlying the CFD positions can move rapidly and large losses may materialise quickly. The need for immediate liquidity to make margin payments can cause liquidity problems which may lead to brokers closing positions.

# 2 Dealing in Equities

Learning objective

3.2.1 **Understand** the purpose, key features and differences between the following: primary issues, secondary issues, issuing, listing & quotation and dual listing.

When a company is formed, the original founder/shareholders (who are known as the subscribers) may choose the type of company created. The initial choice is between a Private Limited Company (Ltd) or a Public Limited Company (plc). The difference between these two legal forms is that only a plc may issue its shares or securities to the public. An important point to note is that although a company may be incorporated as a plc, it is in no way obliged to issue securities to the general public. In fact, over 75% of all plcs do not take this route for finance.

The management of the company then faces a second choice – whether or not to raise finance privately or to issue securities to the public. Should they decide on the latter route they will need to access investors via a stock exchange (i.e. become listed on an exchange).

A stock exchange is an organisation that acts as an intermediary between companies looking to raise capital and investors looking to invest capital. By raising capital this way the company is accessing the primary market.

In addition, the stock exchange provides a platform on which investors can freely buy and sell shares that have already been listed via the primary market. This is known as the secondary market and makes up the majority of stock exchange transactions.

The stock exchange is regulated by the FSA, and, in its role as the UK listing authority is responsible for screening and vetting companies looking to list. This maintains a high quality of entrant and promotes confidence in the market.

## 2.1 The Listing Rules

The UKLA's rules for admission to the Official List are contained in the Listing Rules. These detail threshold conditions for companies and their securities, if they wish to be admitted to the Official List. The basic conditions detailed in the Listing Rules are as follows.

- The expected market value of shares issued by the company must be at least **£700,000**. If the company is to issue **debt**, the expected market value of any such debt is to be at least **£200,000**.
- All securities issued must be freely transferable and the securities will be admitted to trading on a regulated market, such as a Recognised Investment Exchange (e.g. LSE). The company must publish a statement that it has adequate working capital for the next twelve months.
- The shares must be sufficiently marketable. A minimum of **25% of the company's share capital being made available for public purchase** (known as the **free float**) is seen to satisfy this requirement. The lower the free float, the fewer shares are available in the market, leading to, potentially, higher share price volatility. A lower percentage may be acceptable if the UKLA is satisfied that the shares will still be marketable.
- The issue of warrants or options over the stock of a company is limited to **20%** of the existing capital base.

- The UKLA has additional requirements for a company with a **major** shareholder. If the UKLA allows a company with this type of shareholder to come to the market, then the UKLA will need to be assured that there are measures in place to allow the listed company to **operate independently**.
- The company's Articles of Association must contain **pre-emption rights** in relation to issues of new shares for cash. The Listing Rules further provide that whilst shareholders may vote to waive their pre-emptive rights, the maximum period of such a waiver is five years.
- All applicants for listing agree to be bound by the **continuing obligations** of the UKLA.
- Company directors must have appropriate experience and expertise for managing the company.

Technology companies may be able to list without three years of trading record. Technology companies with over £50 million in market capitalisation and be offering at least £20 million of stock to investors. On the LSE technology stocks are listed on techMARK. Technology companies make use of this opportunity to raise capital for development.

A number of larger organisations choose to obtain listings on more than one exchange (i.e. dual listing) which should offer investors greater liquidity and provide the company a greater number of potential investors to take up any issued stock. Legislation such as the Sarbanes-Oxley act which imposes strict reporting accountability upon directors would apply to a company choosing to dual list with one exchange being in the US. This would be a consideration to take into account for directors thinking of dual listing. To increase liquidity, a number of companies chose to list on numerous US exchanges.

### Standard and Premium listings

Since 6th April 2010 the FSA listing regime has allowed two segments of listing. The aim of this change was to 'level the playing field' between UK companies and overseas companies listing in the UK. The two 'segments' are:

- Standard Listing – requires the issuer to only follow those requirements under the EU directive, which allows less comprehensive shareholder standards and disclosure rules.
- Premium Listing – requires an issuer of shares to meet 'super equivalent' obligations. (These include full obligations of due diligence, governance and shareholder rights).

  [Note: 'super equivalence means that the UK has imposed rules over and above those required by the EU directive on listing standards].

Below is a summary of listing rules which shows where the two segments differ:

| | Standard Listing | Premium Listing |
|---|---|---|
| Minimum market capitalisation | £700,000 | £700,000 |
| Shares freely transferable | Yes | Yes |
| Requirement for audited financial information | No | 3 years |
| Requirement for shares in public hands | 25% | 25% |
| Requirement to appoint a sponsor pre-admission | No | Yes |
| Requirement for the issuer to comply with the listing principles | No | Yes |
| Compliance with the model code | No | Yes |
| Requirement to offer pre-emption rights | Not under listing rules but may be imposed by company law | Yes |

[Note: where an exam question simply refers to listing standards assume that reference is being made to a Premium Listed company].

### 2.1.1 Continuing obligations

#### The objectives of the Continuing Obligations

The Continuing Obligations are contained in the Listing Rules and the Disclosure Rules and Transparency Rules. They govern the conduct of directors of listed companies and the disclosure of information necessary to protect investors, maintain an orderly market and ensure that investors are treated fairly. In addition, the Disclosure Rules and Transparency Rules contain over-arching requirements which relate to the timely and accurate dissemination of inside information.

### 2.1.2 Announcements

The first main requirement of the Continuing Obligations is timely disclosure of all relevant information. A listed company has a **general duty to disclose** all information necessary to appraise investors of the company's position and to avoid a false market in its shares. This reinforces S397 of FSMA, which makes it a criminal offence to conceal information dishonestly in order to create a false market in the company's shares. In addition, a company should announce details of any major new developments in its activities which are not known to the public but which may, when known, significantly affect its share price and affect a reasonable investor's decision. This is referred to as Inside Information.

The second requirement is **equal treatment of all shareholders**. This is to ensure that all shareholders receive inside information in the same way at the same time. All regulatory disclosures required must be disclosed to a Regulatory Information Service as soon as possible, prior to being disclosed to third parties.

A **Regulatory Information Service (RIS)** is a firm that has been approved by the FSA to disseminate regulatory announcements to the market on behalf of listed companies. Once an announcement is sent to the RIS, the company's obligation is met. The RIS is then required to release the announcement to the markets through its links with secondary information providers such as data providers, newswires and the news media.

### 2.1.3 Secrecy and confidentiality

Allied to the general principle of equal treatment of all shareholders is the requirement to **prevent leaks of price-sensitive information**. This particularly relates to impending developments or matters in the course of negotiation, where (apart from to advisers) there must be no selective dissemination of information, and matters in the course of negotiation must be kept confidential.

### 2.1.4 Insider lists

An issuer must ensure that it and its agents and advisors draw up a list of those who have access to inside information, whether on a regular or occasional basis. The FSA can request this list at anytime.

Every insider list must contain the following information

- The identity of each person having access to inside information.
- The reason why they are on the insider list.
- The date the list was created and updated.

An insider list must be promptly updated and records kept for five years.

An issuer must take the necessary measures to ensure that its employees on the list acknowledge the legal and regulatory duties entailed (including dealing restrictions) and are aware of the sanctions attaching to the misuse or improper circulation of such information.

### 2.1.5 Vote holder and issuer notification rules

The Disclosure Rules and Transparency Rules implement the requirements of the Transparency Directive that requires shareholders to disclose when they acquire a significant stake in a company. This information will then be published by a listed company so that there is transparency when a potential bidder starts to build up a stake in a target company.

The **initial threshold is 3%** and then transactions that go above or below a further full percentage point must also be disclosed. The holdings include any financial instrument that would give control over a voting security. It therefore includes derivatives such as futures and options on a share. The disclosure must be made by the end of second business day after the transaction (known as T + 2).

The following example transactions by the same shareholder illustrate the notification requirements:

| Transactions (all same shareholder) | Notification requirements |
|---|---|
| 0% to 2.5% holding in shares | None (below 3% threshold) |
| Additional 0.6% via options on shares | Notify issuing company by T + 2 (total now 3.1%) |
| Acquire additional 0.5% shares | None (total 3.6% so same full percentage point of 3) |
| Acquire additional 2.5% | Notify issuing company by T + 2 (total now 6.1%) |
| Dispose of 3% of shares | Notify issuing company by T + 2 (total now 3.1%) |
| Dispose of 0.6% held via options | Notify issuing company by T + 2 (total now 2.5%) |
| Sell remaining 2.5% of shares | None (below 3% threshold) |

There are exceptions of non-UK listed companies where notification is required at 5% steps up to 30% then 50% and 75% by T + 4.

Fund managers only have to disclose holdings at 5% and 10% and then at every single percentage point change above 10%.

A further requirement is that directors and employees holding 1% or more of shares must avoid selling for at least one year after issue.

### 2.1.6 Compliance with the Continuing Obligations

Failure to comply with the requirements of the Listing Rules, Prospectus Rules or Disclosure Rules and Transparency Rules may lead to

- Unlimited fines by the UKLA.
- Censure by the UKLA.
- Publication of the censure.
- Suspension or cancellation of a company's listing.

The last of these will mean that the company will be unable to use the facilities of the market.

In addition, any offending directors of the company may be censured and the UKLA may require their removal from the board as a condition for the company to retain its listing.

Companies should also be aware that in certain cases, failure to comply with the Listing Rules could also constitute an statutory offence under FSMA, particularly in relation to the market abuse regime.

## 2.2 The Role of the London Stock Exchange, the Companies Act and the FSA (UKLA)

earning objective

**3.2.3 Understand** the structure of the London Stock Exchange, the types of securities traded on its markets, and the criteria and processes for companies seeking admission: main market, AIM, PLUS markets, Market participants and implications for investors.

The London Stock Exchange (LSE) is a company whose purpose is to run an **orderly market place in securities**. The Financial Services Authority (FSA) regulates the LSE, and has granted it the status of a Recognised Investment Exchange (RIE). The LSE publishes rules governing the trading in securities in the secondary markets and, to some extent, in the primary markets. Specific legal requirements for companies are also detailed in the Companies Act including the requirement for annual accounts and meetings.

In May 2000 the FSA took on the statutory role of the **competent authority**. This obliges it to maintain the Official List – the list of companies whose securities are admitted to the LSE. Through a division called the UK Listing Authority (UKLA), it determines which companies may be listed on the LSE, monitors their continuing eligibility, and imposes strict standards of conduct for companies and their advisers in the UKLA Listing Rules.

The UKLA's role also includes the implementation of certain EU Directives and the listing of gilts.

At present, there are two levels of entry into the stock market, namely through the **Official List** and through the **Alternative Investment Market (AIM)**. Of the two, the Official List (often referred to as the Full List) is the senior market, and membership demands more onerous responsibilities. Although the UKLA regulates the Full List, the LSE regulates AIM, publishing the AIM Rules and monitoring compliance with them.

The day-to-day trading rules for both Full List and AIM Companies' securities is covered by the exchange rule books issued by the LSE.

### 2.2.1 Free float

Broadly stated, free float represents the number of shares freely available for trading. Thus, it excludes any shares held by directors of a company or its subsidiaries, individuals connected with those directors or any person holding 5% or more of the shares. Liquidity of a company is directly affected by the number of shares available for trading and generally a free float of 25% - 50% is considered adequate liquidity in a company.

### 2.2.2 Advisors

All applicants for listing must appoint a UKLA-approved **sponsor or listing agent whose role is to**

- Ensure the company and its directors are aware of their obligations.
- Ensure the company is suitable for listing and satisfy UKLA of this fact.
- Liaise with UKLA and submit documentation to them as required.
- Co-ordinate the listing process.

All UK listed companies must retain a corporate broker. The corporate broker acts as a long term advisor, offering the following services:

- Providing equity market-related advice
- Executing equity related transactions
- Co-ordinating institutional investor relations services
- Liasing with the London Stock Exchange and UK Listing Authority on regulatory issues facing listed companies

The sponsor will advise on the preparation of the listing documents which must be submitted to the UKLA 48 hours before a hearing that will determine if a listing application is successful.

### 2.2.3 Issuer's obligations

Companies must also produce a prospectus containing full details on the company's past and present activities and performance, directors, capital structure and future prospects.

Once listed, a company must produce interim (six-monthly) accounts and annual accounts. Price sensitive information must also be rapidly provided to the market, the purpose of reporting being to keep investors informed at all times.

### 2.2.4 Corporate governance

Once a company elects to have its securities listed, it will be more than ever required to adhere to good practices of corporate governance. Having separation of control between chairman, CEO, directors and non-executive directors are example of good governance.

## 3 UK Regulatory Framework

**Learning objective**

**3.2.2** **Understand** the main regulatory, supervisory and trade body framework supporting UK financial markets; companies acts, The financial services Authority (FSA) and the UK Listing Authority (UKLA) HM Treasury, The Panel on Takeovers and Mergers (POTAM), exchange membership and rules and relevant trade associations and professional bodies.

## 3.1 The Companies Act 2006

The Companies Acts contains complex pieces of legislation designed to achieve a number of ends. In particular, they look to protect shareholders from the directors and the general public from the abuse of limited liability. The Act covers requirements about Articles and Memoranda of Association. The various required company meetings and the other means by which directors communicate with shareholders are also covered. The Companies Act 2006 will ultimately replace previous Acts but is being gradually implemented.

The Department for Business, Innovation and Skills (BISS), keeps businesses up to date on any changes in the Companies Act.

## 3.2 HM Treasury

The Memorandum of Understanding establishes what is known as tripartite responsibility in the UK between the FSA, the Treasury, and the Bank of England. Under this arrangement, the Treasury has responsibility for the overall institutional structure of financial regulation and the legislation which govern it, including the negotiation of EC Directives. It must also inform Parliament of the management of serious problems in the financial system and any measures used to resolve them, including any Treasury decision concerning exceptional official operations. HMT must also account for financial sector resilience to operational disruption within government.

## 3.3 UK competition regulation

### Overview of competition regulation

**Statutory Merger Control**

**Office of Fair Trading**

Looks at current takeovers and mergers to ascertain if there has been a substantial lessening of competition

May clear (i.e. bid can go ahead) or refer the bid to Competition Commission

↓

**Competition Commission**

Commission investigates the bid and recommends whether there has been a substantial lessening of competition

↙ ↘

**Bid is block** **Bid is cleared**

UK competition regulations are designed to ensure mergers and acquisitions are not going to result in uncompetitive practices or a **substantial lessening of competition**.

Competition investigations have a two-tier approach involving Office of Fair Trading (OFT) investigation followed by possible reference to the Competition Commission for a second-stage, in-depth investigation where necessary.

The only exception to this is where **Secretary of State for Business, Innovation and Skills** intervenes in cases of national security. The Secretary of State is head of the Department for Business, Innovation and Skills (BIS).

The main statutory rules on competition are within the **2002 Enterprise Act**.

As guidance, the following scenarios will qualify for investigation.

- The combined enterprise **controls at least 25%** of the goods or services in the sector in the UK, or
- The turnover of the entity being acquired **exceeds £70 million**.

While the Panel is swift in making its decisions, the CC is not. The OFT can investigate **four months** from when the transaction is made public. Cases referred to the Competition Commission must normally be investigated **within 24 weeks** of the date of reference.

The Competition Commission has the power to **impose fines** for failure to comply with any request for information.

The Competition Commission will publish preliminary findings prior to its final decision and will consult on, and give reason for, its conclusion. Appeals against this decision may be made to the **Competition Appeal Tribunal,** a separate judicial body.

## 3.4 The Panel on Takeovers and Mergers (POTAM)

The Takeover Panel is a grouping of all the important organisations in the City of London. It is an independent body and its duty is to monitor adherence to the general principles laid down in the Takeover Code (**'The Blue Book'**). Its major weapon to enforce the Code is to withdraw the facilities of the market from anyone who breaks those rules. This is referred to as 'cold shouldering' and is such a powerful weapon that it seldom has to be used – the mere threat of it tends to bring people into line with the rules and regulations.

In very much the same way as the FSA rulebook has been written, the Takeover Code begins with six general principles governing the conduct of takeover activity in the UK. This is then followed by a series of detailed rules which add guidance on the application of the principles, as well as provisions on specific aspects of takeover procedure.

### 3.4.1 The general principles

The six general principles are as follows.

1. All holders of the securities of an offeree company of the same class must be afforded **equivalent treatment**; moreover, if a person acquires control of a company, the other holders of securities must be protected.
2. The holders of the securities of an offeree company must have **sufficient time and information** to enable them to reach a properly informed decision on the bid; where it advises the holders of securities, the board of the offeree company must give its views on the effects of implementation of the bid on employment, conditions of employment and the locations of the company's places of business.
3. The board of an offeree company must act in the **interests of the company as a whole** and must not deny the holders of securities the opportunity to decide on the merits of the bid.
4. **False markets** must not be created in the securities of the offeree company, of the offeror company or of any other company concerned by the bid in such a way that the rise or fall of the prices of the securities becomes artificial and the normal functioning of the markets is distorted.

5. An offeror must announce a bid only after ensuring that he/she can **fulfil in full** any cash consideration, if such is offered, and after taking all reasonable measures to secure the implementation of any other type of consideration.

6. An offeree company must **not be hindered** in the conduct of its affairs for **longer than is reasonable** by a bid for its securities.

These are the guiding principles of the Code. Where there is doubt as to the application of a rule then reference should always be made to the principles. A breach of a principle, even when in strict accordance with the rules, is deemed to be a breach of the Code itself. The Panel will apply the General Principles in accordance with their spirit to achieve their underlying purposes.

### 3.4.2 The role of the panel

The basic purpose of the Panel and the Takeover Code is to **protect shareholders** in the target company and to ensure that there is a level playing field in takeover activity in the UK. The principles and rules contained in the Blue Book ensure that this takes place.

The Blue Book regulates offers for shares in **all public limited companies** (not just listed plcs) and some private limited companies, where the public may have had an opportunity to buy shares in the past.

It is important to note that it is a requirement of the Blue Book that both the **spirit** as well as the letter of the Takeover Code are observed.

The Panel is funded by a flat levy on share transactions **over £10,000**. **Both** parties to these types of transactions (i.e. the buyer and the seller) each pay a flat amount, which is currently **£1**.

In very much the same way as the FSA rulebook has been written, the Takeover Code begins with six general principles governing the conduct of takeover activity in the UK. This is then followed by a series of detailed rules which add guidance on the application of the principles, as well as provisions on specific aspects of takeover procedure.

### 3.4.3 Mandatory bids

In reality, legal control is achieved when a shareholder breaks through the 50% barrier. However, as far as the Panel is concerned, effective control is achieved at 30% and, under the rules of the Panel, **if a shareholder takes their stake to a 30% level or more, then they will be required to make a mandatory offer**. In some circumstances, a shareholder may already have a stake of between 30% and 50%. Such shareholders will be required to make a mandatory offer if they increase their holding without Panel consent.

It should be noted that there are only very limited circumstances in which a person is permitted to acquire 30% or more of a company anyway. In most circumstances, a person is forbidden to acquire 30% or more.

Under the terms of a mandatory offer, much of the offeror's discretion is removed. A mandatory bid must be at the **highest price** at which the offeror has purchased shares **within the last 12 months**. In addition, the offer must be for cash or have a cash alternative. For an ordinary bid, the bid need only be at the best price the offeror has paid in the past three months unless the Panel feels, at its discretion, that 12 months would be more appropriate. In addition, cash or a cash alternative is not usually required.

In an ordinary offer, the offeror sets the acceptance level and may specify an acceptance level of 90% prior to the bid going unconditional (it cannot, however, usually be less than **50%**). In a mandatory bid, the only acceptable level is 50%, which may mean that the offeror acquires a company with a substantial minority interest that may, to an extent, limit the offeror's powers of control.

## 3.5 Trade organisations and professional bodies

### 3.5.1 The Chartered Institute for Securities and Investment (CISI)

The CISI website puts forward the following charitable objectives of their organisation:

- To promote, for the public benefit, the advancement and dissemination of knowledge in the field of securities and investments.
- To develop high ethical standards for practitioners in securities and investments and to promote such standards in the UK and overseas.
- To act as an authoritative body for the purpose of consultation and research in matters of education or public interest concerning investment in securities.

The CISI further describe their aim to be:

"To set standards of professional excellence and integrity for the investment and securities industry, providing qualifications and promoting the highest level of competence to our members, other individuals and firms."

### 3.5.2 The British Bankers' Association (BBA)

The British Bankers' Association is a trade association for UK banking and financial services sector.

Their stated objective is to promote a legislative and regulatory system for banking and financial services – in the UK, Europe and internationally. They engage with governmental, devolved administration and European institutions to put forward the views of the UK banking industry. According to their website, the BBA represent over 200 member banks, which collectively contribute £50 billion annually to the UK economy.

### 3.5.3 The Investment Management Association (IMA)

The IMA is a trade association who represent the interests of the UK investment management industry. They state that they have 185 members who collectively account for more than 90% of the UK industry.

### 3.5.4 The Association of Private Client Investment Managers and Stockbrokers (APCIMS)

The APCIMS is a trade association of wealth managers and broking firms who provide services to private investors. Their objectives as stated on their website are:

- To promote the interests of our members with governments, regulators, financial institutions and all participants in financial services.
- To provide information and assistance to our members across a wide range of regulatory, market and business issues.
- To communicate industry change to our members.
- To lead the debate in Europe in the development of the European securities industry.

# 4 The Role of Stock Exchange Member Firms

All member firms of an exchange are **broker-dealers**. Broker-dealers have **dual capacity**, giving them the choice to either act as **agents** on behalf of customers, or to deal for themselves as **principals**, dealing directly with customers.

Some broker-dealers can elect to take on board an additional level of responsibility through one of the following roles.

| | |
|---|---|
| **Market Makers** | Market makers are the focus of market activity and their obligation is to ensure that there is always a two-way price in the securities in which they are registered (NB: specific obligations for different types of security will be detailed in this chapter and are required to be learnt). |
| **Inter-Dealer Brokers** | Inter-dealer brokers (IDBs) act as an escape valve for market makers, providing them with an anonymous dealing service to unwind positions. |
| **Stock Borrowing and Lending Intermediaries** | Stock Borrowing and Lending Intermediaries (SBLIs) provide a service allowing market makers to borrow securities in order to settle a 'short' transaction, i.e. selling shares they do not own. |

## 4.1 The markets of the London Stock Exchange

Membership of the LSE offers what the LSE describe on their website as being the 'deepest pool of liquidity with trading in UK equities, International Depositary Receipts, Exchange Traded Funds and Commodities, Covered Warrants and Investment Trusts.'

The benefits of becoming an LSE member firm include access to the TradeElect trading system, and the ability to 'establish valuable new relationships in our global community of brokers and listed companies, giving you the opportunity to grow your business and company profile in parallel.'

The LSE website details the key considerations for membership:

**Eligibility**

Membership is available to investment firms and credit institutions authorised in the European Economic Area. You may also be eligible if you are not EEA regulated and should speak with the membership team for further details. Members may be eligible for Stamp Duty Reserve Tax exemption and may apply for this as part of their application.

**Connectivity**

Firms can connect directly to the exchange's markets. The exchange currently offers several types of connectivity options with varying levels of management and performance. These range from full host-to-host solutions to vendor access network connections. Each firm will have different requirements and we can help you choose the right form of access for your firm.

**Clearing and Settlement**

If you choose to connect directly to the exchange you will need to have in place appropriate clearing and settlement arrangements. Members of the London Stock Exchange benefit from an efficient and competitive clearing and settlement infrastructure across its domestic and international markets.

The LSE has come to the conclusion, given that the diversity of shares on offer is so wide, that one single market structure for trading shares is inappropriate. Consequently different types of shares, with varying levels of liquidity, will trade either on SETS or SETSqx. Normal market size (NMS) represents 2.5% of the daily average volume of shares traded over the last year.

Note: the lowest NMS is 100 and the highest is 200,000.

While there are numerous benefits to obtaining a full listing such as the improved liquidity of securities, and the ability to raise less expensive capital, there are however certain disadvantages, such as the cost implications plus the loss of control which comes with share issues.

## 4.2 Order driven v Quote driven

**Learning objective**

**3.3.2** **Understand** the key features of the main trading venues: whether quote or order driven.

Before looking at the detailed mechanics of each of the trading platforms, it is worth considering the fundamental differences between an order driven and quote driven market.

Where a market is order driven, the relevant trading system will match buyers and sellers automatically, provided they are willing to trade at prices compatible with each other. This is essentially the function which SETS performs. Prices of securities which trade on SETS are, therefore, purely driven by the buyers and sellers in the market themselves.

A platform that has a quote driven feature, such as SETSqx, requires certain market participants (market makers) to take responsibility for acting as buyers and sellers to the rest of the market so that there will always be a price at which a trade can be conducted. For such a market to operate efficiently, up-to-date prices at which market makers are willing to trade need to be made available to other market participants.

The SETSqx platform combines the automatic functionality of an order driven system with the price support offered by market makers.

## 4.3 The Alternative Investment Market (AIM)

On 19 June 1995, the LSE introduced the **Alternative Investment Market (AIM)**. This forum for trading a company's shares enables companies to have their shares traded through the LSE in a lightly regulated regime. In contrast to the main market, which is regulated by the UKLA, AIM is regulated by the London Stock Exchange (by permission of the FSA due to the LSE being a Recognised Investment Exchange). AIM is classified as an 'exchange regulated market', whereas the Full List is classified as an 'EU regulated market'. Both Ordinary and Preference shares may be listed.

### 4.3.1 Conditions for admission to AIM

A summary of the main conditions that companies must meet in order to secure admission to AIM is as follows.

- All securities must be **freely transferable**.
- AIM companies must have a **Nominated Advisor** (NOMAD), **approved by the LSE**, to advise the directors on their responsibilities, and guide them through the AIM process. The NOMAD is retained to advise the directors once an AIM listing is granted. Should the company lose its NOMAD, it must appoint a new one (otherwise the listing will be suspended). If the company fails to reappoint a NOMAD within one month, its AIM admission will be cancelled.
- AIM companies must at all times have a nominated broker (who must be an Exchange Member) to support trading in the company's shares, and to assist in pricing and marketing in a flotation.
  - AIM companies must comply with **ongoing obligations** to publish **price-sensitive information** immediately and to disclose details of **significant transactions**. The NOMAD has a duty to ensure the AIM company meets its ongoing obligations.
  - To satisfy corporate governance requirements, the company must have independent non-executive directors, acting for the interests of shareholders.
- Companies with a track record of less than **two years** must agree to a **'lock-in'**, whereby the directors, significant shareholders and employees with 0.5% or more of their capital, agree **not to sell their shares for a year** following admission. The company does not require its shareholders' approval for an AIM admission.

For AIM companies, there is no minimum level of free float (shares available for purchase by the public), no minimum market value for their securities and no minimum trading history.

However, they must produce a prospectus, which is considerably less detailed than for a full listing, and is known as an Admission Document.

### 4.3.2 PLUS Markets

PLUS Markets plc ('PLUS') is a recognised investment exchange (RIE) that provides a rival primary and secondary market to the LSE. There are three segments to the PLUS market:

- **PLUS Listed** refers to the primary market for **securities** that have been granted a listing by the UK Listing Authority. Part of the requirement of obtaining a listing is confirmation that the securities concerned will be admitted to trading on an RIE in an **EU regulated market**.
- **PLUS Quoted** refers to the primary market for smaller companies that are unable to, or do not wish to, comply with the Full List requirements of the UKLA. It is therefore referred to as an 'exchange regulated' market as the admission criteria are determined by PLUS itself. PLUS Quoted is therefore a direct rival to the LSE's Alternative Investment Market (AIM).
- **PLUS Traded** refers to the secondary market for securities that are listed or quoted on other markets but also traded on PLUS.

## 5 When a Prospectus is Required in the UK

earning objective

**3.2.4 Understand** the process of issuing securities in the UK without a prospectus: Principles of exemption established under the Prospectus Directive (PD), Purpose of the FSA Qualified Investor Register (QIR), Eligibility and registration criteria for Natural Persons and SMEs and Terms of access for issuers seeking to use the Qualified Investor Register.

The Prospectus Directive, implemented in the UKLA Prospectus Rules (remember that the UKLA is the FSA), require a prospectus to be issued when securities are offered to the public, or admitted to trading on a regulated exchange. In June 2010, the European Parliament passed changes to the European Prospectus Directive. These were required to be enacted by member state governments within 18 months. The main changes were that:

- The threshold requirement to produce a prospectus was raised from €2.5 million to €5 million. This should be of benefit to smaller firms.
- Employee share scheme offers are made exempt from prospectus requirements.
- A proportionate disclosure regime is introduced for public offers by certain companies.

A prospectus may not be required in certain circumstances, in particular

- A bonus or capitalisation issue.
- The exercise of conversion rights or warrants.
- Shares issued in place of shares already listed, so long as the nominal value in total does not increase as a result, e.g. a share split or consolidation.
- Small issues of securities, which would not increase the class of securities in issue by 10% or more, or by more than €100,000 consideration over a year.

- Where offer is made only to qualified investors (QIs), or to fewer than 100 persons per EU Member state, excluding qualified investors. This exemption is only available when securities are not being admitted to trading on a regulated market, e.g. AIM placings.
- Issues of wholesale securities, i.e. where the minimum subscription or denomination of the securities is €50,000. This would only realistically apply to corporate bond issues.

The rules regarding qualified investors as given by the FSA are outlined below.

## 5.1 Qualified Investors (QIs)

Qualified investors are legal entities authorised to operate in the financial markets (e.g. investment firms and insurance companies), governments, supranational institutions, as well as natural persons and small and medium sized enterprises (SMEs) that certify that they meet the required criteria.

The Prospectus Directive allows the FSA to maintain a register of QIs which must then be available to all issuers and offerors. The information held on the Qualified Investor Register (QIR) is solely to facilitate the issuance of securities without the requirement to publish a prospectus under the PD.

Natural persons and SMEs can only be recognised as QIs if they meet the criteria specified below and are registered on the QIR.

QIs will be removed from the QIR annually and so QIs must specifically request that their details appear on the new register every year. Amendments can be carried out at any time by contacting their register team.

The following will help you register as a QI or obtain a copy of the QIR.

## 5.2 Natural persons seeking inclusion on the Qualified Investor Register

It is necessary to meet at least two of the following three criteria to qualify for inclusion on the QIR:

1. One must have carried out transactions of a significant size (at least €1,000) on securities markets at an average frequency of, at least, ten per quarter for the last four quarters.
2. The security portfolio exceeds €0.5 million.
3. One works – or has worked for at least one year – in the financial sector in a professional position which requires knowledge of securities investment.

The Qualified Investor Register is only available to issuers/offerors or their agents and exclusively for the purpose of making an offer of securities to a Qualified Investor.

## 5.3 Small and medium size enterprises (SME) seeking inclusion on the Qualified Investor Register

SMEs must self-certify. However, at least two of the following three criteria must be fulfilled to qualify for inclusion on the QIR:

1. Average number of employees is less than 250.
2. Total balance sheet does not exceed €43,000,000.
3. Annual net turnover does not exceed €50,000,000.

## 5.4 Issuers/Offerors seeking access to the Qualified Investor Register

The information held on the QIR is to be used solely for issuing securities without publication of a prospectus (see the terms of consent in the application form for inclusion in the QIR and the terms of access in the application form for access to the register).

The following information is included on the QIR for individuals:

1. QI's name
2. QI unique reference number
3. A contact address (this can be the address of their representative/legal, financial or other adviser or a P.O. Box address) or broker name and identification number with that broker.

The following information is included on the QIR for SMEs:

1. The company name;
2. A contact name and position; and
3. The registered office address.

Using the information held on the QIR for any other purpose than to facilitate issuance of securities without publication of a prospectus under the PD contravenes the Prospectus Rules under Part VI of FSMA and section 348 of FSMA and may result in a fine or imprisonment or both.

# 6 Initial Public Offerings (IPOs)

arning objectives

**3.2.5 Understand** the purpose, structure and stages of an initial public offering (IPO), and the role of the origination team, benefits for the issuer and investors, structure: base deal plus green shoe, stages of an IPO, underwritten versus best efforts and principles and process of price stabilisation.

The Initial Public Offering will potentially raise large sums of money and result in new shareholders. A company undertaking an IPO will generally have a base number of shares intended for issue. A successful issue where interest outstrips this base number of shares may be supplemented if green shoe options are issued allowing a further issue of shares.

The stages of an IPO begin with the company coming to the decision that an IPO is the most appropriate method of raising capital, and the subsequent beginnings of the origination team. A prospectus will be required with the sponsor leading the preparation of this document. The syndicate if used will then undertake the sale of the securities often to known clients. The investment banks agreeing to sell the securities may guarantee to buy unwanted shares at an agreed price. This process is referred to as underwriting. Alternatively, the agreement may be for 'best efforts' where no guarantees are in place to buy back securities, but rather an understanding that the lead manager will aim to maintain their good name by selling all securities.

## 6.1 Offer for subscription

**Offer for Subscription**

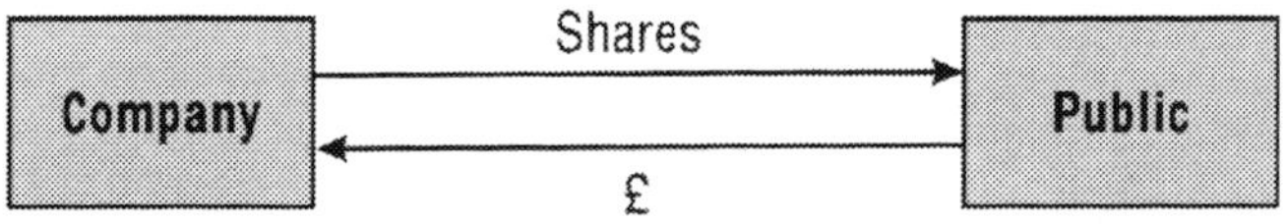


An offer for subscription is where the company issues new shares directly to the public. Most companies are not capable of organising and running an issue themselves, or do not wish to spend management time in doing so. Consequently, there are very few offers for subscription. More commonly, companies appoint an agent to act on their behalf. This is described as an offer for sale.

## 6.2 Offer for sale

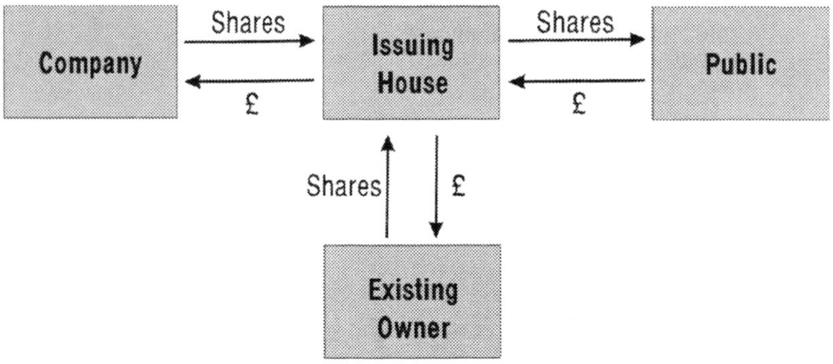


With an offer for sale, the company appoints an issuing house to deal with the public on its behalf. The issuing house advertises the security, obtains acceptances from the public, processes and allots shares and then sends the money to the company after the deduction of a fee. An offer for sale need not revolve around the issue of new securities; it can equally be used by a large shareholder selling a stake into the market place. Privatisations launched by the government have been offers for sale where a broking house has acted on the government's behalf to sell a large block of the shares in a company.

With both offers for sale and offers for subscription, there is the problem of knowing how to price the issue. There are two main solutions.

- A fixed price offer.
- A tender offer.

## 6.3 Fixed price offer

Under a fixed price offer, the issuing house establishes a fair price for the security. This price is frequently based on the price of similar company securities already trading in the market. Once the price has been arrived at, the offer is made to the public on the basis that potential purchasers state the number of shares they wish to buy at the fixed price. In the event of over-subscription, allocations are dealt with on a pro rata basis in line with the terms contained in the offer document.

It is frequently the intention of the company that the offer price should be artificially low so that potential purchasers can foresee an immediate rise in the share price. It is hoped that this will generate goodwill amongst purchasers which, in future, guarantees the company's access to new finance. Investors who purchase shares in a new issue in the belief that the share will rise due to its underpricing are called **stags**.

## 6.4 Tender offer

Under a tender offer, the potential purchasers are asked to divulge the number of shares they wish to buy and the price they are prepared to pay. The issuing house then receives their application forms that are ranked in order of the prices purchasers are prepared to pay – highest first.

## Example

A company wishes to issue 20 million shares and states that there is a minimum price of £1.00. Bids are received from potential shareholders in the following sequence.

1 million @ £1.50

3 million @ £1.45

7 million @ £1.40

11 million @ £1.35

10 million @ £1.30

17 million @ £1.25

Progressing down the list, the offer can be filled at the point where the price is £1.35, since there are more than 20 million applicants. However, a company will frequently establish the price at a lower value, say £1.30, as this will again encourage the market to rise on issue, ensuring both profit and investor goodwill. Note that within this structure, all the shareholders applying for shares pay the common strike price set by the company, be it £1.35 or £1.30. Even those applicants who entered at £1.45 will only pay the common strike price.

The tender method is by far the more complicated of the two methods available and, consequently, the tendency is for the fixed price offer to be the dominant issue method.

## 6.5 Placing

By far the cheapest route open to a company is to elect for a placing. Under a placing, the company sells its shares to a particular broker who then sells the securities to its client base. This removes most of the requirement for advertising, and is also the most efficient method of issuing shares. A placing must be carried out in such a way to **ensure marketability**.

**Placing**

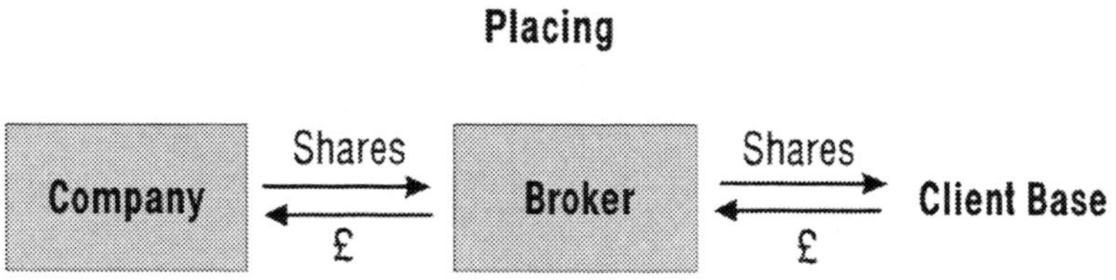


Where a number of brokers are involved in placing an issue with their own clients, widening the investor base, it is known as an **intermediaries offer**.

### 6.5.1 Introduction

Issuing shares to raise capital are described as **marketing operations**. An introduction however, does not raise additional finance for the company, it merely allows the company's shares to be traded on the market place.

## 6.6 The origination team

A company wishing to list securities will form an 'origination team' to assist with the flotation. The origination team will provide expert professional advice to the company and will be made up of a number of parties:

- The company to be listed will require a 'sponsor' who will usually be an investment bank or accounting firm. The sponsor advises on preparation of a prospectus and the best means of bringing the securities to the market.
- PR consultants will offer marketing skills to portray the company and securities in the best light to the market.
- Legal advisors will ensure that materials contained within the prospectus are correct.
- Reporting accountants act together with legal advisors to provide assurance that statements in the prospectus satisfy 'due diligence'.
- A corporate broker will be appointed to facilitate trading in the securities once listed.

## 6.7 The syndicate group

Where the size of the issue is large, companies may elect to work with 'a syndicate' of investment banks and stockbrokers to offer the securities to the market.

The company sponsor or another of the syndicate will act as the 'lead manager' and will co-ordinate the appointment of a team of co-managers. If the issue is very large co-lead managers may be appointed.

The syndicate work together assessing the price that the market will be prepared to pay for securities. This process is known as bookbuilding and starts with an indicative price being suggested and then following market reaction a firm price will be set shortly before publication of the prospectus.

## 6.8 Underwriting

Underwriting refers to an arrangement through which a company is guaranteed that an issue of shares (or bonds) will raise the desired level of cash. A firm agreeing to underwrite an issue will commit itself to subscribe for any part of the issue not taken up by the investing public.

The price paid by the issuing company for this underwriting facility is a small commission, which is payable to the underwriters whether they are required to acquire shares or not.

**There is no obligation for a company to use underwriters in an issue. Deep discounted rights issues** often do **not** require any underwriting facility as there is relatively little chance of the issue being unsold.

There is **no limit** to the number of underwriters who can participate in the purchase of shares in an underwriting syndicate, although the **lead manager** will retain overall responsibility.

## 6.9 Stabilisation

Stabilisation is the practice in which the lead manager, or issuing brokers, ensures that in the immediate market following the issue of the shares or bonds, the price remains stable, or certainly above a minimum floor value. Stabilisation is achieved by the lead manager purchasing, if needs be, stock in the secondary market to support the price.

In itself this may seem like a misleading market practice, but the important thing about stabilisation is that the market must be informed that it is taking place.

The stabilisation regulations are set out in the Market Conduct (MAR) Sourcebook in the FSA's Handbook. There is a minimum period of 30 to 60 days for the stabilisation.

The advantage for the issuing company is that investors have a limited downside and so should be more willing to participate in an initial public offer. This increased demand should raise the issue price and may be cheaper than underwriting fees. The issuing company may grant a green shoe option (or over allotment provision) to the lead manager to facilitate the stabilisation, this allows the lead company to over allocate the issue by the amount of green shoe options available up to an extra 15% of the shares. If the offer is a success and shares are fully taken up then the lead manager exercises the green shoe options to meet the demand. If the share price falls then the lead manager buys back the over allocation of shares at an agreed price which is the process of stabilisation.

# 7 Equity Markets and Trade Execution

arning objectives

**3.3.1 Apply** fundamental UK regulatory requirements with regard to trade execution and reporting: Best Execution, Aggregation and allocation, Prohibition of conflicts of interests and front running

**3.3.2 Understand** the key features of the main trading venues: Regulated and Designated Investment Exchanges, Recognised Overseas Investment Exchanges, Structure and size of markets, Whether quote or order driven, Main types of order – limit, market, iceberg, named, Liquidity and transparency and Participants.

As noted earlier, a secondary market is a market that allows shareholders to trade the securities that are in issue. For companies with listings, the LSE acts as both:

- Primary market – a market where companies issue new shares to raise finance
- Secondary market – a market where existing shares can be traded

To operate in this capacity in the UK, an entity must be a Recognised Investment Exchange under FSA regulations, and currently there are only two such exchanges for equities:

- The London Stock Exchange (LSE)
- PLUS Stock Exchange (PLUS-SX)

When placing trades for clients, advisers must comply with their obligation of best execution. The general FSA rules here are:

- A firm must take all reasonable steps to obtain, when executing orders, the best possible result for its clients
- A firm must take into account the characteristics of:
  - The client including the categorisation of the client as retail or professional
  - The client order
  - Financial instruments that are the subject of that order
  - The execution venues to which that order can be directed

When arranging transactions for retail clients, best execution is measured by reference to total consideration taking into account price, dealing costs and any other expenses. A firm must have a best execution policy explaining the firm's approach and providing information on execution venues, and clients must be informed of this policy. The firm should monitor adherence to this policy and be able to show that a client's transaction has been correctly handled. For professional clients total consideration is, again, the measure though there may be circumstances when other factors need to be considered, including speed of execution, settlement timings, size of deal.

*NOTE: The syllabus does not explicitly require knowledge of the operation of the LSE. We have included the discussion of the trading procedures and platforms used to enable a fuller understanding of the subject.*

## 7.1 The Electronic Trading Service (SETS)

The LSE, SETS platform is described on the LSE website as being the 'London Stock Exchange's flagship electronic order book. The LSE then lists the securities which are offered on SETS as being :, 'FTSE100, FTSE250, FTSE Small Cap Index constituents, Exchange Traded Funds, Exchange Trading Products as well as other liquid AIM, Irish and London Standard listed securities.'

### Trading hours

The SETS system operates from **07:00 to 17:15**. The term '**trading day**' refers to the period during which trade reports may be entered into the system, i.e. from 07:15 to 17:15.

| | |
|---|---|
| 07:00 | SETS opens. |
| 07:15 | Member firms can begin entering trade reports (see Section 10) |
| 07:50 | Start of the opening auction call period. SETS participants may input and delete limit, market and iceberg orders only. |
| 08:00<br>+ random start<br>+ extensions | PLUS a random delay of between 0 and 30 seconds to discourage removal of misleading orders in the last few seconds.<br>SETS runs the uncrossing algorithm to determine the opening price at which the maximum volume of trades will result. **During** the uncrossing program, **no input or deletion of orders is permitted**.<br>However, the auction call period may be extended for unfulfilled market orders and large price variations (see below).<br>Following completion of the uncrossing algorithm automatic matching commences. All order types except market orders may now be entered. |
| 16:20 | The volume weighted average price (VWAP) of all automatically executed trades from 16:20 to 16:30 (i.e. in the last 10 minutes) will be calculated for a reference price in the closing auction. |
| 16:30 | Automatic matching ceases. Closing call auction period commences. Only limit, market and iceberg orders may be entered. |
| 16:35<br>+ random end | Closing auction ends. Uncrossing algorithm run and this sets the closing price. If there are overhanging market orders, a market order extension will operate for two minutes.<br>To avoid large price swings in the closing price, there will be price and volume checks.<br>A price monitoring extension of at first five minutes and then a further five minutes plus random ends will occur if the potential closing price would be greater than 5% away from the VWAP.<br>If at the end of the price monitoring extension the uncrossing price is still greater than 5% away from the VWAP, SETS will check there is sufficient volume to justify this large price swing. The uncrossing volume must be at least ½ × NMS (Normal Market Size), otherwise the closing auction will be cancelled, no trades will execute and the closing price will be the VWAP. |
| 17:00 | Any unexecuted orders can be deleted up to 17:00. The period from the end of the closing auction until 17:00 is known as the Order Management Period. |
| 17:15 | SETS closes. From 17.00 to 17:15, SETS remains open for trade reporting purposes. |

Note: 08:00-16:30 is termed **'Normal Market Hours'**.

### 7.1.1 Call period extensions

- **Market order extension**

  If there are insufficient limit orders to match with market orders, then a two-minute market order extension is run to allow the entry of more orders to fill the overhanging market orders.

- **Price monitoring extension**

  If the opening auction uncrossing price would be more than 5% away from the last automated trade of the previous day, then a five-minute price monitoring extension is run.

  Opening call extension periods have random ends of 0 to 30 seconds. Both extensions may be required and they would run one after the other.

### 7.1.2 Trading abnormalities

- **Share suspension** – If the LSE suspend dealings in a share, automatic matching will cease and firms may **not enter or delete** orders onto or from the order book (nor may they enter transactions in that share away from the order book, i.e. on the telephone).
- **Other trading halts** – Automatic matching via SETS will be halted if
  - The traded price of a share moves by more than **5%** from the previous automatic trade, in which case trading in that share will halt for **five** minutes.
  - There is an LSE system fault.
  - The LSE considers it appropriate.

  During a halt for any of the above reasons, input and deletion of limit and market orders is still permitted and hence the uncrossing algorithm must be rerun before automatic matching recommences. Trading away from the order book can still continue. There will be a random start and the potential for a market order extension.
- **Fast market** – In the event that the market is moving dramatically and the system is having difficulty coping with the volumes, the LSE will firstly warn the market that the system is under pressure and that consequently there may be some delay before matching takes place. If the situation continues, the LSE may suspend the ability of firms to input orders. Once the backlog has been resolved the system will start again. There will be no need to run the uncrossing algorithm since at no time will automated matching have been suspended.
- **Blank order book** – In a normal trading situation, the official best price is derived from the order book and will represent the best bid and offer price currently available. If there are no bids or offers available on stock, zeros will be broadcast.

### 7.1.3 Trading outside the order book

Use of the order book is not mandatory and it is possible to execute trades outside the SETS system. These trades would be negotiated between the firms directly with no exposure to the market and no need to consider, other than for the purpose of assessing best execution, the outstanding limit orders on the system. The requirement of trade reporting with three minutes to the exchange still holds for LSE member firms.

### 7.1.4 The SETS order book

The SETS screen displays **limit orders** (orders to buy shares with a maximum price stated and orders to sell shares with a minimum price stated). Member firms of the LSE can enter an order to be matched automatically with the limit orders displayed, in order to buy or sell shares.

Below is an example **order book** for a SETS security. 'The order book' is an alternative name for the SETS screen.

| Buy | | | Sell | | |
|---|---|---|---|---|---|
| **Time** | **Volume** | **Price** | **Price** | **Volume** | **Time** |
| 09:03 | 12,000 | **① 174** | **① 175** | 1,100 | 09:15 |
| 10:08 | 5,000 | **174** | **176** | 1,400 | ② 09:12 |
| 09:31 | 11,000 | **173** | **176** | 12,530 | 09:45 |
| 09:32 | 4,500 | **173** | **176** | 2,721 | 09:52 |
| ② 09:20 | 8,350 | **172** | **177** | 12,000 | 10:00 |
| 09:24 | 12,050 | **172** | **177** | 4,290 | 10:02 |
| 09:40 | 4,933 | **172** | | | |

Orders will appear on the SETS screen in ① **price order**. For example, on the buy order side of the screen, the highest prices appear first starting with 174 and then moving down. On the sell order side of the screen, the lowest prices appear first, starting with 175 and then moving up.

If there are several orders at the **same** price then orders are prioritised by ② **time of input**. For example, there are three sell orders at 176 prioritised by time of input. There are also three buy orders at 172 prioritised by time of input.

Size of the transaction of order is not a factor in prioritising orders.

If a member firm places an order to sell shares at 174 then the order will be automatically matched with the buy orders at 174. Matching will always occur with the limit orders at the top of the list (this guarantees **best execution**). Once matched, the orders are removed from the screen.

It should be noted that counterparties' names are not displayed on the system, nor when a trade is automatically executed are the relevant parties informed as to the identity of their counterparty. This is because the **London Clearing House** (LCH Clearnet Limited) becomes the **central counterparty** to all SETS trades. All automatically executed trades **novate** to the LCH such that the buyer buys from the LCH, and the seller sells to the LCH. This provides pre- and post trade anonymity and reduces default risk. There is more information on the Central Counterparty Participant (CCP) in the chapter entitled Settlement, Safe Custody and Prime Brokerage.

When a member firm, or firms, undertake a trade on the LSE, one of the parties will normally be required to issue a trade report to the LSE in order for the trade to be published. However, trades which are executed via the SETS system are **automatically trade reported**, thereby fulfilling the obligations of the relevant member firm.

### 7.1.5 Types of order

All member firms of the LSE will be able to input orders into the system. There are a variety of different types of order that can be input by members of the LSE.

- **Limit orders** – These are orders in which a worst acceptable price is specified. These are the **only** orders which will **appear on the screen** (with the exception of market orders during auction calls, and iceberg orders).

For example, if a member firm entered a buy order for 20,000 shares with a limit price of 176, this would match with the limit orders to sell as follows.

| | | |
|---|---|---|
| 1,100 | shares at 175 | **A multiple fill** |
| 1,400 | shares at 176 | |
| 12,530 | shares at 176 | |
| 2,721 | shares at 176 | |
| 17,751 | | |

The unexecuted proportion of the deal (20,000 – 17,751 = 2,249 shares at 176) will then appear as the top buy order on the buy side of the order book.

Limit orders may specify an expiry time and date (up to a **maximum of 90 calendar days**). If no expiry date or time is specified, then the system will assume the end of the current trading day as the expiry.

- **At best order** – These are orders to buy or sell at whatever the best market price is. For example, an at best order to buy 10,000 shares, will buy the 10,000 cheapest shares on offer in the system. In our example, this will give an execution pattern of 1,100 shares at 175 and also 8,900 shares at 176. Partial execution is possible but **any excess will be eliminated**, as only limit orders remain on the system during normal market hours.
- **Market orders** – These are 'at best' orders that are entered into the system during an **auction call period**. They specify a volume to buy or sell but no price limit. They will have the highest priority for matching at the end of the auction call period in time entry order and will be executed at the **uncrossing price**.
- **Execute and eliminate order** – Similar to an 'at best' order, but with this type a limit price is also specified and a partial execution is possible. As much of the order as possible will be executed immediately and the **remainder will be rejected**. For example, if the order were to require the purchase of 4,000 at best, but subject to a maximum price of 175, then the system would partially execute the bargain against the sell order for 1,100 shares at 175 and eliminate the remaining 2,900 shares, since it cannot at this stage be executed.
- **Fill or kill order** – These are a variant of the at best or execute and eliminate orders (where a limit price would be specified). If the order is entered as a fill or kill, **no partial execution is possible**. The order is either executed in full or entirely eliminated.
- **Iceberg order** – An iceberg order is similar to a limit order but can be **partially hidden** from market view. It is therefore necessary to specify the total order size, limit price and the visible 'peak' size. The peak size is the maximum volume that will be seen on the order book at any given time. The minimum peak size is 10% of the stock's NMS. When an iceberg is entered onto the order book, the maximum possible volume is executed against compatible orders immediately. Any remaining volume of the order will then be shown to the market in peaks. Each peak is effectively treated as a limit order, with its own time-stamp. Only when an individual peak is executed in full will the next peak be revealed and allocated a time-stamp. This means that other (visible) limit orders at the same price will be executed before the hidden volume of an iceberg order. However, the total volume (visible and hidden) of an iceberg order still has priority over other orders at a worse price.

## Example

As an example, let's imagine an iceberg order is entered at 10:10 onto the same example screen above, to buy 100,000 shares at a price of 175p, with a peak size of 10,000 shares.

The iceberg order will immediately match against the 1,100 shares at 175p on the sell side. This leaves an iceberg size of 98,900 shares, of which the first peak of 10,000 appears on the order book as a conventional limit order:

| Buy | | | Sell | | |
|---|---|---|---|---|---|
| **Time** | **Volume** | **Price** | **Price** | **Volume** | **Time** |
| 10:10 | 10,000 | **175** | **176** | 1,400 | 09:12 |
| 09:03 | 12,000 | **174** | **176** | 12,530 | 09:45 |
| 10:08 | 5,000 | **174** | **176** | 2,721 | 09:52 |
| 09:31 | 11,000 | **173** | **177** | 12,000 | 10:00 |
| 09:32 | 4,500 | **173** | **177** | 4,290 | 10:02 |
| 09:20 | 8,350 | **172** | | | |
| 09:24 | 12,050 | **172** | | | |
| 09:40 | 4,933 | **172** | | | |

Only when this 10,000 has been executed **in full** will the next 10,000 appear on the screen. Therefore, if another trader enters at 10:12, a limit order to buy, say, 6,000 at 175p (before the initial peak is executed), it will appear in its usual way on the screen.

| Buy | | | Sell | | |
|---|---|---|---|---|---|
| **Time** | **Volume** | **Price** | **Price** | **Volume** | **Time** |
| 10:10 | 10,000 | **175** | **176** | 1,400 | 09:12 |
| 10:12 | 6,000 | **175** | **176** | 12,530 | 09:45 |
| 09:03 | 12,000 | **174** | **176** | 2,721 | 09:52 |
| 10:08 | 5,000 | **174** | **177** | 12,000 | 10:00 |
| 09:31 | 11,000 | **173** | **177** | 4,290 | 10:02 |
| 09:32 | 4,500 | **173** | | | |
| 09:20 | 8,350 | **172** | | | |
| 09:24 | 12,050 | **172** | | | |
| 09:40 | 4,933 | **172** | | | |

If, at 10:14 , an 'at best' order is entered to sell 12,000 shares, all 10,000 in the visible peak of the buy order will be executed, along with 2,000 of the next order down. As the initial peak has now been executed, the next part appears on the screen, with a new time of 10:14.

| Buy | | | Sell | | |
|---|---|---|---|---|---|
| **Time** | **Volume** | **Price** | **Price** | **Volume** | **Time** |
| 10:12 | 4,000 | **175** | **176** | 1,400 | 09:12 |
| 10:14 | 10,000 | **175** | **176** | 12,530 | 09:45 |
| 09:03 | 12,000 | **174** | **176** | 2,721 | 09:52 |
| 10:08 | 5,000 | **174** | **177** | 12,000 | 10:00 |
| 09:31 | 11,000 | **173** | **177** | 4,290 | 10:02 |
| 09:32 | 4,500 | **173** | | | |
| 09:20 | 8,350 | **172** | | | |
| 09:24 | 12,050 | **172** | | | |
| 09:40 | 4,933 | **172** | | | |

There now remains a total of 88,900 of our iceberg.

At 10:16, a further 'at best' order is entered to sell 45,000 shares. Of the 45,000, the first 4,000 are matched with the 10:12 order, the next 10,000 with the visible peak of our iceberg. But the remaining 31,000 are not matched with any other visible orders (as these are at an inferior price to the hidden part of the iceberg). The 31,000 shares are therefore matched off against the next three full peaks of 10,000, and partially against a fourth peak, leaving 9,000 visible.

| Buy | | | Sell | | |
|---|---|---|---|---|---|
| Time | Volume | Price | Price | Volume | Time |
| 10:16 | 9,000 | **175** | **176** | 1,400 | 09:12 |
| 09:03 | 12,000 | **174** | **176** | 12,530 | 09:45 |
| 10:08 | 5,000 | **174** | **176** | 2,721 | 09:52 |
| 09:31 | 11,000 | **173** | **177** | 12,000 | 10:00 |
| 09:32 | 4,500 | **173** | **177** | 4,290 | 10:02 |
| 09:20 | 8,350 | **172** | | | |
| 09:24 | 12,050 | **172** | | | |
| 09:40 | 4,933 | **172** | | | |

We now have 47,900 remaining in our iceberg, of which 9,000 are visible.

### 7.1.6 Summary of the order types

| Order Type | Limit Price Required? | Partial Execution Allowed? | Unexecuted Portion Added to the Order Book? |
|---|---|---|---|
| Limit Order | Yes | Yes | Yes |
| At Best Order | No | Yes | No |
| Execute and Eliminate Order | Yes | Yes | No |
| Fill or Kill Order | Optional | No | No |
| Market Order | No | Yes | Yes |

### 7.1.7 Order conditions (conditions set by the LSE to ensure an orderly market)

There are a number of restrictions to the orders which can be input.

- **Tick size** – The tick size (minimum price movement) is set in bands for securities depending upon their price.

| Security Price | Tick Size |
|---|---|
| Below 500p | 0.25p |
| 500p to 1,000p | 0.5p |
| Over 1,000p | 1.0p |

  The tick size will not change in line with the daily market price but is re-fixed on a quarterly basis.

- **Standard settlement** – Trades executed via the order book will be on standard settlement and trading terms (T + 3 for shares, T + 1 for nil paid rights or when issue trading, and on standard cum div and ex-div terms only. These are explained in more detail in the chapter on Settlement,

Safe Custody and Prime Brokerage). Any trades done on special terms must be executed outside the order book subject to the LSE's maximum special settlement terms of **T + 25**.

- **Order sizes** – There are no minimum or maximum order sizes. In technical terms the maximum order size is 99,999.99 × NMS! However, in a practical sense the maximum trade which could be executed immediately in full will be determined by the **size of the order book**, i.e. the volume of all the unexecuted orders with which the order can be matched.

## 7.2 The Stock Exchange Electronic Trading Service (SETSqx)

### Quotes and Crosses

SETSqx is the LSE's trading service for less liquid securities (those not traded on SETS). SETSqx replaced the Stock Exchange Alternative Trading service (SEATS plus) in June 2007 and in October 2007 it replaced the Stock Exchange Automated Quotations system (SEAQ) for all main market securities.

The SETSqx system combines market maker quotes with periodic auctions. The order types are committed to principal quotes placed by market makers, and anonymous limit orders. Both market makers and non-market makers can participate in auctions, which take place at 08:00, 11:00, 15:00 and 16:35.

There is a Mandatory Quotation Period for market makers from 08:00 until the end of closing auction, during which time they have an obligation to quote a committed principal quote of a minimum of 1 × NMS. However, it is possible that there are no market makers available for the less liquid stocks. Non market makers can place anonymous limit orders which will match during the auctions. These auctions can be subject to price monitoring extensions.

## 7.3 The International Order Book (IOB)

The International Order Book (IOB) is the trading place for international securities in the form of **American Depository Receipts (ADRs)** and **Global Depository Receipts (GDRs)**. Additionally, some international equities are directly traded on the IOB, though most of these will trade on the International Bulletin Board instead.

The IOB is an order matching system which works in a similar fashion to SETS, with all depository receipts quoted in US dollars. (The few equities quoted directly on the IOB trade in Hong Kong dollars).

As with SETS, only LSE members can access the IOB and ITBB.

A summary of the IOB trading day is as follows (all times are London time).

| | |
|---|---|
| 07:00 | Market opens |
| 07:15-08:50 | Trade reporting only |
| 08:50-09:00 | Opening auction (subject to random ends and extensions, as for SETS) |
| 09:00-15:30 | Continuous trading (automatic matching) |
| 15:30-15:40 | Closing auction (subject to random ends and extensions) |
| 15:40-17:00 | Price advertising period (firms can enter and delete 'named orders' advertising prices at which they are willing to trade, but which will not be automatically executed) |
| 17:15 | Market closes |

Less liquid IOB securities follow a slightly different timetable – the 'Auction Only Trading Day' – where members input limit or market orders between 08:50 and 15:40 and these are uncrossed three times a day at 11:00, 14:00 and 15:40, effectively creating three long auction periods.

There is a minimum order size of 50 securities on the IOB and any trade of size greater than 50× NMS is called a 'Block Trade'. Such a trade may have its publication delayed for up to five business days or until 90% of the trade is offset.

# 8 Other Trading Systems

Learning objective

**3.3.4 Understand** the key features of alternative trading venues: Multilateral Trading Facilities (MTFs), Systematic Internalisers and Dark Pools.

On 6 of May 2010 at around 14:30, the US market experienced a short dramatic fall of about 5% in the equities and futures markets in just a few minutes. Labelled by the press as a 'flash crash', this caused concerns in Congress, the SEC and the wider markets as a whole. In an SEC and CFTC report released shortly afterwards, the involvement of high frequency electronic trading now widespread in the market was considered. It notes that high frequency trading has largely replaced the role of specialists and market makers.

The development of trading platforms has been rapid in recent years from the more conventional form of trading exchange to electronic networks using the latest technology allowing much faster and at times less transparent trading between the largest participants. These trading networks often rely on sophisticated algorithms which have implications for the market as a whole.

## 8.1 Market transparency

Trading on an exchange is subject to transparency rules of the exchange, as governed by regulatory provisions. MiFID is backed up by the **Transparency Directive** in its efforts to create a single capital market for the EEA.

The Transparency Directive requires pre- and post-trade transparency in the markets so that investors can easily compare execution venues and therefore select the best market to trade financial instruments in, rather than having to use their own monopolistic national exchange.

## 8.2 Electronic Communication Networks (ECNs)

Electronic Communication Networks (ECNs) are electronic trading systems that automatically match purchase and sale orders at a specified price without the requirement to go through a market maker.

These ECNs have given individual investors the opportunity to trade equities and other securities with increased flexibility, particularly with respect to after hours trading. However, after hours trading does involve additional risk for the investor due to increased price volatility and reduced liquidity. Individual investors will normally place limit orders, that limits the buying or selling price, and these are then matched automatically by the ECN for execution purposes.

The development of ECNs in the UK market has increased the choice of trading mechanisms to UK investors and placed greater competitive pressure on traditional exchanges.

It is important to note that ECNs are not classed as Recognised Investment Exchanges (RIEs) by the FSA, and are therefore not exempt from the need to seek authorisation.

The SEC authorised the use of ECNs in 1998 with an objective of increasing competition and thus reducing costs.

## 8.3 MTFs and 'dark pools'

The **Markets in Financial Instruments Directive (MiFID)** has encouraged the development of many new trading and reporting systems.

**Multilateral Trading Facilities (MTFs)** are systems bringing together multiple parties to buy and sell financial instruments, which are encouraged by the more liberalised rules under MiFID.

MTFs may be crossing networks or matching engines that are operated by an investment firm or a market operator. Instruments traded on a MTF may include shares, bonds and derivatives. MiFID requires operators of MTFs to ensure their markets operate on a fair and orderly basis. It aims to ensure this by placing requirements on MTF operators regarding how they organise their markets and the information they give to users. Additionally, MiFID provides for the operators of MTFs to **passport their services** across borders.

Examples of MTFs include **Turquoise**, **Chi-X**, **PEX** (Portugal) and **Nordic MTF**. **BATS Europe**, operated by the US platform BATS Trading, and **Nasdaq OMX Europe**, an equities platform of the US-based NASDAQ OMX, were both launched in 2008. The European unit of Liffe partnered with HSBC and BNP Paribas to launch **Smartpool**, for large order execution of European stocks. **SIX Swiss Exchange** (formerly SWX Europe) has been in partnership with Nyfix Millennium of the US to create **Swiss Block**, for Swiss blue chip stocks. Nyfix also operates **Euro Millennium™**. **Equiduct** is another MTF.

## 8.4 Dark liquidity pools

This new generation of platforms offers the prospect of firms making use of internal crossing networks – more often now called **dark liquidity pools** or '**non-displayed liquidity venues**', whereby firms can buy and sell blocks of shares away from the public domain. This offers trading anonymity, without pre trade prices being displayed on the public order book usually found on exchanges. There are more than 40 dark pools operating in the US, the largest being Goldman Sachs' Sigma X and Credit Suisse's CrossFinder. By mid-2008, dark pools were estimated to account for 12% of US daily stock trading volume. In the past, **stock exchanges** have viewed off-exchange trading as their main source of competition. The moves by **Liffe** and **SIX Swiss Exchange** to form links with dark pools can be seen as a case of 'If you can't beat 'em, join 'em'.

Some exchanges have adapted their technology to handle the need for large orders to be hidden from the market: LSE and Liffe both offer an **iceberg facility** through which only a small part of a large order is displayed at one time. Meanwhile, sell-side brokers have been developing algorithms to help them to detect if an order is being traded away from the market.

More **regulatory attention** could be paid to the growing use of dark pools in the future, in case of any systemic risk that they might present.

## 8.5 Systematic internalisers

A **systematic internaliser (SI)** is an investment firm which deals on its own account by executing client orders outside a regulated market or a MTF. MiFID requires such firms to publish firm quotes in liquid shares (for orders below 'standard market size') and to maintain those quotes on a regular and continuous basis during normal business hours.

# 9 International Markets

earning objective

**3.3.5 Apply** knowledge of key differences in the developed markets of UK, Germany, USA and Japan, and emerging markets of Brazil; China, India and Russia (BRIC), both on and off exchange: Regulatory and supervisory environment Structure and size of markets, Liquidity and transparency and Access and relative cost of trading.

## 9.1 Germany

### 9.1.1 Federal Financial Supervisory Authority (Bundesanstalt für Finanzdienstleistungsaufsicht - BaFin)

BaFin is the German regulatory authority, whose stated aim is to ensure the 'proper functioning, stability and integrity of the German financial system.'

On its website it explains that under its solvency supervision: 'BaFin ensures the ability of banks, financial services institutions and insurance undertakings to meet their payment obligations. Through its market supervision, BaFin also enforces standards of professional conduct which preserve investors' trust in the financial markets. As part of its investor protection, BaFin also seeks to prevent unauthorised financial business.'

BaFin is organised into three 'Directorates' which are:

- Banking supervision
- Insurance supervision
- Securities supervision

### 9.1.2 Deutsche Börse

The Deutsche Börse group describes itself on its website as offering the following activities:

- Operates the Frankfurt Stock Exchange, which, with Xetra and floor trading, is by far the largest German securities exchange.
- Organizes the world's largest derivatives market via Eurex and the International Securities Exchange (ISE).
- Has one of the world's leading clearing houses with Eurex Clearing.
- Distributes information generated by its trading platforms and makes trading activity transparent by offering market data such as DAX® and numerous prices and further indices.
- Offers a wide range of post-trading services, such as settlement, custody and banking services, through Clearstream.
- Provides technology to its own markets and to customers worldwide through its IT subsidiaries Deutsche Börse Systems and Clearstream Services.

More than 400,000 financial instruments trade on the Frankfurt stock exchange including:

- Shares
- Bonds
- ETFs (exchange traded funds)
- ETCs (exchange traded commodities)
- Mutual funds
- Warrants
- REITs (real estate investment trusts)

### 9.1.3 Clearstream

As seen above, Clearstream is now a part of the Deutsche Börse group, following a merger of Cedel International and Deutsche Börse Clearsing. In addition to offering clearing services, the company also offers safekeeping and administration of securities, in its role as a depositary. It states that 'Over 300,000 domestic and internationally traded bonds, equities and investment funds are currently deposited with Clearstream'.

## 9.2 USA

### 9.2.1 Key regulators

In the USA, there are two main relevant regulatory bodies, the **Securities and Exchange Commission (SEC)**

The Securities and Exchange Commission (the SEC) has an exemption for overseas broker-dealers that wish to engage in transactions with U.S. customers from having to register with the SEC if US customers have initiated these transactions with the overseas broker-dealers without the business being solicited. The Exchange Act Rule 15a-6 currently provides an exemption from for overseas broker-dealers to register with the SEC that undertake transactions in securities with or for customers that they have not solicited.

and the **Commodity Futures Trading Commission (CFTC)**. US regulations governing derivatives trading originally stem from the Wall Street crash of 1929 and are contained in the **Commodity Exchange Act 1936** which have been updated through the **Commodity Futures Modernization Act 2000**. The SEC primarily regulates derivatives on securities whereas the CFTC primarily regulates commodities.

### 9.2.2 The Federal Reserve System (The Fed)

The Federal Reserve System is the US central banking system and in its present form dates back to the Federal Reserve Act of 1913.It plays a central role in the management of the money supply of the US. It has three objectives in this respect:

- To achieve a long term price stability (control of inflation)
- To achieve maximum employment
- To achieve moderate long term interest rates

The twelve board members of the Federal Open Markets Committee (FOMC) form a key part of the Federal Reserve System. They set the reserve requirements, regulatory and supervisory responsibilities over various banking activities in the US. They also act in the decisions involving discount rate policy.

### 9.2.3 The Federal Deposit Insurance Corporation (The FDIC)

The FDIC which was created in 1933 (soon after the 1929 stock market crash) is an independent agency of the US government, backed by 'the full faith and credit of the US government'. It states on its website that:

The Federal Deposit Insurance Corporation (FDIC) is an independent agency created by the Congress to maintain stability and public confidence in the nation's financial system by:

- Insuring deposits
- Examining and supervising financial institutions for safety and soundness and consumer protection, and
- Managing receiverships.

As with the UK's FSCS, which covers UK deposits, its aims is to avoid people losing confidence in the banks and to stop panic withdrawing of funds by guaranteeing their protection with insurance of $250,000 per depositor per insured bank, for each account ownership category.

### 9.2.4 The Office of Thrift Supervision (OTS)

The mission statement of the OTS is 'to supervise savings associations and their holding companies in order to maintain their safety and soundness and compliance with consumer laws, and to encourage a competitive industry that meets America's financial services needs'.

The OTS has a history dating back to the early 19th century and serves to assist the retail financial services industry. Their key objectives centre around the supervision and facilitation of the process of allowing Americans to buy their own houses. Home ownership is described on the OTS website as being the 'bedrock of the American dream'.

### 9.2.5 The Office of the Comptroller of the Currency (OCC)

The OCC states on its website that it's goal in supervising banks is to 'ensure that they operate in a safe and sound manner and in compliance with laws requiring fair treatment of their customers and fair access to credit and financial products.'

In regulating the national US banks the OCC state their powers to be:

- Examining the national banks.
- Approving or denying applications for new charters, branches, capital or other changes in corporate or banking structure.
- Taking supervisory actions against national banks that do not comply with laws and regulations.
- Issuing rules and regulations, legal interpretations, and corporate decisions governing bank investments, lending, and other practices.

US government bonds settle T + 1, while equities and corporate bonds settle T + 3.

### 9.2.6 The New York Stock Exchange (NYSE)

The NYSE website dates the development of today's New York Stock Exchange back to 1790, when the government issued $80 million in bonds to pay for the war of independence. Trading in these bonds lead to the 'Buttonwood agreement' where 24 merchants and brokers signed an agreement agreeing to trade securities on a commission basis and later moved to the Tontine coffee house to do business. In 1817 the New York Stock and Exchange board was formed, becoming the New York Stock Exchange in 1863. At the time traders who did business on the street were known as curb stone traders and would often trade stocks in smaller companies. Technological developments such as the telegraph and ticker tape adopted by the NYSE gave it the edge over competing stock exchange and over time it came to dominate the market. In 2007 the NYSE merged with Euronext to form the NYSE Euronext Group which now allows investors to list securities in either euros or dollars.

The NYSE group currently offers listing in equities, bonds, and also futures and options via its NYSE Liffe company.

### 9.2.7 NASDAQ

NASDAQ (originally known as the National Association of Securities Dealers Automated Quotations Systems) describes itself as being the largest US electronic stock market. It has according to its website 'approximately 3,200 companies, it lists more companies and, on average, trades more shares per day than any other US market. It is home to companies that are leaders across all areas of business, including technology, retail, communications, financial services, transportation, media and biotechnology. NASDAQ is the primary market for trading NASDAQ-listed stocks.'

## 9.3 Japan

### 9.3.1 The Financial Services Agency (FSA)

The FSA of Japan is a Japanese Government agency which has been given responsibility for ensuring the stability of the Japanese financial system.

It states on its website the affairs that it handles to include the following:

- Planning and policy making concerning the financial system.
- Inspection and supervision of private sector financial institutions, Including banks, insurance companies and Financial Instrument Business Operators, as well as market participants, including exchanges.
- Establishment of rules for trading in markets.
- Establishment of business accounting standards and others concerning corporate finance.
- Supervision of certified public accounts and auditing firms.
- Participation in activities of international organisations and bilateral and multilateral for a on financial issues to develop internationally consistent financial administration.
- Surveillance of compliance of rules in markets.

Japan operates a system involving the use of a market watchdog The Securities and Exchange Surveillance Commission (SESC) states its mission to be 'to ensure integrity of capital markets and to protect investors'. Where statutory violations are found to exist as a result of SESC investigations, the SESC may send recommendations to the Commissioner of the FSA who may then take action.

### 9.3.2 The Tokyo Stock Exchange (TSE)

The Tokyo Stock Exchange (TSE) is the primary Japanese stock exchange. A wide variety of products are offered on the exchange

- Equities
- Bonds
- Convertible bonds
- Exchange traded funds (ETFs)
- Futures and options
- Carbon trading

There is also a joint venture between the TSE and the LSE known as Tokyo AIM (Alternative Investment Market) which started operations in 2009 and offers itself as a new market for growing companies.
The TSE employs a system of price controls which prevent the price of a stock from rising or falling above/below set levels during the trading day. Excessive price swings will cause the exchange to stop trading the stock for a given period of time.

### 9.3.3 The Japanese Securities Depositary Centre (JASDEC)

Whilst Japanese Government bonds (JGBs) and Treasury Bills are cleared centrally by the Bank of Japan (BOJ), Japanese equities are cleared by JASDEC. JASEDC offers clearing services for stocks, corporate bonds, commercial paper and Investment trusts. It also offers custodial services for many securities.

Settlement in Japan is T + 3 for bonds and equities.

### 9.3.4 The Deposit Insurance Corporation of Japan (DICJ)

The DICJ has since April 2005 offers protection for 'current deposits, ordinary deposits and specified deposits' up to a maximum principal deposit of ¥10 million plus accrued interest thereon per depositor per financial institution.

## 9.4 Developing markets

Developing or emerging markets are so described because of their current economic position, with relatively low income compared to the developed countries and stock markets which are only a fraction of the size of the world market.

Developing markets offer investors a number of potential advantages over developed markets, but also a number of risks which must be considered. Advantages include:

- **Rapid growth** – The developing countries have shown rapid economic growth in recent times, with their large populations and access to underexploited natural resources. Coming as they do from a current lower level of GDP growth is predicted to continue as they catch up and overtake many of the current leading economic countries. Investors look to these countries for rapid company and profits growth.
- **Inefficient markets** – while it may seem counterintuitive to be attracted to a market where pricing is inefficient, industry experts see this as an opportunity to access undervalued investments.
- **Low correlation** with developed markets – it has been seen that the returns achieved from investing in developing markets have a low correlation with investments in more developed countries. This is attractive to investors looking to find returns in periods when the developed country investments are performing weakly.

Risks of developing country investments are largely due to the less established infrastructure physical, regulatory, political and social.

- **Regulation** - The regulation of developing markets is still perhaps inevitably less rigorous than those more developed markets and as such the dangers of crime, fraud and weak corporate governance measures add to the investor risk.
- **Currency risk** – The currencies of the developing countries may carry higher risk than other currencies such as the dollar and the euro.
- **Liquidity** – Investments in less developed markets may be more difficult to sell. There may also be difficulties experienced when trying to repatriate assets back to the investors home country.
- **Security** – Settlement and custody arrangements can be more difficult and costly to arrange.
- **Higher volatility** – Historically there has been higher volatility in developing country investments. Moving forward however, this may become less significant as the BRIC and other countries become more economically established.

In recent years a number of these countries have experienced rapid economic growth and in particular the so called BRIC countries (Brazil, Russia, India and China) with their large populations and valuable resources have shown very strong growth. Combined population of the BRIC countries adds up to around 40% of the world. In June 2009, the BRIC countries held their first official summit in Yekaterinburg Russia. It should be noted however that a number of commentators have pointed out that China is the dominant BRIC country, with much greater economic and political power than the other BRIC members. Goldman Sachs has suggested that by 2050, these four countries might be among the four most dominant in the world given their current and projected growth.

## 9.5 Brazil

### 9.5.1 The BM&F Bovespa exchange

BM&FBOVESPA was formed in 2008 from the merger of the São Paulo Stock Exchange (Bolsa de Valores de São Paulo) together with the Brazilian Mercantile & Futures Exchange (Bolsa de Mercadoria e Futoros)

It offers trading in:

- Equities
- Commodities and Futures
- Foreign exchange
- Securities
- ETFs
- Carbon market
- Corporate bonds

The Bovespa Index is made up of 50 stocks, traded on the São Paulo Stock Exchange.

### 9.5.2 The Securities and Exchange Commission of Brazil (CVM)

The CVM is Brazil's regulatory authority.

The CVM describes the law that brought it into being and states that the objectives of this law were as follows:

- To assure the proper functioning of the exchange and over-the-counter markets.
- To protect all securities holders against fraudulent issues and illegal actions performed by company managers, controlling shareholders, or mutual fund managers.
- To avoid or inhibit any kind of fraud or manipulation which may give rise to artificial price formation in the securities market.
- To assure public access to all relevant information about the securities traded and the companies which have issued them.
- To ensure that all market participants adopt fair trading practices.
- To stimulate the formation of savings and their investment in securities; and
- To promote the expansion and efficiency of the securities market and the capitalization of Brazilian publicly held companies.

## 9.6 India

### 9.6.1 The National Stock Exchange of India (NSE)

As described in its 'fact book' the NSE was incorporated in November 1992 and, under the Securities Contracts (Regulation) Act, it received recognition in 1993. It describes its market segments and products as:

'NSE provides a trading platform for of all types of securities for investors under one roof – Equity, Corporate Debt, Central and State Government Securities, T-Bills, Commercial Paper (CPs), Certificate of Deposits (CDs), Warrants, Mutual Funds (MFs) units, Exchange Traded Funds (ETFs), Derivatives like Index Futures, Index Options, Stock Futures, Stock Options Currency Futures and Interest Rate Futures. The Exchange provides trading in four different segments *viz.*, Wholesale Debt Market (WDM) segment, Capital Market (CM) segment, Futures & Options (F&O) segment and the Currency Derivatives Segment (CDS).

The ***wholesale debt market*** segment provides the trading platform for trading of a wide range of debt securities which includes State and Central Government securities, T-Bills, state development loans (SDLs), bonds issued by public sector undertakings (PSUs), floating rate bonds (FRBs), zero coupon bonds (ZCBs), index bonds, commercial papers (CPs), certificate of deposits (CDs), four corporate debentures, SLR and non-SLR bonds issued by financial institutions (FIs), bonds issued by foreign institutions and units of mutual funds (MFs).'

### 9.6.2 The Bombay Stock Exchange (BSE)

The BSE is Asia's oldest stock exchange, being established in1875. The BSE states itself as being 'the world's number 1 exchange in the world in terms of the number of listed companies (over 4,900). It is the world's fifth most active in terms of number of transactions handled through its electronic trading system. It is also in the top ten of global exchanges in terms of the market capitalization of its listed companies (as of December 31, 2009). The companies listed on BSE command a total market capitalization of USD trillion 1.28 as of Feb, 2010.'

### 9.6.3 Regulation in the Indian markets

- The Forward Markets Commission (FMC) - The Indian commodity derivative markets is regulated by the FMC.
- The Securities and Exchange Board of India (SEBI) - SEBI was established in 1992 under the terms of the Securities and Exchange Board of India Act. It has the aim of protecting the interests of investors and to regulate the securities market.

### 9.6.4 The Reserve Bank of India

The RBI is the central bank of India, established in 1935 and the RBI describe their activities to include the key roles of

- Monetary authority
- Issuer of currency
- Banker and debt manager to government
- Banker to banks
- Regulator of the banking system
- Manager of foreign exchange
- Regulator and supervisor of the payment and settlement systems
- Developmental role

### 9.6.5 The Ministry of Finance

The Indian ministry of finance is composed of five departments:

- The department of economic affaires
- The department of expenditure
- The department of revenue
- The department of disinvestment
- The department of financial services

The MOF plays a key role in the enacting of Indian financial legislation.

## 9.7 China

### 9.7.1 The Shanghai Stock Exchange (SSE)

The SSE was founded in 1990, and directly regulated by the China Securities Regulatory Commission (CSRC). It describes itself on its website as being Mainland China's pre-eminent stock exchange in terms of the number of listed companies, number of shares listed, total market value, tradable market value, securities turnover in value, stock turnover in value and the T-bond turnover in value. As at the end of 2009, SSE boasted 1,351 listed securities and 870 listed companies, with a combined market capitalization of RMB 18,465.523 billion and a total of 89.6543 million trading accounts. In 2009, listed companies raised RMB 334.315 billion on SSE through IPO and new share placement.

The SSE categorises securities into four groups: stocks, bonds, funds and warrants.

It divides stocks into two categories, A shares which are limited to only domestic investors and B shares which are available to domestic and overseas investors. The SSE website states that by the end of 2008, there were 854 A shares and 54 B shares listed on SSE.

### 9.7.2 The Hong Kong Stock Exchange (HKEx)

The HKEx was formed following a 1999 market reform. The reform brought together the Stock Exchange of Hong Kong Limited (SEHK), the Hong Kong Futures Exchange Limited (HKFE) and the Hong Kong Securities Clearing Company Limited (HKSCC), which merged under a single holding company, HKEx.

It is one of the world's largest securities exchanges.

### 9.7.3 The Shenzen Stock Exchange

The Shenzen stock exchange was established in 1990. It states on its website, that by June 2010, 'SZSE was home to 1,012 listed companies, with 485 on the main board, 437 on the SME board and 90 on the ChiNext market. The total market capitalization was valued at 5.6 trillion yuan (US$828.7 billion).'

### 9.7.4 Regulation in China

#### The China Securities Regulatory Commission (CSRC)

The CSRC is the main regulator of securities in the People's Republic of China

#### The China Banking Regulatory Commission (CBRC)

The Chinese Banking Sector is regulated by the CBRC

## 9.8 Russia

### 9.8.1 The Russia Trading System Stock Exchange (RTS)

The RTS stock exchange was the first regulated stock exchange. It offers a range of products, including:

- **RTS Standard** – which is an equity market aimed at the most liquid Russian securities. It employs CCP technology and standard T + 4 settlement in roubles.
- **RTS Classica** – This trading platform allows both rouble and foreign currency settlement. RTS Classica is accessible by foreign investors in addition to Russian investors. The RTS website states that over 500 securities list on this market. T + 4 DVP settlement.
- **RTS T + 0 market** – Securities trading for retail investors with full preliminary deposit of assets and with ruble settlement.

- **RTS Board** – This is the quote driven market for unlisted stocks and bonds.
- **FORTS** – This is a rouble settled market in futures and options.
- **RTS Index** – the index which was first calculated in 1995 and is based upon 50 of the RTS exchange's most liquid and capitalised shares.

### 9.8.2 The Moscow Interbank Currency Exchange (MICEX)

The MICEX stock exchange is Russia's leading stock exchange with over 80% share of the Russian on-exchange equities market. (If the over the counter market is included about 60%) The MCIEX website states that 'in 2009, the total volume of trading on the MICEX Stock Exchange amounted to 41 trillion roubles (1,304 billion USD). Trading in shares (including repos) accounted for 26 trillion roubles (836 billion USD).'

The MICEX index is Russia's main stock market indicator, comprising 30 of the most liquid stocks and the largest and most rapidly developing Russian companies.

### 9.8.3 Regulation in the Russian market

#### The Bank of Russia

The Bank of Russia is the main regulator of Russia's banking industry.

It has responsibility for banking licences, accounting standards and the lender of last resort in a similar fashion to the BOE in the UK. It is responsible for carrying out Russia's monetary policy and setting interest rates and in doing so protecting the value of the rouble.

## 10 Trading Cum and Ex-div and Normal Settlement

earning objective

**3.3.4 Understand** the concepts of trading cum, 'ex-div' and 'cum-div', cum, special ex, special cum, and ex rights and effect of late registration.

It is the investor's appearance on the share register which entitles him to the benefits attached to the shares (dividends are paid to investors who are on the register on a specified day, stated by the company). The investor is known as the **'legal owner'** if his name is on the share register.

Shares normally trade in the market on the basis of **cum (meaning 'with') dividend**. This means that any purchaser of the shares is entitled to receive the next dividend. As a share approaches its dividend payment date, a company sets a **books close date** (also known as the 'record date' or the 'on register date'). The company pays the next dividend to all shareholders who are on the register of shareholders on the books close date. The books close date will be some time before the dividend payment date to make administration easy for the company.

The problem of **late registration** occurs when a shareholder buys a share cum dividend and fails to have his name entered on the register of shareholders by the books close date. The company registrar will send the dividend cheque to the previous shareholder as their name is still on the register on the record date. The previous shareholder must then write a cheque to their own broker for the total dividend. The **buyer's broker will then claim the dividend from the broker of the original shareholder**.

In order to avoid this problem, the LSE has developed a system whereby shares will commence trading **ex-dividend** (**without** the dividend) on the LSE **two business days** prior to the books close date. Beneficial entitlement to dividend stems from when a share was **traded**, not settled. The books close date will usually be a Friday; therefore the ex-dividend date will usually be a Wednesday. This effectively means that the

Tuesday of that week will be the last day you may buy a share with beneficial entitlement to the dividend. Normally, we expect the price of the share to fall by the dividend amount on Wednesday.

Trades conducted on the last cum div date (the Tuesday of that week) will, therefore, settle on the Friday books close date (given normal settlement of three business days after the trade). Hence, cum div buyers will receive the dividend from the company. Similarly, anyone dealing ex-div on the first ex-div date (Wednesday) would not be entered in the register by the books close date (Friday of the same week), as settlement would take place three business days (T + 3) after the transaction, which would be the Monday of the following week.

## Illustration

**Ex-Div Timetable**

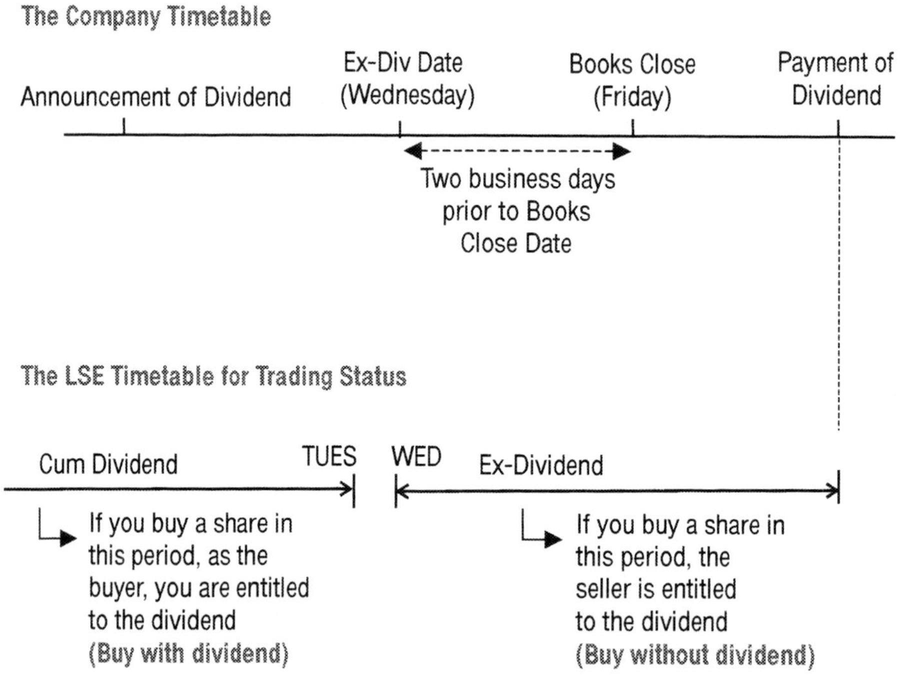


As can be seen, the share will trade ex-dividend from the ex-div date up to when the dividend is paid, **including** the dividend payment date.

## 10.1 Special cum and special ex-dealing for shares in the UK

In addition to the rules on cum and ex-trading, the LSE also has rules for **special cum** and **special ex-trading**. In this situation, the 'special' refers to being able to trade cum when the stock is normally trading ex, and *vice versa*. It is allowable for special settlement to occur provided both parties to the transaction agree.

### 10.1.1 Special cum

The special cum period occurs where shares are normally trading ex-div. The effect of this is to extend the cum-div period up to, but **not** including, the dividend payment day.

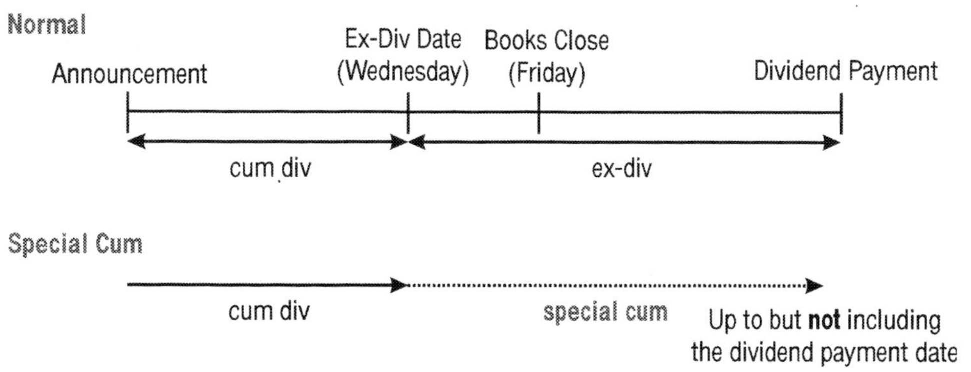


The implication of trading special cum is that the buyer will still ultimately receive the dividend although he is purchasing the shares after the books close day and would normally not be entitled to the dividend. The buyer will be paying 'extra' for the dividend when he settles the transaction, which will enhance the seller's income flow.

### 10.1.2 Special ex

The special ex period commences ten business days prior to the ex-div date (Wednesday). The effect of this is to extend the ex-dividend period by up to ten business days.

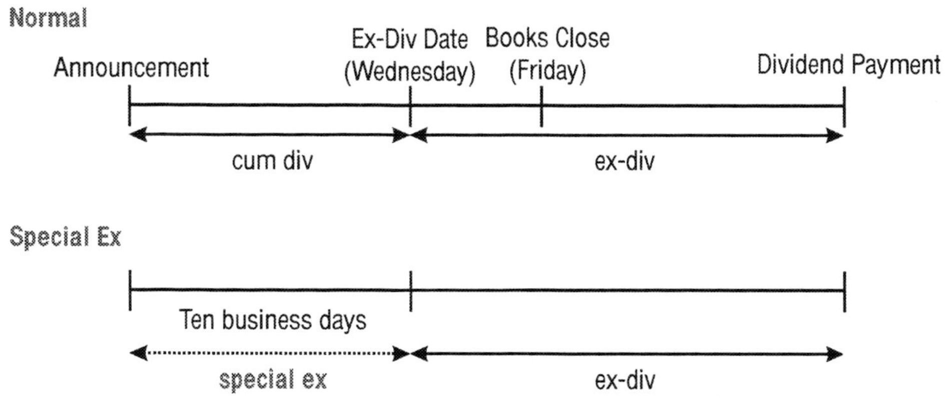


This would suit a buyer who did not want to pay extra up front for a dividend received weeks later.
It may also have tax advantages as the buyer will not receive a dividend on which they would have to pay income tax. Instead they will have bought the share at a lower price leading to a higher capital gain on sale of the share.

### 10.1.3 Summary of special settlement

Shares may be traded special ex (when they are normally cum) in the **ten business days before** they are marked ex, and special cum at all stages when they are being traded ex-div, **except** on the **payment date**.

With **corporate bonds** the special ex period is **five business days** prior to the ex-div date. The special cum period will run from when the bond trades ex up to, but not including, the payment date.

| Security | Normal ex-div date | Special ex | Special cum |
|---|---|---|---|
| **Shares** | Two business days prior to books close date | Ten business days prior to ex-div date | Cum div period extended up to, but not including, the payment date |
| **Corporate bonds** | No norm, depends on the bond | Five business days prior to ex-div date | Cum div period extended up to, but not including, the payment date |
| **Gilts** | Seven business days prior to coupon date* | Not allowed | Cum div period extended up to, but not including, the payment date |

* The 3½% War Loan goes ex-div ten business days prior to coupon date.

# 11 Equity Indices

**Learning objective**

**3.3.6 Assess** how the following factors influence equity markets and equity valuation:

- Trading volume and liquidity of domestic and international securities markets
- Relationship between cash and derivatives markets, and the effect of timed events
- Market consensus and analyst opinion
- Changes to key pricing determinants such as credit ratings and economic outlook
- Regulatory environment including market abuse regime

**3.3.7 Understand** the purpose, construction, application and influence of indices on equity markets: Developed and emerging market regional & country sectors, Market capitalization sub sectors, Free float and full market capitalization indices and Fair value adjusted indices.

## 11.1 What is an index?

An index is a number that gives the value of something relative to some base value. We have probably all heard of the Retail Price Index (the RPI), which is used as a measure of inflation. It measures prices now relative to those in a base year.

However, indices are also frequently used in relation to stock markets to describe how prices of securities in general have moved over time.

In general terms for any index, a base date is established and ascribed an index value of, say, 100. Subsequent valuations of the items will be carried out and compared to the original base value to establish the revised index value.

There are no rules in relation to the selection of a base date, though it would be more useful if it did not have an extreme or unusual value.

Indices may be used for a variety of reasons. Historically, their purpose was to give an indication of the mood of the market. More frequently now, they are used as a benchmark for performance assessment.

To be appropriate for benchmarking purposes, an index must be indicative of the performance that could realistically have been achieved.

The characteristics that are required to render an index suitable as a benchmark are, therefore, that it is

- Specified and unambiguous.
- Appropriate to the preferences of the fund (e.g. a UK large market capitalisation fund may utilise the FTSE 100 index).
- Appropriate to the currency of the fund.

- Investable, i.e. composed of investments that could conceivably be held in the fund.
- Measurable, i.e. the return can be calculated on a frequent basis as required.
- Representative of achievable performance, i.e. it has an arithmetic weighted composition (remember that the return of a portfolio is an arithmetic weighted average of the individual stock returns).
- Measures the relevant component of performance, i.e. total return indices for total return performance and capital value indices for capital growth.

## 11.2 Index construction

The great majority of indices (such as the FTSE100) are constructed as market weighted indices, where the market capitalisation (Share price x Number of outstanding) shares is calculated for each constituent element of the index then (in an arithmetic index) these are added and divided by the index divisor to give the index value. This leads the index to be biased towards the larger companies by market capitalisation, (i.e. a percentage change in a large company will impact the index by an equivalent percentage change in the share value of a smaller company).

There are exceptions to this rule however, the Dow Jones Industrial Average (DJIA30), for example is not capitalisation weighted and is calculated by simply summing the price of a single share of each company on the numerator of the calculation rather than the market cap of each company. This means that the index is more influenced not by the largest company in the index but rather that with the highest dollar market price.

## 11.3 Changes in the constituents of indices

From time to time, it is necessary to replace a share in a share index, perhaps as a result of a closure, merger or takeover, or a bond in a bond index as a result of one reaching maturity or a new bond being issued.

The important point when this occurs is that the index value should **not be altered** by the change. We do not want any discontinuities in the index that will prevent it from being useful.

To avoid this, we need to establish a new divisor (denominator) for the index that will maintain the index value without the old component and with any new component.

### Example

Suppose that the above unweighted arithmetic index related to four shares. Share D is to be removed from the index and replaced by Share E, which has a current price of £1.00. The current index must still be 205.3 following the change, since the market as a whole has not moved; we have simply changed the constituents of the index.

As a result, we must have

$$205.3 = \frac{5.00 + 2.40 + 2.20 + 1.00}{\text{New divisor}} \times 100$$

Hence

$$\text{New divisor} = \frac{5.00 + 2.40 + 2.20 + 1.00}{205.3} \times 100 = £5.163$$

Originally, we were dividing by the unweighted base date value of £5.70 in calculating the index. Now, we are calculating the index by dividing by £5.163, which is not the base date value of the new constituents.

This type of adjustment is required for all types of index (arithmetic and geometric), the result being that the divisor for any stock index calculation is unlikely to be simply the base value of shares or bonds in the index.

## 11.4 Changes in the share capital of constituents

If the issued share capital of any of the constituents of an index changes, then this must be dealt with in exactly the same way. When the issued share capital of constituents of an index changes, a new denominator must be calculated based on the new weightings, in order to ensure that the level of the index itself is unaltered by that change.

## 11.5 Free-float indices

The idea underlying 'free-float' indices is to ensure that the index satisfies the benchmark requirement of being investable. For example, if only 10% of the shares of a company are available to investors at large, then its index weighting should only reflect this investable proportion rather than the full market capitalisation of the company concerned.

If this were not the case, and a full 100% weighting were given to this security within the index, then there would be significant demand for the few available shares (if only from trackers trying to replicate this weighting from the limited supply available) distorting the price upwards, hence distorting the index.

Most major indices are now prepared on a free-float basis.

$$\text{Index level} = \frac{\sum(\text{Market price of stock} \times \text{number of shares}) \times \text{Free float factor}}{\text{Index divisor}}$$

Where the 'free float factor' represents the fraction of shares in the free float as a proportion of the issued shares. [Note: Free float includes all shares expect those which are restricted i.e. held by directors of a company or its subsidiaries, individuals connected with those directors or any person holding 5% or more of the shares.]

### Share indices

In the UK and worldwide, equity indices developed in the 1960s and there are now a number of universally accepted indices that may be used for share performance evaluation in various countries.

Share indices generally measure the appreciation (or otherwise) of the **capital value** of the relevant shares, taking no account of the income generated. As a result, they will provide a useful benchmark for comparing portfolio capital gains, but not dividend income. To reflect the different sizes of companies in the index the most common construction is arithmetic weighted.

## 11.6 International stock indices

| | Market (Stock Exchange) | Number of Shares | Arithmetic (A) Geometric (G) Weighted (W) Unweighted (U) | Currency | Notes |
|---|---|---|---|---|---|
| **FT Ordinary Share Index** | UK (London) | 30 | GU | £ | |
| **FTSE 100** | UK (London) | 100 | AW | £ | Based at 1,000 at 30 December 1983. The FTSE 100 Index represents approximately 70% of the market value of UK listed shares. |
| **FTSE 250** | UK (London) | 250 | AW | £ | |
| **FTSE 350** | UK (London) | 350 | AW | £ | Combines the FTSE 100 and FTSE 250 shares. |
| **FTSE Small Cap** | UK (London) | c. 550 | AW | £ | All shares in the FTSE all shares index not in the FTSE 350. |
| **FTSE Actuaries All Share** | UK (London) | c. 900 | AW | £ | |
| **FTSE Eurotop 100** | UK & Continental Europe | 100 | AW | € | |
| **FTSE Eurotop 300** | UK & Continental Europe | 300 | AW | € | Calculated by both region and sector. |
| **FTSE Private Investor Indices** | UK | | | £ | Based on typical private client asset split. |
| **Dow Jones Industrial Average** | US (New York) | 30 | AU | $ | Possibly the most widely quoted US index. |
| **Standard and Poor's 500** | US (New York) | 500 | AW | $ | |
| **CAC 40** | France (Paris) | 40 | AW | € | |
| **Nikkei 225** | Japan (Tokyo) | 225 | AU | ¥ | |
| **Nikkei 300** | Japan (Tokyo) | 300 | AW | ¥ | |
| **Hang Seng** | Hong Kong | 33 | AW | HK$ | |
| **DAX** | Germany (Frankfurt) | 30 | AW | € | |

# 12 Dealing Regulations

| Learning objective 3.3.1 | **Apply** fundamental UK regulatory requirements with regard to trade execution and reporting: Best Execution, Aggregation and allocation, Prohibition of conflicts of interests and front running |
|---|---|

## 12.1 Best execution

The basic COBS rule of **best execution** is as follows.

A firm must take all reasonable steps to obtain, when executing orders, the best possible result for its clients taking into account the execution factors.

When a firm is **dealing on own account with clients**, this is considered to be execution of client orders, and is therefore subject to the best execution rule.

If a firm provides a best quote to a client, it is acceptable for the quote to be executed after the client accepts it, provided the quote is not manifestly out of date.

The obligation to obtain best execution needs to be interpreted according to the particular type of financial instrument involved, but the rule applies to **all types of financial instrument**.

The **best execution criteria** are that the firm must take into account **characteristics of**:

- The client, including categorisation as retail or professional
- The client order
- The financial instruments
- The execution venues

The '**best possible result**' must be determined in terms of **total consideration** – taking into account any costs, including the firm's own commissions in the case of competing execution venues, and not just quoted prices. (However, the firm is not expected to compare the result with that of clients of other firms.) Commissions structure must not discriminate between execution venues.

### 12.1.1 Order execution policy

#### Policy requirements

The firm must establish and implement an **order execution policy**, and it must monitor its effectiveness regularly.

The policy must include, for each class of financial instruments, information on different execution venues used by the firm, and the factors affecting choice of execution venue.

The firm should choose venues that enable it to obtain on a consistent basis the best possible result for execution of client orders. For each client order, the firm should apply its execution policy with a view to achieving the best possible result for the client.

If orders may be executed outside a regulated market or multilateral trading facility, this must be disclosed, and clients must give prior express consent.

A firm must be able to demonstrate to clients, on request, that it has followed its execution policy.

### 12.1.2 Client consent and clients' specific instructions

The firm must provide a **retail client** with details on its execution policy before providing the service, covering the relative importance the firm assigns to execution factors, a list of execution venues on which the firm relies, and a clear and prominent warning that **specific instructions** by the client could prevent the firm from following its execution policy steps fully.

If the client gives **specific instructions**, the firm has met its best execution obligation if it obtains the best result in following those instructions. The firm should not induce a client to gives such instructions, if they could prevent best execution from being obtained. However, the firm may invite the client to choose between execution venues.

The firm must obtain the **prior consent** of clients to its execution policy, and the policy must be **reviewed annually** and whenever there is a material change in the firm's ability to achieve the best possible result consistently from execution venues.

### 12.1.3 Portfolio management and order reception and transmission services

Firms who act as **portfolio managers** must comply with the **clients' best interests rule** when placing orders with other entities. Firms who provide a service of **receiving and transmitting orders** must do the same when transmitting orders to other entities for execution. Such firms must:

- Take all reasonable steps to obtain the best possible result for clients
- Establish and maintain a policy to enable it to do so, and monitor its effectiveness
- Provide appropriate information to clients on the policy
- Review the policy annually or whenever there is a material change affecting the firm's ability to continue to obtain the best possible result for clients

### 12.1.4 Dealing ahead of publication (front running)

More commonly known as 'front running of research', this rule outlines the circumstances in which the firm can use its knowledge of the publication of research prior to its release to customers. For example, when might the firm, which is just about to publish a buy recommendation to customers, use this research for its proprietary trading?

If a firm or its associate intends to publish a written recommendation or a piece of research or analysis to customers relating to designated investments, the firm must:

- Not undertake any own account transactions in the relevant investment (or related investment, e.g. derivatives), and
- Take all reasonable steps to ensure that its associates do not undertake any own account transactions in the relevant security (or related investment)

Until the customers for whom the research was principally intended have had a reasonable opportunity to act upon it.

As may be seen, the starting point of the rule is to prohibit such transactions.

Two exceptions:

- Front running is allowed if the firm or its associate is market making in good faith
- Dealing is allowed to satisfy an unsolicited customer order

### 12.1.5 Aggregation and allocation

Aggregation is the practice of grouping together orders with those of other customers and of the firm itself. Although common in many markets, it is more prevalent in equity dealings where brokers bundle together the small orders of many customers.

A firm may not aggregate a customer order with an own account order or with another client's order unless the following two conditions are satisfied.

- It is not likely to disadvantage each customer.
- Any possible disadvantage has been disclosed to each customer, either orally or in writing. This can be done specifically on each transaction, or generally in the terms of business letter.

A danger of such aggregation is that, while it must always be thought to be in the best overall interests of customers generally, it may of course, disadvantage some. Hence, there is a requirement to disclose the possible disadvantage to each customer.

### 12.1.6 Fair allocation

This rule requires that no unfair preference be given to any of those for whom the firm dealt. Fairness is gauged in two ways price and size.

The rule requires that customer orders are prioritised unless the firm can demonstrate on reasonable grounds that the transaction would not have happened on such favourable terms (or indeed at all) without the firm's involvement.

#### Timely allocation

Having dealt with fair allocation, consideration needs to be given to timely allocation. Where a firm has aggregated a customer order with its own or other clients' orders, it must promptly (normally T+1) allocate back to the customer.

### 12.1.7 Preventing Conflicts of interest and Personal account dealing

Personal account dealing relates to trades undertaken by the staff of a regulated business for themselves. Such trades can create **conflicts of interest** between staff and customers.

A firm conducting **designated investment business** must establish, implement and maintain adequate **arrangements** aimed at preventing employees who are involved in activities where a conflict of interest could occur, or who has access to inside information, from:

- Entering into a transaction which is prohibited under the **Market Abuse Directive**, or which involves misuse or improper disclosure of confidential information, or conflicts with an obligation of the firm to a customer under the regulatory system
- Except in the course of his job, advising or procuring anyone else to enter into such a transaction
- Except in the course of his job, disclosing any information or opinion to another person if the person disclosing it should know that, as a result, the other person would be likely to enter into such a transaction or advise or procure another to enter into such a transaction

The **firm's arrangements** under these provisions must be designed to ensure that:

- All relevant persons (staff involved) are aware of the personal dealing restrictions
- The firm is informed promptly of any personal transaction
- A service provider to whom activities are outsourced maintain a record of personal transactions and provides it to the firm promptly on request
- A record is kept of personal transactions notified to the firm or identified by it, including any related authorisation or prohibition


BPP LEARNING MEDIA

The rule on personal account dealing is **disapplied** for personal transactions:

- Under a discretionary portfolio management service where there has been no prior communication between the portfolio manager and the person for whom the transaction is executed
- In UCITS collective undertakings (e.g. OEICs and unit trusts) where the person is not involved in its management
- In life policies
- For successive personal transactions where there were prior instructions in force, nor to the termination of the instruction provided that no financial instruments are sold at the same time

# Chapter Roundup

## Characteristics

- The shareholders of the company are the owners of the company. As the owners they have a right to vote and to dividend payments when they are distributed.
- UK companies may be either public companies (who can issue shares to the public), or private companies (who can not issue shares to the public).
- The majority of shares are 'ordinary' shares with equal rights to votes and to share in the profits.
- Preference shares pay a fixed dividend which must be paid before the company can pay out an ordinary dividend. They also have priority over ordinary shareholders in the event of a company winding up. They have no voting rights unless there is five years dividend arrears. Sub classes include
  - Redeemable.
  - Convertible.
  - Participating.
- ADRs allow UK shares to trade in the US, GDRs allow shares listed in one country to be traded in another.
- There are several ways of issuing new shares to investors. These include an offer for subscription, an offer for sale, a placing and an intermediaries offer.
- The Companies Acts provide existing shareholders with first rights over any new shares that are issued (pre-emption rights).
- Bonus issues and stock splits are methods of cosmetically reducing the share price to increase liquidity in the shares, they do not raise finance.
- Rights issues are issue to current shareholders at a discount to the current share price. They do raise finance.
- You must be able to calculate the theoretical price after an issue.

## Transaction costs

| Cost | Purchase transaction | Sale transaction |
|---|---|---|
| Commission | Yes – negotiable | Yes – negotiable |
| Stamp duty/SDRT* | 0.5% | N/A |
| PTM Levey | £1.00 Transactions > £10,000 | |

* Stamp duty is payable on certificated transfers and is *rounded up* to the nearest £5. SDRT is payable on electronically registered transfers and is rounded to the *nearest* 1p.

- MTF = Multi-lateral trading facility introduced by MiFID that is expected to reduce equity transaction costs.
- $\text{Conversion prem. or dic.} = \left(\frac{\text{Conversion Ration} \times \text{Market Price of Convertible Shares} - 1}{\text{Market Price of Ordinary Shares}} - 1\right) \times 100$
- Dividends on UK shares are received net of a 10% tax credit.
- Warrants are similar to call options and give the right but not the obligation to buy a company share at a given price.
- Warrant exercise will result in the issue of a new share by the issuing company (unlike a call option).

- Warrants are issued by the company in whose shares the warrant is written, covered warrants are issued by a third party.
- American Depositary Receipts (ADRS) are:
  - Bearer form
  - Denominated in US dollars
  - Pay dividends in US dollars
  - Trade on numerous exchanges
  - May trade 'pre-release' for up to three months
  - Settle T + 3
- UKLA listing requirements for the official list are that:
  - The company must offer at least £700,000 in shares (and £200,000 in debt if they issue debt).
  - Shares must be freely transferable.
  - Shares must be sufficiently marketable (at least 25% of the company's capital is available for public purchase).
  - The issue of warrants is limited to 20% of existing capital base.
- UK takeovers are monitored by the Panel on Takeovers and Mergers (POTAM), which issues six general principles in its 'blue book'.
- Member firms of an exchange act as broker dealers (dual capacity).
- The Alternative Investment Market (AIM) admission rules are:
  - All securities must be **freely transferable**.
  - AIM companies must have a **Nominated Advisor** (NOMAD), **approved by the LSE**, to advise the directors on their responsibilities, and guide them through the AIM process. The NOMAD is retained to advise the directors once an AIM listing is granted.
  - AIM companies must at all times have a nominated broker (who must be an Exchange Member) to support trading in the company's shares, and to assist in pricing and marketing in a flotation.
- A prospectus may not be required in certain circumstances including
  - A bonus or capitalisation issue.
  - The exercise of conversion rights or warrants.
  - Shares issued in place of shares already listed, so long as the nominal value in total does not increase as a result, e.g. a share split or consolidation.
  - Small issues of securities, which would not increase the class of securities in issue by 10% or more, or by more than €100,000 consideration over a year.
  - Where offer is made only to qualified investors (QIs), or to fewer than 100 persons per EU Member state, excluding qualified investors. This exemption is only available when securities are not being admitted to trading on a regulated market, e.g. AIM placings.
  - Issues of wholesale securities, i.e. where the minimum subscription or denomination of the securities is €50,000. This would only realistically apply to corporate bond issues.
- IPOs (initial public offerings) involve the offer of new shares to new investors.

# Test Your Knowledge

*Check your knowledge of the chapter here, without referring back to the text.*

1. Name three special types of preference share.

2. What is an ADR?

3. An introduction is a method of raising finance. *True or false?*

4. 20,000 shares are bought in A plc at a price of 56p and 4,000 are sold in B plc at a price of £3.20. If the broker charges 0.2% commission what is the total cost and net revenue from each transaction.

5. What is the minimum offer of equity for a company wishing to be admitted to the official list?

6. What are the objectives of the CISI?

7. What is a 'NOMAD'?

8. What are the three segments to the PLUS market?

9. What is required for a natural person to be included on the Qualified Investor Register?

# Test Your Knowledge: Answers

1. Participating, conversion and redemption.

   **(See Section 1.2.2)**

2. American Depository Receipt.

   **(See Section 1.7)**

3. False. An introduction merely allows a company's shares to be traded on the market.

   **(See Section 6.5.1)**

4. **A plc**

| | | £ |
|---|---|---|
| Cost of shares (20,000 × 56p) | | 11,200.00 |
| Add: | Broker fee (11,200 × 0.2%) | 22.40 |
| | SDRT (11,200 × 0.2%) | 56.00 |
| | PTM Levy | 1.00 |
| Total cost | | 11,279.40 |

| | | £ |
|---|---|---|
| **B plc** | | |
| Sale proceeds (4,000 × £3.20) | | 12,800.00 |
| Less: | Brokers fees paid (12,800 × 0.2%) | (25.60) |
| | PTM Levy | (1.00) |
| Net proceeds after deducting costs | | 12,773.40 |

   **(See Section 3.3.2)**

5. £700,000. (and £200,000 debt, if they chose to issue debt)

6. The Chartered Institute for Securities and Investments puts forward the charitable objectives of:

   - To promote, for the public benefit, the advancement and dissemination of knowledge in the field of securities and investments
   - To develop high ethical standards for practitioners in securities and investments and to promote such standards in the UK and overseas
   - To act as an authoritative body for the purpose of consultation and research in matters of education or public interest concerning investment in securities

   **(See Section 3.4.1)**

7. AIM companies must have a **Nominated Advisor** (NOMAD), approved by the LSE, to advise the directors on their responsibilities, and guide them through the AIM process.

   **(See Section 4.3.1)**

**8.** PLUS Listed

PLUS Quoted

PLUS Traded

**(See Section 4.3.2)**

**9.** It is necessary to meet at least two of the following three criteria to qualify for inclusion on the QIR:

1. One must have carried out transactions of a significant size (at least €1,000) on securities markets at an average frequency of, at least, ten per quarter for the last four quarters.
2. The security portfolio exceeds €0.5 million.
3. One works – or have worked for at least one year – in the financial sector in a professional position which requires knowledge of securities investment.

**(See Section 5.2)**

# 4 Settlement, Safe Custody and Prime Brokerage

## INTRODUCTION

The term settlement refers to the process of transferring ownership to the buyer and funds to the seller following a trade. The three main elements to settlement are timing, the legal documentation required to transfer ownership and the physical mechanisms required for transferring the securities.

This chapter explains settlement characteristics in more detail with focus on cum and ex-dividend periods for shares, security ownership, stamp duty, stamp duty reserve tax (SDRT), CREST and the settlement of overseas shares and bonds.

### CHAPTER CONTENTS

# Chapter Learning Objectives

## Settlement, Safe Custody and Prime Brokerage

### 4.1 Clearing, Settlement and Safe Custody

**4.1.1** **Understand** how fixed income, equity, money market and foreign exchange transactions are cleared and settled in the UK, Germany, USA and Japan:

- Principles of Delivery versus Payment (DVP) and Free Delivery
- Trade confirmation process
- Settlement periods
- International Central Securities Depositories (ICSD) - Euroclear & Clearstream International
- Exchanges

**4.1.2** **Understand** how settlement risk arises, its impact on trading and the investment process, and how it can be mitigated:

- Underlying risks: default, credit and liquidity
- Relative likelihood of settlement- based risks in developed and emerging markets
- Effect of DVP and Straight through Process (STP) automated systems
- Risk mitigation within markets and firms
- Continuous Linked Settlement

**4.1.3** **Understand** which transactions may be subject to or exempt from UK stamp duty/SDRT

**4.1.4** **Understand** the principles of safe custody, the roles of the different types of custodian, and how client assets are protected:

- Global
- Regional
- Local
- Sub custodians
- Clearing & settlement agents

**4.1.5** **Understand** the implications of registered title for certified and uncertified holdings:

- Registered title versus unregistered (bearer)
- Legal title
- Beneficial interest
- Right to participate in corporate actions

**4.1.6** **Understand** the function of nominees:

- Designated nominee accounts
- Pooled nominee accounts
- Corporate nominees
- Details in share register
- Legal ownership
- Effect on shareholder rights of using a nominee

### 4.2 Prime brokerage and equity finance

**4.2.1 Understand** the purpose, requirements and implications of securities lending:

- Benefits and risks for borrowers and lenders
- Function of market makers, intermediaries and custodians
- Effect on the lender's rights
- Effect on corporate action activity
- Collateral

**4.2.2 Understand** the purpose and main types of Prime Broker equity finance services and their impact on securities markets:

- Securities lending and borrowing
- Leverage trade execution
- Cash management
- Core settlement
- Custody
- Rehypothecation
- Repurchase agreements
- Collateralized borrowing
- Tri-party repos
- Synthetic financing

# 1 The Settlement Process

## 1.1 Introduction to clearing and settlement

Learning objective

**4.1.1 Understand** how fixed income, equity, money market and foreign exchange transactions are cleared and settled in the UK, Germany, USA and Japan: Principles of Delivery versus Payment (DVP) and free delivery, trade confirmation process, settlement periods and international Central Securities Depositaries (ICSD) – Euroclear & Clearstream, International Exchanges.

The terms clearing and clearance have exactly the same meaning. They refer to the practice post-trade and pre-settlement of defining settlement obligation and assigning responsibility for effecting settlement.

Following a trade, each counterparty submits trade instructions to a clearing house. This is an organisation that performs the gathering and matching of settlement instructions on behalf of market participants. The computerised system utilised for this purpose is called a clearing system.

The clearing house will

- Match delivery instructions with the corresponding receipt instruction
- Report the matched results to the participants

The clearing house matches both sides of the transaction. Trades that match are held in a pending file by the clearing house until settlement. If a trade does not match then it cannot settle and remedial action will be required. The problem must be resolved and the trade resubmitted to the clearing house for further matching. A pre-settlement report will be sent to the counterparties. This will list those transactions that have matched and those that remain unmatched.

Trade date is the date when the counterparties 'do the deal'. This means that dealers agree the quantity and prices of the stock and the delivery date.

Settlement date is when the stock and cash physically change hands. Intended settlement date takes place at T + 3 for UK equities, e.g. a transaction executed on a Wednesday will settle the following Monday, assuming no public holidays intervene.

There are three basic elements to any settlement regime.

- Timing.
- Legal documentation required to transfer ownership.
- Physical mechanisms for transferring the securities.

## 1.2 Settlement Agencies

A settlement agency facilitates settlement. The role and mechanics of each settlement agency vary around the world but the underlying principles and basic services are the same.

The settlement agency will assist with the pre-matching stage by collating the information from the counterparties and producing matched/unmatched reports. In order to keep high standards in the market and ensure that trades settle on time, it is imperative that matching happens on a timely basis. The settlement agency might fine the financial institutions for failing to meet matching targets.

Some settlement agencies will act as a central counterparty. Customer A will transact with Customer B but the trade will actually settle between Customer A and the settlement agency and Customer B and the settlement agency. This speeds up the matching process and assists the settlement process. It reduces risk as the central counterparty is always more reliable than a counterparty. Derivatives exchanges for futures and options always use a clearing house as a central counterparty, examples are LCH.Clearnet in the UK and Options Clearing Corporation in the United States.

Settlement agencies facilitate the securities movement because the securities are immobilised by the agency (DTCC and Euroclear) or the securities are electronic/dematerialised (CREST). The more sophisticated settlement agencies can resolve interdependent links and blockages to ensure that an optimum number of trades settle (the equivalent of a policeman directing traffic at a congested roundabout). This is known as circles within CREST.

Settlement agencies can provide additional functionality including stock borrowing/lending, processing corporate actions, collecting and paying taxes and performing reconciliations.

### 1.2.1 Euroclear UK & Ireland (formerly CRESTCo Ltd)

On 1 April 2007 CrestCo Ltd changed its name Euroclear UK and Ireland. References to 'CREST' as the company's processing system will continue until 2009/2010. Over 98% of CREST trades settle on the intended settlement date.

CREST holds securities in a dematerialised format. The CREST system maintains a cash Memorandum Account which keeps track of cash movements for each firm and cash is held outside CREST by guarantee banks. At the end of the day, there is a net receipt or payment. CREST has a special function which runs an algorithm called circles throughout the day to reduce settlement backlogs. Through CREST it is possible to reach 14 overseas Central Securities Depositaries (CSDs) using links that CREST has established through its Euroclear parent and via other relationships. The full country list is Autria, Belgium, Denmark, Finland, France, Germany, Italy, Netherlands, Norway, Portugal, Spain, Sweden, Switzerland and the USA.

In August 2006, Euroclear Uk and Ireland launched the Single Settlement Engine (SSE) which will consolidate the settlement function of al Euroclear group entities. They, in effect, have two systems supporting the core processing of the UK and Irish markets, namely the 'legacy' CREST system and the new Euroclear SSE.

### 1.2.2 Settlement in the USA

In the USA, there are two inter-related and coordinated clearance and settlement systems, one for dealer traders and the other for institutional customer transactions.

### 1.2.3 National Securities Clearing Corporation (NSCC)

Part of the DTCC group, the main function of the NSCC is to act as a checking and clearing service for dealer-traders and members of the exchange. It creates the underlying records on which transactions are settled and, where appropriate, generates book entry transfer system rather than the electronic holding.

Any securities not held in the DTCC tend to be registered in the name of a broker as nominee, theses being referred to as 'street names'. It is always possible for an individual to insist on registration in their own name, but in practice it is a very rare occurrence.

### 1.2.4 Euroclear and Clearstream

Euroclear and Clearstream both settle transactions in a large number of securities including all kinds of Eurobonds, domestic and foreign bonds, US Treasury and Agency bonds, short-term instruments (euro notes, CDs, bank bills, etc) and international and domestic equities and American/global depositary receipts. Settlement is on a T + 3 basis. Clearstream and Euroclear operate an electronic bridge between each other.

Within Euroclear and Clearstream, the stocks are physically immobilised within secure vaults in comparison to CREST where the shares are held electronically. On settlement date there is a book entry transfer to move stock from one account to another.

### 1.2.5 Euroclear Bank

The core Euroclear Bank service is the settlement of cross border securities transactions on behalf of participants. Over 210,000 different securities are accepted through Euroclear, the majority of which are domestic securities from over 32 markets.

Settlement-related services such as wholesale custody, money transfer in over 50 currencies, and securities lending and borrowing meet the changing needs of securities professionals. Moreover, all services are seamlessly integrated within the settlement process.

Collateral management opportunities are offered to Euroclear participants to help them optimise their asset usage.

Euroclear is deemed to be the market leader and is forced by competition from Clearstream to keep pace with market changes and provide innovative responses to participants' needs and make steady investments in research and development for future services.

Added value comes from the provision of timely and accurate information, delivered through flexible and rapid means of communication at a competitive cost.

### 1.2.6 Clearstream

Clearstream is part of the Deutsche Börse group. It has two divisions – Clearstream Banking Luxembourg (the international Central Securities Depository or ISCD) and Clearstream Banking Frankfurt – the German domestic CSD. Clearstream offers settlementand custody services to more than 2,500 customers in 94 countries, covering more than 150,000 domestic and internationally – traded bonds and equities. They settle half a million transactions daily across 40 markets. Acting as custodians, they take care of any rights attached to the securities that their customers keep with them.

Clearstream's core business is to ensure that cash and securities are promptly and effectively delivered against each other in clearing and settlement market transactions.

Clearstream is now a settlement location for 22 trading platforms and Central Counterparties (CCP), in addition to the trading platforms and CCP run by Deutsche Börse Group. These includes a recent link with LCH.Clearnet and two similar relationships opened in late 2003 to BrokerTec and MTS Deutscheland.

### 1.2.7 Japan

Settlement is handled by the Japan Security Depositary Centre (JASDEC). The role of clearing and central counterparty is handled by Japan Securities Clearing Corperation (JSCC). All quoted shares are in registered form and bonds can be either bearer or registered. Securities cannot be held outside Japan and therefore local safe custody facilities are obligatory for non-residents wishing to deal in Japanese securities. There are five Stock Exchanges in different cities, the Tokyo Stock Exchange being the largest. Nearly all (99% of transactions settle on T + 3 (regular settlement).

### 1.2.8 Summary of settlement

| Region | Securities | Settlement | System employed |
|---|---|---|---|
| UK | Gilts<br>Listed Equities<br>Corporate bonds | T + 1<br>T + 3 | Euroclear UK & Ireland ~ (CREST) |
| US | Government bonds<br>Listed Equities | T + 1<br>T + 3 | DTCC |
| EU | Government bonds<br>Listed German equities | T + 1<br>T + 3 | Clearstream/Euroclear<br>Clearstream |
| Japan | Listed equities and convertible bonds<br>Japanese Government Bonds JGBs | T + 3 | JASDEC<br>Bank of Japan BOJ |

## 2 Settlement Risk

**Learning objective**

**4.1.2 Understand** how settlement risk arises, its impact on trading and the investment process, and how it can be mitigated; Underlying risks; default, credit and liquidity, relative likelihood of settlement-based risks in developed markets effect of DVP and straight through process (STP) automated systems, risk mitigation within markets and firms and continuous linked settlement.

The key to any successful settlement system must be the level of confidence and security the participants have in the process. Confidence is normally achieved through the centralisation of the settlement process into the hands of a single authority, e.g. Euroclear UK and Ireland or LCH.Clearnet. However, some counterparties will be happy to coordinate transfer of ownership between themselves (inter-office settlement).

**Cash Against Document (CAD)** is the simplest method of achieving this level of satisfaction. Under this structure, whilst the central facility or individual broker holds the cash or documents, they will not be released until both sides of the transaction are ready to settle. Therefore the seller does not relinquish their security until the cash is available to settle the transaction and *vice versa*. This is also referred to as **Delivery versus Payment (DVP)**.

In certain circumstances, e.g. where there is a relationship of trust between the two counterparties, participants will settle one part of the deal without the other side. These trades are frequently referred to as **Free Delivery or Free Payment**.

Internationally, markets are moving towards computerised book entry systems. **Book entry systems** do away with the need for documentation by holding the records of ownership on computer. Transfers between account holders are simply reflected in adjusted account balances, in much the same way as bank accounts. As such they are invariably cheaper and faster than the older paper driven systems, where individuals held certificates as evidence of their ownership of the security.

## 2.1 Settlement accounting

Custodians have **two options,** in accounting for transactions, which will produce different results in the event of delayed or failed settlement.

### Actual settlement date accounting (ASDA)

Under **Actual Settlement Date Accounting (ASDA)** sale proceeds and purchase costs are recognised in the investor's cash accounts only when the **trade actually settles**. Delays in settlement can therefore mean that either the investor retains use of the funds for longer (if a purchase) or does not have the expected funds available (if a sale). This latter problem could mean there are insufficient funds available to settle other purchase transactions and thereafter cause additional failed settlement. Here, the **investor** carries the **risk of delayed settlement**.

### Contractual settlement date accounting (CSDA)

Under Contractual Settlement Date Accounting (CSDA), the investor's cash accounts are debited or credited with good value on the **intended settlement date**, regardless of the actual settlement date. This will remove, to some extent, causes of further failed settlement. Here, the **custodian** carries the **risk of delayed settlement**.

However, the custodian may **not** provide CSDA where

- A country has a sub-standard settlement infrastructure.
- Investors' instructions are received late.
- Investors attempt to sell securities they do not have available to deliver (i.e. short selling).

The custodian may also reserve the right to reverse entries that do not actually settle within a given time limit after the contractual settlement date.

## 2.2 Processing settlement instructions

With the move to T + 3 settlement for all securities, and the difficulty of different time zones for global investors and custodians, settlement instructions must be processed quickly to avoid settlement delays. The industry has moved towards electronic instruction, e.g. the **SWIFT** (Society for Worldwide Interbank Financial Telecommunications) **automated telecommunication system**, where investors send settlement instructions to their global custodian via an electronic link (**Electronic Trade Confirmation**). The global custodian then passes the instruction onto its sub-custodian in the local market.

The industry is currently working to allow **'straight through processing'**. This uses common technology and standardised settlement instructions, and aims to allow investor instructions to be passed straight to the custodian's computer system without further intervention.

In addition, the G30 have recommended that securities should have an international identification code and that all countries should adopt the International Securities Identification Numbering System (**ISIN**). This removes language barriers to global settlement.

## 2.3 Continuous Linked Settlement (CLS)

Whilst volumes in global FX transactions have increased considerably in recent times, the method of settlement has remained largely the same. Before Continuous Linked Settlement (CLS), each side of a trade was paid separately. Taking time zone differences into account, this increased the risk of either party defaulting.

This is known as **Herstatt risk**, after Bankhaus Herstatt, a small German bank which went into liquidation in 1974. Its accounts were frozen after it had received amounts in US dollars for foreign exchange transactions, but before it had made its own payments on the Deutschmark side of the trades, resulting in considerable losses for several counterparties.

CLS is a means of settling foreign exchange transactions finally and irrevocably. It eliminates settlement risk by linking the receipt of one currency to the payment of the other. It also improves liquidity management, reduces operational banking costs and improves operational efficiency and effectiveness.

CLS aims to settle both currency legs of a trade simultaneously, irrespective of time zones, through **CLS Bank**, which has been established in New York. In order to settle transactions directly within the system, banks must be Settlement Members of CLS. However, smaller banks can use the system indirectly by settling their trades via a CLS member bank.

A brief outline of the different stages in the process is as follows.

1. Settlement members input instructions for amounts to be settled on a given day in the CLS system. This will result in each member having a net amount payable or receivable daily in each currency. Members must submit their instructions by 06:30 CET (Central European Time). At this time members receive a schedule of payments that they must make that day.
2. Settlement members pay in the net funds at the relevant central banks. For the UK, such payments are made through the Bank of England via CHAPS (Clearing Houses Automated Payment System). Payments may be made from 07:00 CET
3. As funds are received, the CLS Bank settles trades on a **Payment Versus Payment** (**PVP**) basis, by ensuring that strict settlement criteria have been met. Essentially, a trade will not settle if it would result in either counterparty having a negative balance in any currency. As this will mean that some trades cannot settle immediately, such trades are put back in the queue and continually revisited until settlement is possible.
4. After the settlement process has been completed each day, net funds receivable by settlement members in each currency are disbursed back to settlement members via the central banks.

# 3 Services Provided by Custodians

**Learning objective**

**4.1.4 Understand** the principles of safe custody, the roles of the different types of custodian, and how client assets are protected: Global, Regional, Local, Sub custodians, Clearing & settlement agents

A custodian provides clients with custody, settlement and reporting services for all classes of financial instrument. As the name suggests, it is the primary role of the custodian to protect the clients' assets. The custodian must have rigorous security measures in place.

Core services are the basic standardised services which a custodian will offer. These may be classified as

- Settlement arrangements, facilitated by the custodian who manages delivery and receipt of securities and also management of cash flows and payments.
- Safekeeping of the clients' assets.
- Following up corporate actions on behalf of the client, e.g. dividend payments, voting rights and takeovers.
- Reporting and regulatory obligations on clients' behalf.

- Withholding tax reclamation, and other tax services.
- Registering and ensuring correct legal title of securities.

Custodians may offer additional or value-added services to clients. These will include services such as stock lending, investment accounting and cross-border proxy voting.

Investors have several options available in structuring their custody services.

Given that investors are likely to invest in a number of markets, both local and international, they are likely to require expert custody knowledge in all of these markets. As such a number of separate custodians may be required.

| | |
|---|---|
| **Domestic Custodian Network** | A different local custodian for each country in which assets are held |
| **Regional Custodian Network** | A custodian for each geographic region (e.g. Europe) where assets are held |
| **Global Custodian Network** | A typical global custodian network is shown below |

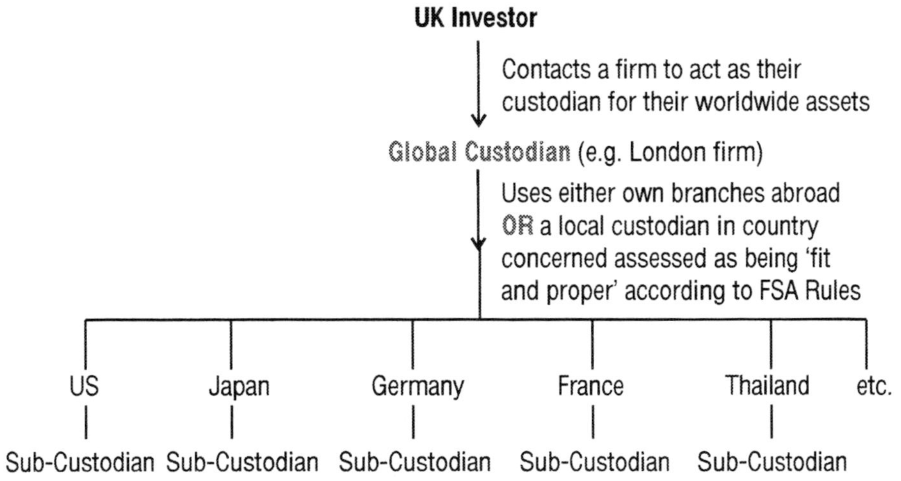


## 3.1 Global custodians

The use of a global custodian will have the advantages for the investor of no language or time zone problems, consolidated reporting and asset reconciliation, and one communication system. However, it will also mean concentration of risk using a single provider, because there is no direct relationship with local custodians in overseas markets.

## 3.2 Sub-custodian

Sub Custodians will offer services to global custodians in the local markets. The global custodian will need specific local contacts and market information, as well as administrative (and local language) skills to operate in local markets. The operation of sub custodians may be possible in one of the global custodians' local offices where possible, or where not they may make use of either, regional custodians or local custodians.

### 3.3 Regional custodian

Regional custodians provide services across a region such as Eastern Europe, or Asia-Pacific. The benefits of employing a regional custodian would include:

- While global custodians work over a large number of markets the regional custodian will be able to operate in a local time zone and with some regional knowledge.
- It may be able to offer consistent reporting, and market information in a standard format.
- Given that it is operating on a larger scale than any one local custodian, it will be able to employ economies of scale to its business. In doing so it will be able to offer a higher level of technology and lower costs.
- The regional custodian being a larger organisation than the local custodians, may be able to commend a higher credit rating.

### 3.4 Local custodian

Local custodians focus their attention solely upon one particular market.

Their key advantage is their detailed local knowledge. This may be of particular value in developing markets, where local politics, regulations and certain unique factors may require relationships and detailed knowledge.

Due to their relatively small size however, local custodians may not be able to employ the technology or economies of scale of larger global custodians. Due to this, global custodians have become relatively fewer in number in recent years.

## 4 Security Ownership

**Learning objective**

4.1.5 **Understand** the implications of registered title for certified and uncertified holdings: Registered title versus unregistered (bearer), Legal title, Beneficial interest and Right to participate in corporate actions.

### Introduction

Securities can exist in either **registered** or **bearer form**.

**Registered form** means it is the investors' appearance on the register (a formal legal document maintained by the company registrar) which entitles them to the benefits attached to the share, e.g. right to dividend, vote at an AGM, rights and bonus issues, sell shares, etc. Registered form is the most common form of ownership used in the UK. The company may also send the investor a share certificate, but this is just ***prima facie*** **evidence** of ownership.

By contrast, **bearer form** of ownership means that the legal owner is the person holding the bearer document. An example of a bearer security is a Eurobond. Bearer instruments carry with them settlement problems of

- Security – they are normally immobilised at an International Central Securities Depository (ICSD), e.g. Euroclear or Clearstream.
- Inconvenience for claiming dividends – dividends are normally distributed via a book entry system operated by Euroclear or Clearstream.

Many investors, for convenience, will allow their broker or custodian to hold their shares in a **nominee account**. This is where the custodian's nominee is registered as the **legal owner** on the company register, but the **investor** is recorded as the **beneficial owner** of the shares by the custodian.

The custodian's nominee is therefore the legal owner in name only and the investor retains all other beneficial rights, e.g. with regard to dividends and voting.

## 4.1 Settlement agencies

A settlement agency facilitates settlement. The role and mechanics of each settlement agency vary around the world but the underlying principles and basic services are the same.

The settlement agency will assist with the pre-matching stage by collating the information from the counterparties and producing matched/unmatched reports. In order to keep high standards in the market and ensure that trades settle on time, it is imperative that matching happens on a timely basis. The settlement agency might fine the financial institutions for failing to meet matching targets.

Some settlement agencies will act as a central counterparty. Customer A will transact with Customer B but the trade will actually settle between Customer A and the settlement agency and Customer B and the settlement agency. This speeds up the matching process and assists the settlement process. It reduces risk as the central counterparty is always more reliable than a counterparty. Derivatives exchanges for futures and options always use a clearing house as a central counterparty, examples are LCH.Clearnet in the UK and Options Clearing Corporation in the United States.

Settlement agencies facilitate the securities movement because the securities are immobilised by the agency (DTCC and Euroclear) or the securities are electronic/dematerialised (Euroclear UK and Ireland). The more sophisticated settlement agencies can resolve interdependent links and blockages to ensure that an optimum number of trades settle (the equivalent of a policeman directing traffic at a congested roundabout). This is known as circles within Euroclear UK and Ireland.

Settlement agencies can provide additional functionality including stock borrowing/lending, processing corporate actions, collecting and paying taxes and performing reconciliations.

## 4.2 Euroclear UK and Ireland (formerly CREST Co Ltd)

On 1 April 2007 CREST Co Ltd changed its name to Euroclear UK and Ireland. It is a Recognised Clearing House regulated by the FSA, and is the UK's electronic delivery versus payment book entry settlement system. References to 'CREST' as the company's processing system will continue until 2009.

CREST holds securities in a dematerialised format. The CREST system maintains a Cash Memorandum Account which keeps track of cash movements for each firm in the major currencies (US $, £ and €). The cash itself is held outside CREST by guarantee banks. At the end of the day, there is a net receipt or payment in relation to all of a CREST member's trades made between these payment banks. CREST has a special function which runs an algorithm called circles throughout the day to reduce settlement backlogs. Through CREST it is possible to reach 14 overseas Central Securities Depositaries (CSDs) using links that CREST has established through its Euroclear parent and via other relationships.

In August 2006, Euroclear UK and Ireland launched the Single Settlement Engine (SSE) which will consolidate the settlement function of all Euroclear group entities. They, in effect, have two systems supporting the core processing of the UK and Irish markets, namely the 'legacy' CREST system and the new Euroclear SSE.

## 4.3 LCH.Clearnet

Although LCH.Clearnet is the settlement agency for the UK derivatives market, its role in the securities market is as a **central counterparty**. This means that it acts as the buyer to every seller, and the seller to every buyer in all SETS matched orders. This provides anonymity and reduced credit risk. Settlement still takes place through CREST but as two separate principal-to-principal trades between the original buyers and LCH, and the original sellers and LCH. In order to manage this credit risk, LCH.Clearnet takes a deposit (known as a margin) from each party.

## 4.4 Settlement in the USA and Europe

### USA

In the USA, there are two inter-related and coordinated clearance and settlement systems, one for dealer traders and the other for institutional customer transactions.

### 4.4.1 National Securities Clearing Corporation (NSCC)

Part of the DTCC group, the main function of the NSCC is to act as a checking and clearing service for dealer-traders and members of the exchange. It creates the underlying records on which transactions are settled and, where appropriate, generates book entry transfer system rather than the electronic holding.

Any securities not held in the DTCC tend to be registered in the name of a broker as nominee, theses being referred to as 'street names'. It is always possible for an individual to insist on registration in their own name, but in practice it is a very rare occurrence.

### Europe

Euroclear and Clearstream both settle transactions in a large number of securities including all kinds of Eurobonds, domestic and foreign bonds, US Treasury and Agency bonds, short-term instruments (euro notes, CDs, bank bills, etc) and international and domestic equities and American/global depositary receipts. Settlement is on a T + 3 basis. Clearstream and Euroclear operate an electronic bridge between each other to allow for reconciliations of assets held at either bank.

Within Euroclear and Clearstream, the stocks are physically immobilised within secure vaults in comparison to CREST where the shares are held electronically. On settlement date there is a pool entry transfer to move stock from one account to another.

### 4.4.2 Euroclear Bank

The Euroclear Bank is the settlement arm of the German Deutsche Borse which is based in Luxemburg,. Its primary service is the settlement of cross border securities transactions on behalf of participants. Over 210,000 different securities are accepted through Euroclear, the majority of which are domestic securities from over 32 markets.

Settlement-related services such as wholesale custody, money transfer in many currencies collateral management, and securities lending and borrowing are integrated within the settlement process.

### 4.4.3 Clearstream

Clearstream is part of the Deutsche Börse group. It has two divisions-Clearstream Banking Luxembourg (the international Central Securities Depository or ISCD) and Clearstream Banking Frankfurt – the German domestic CSD. As with Euroclear, Clearstream offers settlement and custody services for major countries, domestic and internationally-traded bonds and equities.

Clearstream's core business is to ensure that cash and securities are promptly and effectively delivered against each other in clearing and settlement market transactions. Acting as custodians, they take care of any rights attached to the securities that their customers keep with them.

Clearstream is now a settlement location for 22 trading platforms and Central Counterparties (CCP), in addition to the trading platforms and CCP run by Deutsche Börse Group. These includes a recent link with LCH. Clearnet and two similar relationships opened in late 2003 to BrokerTec and MTS Deutschland.

### 4.4.4 Settlement in Japan

Settlement is handled by the Japan Securities Depository Center (JASDEC). The role of clearing and central counterparty is handled by Japan Securities Clearing Corporation (JSCC). All quoted shares are in registered form and bonds can be either bearer or registered. Securities cannot be held outside Japan and therefore local safe custody facilities are obligatory for non-residents wishing to deal in Japanese securities. There are eight Stock Exchanges in different cities, the Tokyo Stock Exchange being the largest. Nearly all transactions settle on a T + 3 basis.

### 4.4.5 Settlement summary

| Country | Standard Settlement for Bonds | Standard Settlement for Equity | Main Clearing House |
|---|---|---|---|
| US | T + 1 (T-bond) | T + 3 | Depository Trust Clearing Corporation (DTCC) |
| Germany | T + 3 | T + 2<br>T + 3 | Deutsche Börse Clearing/Clearstream |
| France | T + 3 (OAT)<br>T + 1 (BTAN domestic) | T + 3 | Euroclear France |
| Japan | T + 3 (JGB) | T + 3 | Japan Securities Depository Center (JASDEC) |
| UK | T + 1 (Gilts)<br>T + 3 (Corporate bonds) | T + 3 Secondary market<br>T + 1 New issues<br>T + 1 Rights issues | Euroclear UK and Ireland (CREST) |

# 5 Nominee Accounts

Learning objective

**4.1.6 Understand** the function of nominees: designated nominee accounts, pooled nominee accounts, corporate nominees, details in share register, legal ownership and effect on shareholder rights of using a nominee.

Nominee accounts can be in two forms.

| Pooled Nominee (also known as omnibus) | Individual Designation (also known as segregation) |
|---|---|
| The investor's shares are pooled into a single nominee holding held by the custodian, with separation of ownership recorded only within the custodian's records. | The custodian holds the investor's shares in a separate nominee registered shareholding for each investor. |
| The custodian's nominee name appears on the register, **not** the investor's. The investor is the beneficial owner. | The nominee is listed on the share register as being the legal owner with a specific designation for each client (e.g. an account number). The investor is the beneficial owner. |

### 5.1 Corporate nominees

Occasionally, it will be possible for investors to hold shares in a nominee company sponsored and administered by the actual company in whose shares they are investing. This is known as a corporate nominee company. This gives the investor the benefits of using a nominee, such as enabling electronic ownership of the shares without needing an individual account within Euroclear UK and Ireland, whilst maintaining a direct line of communication between the company and the investor for corporate actions, distribution of accounts, etc.

## 6 Stamp Duty and Stamp Duty Reserve Tax (SDRT) (UK)

Learning objective

**4.1.3 Understand** which transactions may be subject to, or exempt from UK stamp duty / SDRT.

The purpose of stamp duty is to tax the transfer of property between individuals. For example, with regard to certificated shares, the tax is **payable by the buyer** and is charged at a rate of **0.5%** of the consideration **rounded up** to the **next £5**. The legislation refers to the rate as **£5 per £1,000 of the consideration or any part thereof**.

**NB:** Broker's fees are **not** included in the calculation of stamp duty.

### Example

| | | (£) |
|---|---|---|
| Consideration (before broker's charges) | = | 15,030.00 |
| **Stamp duty** payable = 0.5% × £15,030 | = | 75.15 |
| Rounded up | = | **80.00** |

The buyer will send a stock transfer form and the share certificate to HM Revenue and Customs (HMRC) in order to pay the stamp duty, before passing the documents to the Registrar.

### 6.1 Stamp duty reserve tax (SDRT)

Stamp Duty Reserve Tax (SDRT) is a tax that complements the stamp duty provisions and is designed to cover transfers not envisaged by the original legislation (such as the uncertificated transfer of shares within CREST). The rate, by contrast, is a simple 0.5% of the consideration rounded up/down to the nearest penny.

## Example

| | | (£) |
|---|---|---|
| Consideration (before broker's charges) | = | 15,030.00 |
| SDRT payable = 0.5% × £15,030 | = | **75.15** |

As both taxes are based on the amount paid, they are also known as an *'ad valorem'* tax. Note that they are **only paid by the purchaser** and not the seller.

The following table summarises the two taxes and the relevant exemptions.

## 6.2 Stamp duty summary and exemptions

| | Stamp Duty | Stamp Duty Reserve Tax |
|---|---|---|
| Payable by the buyer of | Certificated shares | Uncertificated shares in dematerialised form<br>Shares sold on the same day (so no entry appears on the register)<br>New issues in renounceable form (such as rights letters)<br>Convertible loan stock |
| Rates* | 0.5% consideration rounded up to next £5 | 0.5% consideration rounded to nearest penny |
| Persons exempt from either tax | Intermediaries*<br>Registered charities<br>Recipients of gifts | |
| Instruments exempt from either tax | Gilts<br>Sterling non-convertible UK loan stock<br>Bearer stocks**<br>Foreign registered stocks<br>Foreign mutual funds<br>Units in a unit trust<br>New issues of securities to the original owner | |

* London Stock Exchange members who are not fund managers are granted intermediary status.

** Where shares are converted into bearer depository receipts (which are exempt from stamp duty or SDRT) HMRC make a one-off charge of **1.5%** on the conversion.

It should be noted that whilst transfers of units within a unit trust **are** subject to stamp duty, this is included within the price of a unit. Hence, the fund manager charges stamp duty **within the spread** of buying and selling prices.

# 7 Security Lending

**Learning objective**

4.2.1 **Understand** the purpose, requirements and implications of securities lending: Benefits and risks for borrowers and lenders, Function of market makers, intermediaries and custodians, Effect on the lender's rights, Effect on corporate action activity and Collateral.

## 7.1 Stock lending

Stock lending is in many ways similar to sale and repo agreements (repos). It involves the temporary transfer of ownership of securities from the borrower to a lender in return for cash. It allows those in possession of securities such as funds to gain additional returns on their investments and it allows those who require securities (generally to settle trades) access to securities. The obvious difference between repos and stock lending is that repos are rewarded with interest and stock lending is done in return for a fee paid.

Stock lending is most often undertaken to engage in short selling, which has required in many jurisdictions that it be covered (e.g. Germany no longer allows naked short selling). This means that a short sale will be preceded by the borrowing of shares before they are sold.

The International Securities Lending Association (ISLA) discuss the benefits of stock lending and describe benefits as being:

- To ensure settlement of trades can take place
- To facilitate market making and other trading activities, such as hedging and short selling.

They further describe that:

'Securities lending plays an important role in providing liquidity for the market by facilitating price formation and high settlement success helping to ensure that the financial markets operate efficiently.'

From the lenders perspective:

'Securities lending can be used by certain investors as a way of deriving additional income from their investment portfolios.'

To facilitate this process in the market a service is offered by Stock borrowing and lending intermediaries.

Stock Borrowing and Lending Intermediaries (SBLIs) provide a service allowing market makers to borrow securities in order to settle a 'short' transaction, i.e. selling shares they do not own. The stock is generally borrowed from investors or fund who hold the stock. The lender will charge a fee for the loan of the stock and will retain the rights to receive dividends during the lending period.

In determining appropriate terms and conditions when lending stock, the firm should take into account the specific instructions of customers as well as the requirements of individual markets where lending takes place.

Documentation should also be in place with borrowing counterparties setting out terms and conditions which are appropriate, taking into account

- The customers whose safe custody investments are being lent.
- The markets in which lending takes place (e.g. by reference to the Stock Lending and Repo Committee's Stock Borrowing and Lending Code of Guidance).
- The risks involved in the transaction.
- Other circumstances of the transaction.

If assets are pooled, the firm must ensure that either all customers have consented to assets being lent out, or only assets belonging to customers who have consented can be lent out. Where the custody or settlement system operates an 'automatic' stock lending programme, the firm should maintain a separate account or be able to demonstrate that it maintains adequate systems to differentiate between the safe custody investments of those customers who have not consented to stock lending activity and the designated investments of those that have consented.

Where collateral is required from the borrower, the firm should **consider whether the collateral should be provided in advance**, given the circumstances of the transaction and normal practice in the relevant market. The level and type of collateral should take account of the creditworthiness of the borrower and the market risks associated with the particular collateral.

Any cash or custody assets held in favour of a **customer** for stock lending activity must be held in accordance with the client money rules or custody rules. This includes dividends, stock lending fees and any other payments received in relation to stock lending.

### 7.1.1 Lender's rights

The lender of stock will essentially transfer all rights of ownership to the borrower. This means that the borrower will:

- Receive dividends or coupons – although most lending agreements require 'manufactured dividends' where payments must be transferred to the lender.
- Have voting rights as the legal owner – if the lender wishes to vote they must arrange return of the security before the vote takes place.
- Corporate actions such as rights issues become the decision of the borrower – arrangements are generally made to transfer these rights back to the lender.
- Need to consider tax implications which vary from country to country

### 7.1.2 Global Master Securities Lending Agreement

The Global Master Securities Lending Agreement (GMSLA) has been constructed to provide standardised securities lending terms and conditions in line with English law.

### 7.1.3 The International Securities Lending Association (ISLA)

The International Securities Lending Association (ISLA) is a trade association established in 1989 to represent the common interests of participants in the securities lending industry. It describes its aims for 2009/2010 on its website as being:

- Working with regulators to provide a safe and efficient framework for securities lending.
- Opening up new markets for securities lending.
- Providing information to members about securities lending market developments.
- Developing good industry practices.
- Enhancing the public profile of the securities lending industry.
- Fostering good communication and cooperation with other trade associations.
- Completing ISLA's review of the GMSLA and promoting use of the Agreement.
- Implementing ISLA's model for Agent Lender Disclosure in Europe to meet the needs of securities borrowers under Basel II.

#### 7.1.4 The Securities Lending and Repo Committee (SLRC)

The SLRC has been in existence since 1990, and aims to promote discussion and good practice in the world of stock lending. As described on its website:

'It is a UK-based committee of international repo and securities lending practitioners and representatives of trade organisations, together with bodies such as Euroclear UK and Ireland, the UK Debt Management Office, the London Stock Exchange, and the Financial Services Authority. The committee provides a forum in which structural (including legal) developments in the relevant markets can be discussed by practitioners and the authorities. It continues to be chaired and administered by the Bank of England.'

### 7.2 The Committee on Payment and Settlement Systems (CPSS)

The Bank for International Settlement (BIS) is an international organisation, and has the aim of improving international monetary and financial co-operation. The BIS states on its website that it achieves this aims by acting as: '

- a forum to promote discussion and policy analysis among central banks and within the international financial community
- a centre for economic and monetary research
- a prime counterparty for central banks in their financial transactions
- agent or trustee in connection with international financial operations

The head office is in Basel, Switzerland and there are two representative offices: in the Hong Kong Special Administrative Region of the People's Republic of China and in Mexico City.'

The Committee on payment and settlement systems (CPSS) is a part of the BIS, and in its own words, aims to strengthen 'the financial market infrastructure through promoting sound and efficient payment and settlement systems. The CPSS is a standard stetting body for payment and securities settlement systems. It also serves as a forum for central banks to monitor and analyse developments in domestic payment, settlement and clearing systems as well as in cross-border and multicurrency settlement schemes.' The CPSS / IOSCO have published have published the 'Core principles for systematically important payment systems' and 'recommendations for central couterparties'. In doing so the CPSS states that 'the Committee has contributed to the set of standards, codes and best practices that are deemed essential for strengthening the financial architecture worldwide.'

## 8 PRIME BROKERAGE

| Learning objective | |
|---|---|
| | **4.2.2 Understand** the purpose and main types of prime broker equity finance services and their impact on securities markets: securities lending and borrowing, leverage trade execution, cash management, core settlement, custody, rehypothecation, repurchase agreements, collateralized borrowing, tri-party repos and synthetic financing. |

Prime brokerage describes the bundle of services offered by investment banks to hedge funds. The main benefit of prime brokerage is that it offers a central clearing facility and allows the netting off of collateral for those deals handled by the prime broker.

The prime brokerage services generally offered include:

- Leverage trade execution
- Securities borrowing and lending
- Global custody (including clearing and asset servicing)


BPP LEARNING MEDIA

- Cash management
- Core settlement

Prime brokers will offer a number of ways to raise finance for their hedge fund clients.

## 8.1 Repurchase agreements

A **repurchase agreement** (or repos) allows secured lending, with securities being sold and then repurchased at a later date, with interest being paid to the lender of the cash. The use of securities in the lending agreements adds protection to the lender, and if the borrower fails to pay, then the lender will inherit ownership of the securities.

The cash borrower will be able to get access to funds via a repo which will be considerably cheaper than through unsecured borrowing. Where the value of the securities rises or falls outside a pre-agreed band then **variation margin** is paid to ensure that the value of the money borrowed remains equivalent to the securities provided.

## 8.2 Rehypothecation (tri-party repos)

Repo agreements arranged between two counterparties directly are referred to as direct repos. Direct repos have the inherent risk of default and to avoid this the use of the tri-party repo has become more common. A tri-party agent acts as a counterparty to both borrower and lender. They manage the cash and securities transfer between counterparties and ensure that both counterparties are fully collateralised at all times, managing variation payments as required.

## 8.3 Stock borrowing and lending

Funds with short positions may require securities to be borrowed to cover the fund's position. This together with lending the fund's long positions can be facilitated by prime brokers. The prime brokers may also offer fund lending to bring additional returns to a portfolio.

## 8.4 Synthetic financing

This is the process whereby the prime broker will manufacture exposure to a particular security without having to buy or sell the security itself.

The prime broker will package together derivatives such as swaps or options, into a **synthetic product** that mirrors the characteristics of an underlying asset.

Synthetic financing is popular with hedge funds as it can give them exposure to specific assets at a fraction of the cost and can have significant tax benefits.

## 8.5 Collateralised borrowing

The prime broker will advance cash to hedge fund clients against the security of a fixed charge over the fund's portfolio. This is a useful source of funds for the broker's clients because security provided, in the form of their portfolio, can dramatically reduce borrowing costs.

# Chapter Roundup

- A Clearing House will match delivery instructions with corresponding receipt instructions and will report matched results to the participants.
- There are three elements to the settlement regime: timing, legal documentation and the physical mechanisms for transferring securities.
- There are two methods of achieving satisfactory settlement: Cash Against Document (CAD) also known as Delivery Versus Payment (DVP) when both sides of the transaction settle simultaneously. When each side of a deal is settled independently, it is known as Free Delivery of Free Payment.
- The main overseas clearing houses are:
  - US – Depositary Trust Clearing Corporation (DTCC)
  - Germany – Clearstream
  - France – Euroclear France
  - Japan – Japan Securities Depository Centre (JASDEC)
- Settlement in the UK is conducted by Euroclear UK and Ireland (formerly CREST Co Ltd).
- Stamp duty is payable on certificated purchases of UK shares, whereas SDRT is payable on purchase of dematerialised shares. Both are charged at 0.5% of the consideration. Stamp duty is rounded up to the nearest £5 whereas SDRT is rounded to nearest penny.
- LCH.Clearnet acts as the central counterparty for SETS executed trades and guarantees delivery on the payment of margin.
- Foreign Exchange transactions are settled via Continuous Linked Settlement (CLS) at the CLS Bank in New York. This eliminates any risk to either party – especially Herstatt Risk. UK banks may access CLS via the Bank of England's CHAPS system.
- Custodians provide a number of core services:
  - Settlement arrangements, facilitated by the custodian who manages delivery and receipt of securities and also management of cash flows and payments.
  - Safekeeping of the clients' assets.
  - Following up corporate actions on behalf of the client, e.g. dividend payments, voting rights and takeovers.
  - Reporting and regulatory obligations on clients' behalf.
  - Withholding tax reclamation, and other tax services.
  - Registering and ensuring correct legal title of securities.
- Custodians take the form of:
  - Domestic custodians – dealing in the local market
  - Regional Custodians – Custodian for a geographical region
  - Global Custodian – A network of custodians in numerous regions
- Securities will be held in either registered or bearer form. Those held in bearer form such as Eurobonds will generally be immobilised in a depositary.
- Crest (part of Euroclear UK and Ireland, will settle in US $, £ and €.

- Nominee accounts may take the form of:
  - Pooled Nominee Accounts (Omnibus) – where investor's shares are pooled
  - Individual Designation (segregation) –Where investor shares are held separately from one another
- Stock lending is done in return for a fee.
- During Stock Lending, the Borrower will:
  - Receive dividends or coupons – although most lending agreements require 'manufactured dividends' where payments must be transferred to the lender.
  - Have voting rights as the legal owner – if the lender wishes to vote they must arrange return of the security before the vote takes place.
  - Corporate actions such as rights issues become the decision of the borrower –arrangements are generally made to transfer these rights back to the lender.
  - Need to consider tax implications which vary from country to country.
- Prime brokerage Prime brokerage describes the bundle of services offered by investment banks to hedge funds:
  - Leverage trade execution
  - Securities borrowing and lending
  - Global custody (including clearing and asset servicing)
  - Cash management

# Test Your Knowledge

*Check your knowledge of the Chapter here, without referring back to the text.*

1. What is the standard settlement time for gilts on CREST?

2. Describe an omnibus nominee.

3. Stamp duty is rounded up to what figure?

4. In which currencies may CREST securities be settled?

5. What is the name of the system used for settling foreign exchange deals?

6. What services are generally offered by a prime broker?

7. Describe the process of rehypothecation.

8. What does the SLRC stand for?

9. What is the main difference between a repo agreement and a stock lending agreement?

# Test Your Knowledge: Answers

1. Gilt settlement T + 1

   **See Section 1.2.8**

2. Omnibus refers to pooled nominee accounts, which have investor's securities pooled into a single nominee holding, held by a custodian

   **See Section 4.1.6**

3. Stamp duty is rounded up to the next £5 (and SDRT to the nearest penny)

   **See Section 4.1.3**

4. CREST can settle in sterling, euros and US $

   **See Section 4.2**

5. Continuous Linked Settlement

   **See Section 2.3**

6. Prime brokers may offer:

   - Leverage trade execution
   - Securities borrowing and lending
   - Global custody (including clearing and asset servicing)
   - Cash management

   **See Section 8**

7. A rehypothecation or tri-party agreement has tri party agents acting as a counterparty to both borrower and lender in repo agreements.

   **See Section 8.2**

8. The Securities Lending and Repo Committee or SLRC promotes good practice in the stock lending world.

   **See Section 7.5**

9. A number of differences exist but the key one is probably that the Repo agreement will return interest to the lender, while the stock lending agreement pays a fee.

   **See Section 7.1**

# 5 Securities Analysis

## INTRODUCTION

The primary purpose of financial statements is to provide a medium by which the directors can report to the shareholders on the performance of the company concerned.

The financial statements are, however, frequently used by other interested parties, such as lenders, creditors, potential investors, tax authorities and the government to help them assess their returns and the risk that they may face.

This chapter explains the purpose and format of the three main financial statements, the balance sheet, the income statement and the cash flow statement.

## CHAPTER CONTENTS

# Chapter Learning Objectives

## Securities Analysis

### 5.1 Financial Statement Analysis

**5.1.1 Understand** the purpose, structure and relevance to investors of balance sheets.

**5.1.2 Understand** the purpose, structure and relevance to investors of income statements.

**5.1.3 Understand** the purpose, structure and relevance to investors of cash flow statements.

**5.1.4 Analyse** securities using the following financial ratios:

- Liquidity
- Asset turnover
- Gearing
- Profitability
- Dividend policy

**5.1.5 Analyse** securities using the following profitability ratios:

- Net profit margin
- Equity multiplier
- Return on Capital Employed

**5.1.6 Analyse** securities using the following investor ratios:

- Earnings per share
- Price / Earnings (both historic and prospective)
- Net dividend yield
- Net dividend / interest cover

**5.1.7 Understand** the main advantages and challenges of performing financial analysis:

- Comparing companies in different countries and sectors
- Comparing different companies within the same sector
- Over-reliance on historical information
- Benefits and limitations of relying on third party research

### 5.2 Accounting for Corporate Actions

**5.2.1 Understand** the purpose and structure of corporate actions and their implications for investors:

- Stock capitalization or consolidation
- Stock and cash dividends
- Rights issues
- Open offers, offers for subscription and offers for sale
- Placings

**5.2.2** **Calculate** the theoretical effect on the issuer's share price of the following mandatory and optional corporate actions:

- Bonus/scrip
- Consolidation
- Rights issues

**5.2.3** **Analyse** the following in respect of corporate actions:

- Rationale offered by the company
- Understand the dilution effect on profitability and reported financials

# The Format and Purpose of Financial Statements

A company is a business organisation created in law which is owned by its members or shareholders.

Generally, for listed companies and larger unlisted ones, the shareholders appoint directors to manage the company on their behalf, having little involvement in the day-to-day operations of the companies themselves. The primary purpose of annual financial statements is to provide a medium enabling the directors to report to the shareholders on the performance of the company. The financial statements are, however, frequently used by other interested parties such as lenders, creditors, potential investors, tax authorities, the government, etc. to help them assess the returns they are receiving and the risks that they may face.

In June 2002, the EU adopted a regulation requiring listed companies in Member states (including the UK) to prepare their group/consolidated financial statements using 'adopted International Accounting Standards' for accounting periods beginning on or after 1st January 2005.

The exam has now switched to focusing on **International Financial Reporting Standards (IFRSs)** and their predecessors, International Accounting Standards (IASs). These can be considered to have replaced UK accounting standards in the overall context of UK GAAP, as far as listed companies are concerned.

Note that the requirement to comply with the Companies Acts remains. Furthermore, companies listed on an EU regulated exchange must also follow the Listing Rules.

# 1 The Balance Sheet

## (The statement of financial position)

Learning objective

**5.1.1** **Understand** the purpose, structure and relevance to investors of balance sheets.

### Introduction

The balance sheet is a statement of the financial position of the business at a specific point in time, such as the year-end. IAS 1 has now adopted the term 'Statement of Financial Position' to describe the balance sheet, however the adoption of this nomenclature is as yet not compulsory. (In fact the balance sheet is often referred to simply as the 'statement of financial position', although in this syllabus expect to see it referred to as the balance sheet).

It is the product of the accounting equation that, as its name suggests, it must always equate or balance.

It should always be borne in mind that it is only a picture of the company at the **specific point of time**. Each transaction impacts on the accounting equation, hence the balance sheet just after the year-end may be significantly different from that at the year-end, if a company has undertaken significant transactions between the two dates.

IAS 1 lists the required contents of a company's income statement and balance sheet. It also gives guidance on how items should be presented in the financial statements.

## 1.1 Accounting equation

### Introduction

The **accounting equation** can be stated as

Formula to learn

Assets = Equity + Liabilities

The format usually adopted presents this equation vertically with assets above equity and liabilities, rather than horizontally where they are alongside one another. In outline, an International balance sheet appears as follows.

#### Balance sheet outline

| | £'000 |
|---|---|
| **Assets** | |
| Assets | 400 |
| | 400 |
| **Equity and liabilities** | |
| Share Capital | 100 |
| Reserves | 150 |
| Liabilities | 150 |
| | 400 |

As we can see, the accounting equation holds and the balance sheet balances.

The four categories we have outlined are as follows.

## 1.2 Assets

These represent resources owned or controlled by the company and available for its use, such as inventories of goods for sale or production equipment. These can be subcategorised under two headings.

### 1.2.1 Non-current assets

Assets acquired for **continued use in the business to earn profit**, not for resale. Examples of such items would include office and production buildings, and equipment. Clearly, we intend to use these long term, not simply sell them on at a profit. The asset must have a 'life' in use of more than one year.

### 1.2.2 Current assets

Assets **acquired for conversion to cash** during the ordinary course of business (usually within one year). Examples of such assets would include inventories of goods available for sale to customers, or customers' account balances which will be settled for cash. Cash and cash equivalents (such as short term money market investments) are also defined as current assets.

### 1.2.3 Liabilities

These represent **amounts owed by the company** to outside suppliers and lenders. These too are subcategorised as

- Current liabilities – amounts falling due within one year.
- Non-current liabilities – amounts falling due after more than one year.

The purpose of the above classification is to provide a clear indication of the timescales for settlement.

### 1.2.4 Share capital

This is **money invested in the company** by shareholders, i.e. money subscribed for shares.

#### Reserves

These generally represent **profits earned and retained by the company** since it started to trade, although there may be other types of reserves, as we will see later.

Share capital and reserves 'equity' is also known as shareholders' funds.

### 1.2.5 Format

The general format for a balance sheet is prescribed in the Companies Act, with further guidance provided by IAS 1.

## XYZ plc – Balance sheet as at 31 December 2012

| **Assets** | **2011**<br>**£'000** | **2010**<br>**£'000** |
|---|---|---|
| **Non-current assets** | | |
| Tangible | 1,098 | 1,007 |
| Intangible | 20 | 30 |
| Investments | 231 | 121 |
| | 1,349 | 1,158 |
| **Current assets** | | |
| Inventories | 220 | 204 |
| Accounts receivable | 185 | 123 |
| Investments held for trading | 26 | 161 |
| Cash | 100 | 41 |
| | 531 | 529 |
| **Total assets** | 1,880 | 1,687 |
| | | |
| **Equity and liabilities** | | |
| **Equity** | | |
| Share capital (£1 NV ordinary shares) | 500 | 400 |
| Share premium | 70 | 70 |
| Revaluation reserve | 392 | 392 |
| General reserve | 160 | 157 |
| Retained earnings | 303 | 251 |
| | 1,425 | 1,270 |
| | | |
| **Non-current liabilities** | | |
| Bank loan | 200 | 150 |
| | | |
| **Current liabilities** | | |
| Accounts payable | 195 | 205 |
| Accrued expenses | 17 | 50 |
| Declared dividend | 43 | 12 |
| | 255 | 267 |
| **Total equity and liabilities** | 1,880 | 1,687 |

You will notice that the balance sheet is shown for both the current year and the previous year-end for comparison. The notes referred to above would normally provide further detailed analysis, but here they are being used to provide additional explanations of the terminology.

There are IASs which lay out the required content, but there is no IAS which lays out the order of items in the balance sheet. However the above layout is the preferred format in practice.

## 1.3 Terminology

### 1.3.1 Non-current assets

As already noted, non-current assets are assets **acquired for continued use** within the business and not for immediate resale. As we can see, these should be sub classified into:

- Tangibles
- Intangibles
- Investments

### 1.3.2 Tangible non-current assets – depreciation

These are physical assets that are used within the business over a number of years with a view to deriving some benefit from this use, e.g. through their use in the manufacture of goods for resale. They are often referred to as **'property, plant and equipment'**.

Tangible non-current assets include items such as:

- Freehold land and buildings (including buildings under construction).
- Leasehold land and buildings.
- Plant and machinery.
- Motor vehicles.
- Fixtures and fittings.

It is required by both UK and International Accounting Standards that all fixed assets that have limited useful economic lives must be **depreciated**, but what is depreciation?

Note: This does not include freehold land.

## Example

A company buys some production machinery at a cost of £60,000. It expects, from previous experience, that it will last five years, after which time it will be sold for £5,000. It will therefore cost the company £55,000 (£60,000 cost less £5,000 expected sale proceeds) to use the equipment over these five years.

Applying the matching concept, this £55,000 cost should be spread over the five years, i.e. a depreciation expense of £11,000 charged against the profit each year.

Depreciation is the method by which the cost of using the asset is matched against its related benefit. On the balance sheet fixed assets are usually stated **at net book value (NBV), i.e. cost less the accumulated depreciation provision**. Thus, at the end of each of the next five years the fixed asset will be valued in the balance sheet as follows.

| | Year 1 (£'000) | Year 2 (£'000) | Year 3 (£'000) | Year 4 (£'000) | Year 5 (£'000) |
|---|---|---|---|---|---|
| Cost | 60 | 60 | 60 | 60 | 60 |
| Accumulated depreciation provision | (11) | (22) | (33) | (44) | (55) |
| Net book value | 49 | 38 | 27 | 16 | 5 |

As we can see, the balance sheet net book value of the equipment falls by £11,000 each year (as the amount is charged as an expense – depreciation), until in Year 5 it has dropped to the estimated sales proceeds of £5,000.

Depreciation is an example of the accounting principle known as accrual or matching. Note that the depreciation charge in the income statement, of £11,000 each year, is just an accounting entry and does not appear in the cash flow statement.

A similar procedure is used for intangible non-current assets – it is referred to as 'amortisation.'

### 1.3.3 Intangible non-current assets

Intangibles are literally assets **without physical form**. They cannot be touched. They frequently represent intellectual property rights of the company, or abilities of its staff, that enable it to operate and generate profits in a way that competitors cannot.

The types of intangible assets that most frequently appear on the balance sheet are as follows.

- Development expenditure.
- Patents, licences and trademarks.
- Publishing rights and titles.
- Goodwill.
- Brands.

### 1.3.4 Goodwill

Goodwill is created by good relationships between a business and its customers as the following examples illustrate.

- By building up a reputation for high quality products or high standards of service
- By responding promptly and helpfully to queries and complaints from customers
- Through the personality of the staff and their attitude to customers

Goodwill as illustrated above while it may be very significant, is not however usually valued in the accounts of a business at all. While it has an inherent value, it does not have any objective value.

There is however a key exception to this general rule.

### 1.3.5 Purchased goodwill

When a business is purchased, they will purchase not only the long-term assets and inventory (and perhaps take over its accounts payable and receivable too) but also the goodwill of the business. Purchased goodwill is recognised in the statement of financial position because it has been paid for. It has no physical substance, and so it is an intangible non-current asset.

The goodwill shown by the purchaser in their accounts will be:

**The purchase consideration – Fair valuation of the net assets acquired.**

### 1.3.6 Investments

Where the investment is purchased with a view to holding on to for more than one year, it would be classified as non-current.

These represent long-term ownership of shares in other companies and are usually reported in the balance sheet at historical cost. The notes to the accounts will disclose the market value at the balance sheet date. Additional reporting regulations apply to significant levels of shareholdings that have caused the investments to be classified as either a subsidiary (50%+) or an associated undertaking (20%+).

### 1.3.7 Current assets

Strictly speaking, these are assets other than non-current assets, although perhaps the best description is that current assets are assets held for conversion into cash in the ordinary course of business. The distinction between a non-current asset and a current asset is not what the asset is physically, but for what purpose it is obtained and used by the business.

Current assets are subcategorised into

- **Inventories:** goods held available for sale.
- **Trade accounts receivable:** amounts owed to the company, usually as a result of selling goods on credit. (Shown net of bad and doubtful debts).
- **Prepayments** are amounts paid before the balance sheet date, which relate to the period after that date. Since we have paid the money over, but not yet received the benefit due from the expenditure, we still have an asset at the balance sheet date.
- **Investments held for trading:** shares held in the short term with the intention of reselling, e.g. short-term speculative investments.
- **Cash**.

### 1.3.8 Net Receivable Value (NRV)

As a general rule, assets should not be carried at amounts greater than those expected to be realised from their scale or use. In the case of inventories this amount could fall below cost when items are damaged or become obsolete, or where the costs to completion have increased in order to make the sale.

It is likely to be a fairly straightforward operation to value assets where they are all separately identifiable. Where assets are fungible (all items identical), however and items were purchased or produced over time and at different costs, it may be more difficult to separately identify different assets.

In instances where inventory is identical, there are three choices of how to account for the assets.

**FIFO** (first in first out)

The first in first out basis means literally what it says. i.e. we consider the first units bought to be the first sold. As a result, if we have any inventory at a particular point in time, it must represent the latest units purchased. This will lead to the inventory being the newest stock purchased, and the stock recorded as sold being the older (and in an inflationary environment) the lowest value stock. This in turn will lead to the highest reported profits.

**LIFO** (last in first out)

IAS2 does not allow LIFO to be used. US Gaap however does allow its use. It assumes that the first items taken out of inventory are the last ones purchased. This leads (the reverse of FIFO) to lower reported profits and higher reported inventory.

### AVCO (Weighted average cost)

The AVCO method uses the average cost of all inventories in stock as the cost of items going through the income statement. This results in the profits reported being between that reported under FIFO and that reported under LIFO.

In valuing current assets, the fundamental accounting concept of **prudence** is applied, in that they are valued at the lower of

- Cost.
- Net realisable value (NRV), i.e. estimated selling price less any cost incurred in order to sell.

Thus

- If the NRV exceeds cost, the asset is valued at cost, i.e. no profit is anticipated.
- If the NRV is less than cost, the asset is devalued down to NRV, i.e. a loss is recognised.

### 1.3.9 Current liabilities

Current liabilities are debts of the business that must be paid within a fairly short period of time; i.e. they are liabilities that will be liquidated in the near future.

By convention a fairly short period of time has come to be accepted as one year.

Examples of current liabilities are:

- Loans repayable within one year
- A bank overdraft, which is usually repayable on demand
- **Trade accounts payable** – these represent goods that a business has bought on credit and has yet to pay for
- Taxation payable
- **Accrued expenses** – these are expenses that have been built up by the business (such as electricity charges) but for which no invoice has yet to be received

### 1.3.10 Non-current liabilities

A non-current liability is a debt which is not payable within the 'short term' (ie it will not be liquidated shortly) and so any liability which is not current must be non-current.

A non-current liability is a debt due to someone else which has been put off until some time in the future. Just as short term by convention means one year or less, non-current means more than one year.

Examples of non-current liabilities are as follows.

- Loans which are not repayable for more than one year, such as a **bank loan**.
- Loan stock. These are securities issued by a company at a fixed rate of interest. They are repayable on agreed terms by a specified date in the future. Corporate bonds are often referred to as loan stock.

### Provisions

IAS 37 details the accounting treatment for provisions. As we saw earlier, a liability is an obligation of an enterprise to transfer economic benefits as a result of some past transaction or event. A provision is a liability where the **timing or amount** of the liability is **uncertain**.

The reason there is a distinction between liabilities, such as trade accounts payable, and provisions is due to the element of uncertainty. With a provision there is **greater uncertainty** about the timing or amount of future expenditure.

However, the probability is still that the event will happen.

### 1.3.11 Equity

Equity = Share Capital + Reserves

Equity is sometimes referred to as shareholders' funds and is made up of the share capital plus a number of reserves.

### 1.3.12 Reserves

In most countries a distinction must be made between the following.

- **Statutory reserves**, which are reserves a company is required to set up by law, and which are not available for the payment of dividends.
- **Non-statutory reserves**, which are reserves consisting of profits which are distributable as dividends, if the company so wishes.

### 1.3.13 Share capital

This represents the total **nominal value of the shares in issue** at the year-end, e.g. our company has in issue 400,000 shares, each with a £1 nominal value giving £400,000 share capital.

This is a statutory reserve and UK companies have to ascribe a nominal or par value to each share. This represents

- The **minimum value at which shares can be issued**. The company is not allowed to issue fully paid shares at a price below nominal value.
- The **limits of the liability of the shareholder**. If the company becomes insolvent, shareholders' liability is limited to any unpaid element of this nominal value. Where the share is a fully paid share, the shareholder has no more liability.
- Note there is a distinction between **issued** shares and **authorised** shares. A company may be authorised to issue 500,000 shares but only have chosen to issue 400,000 so far.

### 1.3.14 Share premium account

If a company trades profitably and retains those profits to finance expansion, then its value will grow. As a result, it will be able to raise cash in later years by issuing more shares at a price in **excess of their nominal value**, i.e. at a premium.

## Example

If a company could raise £20,000 by issuing 5,000 new £1.00 ordinary shares at a price of £4.00 each, then there is a premium of £3.00 on each share (full price of £4.00 less nominal value of £1.00).

The company must record the issue of these shares by increasing the share capital account by only the **nominal value** of the shares issued, i.e. £5,000. The premium of £15,000 must be added to the share premium account. This is a statutory reserve. The impact on the accounting equation is

| | £'000 |
|---|---|
| **Impact on assets** | |
| Cash up | +20 |
| | +20 |
| **Impact on equity** | |
| Share capital up | +5 |
| Share premium account up | +15 |
| | +20 |

Therefore, a share premium account is an account into which sums received as payment for shares in excess of their nominal value must be placed.

The share premium account can also be used when a company undertakes a bonus issue. This results in a transfer taking place between the share premium account reserve and the share capital account. This is why a bonus issue is called a capitalisation issue – there is a change in the share capital.

### 1.3.15 Revaluation reserve

Companies are permitted to revalue all assets upwards, other than goodwill, increasing assets and the revaluation reserve.

Where a company does revalue its non-current assets upwards, it would be imprudent to treat this increase in equity as part of the company's realised profits for the year. It has not been generated by the operational performance of the company and it is certainly not represented by cash. It is therefore considered unrealised and **non-distributable**, i.e. the company cannot use the revaluation reserve to pay a dividend.

In this situation, the increase in the net book value of the assets is reflected within the revaluation reserve.

**Impact on assets**: Non-current assets up

**Impact on equity**: Revaluation reserve up

The revaluation reserve may fall, however, if an asset which had previously been revalued upwards suffered a fall in value in the next revaluation. This is a statutory reserve.

### 1.3.16 General reserves

These are a form of non-statutory reserves, which company managers may choose to set up. These may have a specific purpose (e.g. plant and machinery reserve) or not (e.g. general reserve).

The creation of these reserves usually indicates a general intention not to distribute the profits involved at any future date, although legally any such reserves, being non-statutory, remain available for the payment of dividends.

### 1.3.17 Retained earnings

Retained earnings on the balance sheet represents the **accumulated profits made by the company since it started to trade**, which have **not been paid out as dividends** or transferred to other reserves. As such, it is a **distributable reserve** and it can be used to cover the payment of dividends to shareholders.

The separate **income statement details the impact of this year's trading activities on this accumulated figure**. Any profits retained this year which are detailed in the separate income statement will be added to the accumulated retained profits (or reserves) brought forward, giving the accumulated position at the end of the year. This could be viewed like a bank statement, where the statement only shows the movements for the month, but these are added to the opening cash balance to arrive at the closing one.

### 1.3.18 Minority interests

Minority interests arise when a company has a partly owned subsidiary company. For example, XYZ plc may own 80% of ABC Ltd. The balance of the shares in ABC Ltd are owned by other shareholders, referred to as the minority interest.

When XYZ plc prepares its consolidated accounts (covered in section 6 of this chapter) it will include all the assets and liabilities of ABC Ltd on the top half of its balance sheet as being part of the group's assets and liabilities. The reason for this is that it controls all of ABC Ltd's assets, since it has a majority of voting rights.

However, it only owns 80% of ABC Ltd's net assets, with the other 20% being owned by the minority interest. XYZ plc recognises this fact by analysing the total shareholder financing into two separate entities – group shareholders' funds and minority interest. The minority interest shows how much of the net assets belong to the minority shareholders in ABC Ltd.

## 1.4 The Income Statement

Learning objective **5.1.2 Understand** the purpose, structure and relevance to investors of income statements.

The income statement provides a detailed analysis of how the company has generated its profit or loss for the accounting period. As already noted, it reconciles the change in the balance sheet retained earnings figure from one year to the next.

### 1.4.1 The format

The income statement can be considered in two parts:

- A trading account showing gross profit from the sale of goods or services.
- An income and expense account showing the net profit (gross profit less expenses).

The income statement is a statement in which revenues and expenditure are matched to arrive at a figure of profit or loss. Many businesses try to distinguish between a gross profit earned on trading, and a net profit after other income and expenses.

In the first part of the statement (the trading account) revenue from selling goods is compared with direct costs of acquiring or producing the goods sold to arrive at a gross profit figure. From this, deductions are then made in the second half of the statement in respect of indirect costs (overheads) and additions for non-trading income.

The income statement shows in detail how the profit or loss has arisen. The owners and managers of a business need to know how much profit or loss has been made. In order to exercise financial control effectively, managers must know how much income has been earned, what costs have been incurred, and whether the performance of sales or the control of costs appears to be satisfactory.

**XYZ plc**
**Income Statement as at 31 December 2012**

| | **2012** | **2011** |
|---|---|---|
| | **£'000** | **£'000** |
| Revenue (Turnover) | 2,887 | 1,748 |
| Cost of sales | (2,402) | (1,442) |
| **Gross profit** | **485** | **306** |
| Administration expenses | (333) | (223) |
| **Operating profit** | **152** | **83** |
| Interest | (17) | (19) |
| **Profit before taxation** | **135** | **64** |
| Taxation | (40) | (19) |
| **Profit after taxation** | **95** | **45** |
| Dividend | (43) | (17) |
| Retained profit for the year | 52 | 28 |
| Earnings per share | 19 pence | 11.2 pence |

### 1.4.2 Terminology

In accordance with the accruals or matching concept, income and expenses are recognised in the income statement when earned, regardless of when paid. Any difference between the recognition of these items and the corresponding cash flow will be reflected in a balance sheet trade receivable or trade payable.

### 1.4.3 Revenue

The revenue figure represents the total value of goods or services provided to customers during the accounting period whether they have been paid for or not, in accordance with the accruals concept.

### 1.4.4 Cost of sales

The cost of sales represents the total cost to the business of buying or making the actual items sold.

An easy way to calculate cost of sales is to take:

Opening Inventory
  Add: Purchases
  Less: Closing Inventory
Cost of sales

Or: Opening Inventory + Purchases – Closing Inventory = Cost of Sales

You should be able to manipulate this formula to solve an unknown. For example, if the examiner were to ask you to calculate purchases:

Purchases = Cost of sales – Opening inventory + Closing inventory

### 1.4.5 Gross profit

Gross profit is the difference between the value of the sales and the value of the cost of goods sold. One measure frequently used in determining the performance of the business is to consider its gross profit margin, which can be calculated as

**Formula to learn**

$$\text{Gross profit margin} = \frac{\text{Gross profit}}{\text{Revenue}} \times 100\%$$

Clearly, the higher the margin for a particular level of operations, the higher the profit. However, this does not mean that low margins result in low profits. A number of businesses generate very healthy profits through selling very large numbers of items (achieving correspondingly large revenue) at low margins.

### 1.4.6 Administrative expenses

These costs include all other expenses incurred in generating the revenue for the period. This would include rental, electricity and telephone expenses as well as administration and distribution costs.

### 1.4.7 Interest

In common with most other business expenses, any interest payable goes to reduce the company's profit before tax and hence, taxable profit by the gross amount payable. For example, if a company has in issue £100,000 of 10% loan stock, then the interest charge in its accounts each year will be £10,000.

### 1.4.8 Taxation

UK companies pay corporation tax at the appropriate rate on **all** their taxable profits.

### 1.4.9 Dividends

Typically, companies pay out dividends which are less than their profits after tax, i.e. the dividend is being paid from this year's profits and is said to be covered. However, it is **not essential for a dividend to be covered**. It may be financed from previously retained profits which, as we have seen, are accumulated in the retained earnings account on the balance sheet.

In most cases, companies pay dividends in two stages.

- **Interim dividend paid** – this is paid out during the year, based on the half-year's performance.
- **Final dividend paid** – this is paid to shareholders based on the full year's performance.

### 1.4.10 Capital and revenue expenditure

#### Capital expenditure

Capital expenditure is expenditure on acquiring or enhancing fixed assets or their operating capacity. As such, the benefits will be derived from this expenditure over the remaining life of the asset. Hence, this expenditure is added to the value of fixed assets (is capitalised) on the balance sheet and will subsequently be **depreciated** through the income statement.

#### Revenue expenditure

Revenue expenditure is expenditure incurred in

- Acquiring assets to be sold for conversion into cash, e.g. stock.
- Manufacturing, selling, distributing goods, e.g. wages.
- Day-to-day administrative expenses, e.g. electricity, telephone.
- Maintenance of fixed assets, e.g. repairs.

Revenue expenditure is charged directly against profits for the period to which it relates.

## 1.5 IAS 7 – Cash Flow Statement

**Learning objective** **5.1.3 Understand** the purpose, structure and relevance to investors of cash flow statements.

#### Introduction

The balance sheet and income statement are prepared on an accruals basis. They give no indication of the effects of the operations of the business on its cash flows. It should always be noted that profits do not correspond exactly to cash. A company may be very profitable, but almost bankrupt (unable to pay its liabilities as they fall due).

Since cash is such an important figure in determining the continuing existence of a company, we need a statement showing how the company's financial resources have been acquired, and have been used, in order to highlight the liquidity position and trends of the company.

IAS 7, *Cash Flow Statements* lays down the rules to be followed in the preparation of such statements, defining

- **Cash**, i.e. what is and what is not cash.
- The **format** to be adopted in cash flow statements.

Note that only larger reporting entities are required to prepare a cash flow statement.

### 1.5.1 Objective of IAS 7

#### Scope

The aim of IAS 7 is to provide information to users of financial statements about an entity's ability to generate cash and cash equivalents, as well as indicating the cash needs of the entity. The cash flow statement provides historical information about cash and cash equivalents, classifying cash flows between operating, investing and financing activities.

- **Operating activities** are the principal revenue producing activities of the enterprise and other activities which are not investing or financing activities.
- **Investing activities** are the acquisition and disposal of non-current assets and other investments not included in cash equivalents, plus dividends and interest received from investments in the form of cash.
- **Financing activities** are activities that result in changes in the size and composition of the equity capital and borrowings of the entity.

### 1.5.2 Cash and cash equivalents

The standard expands on the definition of 'cash' to include 'cash equivalents'. This includes investments with a maturity date of not more than three months from the date of acquisition.

### 1.5.3 Benefits

The use of cash flow statements is very much in conjunction with the rest of the financial statements. Cash flow statements enhance comparability as they are not affected by differing accounting policies used for the same type of transactions or events.

### 1.5.4 Format

The illustration below shows how a cash flow statement should appear in the accounts of XYZ plc.

| **XYZ plc – Cash Flow Statement** | **2012**<br>**£'000** |
|---|---|
| **Cash flows from operating activities** | |
| Cash receipt from customers | 3,033 |
| Cash paid to suppliers and employees | (2,760) |
| Cash generated from operations | 273 |
| Interest paid | (20) |
| Income taxes paid | (45) |
| Net cash from operating activities | 208 |
| | |
| **Cash flow from investing activities** | |
| Purchase of property, plant and equipment | (700) |
| Proceeds from sale of equipment | 20 |
| Interest received | 200 |
| Dividends received | 200 |
| Net cash used in investing activities | (280) |
| | |
| **Cash flows from financing activities** | |
| Proceeds from issuance of share capital | 100 |
| Proceeds from long-term borrowings | 50 |
| Dividends paid | (19) |
| Net cash used in financing activities | 131 |

| XYZ plc – Cash Flow Statement | 2012 £'000 |
|---|---|
| Net increase in cash and cash equivalents | 59 |
| Cash and cash equivalents at beginning of period | 41 |
| Cash and cash equivalents at end of period | 100 |

### 1.5.5 Profit v Cash

Trade certainly causes cash to flow, for example when customers pay or suppliers are paid, therefore trade does impact on cash flows. However, not all income statement items result in an immediate cash flow or even any cash flow at all, for example

- **Depreciation** – the cash flow arises when the original non-current asset is purchased from the supplier. The income statement depreciation charge is **not** a cash flow.
- **Sales on credit/purchases on credit** – cash flows in relation to these items arise when the amounts are actually received/paid, which is after they have been credited/charged within the income statement.
- **Accrued expenses/pre-paid expenses** – cash flows arise when these expenses are settled which, again, differs from when they are recognised in the income statement.

These differences between accounting entries and movements of the actual cash must be reconciled in the notes to the accounts to show the net cash flow from operations.

In addition to the 'direct' method for computing cash flow from operations, IAS 7 permits another approach. Known as the 'indirect' method, this alternative approach reconciles the operating profit figure in the income statement to obtain cash flow from operations.

This method is undoubtedly easier from the point of view of the preparer of the cash flow statement. The net profit or loss for the period is adjusted for the following.

(a) Changes during the period in inventories, operating receivables and payables.

(b) Non-cash items, e.g. depreciation, provisions, profits/losses on the sale of assets.

(c) Other items, the cash flows from which should be classified under investing or financing activities.

| | 2012 £'000 |
|---|---|
| Operating profit | 152 |
| Depreciation | 35 |
| (Profit)/loss on sale of tangible non-current assets | 109 |
| (Increase)/decrease in inventory | (16) |
| (Increase)/decrease in receivables | (62) |
| Increase/(decrease) in payables | (10) |
| Net cash flow from operating activities | 208 |

### 1.5.6 Free cash flow

#### The purpose of free cash flow

The purpose of the calculation of free cash flow is to identify the surplus cash flow that a company is generating. This free cash flow can be used to evaluate a company. At a simplistic level, the current level of free cash flow can be compared to the value of the company, giving a multiple for comparison with other companies. At a more complex level, free cash flow can be forecast into the future and the present value of the cash flow calculated, giving a valuation of the business.

### Definition of free cash flow

The definition of free cash flow varies quite substantially between companies and analysts, largely because of what they are trying to achieve with their definition. As a result, it is not possible to be exhaustive when defining free cash flow and the various ways in which it may be calculated. We will, therefore focus on two major categories of definitions-free cash flow to equity and free cash flow to the enterprise.

### Enterprise cash flow and equity cash flow

Enterprise cash flow represents the total cash flow generated by a business or enterprise that is available to service all providers of capital, including equity investors, preference shares investors, debt investors and minority interests.

Equity cash flow represents the cash flow generated by a business that is available to service the providers of equity finance.

Although it may seem more appropriate to focus on equity cash flow at first sight since we are trying to assess the business from the point of view of its equity investors, enterprise cash flow has an important part to play in the analysis process. The reason for this is that it ignores the level of gearing and other related financial factors when analysing a business.

In addition, enterprise cash flows is a useful benchmark for comparisons across companies. Since many companies in different countries will have different gearing levels, even though they are in the same industry, it will not be easy to compare their businesses based on equity cash flows. A more appropriate comparison would be to look at multiples based on enterprise cash flow. For example, cash flow multiples based on turnover, research and development costs, number of locations, etc can be calculated and compared across the international sector.

### Free cash flow for equity

If we wish to establish the free cash flow for the equity, the analyst would aim to identify the surplus cash flow available after all the non-discretionary costs have been met. This could therefore be defined as follows.

| | |
|---|---|
| Net cash from operating activities | £x |
| (after tax and interest) | |
| Less: capital expenditure | (£x) |
| Less: preference dividends | (£x) |
| **Free cash flow to equity** | **£x** |

Note that this is not the only possible definition of free cash flow for equity – however, it does aim to highlight the key issues to consider when calculating such a cash flow figure.

### Free cash flow for the enterprise

The free cash flow enterprise is often referred to as 'net operating cash flow' and it can be calculated in the following way.

| | |
|---|---|
| Net cash from operating activities | £x |
| Less: tax payments | (£x) |
| Less: capital expenditure | (£x) |
| **Free Cash Flow for The Enterprise** | **£x** |

The free cash flow is the total amount of cash the company generates after funding purchases of fixed assets and any required increases in working capital, assuming that there is no debt. As such, it represents the maximum amount that a company could pay out to all its investors, assuming that the company is ungeared and has no commitment to pay interest to debt investors.

# 2 Analysis of Accounts

### Introduction

The financial statements, incorporating the profit and loss account statement, the balance sheet, the cash flow statement and all of the associated notes, contain a vast amount of information. The role of ratios is to distil this information into a more usable form for the purpose of analysis.

The financial statements are primarily prepared for company shareholders. However, they may have several other users, such as the Board, suppliers, competitors and employees. Each of these groups will use the accounts to provide an indication of the

- Returns they are receiving.
- Risks they are facing.

A number of fairly standard ratios have been developed to assist with this process, and these can be grouped under three headings:

| Type | Purpose |
|---|---|
| **Profitability ratios** | Ratios that assess the trading or operating performance of the company, i.e. levels of trading profits generated, and the productivity of trading assets. |
| **Financial gearing ratios** | Ratios that assess the risks to the providers of finance, by analysing the company's exposure to debt. |
| **Investors' ratios** | Ratios that assess the returns to the providers of finance, who may be either shareholders or lenders. |

## 2.1 Purpose and limitations

Ratios are rarely useful when viewed in isolation. However, they can be used to assess a company by **comparison** to sector averages, market averages or other similar companies. A company's progress can also be measured by comparing ratios with past in-house figures (for internal assessment) or previous published accounts to give a picture of year-on-year performance.

However, as there are no official rules concerning ratio calculation, there is a risk that, if two ratios from different sources are being compared, slightly different calculation methods may have been used, giving rise to some distortion in the comparison. Also, changes in accounting policies and restatement of prior year figures may lead to changes in ratios, which are not necessarily indicative of underlying performance.

Throughout our review of ratios, we will draw examples from the balance sheet and the income statement data for **Illustration plc**.

## Illustration plc

### Balance sheet as at 31 December

| | £'000 | £'000 |
|---|---|---|
| **Non-current assets** | | |
| Intangible | | 3,926 |
| Tangible | | 18,731 |
| Investments | | 842 |
| | | 23,499 |
| **Current assets** | | |
| Inventory | 19,420 | |
| Receivables | 27,882 | |
| Investments | 3,926 | |
| Cash | 6,425 | |
| | | 57,653 |
| **Total assets** | | **81,152** |
| **Share capital** | | |
| £1.00 NV Ordinary shares | | 17,925 |
| Preference shares | | 837 |
| **Reserves** | | |
| Share premium account reserve | | 2,455 |
| Revaluation reserve | | 2,681 |
| Retained earnings reserve | | 9,143 |
| **Shareholders' funds** | | 33,041 |
| **Creditors due after one year** | | |
| Secured loans | 2,073 | |
| Unsecured loans | 2,372 | |
| | | 4,445 |
| **Creditors due within one year** | | |
| Bank overdraft | 17,079 | |
| Trade payables | 18,702 | |
| Tax | 1,625 | |
| Others | 6,260 | |
| | | 43,666 |
| **Total liabilities** | | **81,152** |

### Income statement account

| | £'000 |
|---|---|
| Revenue | 135,761 |
| Cost of sales | (83,604) |
| Gross profit | 52,157 |
| Distribution costs | (22,961) |
| Administration costs | (22,712) |
| Operating profit | 6,484 |
| Interest received | 365 |
| Interest paid | (3,176) |
| Profit before tax | 3,673 |
| Tax | |
| Corporation tax | (1,372) |
| Profit after tax | **2,301** |

| | |
|---|---|
| Dividends | |
| Ordinary | 1,120 |
| Preference | 84 |
| | 1,204 |
| | |
| Earnings per share | 12.37p |
| Dividend per share | 6.25p |

## 2.2 Profitability ratios

**Learning objectives**

**5.1.4 Analyse securities.** Using the following financial ratios: liquidity, asset turnover, gearing, profitability and dividend policy.

**5.1.5 Analyse securities.** Using the following profitability ratios: Net profit margin, equity multiplier and return on capital employed.

Ratios are very convenient for summarising and presenting information. In general they are very easy to understand and they help to focus attention on the important aspects of business performance and risk.

A ratio is, however, meaningless in isolation. In order to be useful, a ratio must have some reasonable comparative, for example

- Prior year figures
- Competitors' figures
- Budget figures

We can then review how we are doing compared with, say, the previous year. The ratio is not an answer, simply a means to an end. If all of our ratios this year are the same as they were last year, then our returns and risks for all interested parties are unaltered.

Ratios can be used to highlight trends over a number of years, which may not be so apparent from the figures themselves. These trends can then be used by the analyst's client to assess how the company is performing.

When using ratios to focus our attention for analysis purposes, we will essentially be looking for:

**Discontinuities**, i.e. large changes in the ratios from one year to the next, or large variances of the ratio against competitors or budgets. These, in all probability, will be highlighting some anomaly.

**Trends** illustrated by the ratios over a period of time. These may be upward/downward trends in terms of returns being achieved, or the risks people face.

## 2.3 Different users of accounts

It is important to decide before analysing a set of accounts, what the users key concerns are:

**Managers and employees** for example, would be mainly interested in the availability and effectiveness of the use of assets, i.e.

a)Trading Performance – how effective the company has been at generating profits (concentrating on the breakdown of profits and profitability ratios).

b)Trading position – what resources the company has available for the purpose of trade (concentrating on the build up of the statement of financial position assets and liquidity ratios).

**Investors and lenders** would be interested in the breakdown and servicing of financing, i.e.

- Financial performance – how effective the company has been in generating a return to its providers of finance (concentrating on the levels of interest and dividends and related investors' ratios).

- Financial position – how the company is financed (concentrating on the financial build up on the statement of financial position).

## 2.4 Return on capital employed

This is a measure of the level of profitability generated by the management of a company.

### Basic calculation

The return on capital employed is calculated as follows.

Formula to learn

$$\text{ROCE} = \frac{\text{Profit before interest payable and tax}}{\text{Capital employed}} \times 100\%$$

### 2.4.1 Profit

This profit figure can be viewed as **operating profit**, i.e. the profits that management have generated from the resources they have available. This is also known as profit before interest and tax ('PBIT'). It is specifically **before** interest payable since this will clearly be dependent on the financing of the business – the larger the loan, the larger the interest payable.

| | **£'000** |
|---|---|
| Profit before tax | 3,673 |
| **Add back** interest payable | 3,176 |
| Profit before interest payable and tax | 6,849 |

### 2.4.2 Capital employed

Ideally, considering capital employed, we would like to consider the average capital employed throughout the year. Our aim is to match the profits generated throughout the year to the capital or assets that have been used to generate them, or the total financing of the business. It is unlikely, however, that this information will be available, and normally the calculation would be based on year-end figures.

Since we are measuring profit as profit before all interest payable, we should consider everything upon which interest is payable as part of the financing in order to be consistent in this ratio, i.e. in this case, we would treat bank overdrafts as part of the financing of the business.

Capital employed could be viewed from either the financing side as

Capital employed = Share capital and reserves + Loans + Bank overdrafts

£54,565,000 = £33,041,000 + £4,445,000 + £17,079,000

or from the trading side as

Capital employed = Total assets – Current liabilities (excluding overdrafts)

£54,565,000 = (£23,499,000 + £57,653,000) – £26,587,000

This is the most consistent treatment of overdrafts for this ratio.

## Example

$$\text{ROCE} = \frac{£6,849,000}{£54,565,000} \times 100\%$$

ROCE = 12.6%

#### 2.4.3 Potential problems

Ideally, it would be best to use the average capital employed as our aim is to match the profits generated throughout the year to the capital or assets that have been used to generate them, or the total financing of the business.

It is unlikely that this information will be available, and normally the calculation would be based on year-end figures. This can lead to some **major distortions in our ratios**, especially if there have been large changes in capital employed during the year, i.e. from the acquisition of a subsidiary or the raising of funds near the year end.

#### 2.4.4 Analysis points

Having established our return on capital employed, we now need to consider what may have caused any change from one year to the next. This is caused by one of two factors.

- Changes in profit margin.
- Changes in revenue volumes.

We define each of these more fully below, but in outline

$$\text{Profit margin} = \frac{\text{Profit}}{\text{Turnover}}$$

$$\text{Asset turnover} = \frac{\text{Turnover}}{\text{Capital employed}}$$

Hence

$$\text{Profit margin} \times \text{Asset turnover} = \frac{\text{Profit}}{\text{Turnover}} \times \frac{\text{Turnover}}{\text{Capital employed}} = \frac{\text{Profit}}{\text{Capital employed}} = \text{ROCE}$$

### 2.5 Profit margins

A profit margin is a measure of the profit achieved per £1 of sales generated.

**Formula to learn**

$$\text{Profit margin} = \frac{\text{Profits}}{\text{Revenue}} \times 100\%$$

#### 2.5.1 Considerations

We may be tempted to use the profit figure from our earlier ROCE calculation, however, this may bring with it the problem that not all elements of this profit have any relationship to the levels of revenue. For example, this profit is stated after

- Interest receivable.
- Income from non-current asset investments.
- Share of profits of associated undertakings.

None of the above three are related to revenue. In practice it might be better, therefore, to use the trading profit figure only particularly if examining the profit margin in isolation. However, we will continue using our 'full' PBIT figure for now.

## Example

Again, using information contained in our illustration financial statements at the end of this chapter.

$$\text{Profit margin} = \frac{\text{£6,849 (see ROCE above)}}{\text{£135,761}} \times 100\%$$

Profit margin = 5.0%

### 2.5.2 Analysis points

Once we have calculated this ratio, we need to make something meaningful out of it. When doing this, it is important to consider the causes and possible consequences, not just the numbers.

If profit margins are up it may appear to be good news – higher levels of profits. However, these higher profits may mean that the company loses customer loyalty if they perceive that they are being exploited. Alternatively, high prices may attract competitors into the field, in which case the company may lose a substantial amount of market share.

Conversely, margins going down may normally be perceived as bad news. However, it may be as a consequence of a policy of penetration pricing; or it may be that the company is incurring high development costs and future years' profitability will be that much higher as a result.

## 2.6 Liquidity ratios

These ratios attempt to review the ability of a company to repay its debts through a consideration of its **working capital**. The working capital of a business is the net of its current assets and current liabilities (also sometimes referred to as **net current assets**), i.e.

Working capital = Current assets – Current liabilities

A positive working capital figure indicates that if all of the current assets are realised they will be sufficient to cover the current liabilities and the following ratios examine that comparison in more detail.

### 2.6.1 Current ratio

#### Basic calculation

The purpose of this ratio is to see whether the assets existing at the year-end, which are recoverable within one year, are sufficient to cover the liabilities at that date which fall due within that year.

**Formula to learn**

$$\text{Current ratio} = \frac{\text{Current assets due within one year}}{\text{Current liabilities falling due within one year}}$$

#### Considerations

The term current assets normally refers to assets that are recoverable within one year, hence this would normally be a match. However, care should be taken. It may well be the case, for example, that some receivables are recoverable after more than one year. This particular fact will be noted in the accounts if this is the case.

## Example

$$\text{Current ratio} = \frac{£57,653,000}{£43,666,000}$$

Current ratio = 1.32×

### Analysis points

Analysis points when calculating or using this ratio are as follows.

- **Overdrafts** will be included within creditors falling due within one year but are frequently payable after more than one year in practice. Banks frequently allow companies to continue with overdrafts for several years.
- **Realisation of inventory** – inventory is contained within current assets and therefore is almost automatically assumed to be realisable within one year, but this may not necessarily be the case. Unlike receivables there will be no note anywhere indicating the recoverability or likely timescale for the realisation of inventory.
- This ratio completely ignores the **timing of cash flows** within the period. In theory it could be possible that all the liabilities are payable now and all the assets are recoverable in 12 months' time. Although in total terms they match, in actual cash flow terms they do not.

### 2.6.2 Quick (acid test) ratio

### Basic calculation

The quick ratio is an adaptation of the current ratio to remove the problem of inventory. Inventory is a problem, in that it is not easily convertible into cash and therefore may distort the ratio.

**Formula to learn**

$$\text{Quick ratio} = \frac{\text{Current assets excluding inventory}}{\text{Current liabilities falling due within one year}}$$

### Considerations

The quick ratio considers just the readily realisable assets (cash, investments and receivables) and whether they are sufficient to cover the short-term liabilities of the business. Being a modification of the current ratio, it suffers from the same problems, excluding realisability of inventory, of course.

## Example

$$\text{Quick ratio} = \frac{£57,653,000 - £19,420,000}{£43,666,000}$$

$$\text{Quick ratio} = \frac{£38,233,000}{£43,666,000}$$

Quick ratio = 0.875×

Our company has a quick ratio of less than one. This does not mean that it is insolvent and unable to pay off its liabilities. However, depending on the type of business, it may be a sign of liquidity problems.

## 2.7 Asset turnover

The asset turnover ratio assesses the effectiveness of the use of the trading assets available.

**Formula to learn**

$$\text{Asset turnover} = \frac{\text{Revenue}}{\text{Assets (capital) employed}}$$

### 2.7.1 Considerations

Once again, we could take all the capital employed used in our ROCE calculation as the denominator in this calculation. However, again, it may be that some assets bear no relationship to revenue whatsoever, e.g.

- Investment in associated undertakings.
- Short-term investments.

In practice, it may therefore be more appropriate to take just those trading assets that have contributed to revenue.

## Example

Using information from our illustration financial statements (Section 10.9).

$$\text{Asset turnover} = \frac{£135,761}{£54,565 \text{ (see ROCE above)}}$$

Asset turnover = 2.49×

### 2.7.2 Potential problems

Again a problem with this ratio, in common with the problem of return on capital employed, is that we are comparing a full year's transactions (revenue) to a year-end balance sheet figure (assets employed). Unless this year-end figure is representative of the assets employed throughout the year, we will not exactly be comparing like with like and there may be some distortions.

For example, if the company buys a subsidiary or raises new finance close to the year end, then the year-end assets employed would be substantially higher than the general level throughout the year.

Another problem is the impact of accounting policies. If, for example, non-current assets are revalued this year then this will have two effects.

- Profits will be down due to increased depreciation charges.
- Capital assets employed will be up due to the increase in non-current asset NBVs.

The result will be that our return on capital employed and asset turnover figures will be reduced, although the effectiveness of our trade, in truth, may be unaltered. It is very difficult to remove these distorting effects. It is probably more convenient to calculate the ratios but to note any distortions.

### 2.7.3 Analysis points

Again, when considering this ratio, it may be tempting just to state the obvious – but take care. We should **consider the causes**, not just the numbers.

Considering just the numbers, it would be tempting to believe that increased asset turnover is a positive thing. However, it may arise from

- Overtrading, which would result in liquidity problems.
- A deterioration of the capital base, i.e. sales are not rising, rather the asset base is falling.

As the diagram above illustrates, this ratio may be further sub-analysed into, for example, working capital turnover and non-current asset turnover; each of which may be an appropriate ratio for a particular sort of industry. Non-current asset turnover may be an appropriate ratio in a capital-intensive industry where a large amount of the capital of the business is tied up in non-current assets. The analyst needs to decide which ratios to use and how to use them.

## 2.8 Financial gearing ratios

**These ratios deal with the financing side of the balance sheet and consider the** relationships between

- Interest-bearing borrowed capital on which the return (i.e. coupon or dividends) must be paid.
- Shareholders' capital on which the return (i.e. dividend distribution) is optional.

It is generally accepted that high levels of gearing imply high financial risks for the company.

### 2.8.1 Debt to equity ratio

#### Basic calculation

This is a relationship that shareholders would consider as a measure of the risk to their dividends.

**Formula to learn**

$$\text{Debt to equity} = \frac{\text{Interest bearing loans}}{\text{Equity shareholders' funds}} \times 100\%$$

#### Considerations

We consider only interest-bearing debt since this is what is causing the risk to profit before tax, hence ultimately the profits after tax and amounts available for payment as dividends to our shareholders.

Example:

$$\text{Debt to equity} = \frac{£2{,}372{,}000 + £17{,}079{,}000 + £2{,}073{,}000}{£32{,}204{,}000}$$

$$\text{Debt to equity} = \frac{£21{,}524{,}000}{£32{,}204{,}000} \times 100\%$$

Debt to equity = 66.8%

Equity shareholders' funds are given by the equity share capital and all of the reserves.

### 2.8.2 Net debt to equity ratio

This is an alternative to the above, and takes account of the cash that a business may also hold that could be used to repay debt.

**Formula to learn**

$$\text{Net debt to equity} = \frac{\text{Debt (as above)} - (\text{Cash} + \text{Current asset investments})}{\text{Equity shareholders' funds}} \times 100\%$$

#### Considerations

We should consider the ability of the company to use the cash it has available to repay debt.

## Example

$$\text{Net debt to equity} = \frac{£21{,}524{,}000 \text{ (as above)} - £6{,}425{,}000 - £3{,}926{,}000}{£32{,}204{,}000} \times 100\%$$

$$\text{Net debt to equity} = \frac{£11{,}173{,}000}{£32{,}204{,}000} \times 100\%$$

Net debt to equity = 34.7%

## 2.9 Investors' ratios

Learning objective

**5.1.6 Analyse** securities using the following investor ratios: Earnings per share, Price / Earnings, Net Dividend Yield and Net dividend / interest cover.

### 2.9.1 Earnings per share

Earnings per share (EPS) is defined as

Formula to learn

$$\text{EPS} = \frac{\text{Earnings attributable to ordinary shareholders}}{\text{Number of ordinary shares}}$$

Earnings are defined as consolidated profit after

- Tax.
- Minority interests.
- Extraordinary items.
- Preference dividends.

Earnings therefore represent the remaining profits available to the ordinary shareholders.

## Example

$$\text{EPS} = \frac{£2{,}301{,}000 - £84{,}000}{17{,}925{,}000 \text{ shares}}$$

$$\text{EPS} = \frac{£2{,}217{,}000}{17{,}925{,}000 \text{ shares}}$$

EPS = 12.37p

The net basic EPS must always be disclosed in a listed company's accounts.

### Analysis points

We have already noted that current earnings are calculated as profits after interest, tax and preference dividends. However, it is also worth noting that earnings can also be calculated as retained earnings plus ordinary dividends.

While current earnings of different companies can be compared relative to each other, the EPS for one company should not be compared relative to another, as this is affected not only by actual earnings but also by the number of shares in issuance. Therefore, the EPS is not a good measure for comparing two companies against each other.

### 2.9.2 Fully diluted earnings per share

The purpose of the fully diluted earnings per share figure is to warn shareholders of **potential future changes in the earnings per share figure** as a result of potential shares that already exist. There are three possible factors that could cause a fully diluted earnings per share to arise.

- Convertible loan stock or preference shares in issue.
- Options in issue.
- Shares in issue not ranking for a dividend this year.

Each of these circumstances may potentially result in more shares being issued and ranking for a dividend in future years, hence leading to a dilution of the current earnings per share.

## 2.10 Price/earnings ratio (P/E ratio)

The P/E ratio is calculated as follows.

Formula to learn

$$\text{Price/Earnings} = \frac{\text{Current market price per share}}{\text{Earnings per share}}$$

### Considerations

The P/E ratio expresses the number of years' earnings represented by the current market price.

## Example

If we take our current share price as £2.20 and our EPS figure as 12.3p, the P/E ratio is

$$\text{Price/Earnings} = \frac{220\text{p}}{12.3\text{p}}$$

Price/Earnings = 17.9 years

### 2.10.1 Analysis points

The significance of a P/E ratio can only be judged in relation to the ratios of other companies in the same type of business. If the median P/E ratio for an industry sector was 8, a ratio of 12 for a particular company would suggest that the shares of that company were in great demand, possibly because a rapid growth of earnings was expected. Note that **growth** (and therefore a **high P/E**) can be generated by retaining a large proportion of earnings and paying **low dividends** and reinvesting the earnings to grow the business. A **low ratio**, say 4 for example, would indicate a company – not greatly favoured by investors – which probably has **poor growth prospects**.

Alternatively, a high P/E ratio might indicate that a company is overpriced (overvalued), and a low P/E ratio might indicate that a company is underpriced (undervalued).

### 2.10.2 Historic versus prospective price/earnings ratios

If the earnings figures used are the published figures for the last year, this gives the historic price/earnings ratio. Alternatively, an analyst may look at the earnings which been forecast by equity research analysts and calculate a prospective or future predicted price/earnings ratio.

### 2.10.3 Net dividend yield

The dividend yield of an ordinary share is calculated as follows.

**Formula to learn**

$$\text{Net dividend yield} = \frac{\text{Net dividend per share}}{\text{Current market price per share}} \times 100\%$$

## Example

$$\text{Dividend yield} = \frac{6.25\text{p}}{220\text{p}} \times 100\%$$

Dividend yield = 2.84%

### Analysis points

A high dividend yield suggests that the company is paying reasonable levels of income. However, a high yield may be due, in part, to a relatively low share price, indicating that the company has low growth prospects. Investors who believe that the company has good growth prospects would buy the share, driving the price up and reducing the yield.

Therefore, it is also true that companies with high P/E ratios tend to have low dividend yields, and *vice versa*.

## 2.11 Dividend cover

Dividend cover is used to assess the likelihood of the existing dividend being maintained. The dividend cover is calculated as follows.

**Formula to learn**

$$\text{Dividend cover} = \frac{\text{Earnings per share}}{\text{Net dividend per share}}$$

## Example

$$\text{Dividend cover} = \frac{12.37\text{p}}{6.25\text{p}}$$

Dividend cover = 1.98×

A high dividend cover indicates that the company is earning adequate amounts to continue paying equivalent dividend levels in future periods. It may also indicate that the company is retaining a large amount of its earnings, which will in turn suggest that growth in future periods should be strong.

## 2.12 Dividend policy

An unusually high dividend cover implies that the company is retaining the majority of its earnings, presumably with the intention of reinvesting to generate growth.

A company **may** choose to pay a **larger dividend than that year's earnings** (in which case dividend cover will be <1). Where this occurs, the company is drawing on past reserves and is said to be paying an **uncovered dividend**.

Company directors set the dividend level based upon the previous year's profits and their policy on dividends. The proposed dividend is offered to the shareholders with the audited accounts. The shareholders may vote to decrease the dividend but not to increase it.

By altering the dividend declared directors will be sending a message to the market regarding their view on the future prospects and direction of the company. Certain companies will establish themselves as good cash generators who pay out dividends of a certain level, as such they become attractive to investors such as pension funds who look for steady income.

## 2.13 Interest cover

### Basic calculation

This ratio considers gearing from the viewpoint of the income statement and measures the capacity of the firm to meet its interest obligations.

**Formula to learn**

$$\text{Interest cover} = \frac{\text{Profit before interest payable and tax}}{\text{Interest payable}}$$

### Considerations

The interest cover provides a measure of the ability of the company to pay the fixed interest on borrowings from profits for the year. Clearly, the higher the level of interest cover, the less risk there is to either shareholders or lenders. However, there is no optimal level.

### Example

$$\text{Interest cover} = \frac{£6,484 \text{ (see ROCE above)}}{£2,811}$$

Interest cover = 2.31×

## 2.14 Effect of corporation tax on ratios

Most ratios will measure returns to shareholders before the deduction of tax. This will prevent different tax treatments on the same items in two separate companies distorting the ratios.

An example of a different treatment relates to depreciation expenses. Each company charges the depreciation rate they feel is true and fair for their company. However, this is then adjusted by the UK tax authorities (Her Majesty's Revenue and Customs [HMRC]) to give a standard tax depreciation called a capital allowance.

### Effective tax rate

Due to this difference in accounting treatments, we can measure the effectiveness of a company in minimising its tax return.

**Formula to learn**

$$\text{Effective tax rate} = \frac{\text{Tax charge in income statement}}{\text{Profit before taxation}}$$

For Illustration plc $\frac{£1,372,000}{£3,673,000} = 37.35\%$

## 2.15 Common sized financial statements

### 2.15.1 Common sized Balance sheet

The use of 'common size statements' is common when analysing accounts. It involves showing each line of a balance sheet as a percentage of one item referred to as a 'base value'. The most common item selected to be the base value is total assets. The example below shows this in action.

The benefit of using common sized statements is in the observing of trends from year to year. Shifts can be observed below from short term liabilities to longer term liabilities, which may have involved the firm issuing bonds or arranging longer term loans with the bank, which may put them into a stronger position.

| | 2011<br>£000 | Common sized | 2012<br>£000 | Common sized |
|---|---|---|---|---|
| **Assets** | | | | |
| Non-current assets | 23,499 | 28.96% | 27,321 | 31.85% |
| Current assets | 57,653 | 71.04% | 58,453 | 68.15% |
| **Total** | **81,152** | **100.00%** | **85,774** | **100.00%** |
| | | | | |
| **Financing** | | | | |
| Share capital | 18,762 | 23.12% | 18,762 | 21.87% |
| Reserves | 14,279 | 17.59% | 19,432 | 22.65% |
| Shareholders funds | **33,041** | | **38,194** | |
| Creditors due after One year | 4,445 | 5.48% | 16,342 | 19.05% |
| Credit due within One year | 43,666 | 53.81% | 31,238 | 36.43% |
| **Total** | **81,152** | **100.00%** | **85,774** | **100.00%** |

In a fashion similar to that of common sized balance sheets, it is common to make use of common sized income statements. These generally use the revenue figure as their base value.

## 2.16 Common sized Income Statement

| | 2011 | % of revenue | 2012 | % of revenue |
|---|---|---|---|---|
| Revenue | 135,761 | | 158,341 | |
| Cost of sales | (83,604) | | (87,324) | |
| Gross profit | 52,157 | 38.42% | 63,276 | 39.96% |
| Distribution costs | (22,961) | 16.91% | (27,197) | 17.18% |
| Administration costs | (22,712) | 16.73% | (22,967) | 14.50% |
| Operating profit | 6,484 | 4.78% | 13,112 | 8.28% |
| Interest received | 365 | | 413 | |
| Interest paid | (3,176) | | (3,112) | |
| Profit before tax | 3,673 | 2.71% | 10,413 | 6.58% |
| Tax | | | | |
| Corporation tax | (1,372) | 1.01%% | (3,889) | 2.46% |
| Profit after tax | **2,301** | 1.69% | **6,523** | 4.12% |
| | | | | |
| Dividends | | | | |
| Ordinary | 1,120 | | 1,245 | |
| Preference | 84 | | 84 | |
| | 1,204 | | 5,194 | |
| | | | | |
| Earnings per share | 12.37p | | 13.13p | |
| Dividend per share | 6.25p | | 6.31p | |

The use of common size statements allows the use of trend analysis. We can see for example a strong growth in operating profit from 4.78% to 8.28%, which may well be due to control of administrative costs which have fallen to 14.5% from 16.73%.

## 2.17 Challenges in financial analysis

**Learning objective**

5.1.7 **Understand** the main advantages and challenges of performing financial analysis: Comparing companies in different countries and sectors, Comparing different companies within the same sector, Over-reliance on historical information, Benefits and limitations of relying on third party research.

Ratios are useful tools only when used as comparisons with other firms. In isolation they provide little by way of useful information to the analyst. To make appropriate like for like comparisons, it is necessary to compare companies within the same country and sectors and with similar characteristics such as size. Where comparisons are to be made across sectors or of companies in different countries, adjustment factors are made to account for the different risk and taxation levels for example in the different countries.

The fact that many analysts rely for their data upon financial statements, which are themselves historical in nature means that their predictive value for future decisions must be questioned. Where ratios use historical data, forward looking adjustments to predict future results such as sales or costs may be necessary.

Third party research is often used where specialist agencies such as credit rating agencies have access to information and models which may be difficult for a firm to replicate effectively. Over reliance on third party research however may prevent an investor being able to outperform market returns as they are using generally available information, which other investors also have access to.

### 2.17.1 Who is the information for?

We need to satisfy the requirements of our clients and hence concentrate on those areas that are of concern to them. If, for example, our client is a shareholder, then we would probably concentrate initially on the investors' ratios.

However, we should never adopt a blinkered approach to analysis. When looking at an investors' ratio we may consider, for example, the earnings per share figure. The earnings per share figure clearly depends on the profits and the number of shares. If the earnings per share figure is changed because profits have changed, we may well wish to go and consider further the profitability of the business. Hence our client tells us the starting point for our analysis, but we should be prepared to be taken off in different directions depending on what we find being highlighted by the ratios we initially consider.

### 2.17.2 Practical circumstances

In order to appreciate and understand the trends and ratios we are seeing, we need to consider the practical circumstances of the business.

### 2.17.3 Profitability

How did the business make its profits? Is it a 'stack 'em high and sell 'em fast', high volume, low margin retailer or is it a high margin, low turnover business, such as a jeweller?

What is the nature of the earnings and the dependency of those earnings on economic factors such as exchange rates, general state of the economy, recession etc. For example, supermarkets largely provide necessities, hence in a recession we would expect their profits to remain fairly level. However, for luxury car manufacturers, we would expect their profits to decline substantially in a recession as demand for their goods drops.

### 2.17.4 Liquidity

In considering the liquidity of the business under consideration we should try to imagine its working capital cycle. We should try to picture in our minds what we should expect to see or what we can see as the norm by considering the working capital cycle of the peer group. In this way we will be in decent position to comment on what we are actually finding in the company under consideration.

### 2.17.5 Accounting policies

The accounting policy adopted by any company can significantly impact on its ratios.

If we revalue non-current assets, then our depreciation charge will be higher. Hence, profits will be lower, but on the statement of financial position, more non-current assets means a higher capital employed figure. Hence our return on capital employed will be reduced (lower profits divided by higher capital employed).

If we are comparing two companies, one that does revalue non-current assets and one that does not, or if we are comparing one company to a previous year when we have revalued non-current assets in between, then we would expect to see a distortion between the ratios as a result of this accounting policy.

### 2.17.6 Window dressing

Window dressing techniques incorporate some dubious financing methods, hence they are worthy of consideration here.

Window dressing transactions are transactions intended to mislead the user of the accounts. We outline below two basic window dressing transactions types.

### 2.17.7 Circular transactions

In a circular transaction, Company A sells goods to Company B who in turn sells them back to Company A. The purpose of undertaking these transactions is simply to boost reported revenues, which in turn would boost such measures as asset turnover, distorting the view of the user as to the effectiveness of the management of the company.

Clearly, such a transaction is totally fictitious. It is likely that the transactions would have to be disclosed as a result of the rules in IAS 24 Related Party Disclosures, assuming that the two companies are in some way connected.

### 2.17.8 Possible distorting effects

When calculating any ratios, we should always try to look for possible distorting effects that impact on our analysis. Factors to consider would be as follows.

### 2.17.9 Bed and Breakfast transactions

A bed and breakfast transaction is very much like a circular transaction that is undertaken over a year end, i.e. Company A sells to Company B before year end, then repurchases after the year end. This will not only boost Company's revenue for the year but also their reported profits if the goods have been sold at a profit. Again, the transaction is totally fictitious and only designed to mislead the user of the account. As above the transactions are likely to be disclosed as being with a related party.

### 2.17.10 Comparing a full year's transactions to year end balances

One of the biggest possible distortions that is only tackled in the earnings per share calculation as a matter of course, is that we compare a full year's worth of transactions to a year-end statement of financial position figure with a number of the ratios. What we really should be doing is comparing a full year's transaction to a representative balance throughout the year. For example, ideally we should compare the full year's profits to a representative amount of capital employed to get return on capital employed. When analysing a set of financial statements, it is highly unlikely that you will be able to calculate the representative amount of capital employed throughout the year, hence you may only be able to work out the return on capital employed figures. The problem is not only confined to return on capital employed, it is true for any ratio that compares a full year's transaction to a year end figure, for example receivables' collection period, payables' payment period or inventory turnover rate. Hence, these ratios can be distorted by such things as

- **Subsidiary acquired near year end** – profits up only from the date of acquisition, capital up at the year end by the full amount.
- **Funds raised near year end** – capital employed higher, return increased by only a small amount based upon what the funds have managed to generate in the short period of time to year end.
- **Seasonal sale** – the receivables' collection period compares the year end receivables to the year's sales. If sales are seasonal in nature then, depending on when the year end is, the receivables may be very significant or very small compared to the year's revenue.

### 2.17.11 Comparing like with like

All of our ratios should endeavour to compare like-with-like. For example, when considering the payables' payment period, we should try to compare the invoiced payables to the invoiced cost of sales. When calculating profit margins, we should compare the profit to the revenue that has generated that profit.

We should therefore, always be looking for factors that cause distortions in these ratios. For example, income from associated undertakings boosts the profits before tax, however, it has no revenue


BPP LEARNING MEDIA

implications and therefore a simple calculation of profit margins based upon profits before tax and revenue implications will incorporate a distorting effect.

The method of equity accounting for associates on the statement of financial position will similarly distort any asset turnover calculation, since this particular element of capital employed does not contribute to revenue. When considering any ratio the aim should always be to compare like-with-like.

#### 2.17.12 Ability to realise assets

When considering any ratios, in particular liquidity, it may be very difficult for us to get any indication as to the potential ability to realise assets.

#### 2.17.13 Cash

We would normally assume that we can get hold of any cash immediately. However, it is quite possible that a company may have significant amounts of cash held overseas that it cannot remit to the UK for certain reasons particular to the country concerned. Alternatively, a proportion of the cash a company is in possession of may not be freely available for its own use to repay debts. For example, a manufacturer may have received cash in advance that can only be used to fund a specific project and is not available to settle other debts.

#### 2.17.14 Inventory

Inventory is shown on the statement of financial position under the heading current assets, which leads to the reasonable assumption that is likely to be converted into cash within 12 months. However, this may not always be the case. In such industries as high tech, or fashion, inventory may become unsalable very rapidly.

#### 2.17.15 Use of historical information and third party research

Given the common use of financial statements in analysing a company, decisions may be based upon previous years' information. Given the changes in aspects such as the global economy and a specific companies performance in certain conditions, this could lead to highly misleading impressions being arrived at.

Third party research is common, with credit rating agencies and analysts offering there specialist knowledge. Dangers arise however if this is taken too fully on trust, as was seen where a number credit rating agencies failed to fully appreciate the dangers of mortgage backed securities.

# 3 Accounting for Corporate Actions

## 3.1 Rights Issues

arning objectives

**5.2.1** **Understand** the purpose and structure of corporate actions and their implications for investors: stock capitalisation or consolidation, stock and cash dividends, rights issues, open offers, offers for subscription and offers for sale, placing.

**5.2.2** **Calculate** the theoretical effect on the issuer's share price of the following mandatory and optional corporate actions: bonus/scrip, consolidation and rights issues.

**5.2.3** **Analyse** the following in respect of corporate actions: Rationale offered by the company, Understand the dilution effect on profitability and reported financials.

### 3.1.1 Basic details of rights issues

#### Issues to new shareholders

Companies have an obligation under the Companies Act to ensure that any new shares issued for cash are first offered to existing shareholders in proportion to their existing shareholdings. Shareholders may disapply their **pre-emptive rights through a special resolution**.

### 3.1.2 Mechanics of a rights issue

Rights issues are made at a discount to the current market price to encourage existing shareholders to buy the shares and ensure the issue is successful. The greater the discount, the more incentive shareholders have to take up the rights issue, and the greater the chance of success.

## Example

A company carries out a 1 for 3 rights issue at a subscription price of £4.00, when the current market price is £5.00 per share (the **cum rights price**). Each shareholder now has the right to acquire one new share for every three shares he currently owns.

A **Rights Letter** is despatched to each shareholder informing them of their right to subscribe for a certain number of shares. For example, shareholders who currently own 3,000 shares will receive a letter telling them of their right to subscribe for 1,000 new shares at a subscription price of £4.00 each; total £4,000.

The Rights Letter is despatched to all shareholders listed on the register of shareholders on a particular date. The date is set by the company and is referred to as the **on register day**. An example Rights Letter can be found in section 5.5. It is frequently referred to as a PAL (provisional allotment letter).

Once the Rights Letter has been despatched to the owner of the shares, on the 'on register' day, the owner then has four courses of action from which to choose.

1. **To take up the shares and hold them.** Rights are taken up by the shareholder by attaching a cheque to the rights letter for the appropriate amount, and returning them to the company registrar. The company registrar then stamps the rights letter to indicate that the amount due has been paid and returns it to the original owner. From this point, the receipted rights letter acts as a **temporary document of title**, acting as evidence of ownership of the underlying shares. In due course, a real share certificate (a **definitive document of title**) is sent to the shareholder.
2. **To take up the shares and sell them.** In this case, the shareholder returns the rights letter and cheque to the registrar as before. He then renounces his rights to the shares over to a new shareholder. On the reverse of the rights letter are two forms; **Form X** and Form Y. Form X, the Form of Renunciation, states that the owner has transferred the rights attached to the piece of paper to the holders named in **Form Y**, the Registration Application Form. The normal form of transfer in this case is for the original owner to sign Form X and give it blank to the new purchaser. In effect, a bearer document is created, known as American form. The new owner **must register** his or her rights to these shares by a specified date – the **registration of renunciation** – which is generally four weeks prior to the despatch of share certificates.
3. **To sell the rights nil paid. The rights letter gives the holder the right to buy a share at a discounted price. Consequently, the holder can simply sell on their rights letter, without having accepted it themselves.**

   In order to sell the rights nil paid, the original holder once again signs Form X, on the reverse of the rights letter. This time it is done prior to sending off payment for the shares. It is then the responsibility of the purchaser of the rights letter to accept the rights by the **last acceptance and payment date**, which in this example is Monday, 25 March. In doing this, Form Y must also be completed – the **Registration of Renunciation**. The registrar then returns the receipted rights letter in the purchaser's own name.

4. **To do nothing**, allow the rights to expire and the company will then sell the shares in the market place. Any surplus over the subscription price – in this case £4.00 – will then be despatched to the shareholder. It should be noted that this fourth option is subject to administration charges by the company, and may result in a very small payment, if any, to the shareholder.

The shareholder must be allowed **at least 21 calendar days** after the despatch of the rights letter to consider which option to take. If, by the end of this period, the shareholder has not taken up these rights, they will be deemed to have lapsed (point 4 above).

**Example Rights Letter Timings**

| Dispatch of Rights Letter | Last Acceptance and Payment Date | Registration of Renunciation | Dispatch of New Share Certificates |
|---|---|---|---|
| Friday 1 March | Monday 25 March | Friday 26 April | Friday 26 May |

In the example above, the rights letter is despatched on Friday, 1 March. The recipient must accept the rights letter by sending payment by Monday, 25 March (at least 21 calendar days). Failure to do so results in the lapse of the rights. In this event, the company would normally enter the market the following day and sell the shares at the then market price. Any balance (in excess of the subscription price) is returned to the original shareholder.

Once the shareholder has received the receipted rights letter from the company registrar, it can be converted into bearer form. It can then be used to trade, with Form Y still blank, until Friday, 26 April when the Registration of Renunciation takes place. By that time, anyone who has purchased the receipted rights letter in renounceable form must have completed Form Y, and returned it to the registrar. This ensures that the shares are sent to the new holder on Friday, 26 May.

Failure to register the transfer before the registration of renunciation date means that any subsequent transfer must be accompanied by a Stock Transfer Form.

### 3.1.3 Valuation of a rights issue

#### Theoretical ex-rights price

It is important to determine the amount the purchaser pays for the rights nil paid. The first step is to calculate the value of a share after the rights issue, i.e. the **theoretical ex-rights price**.

## Example

A company carries out a 1 for 3 rights issue at a subscription price of £4.00 when the market price (or **cum rights price**) is £5.00 per share.

| | | (£) | |
|---|---|---|---|
| Existing holding | 3 shares @ | 5.00 = | 15.00 |
| Shares issued as a result of the rights issue | 1 share @ | 4.00 = | 4.00 |
| | 4 shares @ | ? = | **19.00** |

As a result of the rights issue, the shareholder now has four indistinguishable (fungible) shares with a total value of £19.00.

Therefore, each share now has a value of $\frac{£19.00}{4}$ = £ 4.75

As a result of the rights issue, the share price will, theoretically, fall from its current market level of £5.00 to £4.75, referred to as the theoretical ex-rights price. This reflects the dilution effect of issuing one new share at £4.00 when the existing market price of the share is £5.00.

### Nil paid values

If the new share price is £4.75, then the maximum price that anybody would be prepared to pay for the rights letter, which gives the right to buy the shares at £4.00, would be **75p**. Anything more would mean that buyers may as well go into the market and buy the shares after the rights issue.

It must be stressed that we are dealing here with a purely **theoretical** situation. In reality, prices might reflect a number of other factors, and rise and fall by different amounts.

### Maximum subscription at nil cost

A final point to consider is that the investor may have insufficient funds available to take up the rights, although he may be very keen to buy as many shares as possible. One solution to this is to split the rights letter into two components. One portion is sold at the nil paid value to raise finance. This money is then used to purchase the shares for as many of the remaining rights as possible. There is a simple formula for working out the number of shares that can be purchased in this fashion.

## Example

If the investor owns 3,000 shares, he will receive the right to purchase an additional 1,000 shares (following the example of a 1 for 3 rights issue).

In order to take up as many rights to shares as possible, it will be necessary to sell the following number of rights.

$$\text{Number of rights available} \times \frac{\text{Subscription price}}{\text{Theoretical ex-rights price}}$$

$$1{,}000 \times \frac{£4}{£4.75} = 842.1\ (843)\ \text{(always round-up)}$$

*Proof*

| | Rights | | | (£) |
|---|---|---|---|---|
| Sell | 843 | @ | 0.75 = | 632.25 |
| Buy/Take up | 157 | @ | 4.00 = | 628.00 |
| | 1,000 | | | 4.25 |

It will be impossible to better this situation. If the investor sold one less right, there would be insufficient funds to take up this extra right.

### 3.1.4 Example rights letter

PROVISIONAL ALLOTMENT LETTER

| | ACCOUNT No. | ALLOTMENT No. |
|---|---|---|
| 00708745 | T4200116 | 15341916 |

IMPORTANT — THIS DOCUMENT IS OF VALUE, IS NEGOTIABLE AND REQUIRES YOUR IMMEDIATE ATTENTION. THE OFFER CONTAINED HEREIN EXPIRES AT 9.30 A.M. (LONDON TIME) ON 15 JUNE 2001. THIS ENTIRE DOCUMENT MUST BE PRESENTED WHEN PAYMENT IS MADE. HOLDERS OF BT SHARES OUTSIDE THE UNITED STATES SHOULD READ THIS PROVISIONAL ALLOTMENT LETTER IN CONJUNCTION WITH THE PROSPECTUS RELATING TO BT, DATED 10 MAY 2001, WHICH ACCORDS WITH THE LISTING RULES MADE UNDER PART IV OF THE FINANCIAL SERVICES ACT 1986 (THE "UK PROSPECTUS"). HOLDERS OF BT SHARES IN THE UNITED STATES SHOULD READ THIS PROVISIONAL ALLOTMENT LETTER IN CONJUNCTION WITH THE REGISTRATION STATEMENT ON FORM F-3, RELATING TO THE NEW BT SHARES, DATED 10 MAY 2001, FILED WITH THE US SECURITIES AND EXCHANGE COMMISSION (THE "US PROSPECTUS"). THE "PROSPECTUS" SHALL MEAN THE UK PROSPECTUS IN THE CASE OF HOLDERS OF BT SHARES OUTSIDE THE UNITED STATES AND THE US PROSPECTUS IN THE CASE OF HOLDERS OF BT SHARES IN THE UNITED STATES AS APPROPRIATE. SHAREHOLDERS SHOULD READ CAREFULLY THE PROSPECTUS BEFORE DECIDING WHETHER TO TAKE UP THEIR RIGHTS.

**All enquiries relating to this provisional allotment letter ("PAL") should be referred to Lloyds TSB Registrars, Antholin House, 71 Queen Street, London EC4N 1SL quoting the account number on this PAL. If you are in any doubt as to the action you should take you are recommended to seek your own professional advice immediately from your stockbroker, bank, solicitor, accountant, fund manager, or other appropriate financial adviser authorised under the Financial Services Act 1986 (the "Act"). If you sell or have sold or otherwise transferred all your existing BT Shares (other than ex-rights) before 21 May 2001, please send this document with Form X completed and the accompanying documents at once to the purchaser or transferee or to the stockbroker, bank or other agent through or by whom the sale or transfer was effected, to be forwarded to the purchaser or transferee. However, this document should not be forwarded in or into Australia, Belgium, Canada, France, Japan or South Africa.**

**BRITISH TELECOMMUNICATIONS PUBLIC LIMITED COMPANY**

*(Incorporated and registered in England No. 1800000)*

RIGHTS ISSUE OF UP TO 1,975,580,052 NEW BT SHARES OF 25 PENCE EACH AT 300 PENCE PER SHARE
payable in full on acceptance not later than 9.30 a.m. on 15 June 2001

60171
MR ANDREW ROBERT DOUGHTY

15341916

| Box 1<br>Registered holding of BT Shares at close of business on 9 May 2001 | Box 2<br>Number of new BT Shares provisionally allotted to you | Box 3<br>Amount payable in full on acceptance at 300 pence per new BT Share not later than 9.30 a.m. on 15 June 2001 |
|---|---|---|
| ***120*** | ***36*** | ***£108.00*** |

All enquiries in connection with this letter should be made to:
Lloyds TSB Registrars
Antholin House
71 Queen Street
London EC4N 1SL
Telephone: 0808 100 4141 (UK only)
+44 20 7864 9074 (International calls)

| Latest time and date for: | 2001 |
|---|---|
| Depositing Nil Paid Rights into CREST | 3.00 p.m. on 11 June |
| Splitting nil paid | 3.00 p.m. on 12 June |
| **Acceptance and payment in full** | 9.30 a.m. on 15 June |
| Depositing fully paid rights into CREST | 3.00 p.m. on 27 June |
| Splitting Fully Paid | 3.00 p.m. on 27 June |
| Registration of renunciation | 3.00 p.m. on 29 June |
| CREST accounts to be credited | 2 July |
| Expected despatch of share certificates | by 16 July |

**TO ACCEPT IN FULL, PLEASE RETURN THE WHOLE OF THIS LETTER WITH A CHEQUE FOR THE AMOUNT SHOWN IN BOX 3 ABOVE (MADE PAYABLE TO "LLOYDS TSB BANK PLC — BT RIGHTS ISSUE" AND CROSSED "A/C PAYEE ONLY") TO LLOYDS TSB REGISTRARS AT THE ABOVE ADDRESS BY 9.30 A.M. ON 15 JUNE 2001. IF YOU WISH TO HAVE THE NEW BT SHARES REGISTERED IN YOUR NAME, YOU DO NOT NEED TO COMPLETE ANY OF THE DETAILS IN THE REST OF THIS LETTER.**

Application has been made to the UK Listing Authority for the new BT Shares to be admitted to the Official List and application has been made to the London Stock Exchange for the new BT Shares to be admitted to trading on its market for listed securities. It is expected that Admission will become effective on 20 May 2001 and that dealings in rights to the new BT Shares will commence, nil paid, at 8.00 a.m. on 21 May 2001. If Admission has not become effective by such time (or such later time and/or date as Cazenove & Co. Ltd and Merrill Lynch International may agree with the Company, not being later than 3.00 p.m. on 29 May 2001) this document shall cease to be of any value and the provisional allotment will lapse and any payments received will be returned without interest. Copies of the UK Prospectus have been delivered to the Registrar of Companies in England and Wales for registration in accordance with section 149 of the Act and may be obtained from or inspected at the offices of Linklaters & Alliance, One Silk Street, London EC2Y 8HQ and the registered office of the Company. Copies of the US Prospectus may also be obtained from or inspected at Morgan Guaranty Trust Company of New York, JP Morgan Service Centre, P.O. Box 842006, Boston MA 02284-2006 ("Morgan Guaranty") or Georgeson Shareholder Communications Inc., 17 State Street, New York, New York 1000Y or the registered office of the Company. Save where the context otherwise requires, words and expressions defined in the Prospectus shall have the same meaning in this PAL.

If you are a holder of BT Shares in the United States and you take up or transfer the rights represented by this Provisional Allotment Letter, you will be deemed to represent that you have received and read a copy of the US Prospectus. If you have not received a copy of the US Prospectus, you should contact, Georgeson Shareholder Communications Inc., 17 State Street, New York, New York 1000Y on +1 888 382 8303 to obtain a copy.

The attention of Qualifying Shareholders who have registered addresses outside the United Kingdom or who are citizens or residents of countries other than the United Kingdom or who are holding BT Shares for the benefit of such persons is drawn to note 7 on page 2 of this document, relating to Overseas Shareholders, and to the section headed "Overseas Shareholders" in paragraph 7 of Part 3 of the UK Prospectus or the paragraph entitled "Non-UK Holders of Shares" on page 32 of the US Prospectus.

If you wish to accept your rights and then wish the fully paid Provisional Allotment Letter to be returned to you, please tick this box. You need to have the fully paid Provisional Allotment Letter returned to you only if you want to deal in your Fully Paid Rights. Otherwise, the next document you receive will be a share certificate for your new BT Shares. ☐ Box 4

| Name and address of lodging agent. (If this box is not completed by the agent lodging this form for payment, this Provisional Allotment Letter will be returned, if requested, to the person(s) named above) | Received the amount payable on acceptance<br><br>For Lloyds TSB Registrars | Account No. T4200116 / Allotment No. 15341916<br>***36***<br>***£108.00***<br>02787537 |
|---|---|---|

PAGE 4

***36***

ACCOUNT No. T4200116

ALLOTMENT No. 15341916

**FORM X** **FORM OF RENUNCIATION**

**To be completed if the original allottee(s) desire(s):**

(i) **to renounce all the Nil Paid Rights or Fully Paid Rights comprised herein (the original allottee may do so up to 3.00 p.m. on 29 June 2001); or**

(ii) **to obtain split Provisional Allotment Letters (the original allottee may do so up to 3.00 p.m. on 12 June 2001 (if nil paid) and up to 3.00 p.m. on 27 June 2001 (if fully paid)); or**

(iii) **(where the original allottee is a CREST member or CREST personal member) to convert the Nil Paid Rights or Fully Paid Rights represented by this letter into uncertificated form (that is, to deposit them in CREST).**

*To the Directors of British Telecommunications public limited company*

I/We hereby renounce my/our right to the new BT Shares comprised in this Provisional Allotment Letter for the purposes of splitting or in favour of the person (s) named in the Registration Application Form (Form Y) or CREST Deposit Form below.

*Notes for completion of this form*

All joint allottees must sign. Any forms completed under a power of attorney must be accompanied by a certified copy of the power of attorney. A company must execute under its common seal which should be affixed in accordance with its articles of association or other regulations. Alternatively, a company to which section 36A of the Companies Act 1985 applies may execute this letter by a director and the company secretary or by two directors of the company signing the letter and bearing the name of the company above their signatures. Each of the officers signing the letter should state the office which he or she holds under his or her signature. Before signing, please read paragraph 7 on page 2 relating to Overseas Shareholders. If all the new BT Shares are to be registered in the name of the person(s) on page 1 of the document this Form X should not be completed. In the case of split letters, this Form X will be endorsed "Original Duly Renounced".

Dated ....................

*Signature(s) of person (s) named on page 1 of this document* { ....................
....................
....................
....................

**CONSOLIDATION LISTING FORM**

| Allotment number of letter | No. of new BT Shares |
|---|---|
| | |
| Total number of allotment letters | Total number of new BT Shares |
| | |

Allotment number of Principal Letter

**FORM Y** **REGISTRATION APPLICATION FORM**

**In the event of renunciation, this Form Y must be completed by or on behalf of the person(s) in whose name(s) the new BT Shares are to be registered unless such person(s) is/are (a) CREST member(s) and wish(es) to hold the new BT Shares in CREST, in which case the CREST Deposit Form below must be completed. THIS FORM Y SHOULD NOT BE COMPLETED IN THE NAME(S) OF THE ORIGINAL ALLOTTEE(S).**

(1) Forename (s) (in full) .................... Surname .................... Mr., Mrs., Miss or title
(2) Forename (s) (in full) .................... Surname .................... Mr., Mrs., Miss or title
(3) Forename (s) (in full) .................... Surname .................... Mr., Mrs., Miss or title
(4) Forename (s) (in full) .................... Surname .................... Mr., Mrs., Miss or title

FULL POSTAL ADDRESS OF FIRST-NAMED APPLICANT OR FULL REGISTRATION DETAILS IF CORPORATE BODY

....................

.................... Postcode ....................

Stamp and/or name and address of agent (if any) lodging this Provisional Allotment Letter for a Share Certificate

For use between 18 June 2001 and 3.00 p.m. on 29 June 2001 (see paragraph 4 on page 2 of this document, relating to Share Certificates).

Name: ....................

Address: ....................

....................

Note: to be completed only if share certificates are to be sent to an address other than shown on page 1 or, if Form Y on this page 4 is completed, other than to the address inserted in Form Y.

**CREST DEPOSIT FORM**

**Before completing this form, please refer to paragraph 4 on page 3 of this letter and to the notes below. This form should only be completed by either: (i) the original allottee(s) (where the original allottee is a CREST member) if he/she wishes to convert the Nil Paid Rights or Fully Paid Rights (as appropriate) represented by this letter into uncertificated form (that is, to deposit them in CREST); or (ii) a person or persons to whom this letter has been renounced and who (being a CREST member) wish(es) to hold the Nil Paid Rights or Fully Paid Rights (as appropriate) represented by this letter in uncertificated form. Form X above must therefore also have been completed. Do not complete Form Y if you are completing the CREST Deposit Form.**

| Counter Location Stamp (a). | SDRN (b). Bar Code or Reference. |
|---|---|
| | |

Full name(s) of the person(s) who wishes to convert Nil Paid Rights or Fully Paid Rights (as appropriate) into uncertificated form or to whom the Nil Paid Rights or Fully Paid Rights have been renounced. Such person(s) must be a CREST member (c).

| Participant ID (d). | Member account ID (d). | Stamp of depositing CREST participant (e). |
|---|---|---|
| | | |

*To the Directors of the Company*

I/we (being the person(s) lodging this form) request you to enter on the relevant register of securities that the Nil Paid Rights or Fully Paid Rights (as appropriate) represented by this Provisional Allotment Letter are held in uncertificated form by the CREST member specified above to whom such rights have been renounced or as a result of conversion of Nil Paid Rights or Fully Paid Rights (as appropriate) from certificated form into uncertificated form.

*Notes for completion of this form*

(a) The Counter Location Stamp identifies the CCSS Counter where this letter has been processed and is applied by the Counter.
(b) The Stock Deposit Reference Number (SDRN) should be written or bar-coded in this space.
(c) No address is required, as the CREST member will be identifiable by its participant ID.
(d) Insert the participant ID of the CREST member to whom this letter has been renounced and the member account ID under which the Nil Paid Rights or Fully Paid Rights will be held in CREST.
(e) This should contain the Broker ID of the depositing CREST participant.

The depositing CREST participant by delivering this letter to CRESTCo authorises CRESTCo to deliver this letter to the Company and agrees to be deemed for all purposes to be the person(s) actually so delivering this letter. CRESTCo is delivering this letter at the direction and on behalf of the depositing CREST participant whose stamp appears herein and does not in any manner or to any extent warrant or represent the validity, genuineness or correctness of the instructions contained herein or the genuineness of the signature(s) of the transferor(s).

0325084

## 3.2 Bonus issues

Bonus issues are also referred to as **scrip issues**, capitalisation issues, cap issues and free issues. Here, the company issues new shares, but does not require a payment for them from the shareholder.

## Example

One for three bonus/scrip issue when market price is £5.00.

| | | | |
|---|---|---|---|
| **Existing holding** | 3 shares | @ £5.00 = | £15.00 |
| **Shares issued as a result of the rights issue** | 1 share | @ free = | £0.00 |
| | 4 shares | @ ? | £15.00 |

As a result, each share now has a diluted value of $\frac{£15.00}{4}$ = £3.75.

Many companies in the UK are now offering the shareholders the right to receive their dividend in the form of shares rather than in the form of cash. This is referred to as a **scrip dividend**.

### 3.2.1 Rationale for bonus issue

The main purpose of bonus issues is to dilute the price of the share in the marketplace by spreading it over a larger number of securities. This is felt to be important in the UK markets, since shares with too high a value may discourage activity, and therefore liquidity, in a stock. Given that a bonus issue will generally increase marketability, the resulting price will usually be above the theoretical ex-bonus level.

In terms of the balance sheet, the effect is

| | |
|---|---|
| **Impact on Net Assets** | None |
| **Impact on Shareholders' Funds** | Share capital up<br>Share premium account down<br>Any surplus over the value of the share premium would have to go to other reserves |

A bonus issue can be financed out of any reserve, not solely from a share premium account.

(b) To write off **preliminary expenses** of forming a company.

(c) To write off **expenses of issue** of shares or debentures.

(d) To charge the **premium on repayment of debentures**.

(e) To charge the **discount on issue of debentures**.

The share premium account can **never be reduced to pay dividends** to the shareholders. It is one of the company's non-distributable reserves.

## 3.3 Stock split

Stock splits have a similar cosmetic effect to a bonus issue in that they create more shares and so reduce the share price. Stock splits differ from bonus issues in that the nominal value of the shares is split.

For example, a company has 200,000 issued shares with a nominal value of £1. The company undertakes a 2 for 1 stock split. This implies the company will be replacing each share with two new shares. We will identify the impact on the share capital account.

Before the stock split the company had

Share Capital £200,000 (representing 200,000 £1 NV shares)

After the stock split the company will have 400,000 shares with a NV of £0.50

Share Capital £200,000 (representing 400,000 £0.50 N.V. shares)

So we can see there has been no impact on the share capital account. Nor has any cash been raised, so again there is no impact on the asset half of the balance sheet.

## 3.4 Open offers

### 3.4.1 What is an open offer?

An open offer is pre-emptive offer to existing shareholders which is not allotted on renounceable documents. This means that the shareholder cannot sell on the right to subscribe for the open offer shares, unlike in a rights issue. An open offer will still be made pro rata to existing shareholdings in the company.

### 3.4.2 Requirements for open offers

The Listing Rules provide that in order to ensure that shareholders have adequate time to claim shares being offered by means of an open offer, there must be at least 15 business days between posting of the application forms to shareholders and when the offer closes.

An open offer will not be permitted where the offer price is at a discount of more than 10% to the middle market price of the shares when the offer is announced, unless the company is in severe financial difficulties or there are other exceptional circumstances and the company obtains shareholder approval.

### 3.4.3 Use of open offers

An open offer is often used in conjunction with a secondary placing, when it may be described as a 'placing with clawback'. Here, the offer shares are first placed conditionally with institutional investors, and then offered on a pre-emptive basis to the company's existing shareholders. To the extent that shareholders take up their entitlement to new shares, these shares are 'clawed back' from the institutional places. This structure has the effect of an underwriting of the open offer.

Where an 'offer for sale' method is employed, shares are offered to the public by the sponsoring investment bank who is acting as an intermediary.

Where an 'offer for subscription', shares are offered to the public by the issuing company, without the use of an intermediary firm.

In both instances, either a fixed offer, where the price is decided in advance, or a tender offer, where bids are requested, may be employed.

# Chapter Roundup

## Financial statements

- A company is a separate legal entity, ie an individual in law.
- A company is owned by its shareholders or members but managed on a day to day basis by its directors.
- In small companies the shareholders may be the directors, but in larger businesses the directors are appointed by the shareholders to manage the business on their behalf.
- The core financial statements are the balance sheet, the Income statement and the cash flow statement.
- The International Accounting Standards Board sets international accounting standards. They work closely with the Accounting Standards Board in the UK, who set standards for firms following UK standards.

## Balance sheet

- The balance sheet is a statement of the financial position of the business at a specific point in time.
- It is a product of the accounting equation that may be stated as either:
  - Assets = Liabilities + shareholders' funds
  - Net assets (Assets – Liabilities) = shareholders' funds
- Assets are distilled into non-current (fixed) and current. Liabilities are also broken down into long term non-current (long-term) and current. The distinction is to aid the users of accounts and make the accounts useful.
- Any business expenditure will be either
  - Capital expenditure = buying assets
  - Revenue expenditure = paying business expenses

## Non-current assets

- All non-current (fixed) assets with a finite useful life must be depreciated in order to match the cost of the asset to the benefit from its use.
- Depreciation may be either:
  - Straight line: $= \frac{\text{Cost} - \text{Residual value}}{\text{Expected useful life}}$

  Balance sheet value = Net book value (NBV) = Cost – Accumulated depreciation
- If a non-current asset is sold at a price that differs from NBV a profit or loss arises.

## Current assets

- All current assets are valued at the lower of:
  - Cost = Historical purchase price
  - NRV = Anticipated sales price – Selling costs
- Inventory cost allocation methods include:
  - FIFO
  - LIFO – (use not permitted in the UK)

- Weighted average
- Any other similar method

### Liabilities

- Amounts payable by the company that are split on the balance sheet between:
  - payable within one year.
  - payable after more than one year.
- Provision = Amount set aside to meet the probable future costs of a past event (usually a known but unquantified liability).
- Contingency = Uncertain liability/possible obligation arising from past events.
- Any pension scheme net assets or liability appears on the balance sheet.

### Other balance sheet items

- Post balance sheet event may be:
  - Adjusting = New information about balance sheet date values.
  - Non-adjusting = Relating to conditions not existing at the balance sheet date.

### Share capital

- Bonus/scrip issue and split = Increase number of shares but do not raise finance, hence NAs and SFs values unaltered.
- Rights issue raises new finance, increasing NAs and SFs.
- Share repurchases consume finance, reducing NAs and SFs.

### Reserves

- Retained earnings = Accumulated retained profits since the business started.
- Share provision account = non-distributable reserve representing the excess received on issuing shares above their nominal value. May be used to:
  - issue fully paid bonus shares.
  - write off preliminary expenses.
  - write off expenses of issuing shares/debentures.
  - write off the premium on redemption or discount on issue of debentures.
- Revaluation reserve = Non-distributable reserve reflecting any change in the value of non-current assets when they are revalued.

### Income statement

- The income statement provides detail on revenue and expenses to show how the company has generated its profit or loss.
- Revenue should be recognised if:
  - product/service has been provided to the buyer.
  - the value of the goods/services has been established.
  - the buyer has recognised his liability to pay.
  - the buyer is willing to pay.

- Profit may be measured at a number of levels as follows:

| | |
|---|---|
| Revenue | X |
| Cost of sales | (X) |
| Gross profit | X |
| Other trading/operating expenses | (X) |
| Operating profit | X |
| Non-trading expenses (eg interest) | (X) |
| PBT | X |
| Tax | (X) |
| PAT | X |

- The statement of changes in equity shows how the equity shareholders' funds have changed from one year to the next due to:
  - Generation of profits.
  - Payment of dividends.
  - Issue/repurchase of shares.
  - Revaluation of property.

## Cash flow statement

- The cash flow statement reconciles the movement in cash on the balance sheet. The statement breaks down into three headings.
  - Operating activities.
  - Investing activities.
  - Financing activities.
- Cash flow from operations may be calculated using either the direct or indirect method.

**Indirect method**

| | |
|---|---|
| Operating profit | X |
| Add: Depreciation | X |
| Working capital adjustments | |
| – (Increase)/Decrease in inventory | X |
| – (Increase)/Decrease in receivables | X |
| – Increase/(Decrease) in payables | X |
| Increase in cash from operations | X |

## Ratio analysis

- Ratios are useful for condensing down information which may be used to identify changes in a company's performance from year to year, or to compare the company's performance against other companies in the same industry.
- Ratios broadly go under the heading of profitability, liquidity, investor and gearing.

## Profitability

- Profitability ratios assess the trading or operating performance of the company.

$$\text{ROCE} = \frac{\text{Profit before interest payable and tax}}{\text{Capital employed}} \times 100\%$$

$$\text{Profit margin} = \frac{\text{Profits}}{\text{Revenue}} \times 100\%$$

### Liquidity

- Liquidity ratios measure the risk of a company being able or unable to pay its creditors.

$$\text{Current ratio} = \frac{\text{Current assets due within one year}}{\text{Current liabilities falling due within one year}}$$

$$\text{Quick ratio} = \frac{\text{Current assets excluding inventory}}{\text{Current liabilities falling due within one year}}$$

### Gearing

- Gearing ratios measure the risks to the providers of debt and equity finance.

$$\text{Debt to equity} = \frac{\text{Interest-bearing loans}}{\text{Equity shareholders' funds}} \times 100\%$$

$$\text{Net debt to equity} = \frac{\text{Debt (as above)} - \text{Cash and current asset investments}}{\text{Equity shareholders' funds}} \times 100\%$$

$$\text{Interest cover} = \frac{\text{Profit before interest payable and tax}}{\text{Interest payable}}$$

### Investors

- Investors ratios measure and assess the returns to the providers of finance.

$$\text{EPS} = \frac{\text{Earnings attributable to ordinary shareholders}}{\text{Number of ordinary shares}}$$

$$\text{Price/Earnings} = \frac{\text{Current market price per share}}{\text{Earnings per share}}$$

$$\text{Earnings yield} = \frac{\text{Earnings per share}}{\text{Current market price per share}} \times 100\%$$

$$\text{Dividend yield} = \frac{\text{Dividend per share}}{\text{Current market price per share}} \times 100\%$$

$$\text{Dividend cover} = \frac{\text{Earnings per share}}{\text{Dividend per share}}$$

$$\text{Net asset value} = \frac{\text{Net assets attributable to ordinary shareholders}}{\text{Number of ordinary shares in issue}}$$

# TEST YOUR KNOWLEDGE

*Check your knowledge of the Chapter here, without referring back to the text.*

1. The balance sheet shows the company's position at a specific point in time. *True/False*?

2. What is the accounting equation?

3. Name three types of non-current asset.

4. Name three types of current asset.

5. What impact will a bonus issue have on the share premium and share capital account?

6. You are provided the following information regarding inventories.

| *Item* | *Cost* | *Selling price* | *Selling cost* |
|---|---|---|---|
| A | 12 | 15 | 2 |
| B | 21 | 24 | 4 |
| C | 18 | 17 | 3 |

Determine the balance sheet value for inventories.

7. The following inventory transactions have occurred.

| | |
|---|---|
| 1 Jan | Buy 100 items at £20 each |
| 3 Jan | Sell 60 items |
| 8 Jan | Buy 40 items at £22 each |
| 10 Jan | Sell 50 items |
| 15 Jan | Buy 40 items at £24 each |

Calculate the cost of the closing inventory on

- FIFO basis
- LIFO basis

8. Receivables are shown on the balance sheet net of bad and doubtful debts. *True/False*?

9. The indirect method of calculating cash flow from operations requires depreciation to be deducted from operating profit. *True/False*?

10. Calculate the cash from operating activities for this year from the following information.

| | *Last year* | *This year* |
|---|---|---|
| Operating profit | 100,000 | 120,000 |
| Depreciation | 15,000 | 16,000 |
| Inventories | 25,000 | 28,000 |
| Receivables | 39,000 | 37,000 |
| Payables | 31,000 | 36,000 |

11. How is return on capital employed calculated?

12. How is the debt-to-equity ratio calculated?

13. A low price to earning ratio indicates that a company is highly rated in the eyes of shareholders. *True/False*?

14. How is the dividend yield calculated and what does it tell us about the growth prospects of the company?

15. You are given the following information.

**Balance sheet**

| | *Last year* | *This year* |
|---|---|---|
| Non-current assets | 200 | 220 |
| Current assets | 100 | 120 |
| Creditors | (80) | (90) |
| Loans | (120) | (130) |
| | 100 | 120 |
| Share capital | 50 | 50 |
| Retained profits | 50 | 70 |
| | 100 | 120 |

**Income statement**

| | | |
|---|---|---|
| Revenue | 100 | 140 |
| Cost of sales | (60) | (80) |
| Gross profit | 40 | 60 |
| Operating cost | (25) | (30) |
| Operating profit | 15 | 30 |
| Tax | (5) | (10) |
| Profit after tax | 10 | 20 |

Calculate the following ratios:

- ROCE
- Gross profit margin
- Current ratio
- Debt to equity


BPP LEARNING MEDIA

# TEST YOUR KNOWLEDGE: ANSWERS

1. True

   **(See Section 1)**

2. Assets = Liabilities + Shareholders' funds
   Net assets = Shareholders' funds

   **(See Section 1.1)**

3. Property, plant and equipment
   Intangibles
   Investments

   **(See Section 1.3.1)**

4. Inventory, receivables and cash

   **(See Section 1.3.7)**

5. Reduce share premium and increase share capital

   **(See Section 3.2.1)**

6.

| *Item* | *Cost* | *NRV* | *BS value* |
|---|---|---|---|
| A | 12 | 13 (15 – 2) | 12 |
| B | 21 | 20 (24 – 4) | 20 |
| C | 18 | 14 (17 – 3) | 14 |
| | | | 46 |

   **(See Section 1.3.8)**

7.

| | |
|---|---|
| Total purchases | 180 units |
| Total sales | 110 units |
| Inventory | 70 units |

   **FIFO**

   Cost = Cost of most recently purchased items, ie

| | |
|---|---|
| 40 @ 24 = | 960 |
| 30 @ 22 = | 660 |
| | 1,620 |

   **LIFO**

   At each sale, units sold = most recently purchased

| | *Purchase* | *5 Jan sale* | *10 Jan sale* | *Inventory* | *Price* | *Cost* |
|---|---|---|---|---|---|---|
| 1 Jan purchase | 100 | (60) | (10) | 30 | 20 | 600 |
| 8 Jan purchase | 40 | | (40) | 0 | 22 | 0 |
| 15 Jan purchase | 40 | | | 40 | 24 | 960 |
| | | | | | | 1,560 |

   **(See Section 1.3.8)**

8. True

   **(See Section 1.3.7)**

9. False

   **(See Section 1.5.5)**

10.

| | |
|---|---|
| Operating profit | 120,000 |
| Add: Depreciation | 16,000 |
| Increase in inventories | (3,000) |
| Decrease in receivables | 2,000 |
| Increase in payables | 5,000 |
| Cash from operating activities | 140,000 |

   **(See Section 1.5.5)**

11. Profit before interest payable and tax/capital employed.

   **(See Section 2.4)**

12. Interest-bearing loans/equity shareholders' funds.

   **(See Section 2.8.1)**

13. False. A low P/E ratio indicates investors are prepared to pay only a relatively low amount relative to the current year's earnings of the business.

   **(See Section 2.10.1)**

14. Dividend/share price.

   A high dividend yield often indicates a company with low growth prospects, since the company is likely to be paying out a large proportion of its profits as dividends, and so only retaining a small proportion.

   **(See Section 2.10.3)**

15. ROCE = $\frac{15}{220}$ = 0.068 or 6.8%

   **(See Section 2.4)**

   Gross profit margin = $\frac{60}{140}$ = 0.429 or 42.9%

   **(See Section 1.4.5)**

   Current ratio = $\frac{120}{90}$ = 1.33×

   **(See Section 2.6.1)**

   Debt to equity = $\frac{130}{120}$ = 1.08 or 108%

   **(See Section 2.8.2)**

# 6 Collective Investments

## INTRODUCTION

Most ordinary investors cannot easily gain exposure to a number of different shares or different sectors conveniently and without incurring relatively high costs. The sectors of financial services industry that offer 'pooled' investment products can help.

In the UK, the main types of pooled investment are unit trusts, open ended investment companies, investment trusts and exchange-traded funds. In this chapter, we explain each of these types of fund in turn.

### CHAPTER CONTENTS

# Chapter Learning Objectives

## Collective Investment

### 6.1 Characteristics of Collective Investment Funds and Companies

**6.1.1** **Analyse** the key features, accessibility, risks, tax treatment, charges, valuation and yield characteristics of open-ended investment companies (OEICs)/Investment Companies with Variable Capital (ICVCs).

**6.1.2** **Analyse** the key features, accessibility, risks, tax treatment, charges, valuation and yield characteristics of unit trusts.

**6.1.3** **Analyse** the key features, accessibility, risks, tax treatment, charges, valuation and yield characteristics of investment trusts.

**6.1.4** **Analyse** the key features, accessibility, risks, tax treatment, charges, valuation and yield characteristics of real estate investment trusts (REITs).

### 6.2 Exchange-Traded Funds

**6.2.1** **Analyse** the key features, accessibility, risks, tax treatment, charges, valuation and yield characteristics of the main types of Exchange Traded Funds (ETFs).

### 6.3 Structured Products

**6.4.1** **Analyse** the key features, accessibility, risks, valuation and yield characteristics of the main types of retail structured products and investment notes, compared with other forms of direct and indirect investment:

- Structure
- Income and capital growth
- Investment risk and return
- Counterparty risk
- Expenses
- Capital protection
- Tax efficiency

### 6.4 Analysis of Collective Investments

**6.4.1** **Analyse** the factors to take into account when selecting collective investments:

- Quality of firm, management team, product track record and administration
- Investment mandate – scope, controls, restrictions and review process
- Investment strategy
- Exposure, allocation, valuation and quality of holdings
- Prospects for capital growth and income
- Asset cover and redemption yield
- Track record compared with appropriate peer universe and market indices
- Location/ domicile/ Passporting arrangements
- Tax treatment

- Key man risk (KMR) and how this is managed by a firm
- Shareholder base
- Measures to prevent price exploitation by dominant investors
- Total expense and turnover ratios
- Liquidity, trading access and price stability

## Collective Investment Vehicles

Collective investment vehicles are return maximising funds. They are operations where a large number of small investors pool their money together to achieve a large fund which is placed under professional investment management. These funds can be in either of the following forms.

- Unit trusts
- Open-ended investment companies (OEICs), also known as Investment Companies with Variable Capital (ICVCs)
- Investment trusts
- Exchange traded funds

Each of these is slightly different.

# 1 Open-Ended Investment Companies (OEICs)

arning objectives

**6.1.1** **Analyse** the key features, accessibility, risks, tax treatment, charges, valuation and yield characteristics of open-ended investment companies (OEICs)/Investment Companies with Variable Capital (ICVCs).

The Treasury introduced regulations in connection to OEICs in early 1997. These created a third type of investment product with many (the best) of the features of both unit and investment trusts. The OEICs are included within the UCITS (Undertaking for Collective Investments in Transferable Securities) Directive. In line with UCITS, the schemes may only invest in transferable securities, and must be open ended.

It is envisaged within the regulations that many existing unit trusts will wish to convert into this new more flexible format. This will be possible without any tax implications on transfer.

In order to accommodate the OEICs into the system, a special company structure has been introduced in order to allow a company to continually issue and redeem its own shares, making it **open-ended**. The end result should be an investment product that is more flexible and more appealing to the European market. As for unit trusts, this open-ended structure ensures that the price of any OEIC shares is directly related to the prices of any underlying assets held. OEICs are be able to issue both **bearer and registered** shares. Several classes of shares are possible and within each class it will be possible to have both large and small denomination shares.

They are sometimes known by the alternative name '**Investment Company with Variable Capital**' or ICVCs. This is a special company structure, which has been introduced in order to allow a company to continually issue, and redeem, its own shares, and hence their capital structure will vary over time. The end result should be an investment product which is more flexible and more appealing, in particular to the Continental European market.

The shareholders of the OEIC are entitled to vote and to attend shareholder meetings.

A recent development by the London Stock Exchange has been the development of its **extraMARK** market, which allows certain OEIC shares to be traded on SETSqx. These OEIC shares are known as **Exchange-Traded Funds (ETFs)**, and are discussed later in this chapter.

Another form of OEIC is an umbrella fund, which allows investors to switch between various sub-funds within one OEIC. OEICs are thus a very flexible form of investment, since sub-funds can be added to an OEIC very quickly, which is another attraction of this structure.

## 1.1 Operation of OEICs

An OEIC must have a board to govern its affairs, one member of which must accept the responsibility of **Authorised Corporate Director** (ACD). The ACD's responsibilities include managing the company's investments, buying and selling its own shares on demand and ensuring the accurate **pricing of shares at net asset value**. This role is thus similar to that of the unit trust manager. The ACD will be FSA authorised.

The role of trustee is to safeguard the assets in an OEIC is performed by a **Depositary**. The role of depositary is generally undertaken by a bank and will be FSA authorised. The depositary will be independent of the OEIC and its directors. If the depositary makes use of sub-custodians, the depositary will retain responsibility for compliance and safekeeping.

Being FSA authorised, the ACD and depositary will be obliged to follow the FSA rulebook.

## 1.2 OEIC pricing

OEICs are regulated predominantly by the FSA, from whom they will require authorisation in a similar way, and following similar rules, to unit trusts. The most significant difference, however, is the requirement for **single pricing**, i.e. the ACD must give one single price at which investors both buy and sell the shares in the OEIC. The price is derived in the same way as for unit trusts, i.e. based on asset value per share at the valuation point.

The price reflects the value of the underlying investments without discount or premium, with any initial charge reflecting dealing costs and management expenses being disclosed separately. As with unit trusts, discounts may be offered on the usual initial charges, e.g. for direct sales or sales through fund supermarkets. The charges with OEICs may be lower than for unit trusts, particularly in respect of cost of entry (setting up) and exit (encashing the investment) due to single pricing.

Annual management costs are not set out as a separate charge as they are with unit trusts. It is however possible to quantify the costs by looking at the total expense ratio (TER) of the company. Figures for this are available in the public domain, allowing investors to make comparisons between investment managers.

Where the ACD is 'running a box', the ACD will keep shares sold back to them to resell later. Running a box reduces creation and cancellation requirements.

Thus, the price of OEICs is influenced partly by the value of the underlying investments, but may also be influenced by the perceived skill of the manager of the fund and general market conditions.

## 1.3 Taxation of OEICs

OEICs / ICVCs face a tax regime similar to that faced by unit trusts. Interest, rent and foreign dividends not taxed at source will be subject to a corporation tax charge. UK dividends received will suffer no further tax other than the 10% deducted at source. Capital gains are exempt from CGT.

Distributions (dividends) paid to investors in an OEIC are taxable in the same way as the distributions from unit trusts. Dividends are paid with a tax credit of 10% that satisfies the tax liability for basic starting rate tax payers.

For investors' OEIC holdings outside a tax-advantaged wrapper such as an ISA, capital gains tax will be chargeable on disposals.

Stamp duty is not paid on purchase of an OEIC.

Where an OEIC is based offshore, the distributions will not be taxed internally. This can be helpful for non-taxpaying investors, and can offer a cash flow advantage to tax paying investors.

## 1.4 ICVCs and SICAVs

Investment Companies with Variable Capital (ICVCs) is a term that is interchangeable with OEICs. Basically, in the UK we are more likely to use the phrase OEIC but ICVC is better understood in continental Europe because this is the UK version of a SICAV.

Société d'investissement à capital variables (SICAVs) were originally created in Luxembourg but are now common in Western Europe. As we have seen, they combine many of the features of unit trusts and investment trust companies.

## 1.5 The role of fund supermarkets

A fund supermarket is typically a website that can provide an alternative, more convenient way of investing in collective investment funds. The 'supermarket' term reflects the way in which they operate; a variety of funds can be purchased from a number of different management groups in one online place. Similar to real life supermarkets, the online counterparts have different goods on offer and services, size and cost vary greatly.

Fund supermarkets, pioneered in America, were introduced to the UK investor at the end of 1999. Since their appearance in the market the choice has become almost overwhelming. The UK is likely to be a springboard for fund supermarkets to launch in to Europe.

The regulators are watching the development of supermarkets closely to ensure investor protection is maintained. In particular, security surrounding the use of the internet to process transactions is an area to which the regulators will pay a great deal of attention.

Thus the price of OEICs is greatly influenced partly by the value of the underlying investments, but may also be influenced by the perceived skill of the manager of the fund and general market conditions.

# 2 Unit Trusts

earning objective

**6.1.3 Analyse** the key features, accessibility, risks, tax treatment, charges and valuation and yield characteristics of Unit Trusts.

### The nature of a unit trust

A **unit trust** is a legal trust. Under its terms, individuals pool their money, which is then invested by the trustees with a fund manager who manages the money. The funds relating to the trust are held in a trust fund, which is run in accordance with the rules laid down in the trust deed.

- Investors can buy units, each of which represents a specified fraction of the trust
- The trust holds a portfolio of securities
- The assets of the trust are held by trustees and are invested by managers
- The investor incurs annual management charges and possibly also an initial charge

The premise of an authorised unit trust (AUT) is that there are single undivided units. It is possible to create variations to this simple form with income units which pay out distributions and accumulation units roll up income into the capital value.

The assets of the trust are legally owned by a **trustee** on behalf of beneficiaries, who are known as the unit holders. They must be independent to the unit trust itself and given that they require assets of over £4 million, they are likely to be a bank or insurance company. While the trustee acts to protect the asset, the investor is the beneficiary.

A **fund manager** (who runs the fund and makes the day-to-day investment management decisions). The manager markets the unit trust, and manages the assets in line with the trust deed, and take responsibility for regulatory requirements. They also appoint the trustee. The job of the trustee is to protect the investor's interests by ensuring that the manager adheres to the rules and regulations that are stipulated in the trust deed. Therefore, we have seen that there are two parties to a unit trust, the manager and the trustee. To prevent conflicts of interest, it is necessary that the manager and the trustee are independent of each other.

As we will see later in this section, all trading takes place through fund managers, and if an individual wishes to add money to the fund he will receive a receipt in return, referred to as a unit in the fund. The fund manager makes a market in these units and may well have second-hand or redeemed units which he can sell to new investors (known as **box management**). Unit trusts in the UK are described as **open-ended** funds as there is no limit to the amount of money which can be invested. If no second-hand units are available, the fund is permitted to create more units and expand the fund.

## 2.1 Regulation of unit trusts

Some unit trusts are regulated by the Financial Services Authority (FSA) and acquire the status '**regulated'**. Only regulated unit trusts may be freely marketed to the public. Once a trust is authorised and regulated, it must abide by the FSA rules. These rules limit both the types of investment that can be entered into within a specific trust and the amounts of those investments compared to the size of the fund.

The rules and regulations are designed to ensure that the investors take a limited amount of risk. Should an investor wish to take more risk within the auspices of a collective investment scheme, there are a number of alternative authorised funds, which provide a range of risk profiles.

The FSA also requires a formal trust deed to be established which again will place limits on the powers of the trustees and the fund managers. Normally, unit trusts specify the nature of the investments into which they will enter, for example, Korean equities. The trust deed will also cover administrative matters such as the fees the fund manager is able to take from the fund each year, and the precise method of calculating the bid and offer prices at which units will be traded.

## 2.2 Buying and selling units

There is **no secondary market** in the units themselves. An individual can only buy or sell units directly with the **fund manager or through an intermediary**, such as an independent financial advisor (IFA). The price of units is based on the asset value of the fund. For example, if the fund has assets under management of £200m and there are 100m units in issue, each unit has a value of £2.00.

However, the fund manager will be able to make a spread (i.e. the difference between bid and offer) around that price. The spread formula is controlled by the FSA and allows for a spread between the bid and offer prices of no more than 15%. This may seem a substantial spread but it does allow the fund manager to be compensated for costs incurred in dealing with the fund, such as stamp duty and other dealing fees. The ability to set two different prices, one for buying (bid) and one for selling (offer), is known as **dual pricing.**

## 2.3 Bid and offer basis

Pricing of unit trusts begins with the **creation price**, which is simply the price the manager must pay to the trustee in order to create a new unit. It is a reflection of the value of the underlying investments the fund manager has made, based upon the valuation within the previous two hours.

Whilst the fund manager is allowed a **spread of up to 15%**, in reality most fund managers operate on a narrower bid to offer basis towards one end of the range.

For example, in pricing the unit above, using a spread of 15% would allow a spread of £1.85 to £2.15. When there are many investors selling the units of the fund, it is likely that the manager of the unit trust will price around the cancellation price (the lowest price). This is sometimes known as the **bid basis.** The bid basis might be £1.85 to £1.90. Operating on a bid basis encourages new money to come into the fund, and discourages money from leaving the fund.

If it is likely that lots of investors want to buy into the fund, the manager will price around the creation price (the highest price). This is sometimes known as the **offer basis**, say, £2.10 to £2.15.

Whilst the fund manager may operate at any point within that spread range, the **cancellation price** must be available on request. The cancellation price will be at the bottom end of the range, which in this case is £1.85.

Unit trusts are also permitted to apply an **exit charge** for investors cancelling their units. Funds that make such a charge are indicated by an **E** in the *Financial Times.*

When an investor wishes to exit the fund and sell his units, the fund manager may either cancel his holding or keep the units, placing them instead in a box. These units can then be reissued to a new investor, thus eliminating the need to create new additional units for investors buying into the fund **(box management)**.

## 2.4 Historic pricing and forward pricing basis

Prices will be set on a historic or forward pricing basis.

- Where the price the investor pays is based on the previous valuation point, the pricing is described as historic. All units purchased up to the valuation point on the following day will be at the same, previous price.
- Where the investor pays a price based on the next valuation point, it is called forward pricing. All units purchased up to next valuation point will be at that price.

Each system has its merits. With historic pricing, the investor knows the price he will pay for units, but the value of the underlying securities may not be reflected in the price paid. This is good if prices have moved up, but bad if they have moved down. Investors find future pricing confusing, as it is not possible to determine in advance the price they will pay, but the price will be more reflective of the underlying value of the securities.

- On a historical pricing basis, the manager creates units at the valuation point according to the amount of sales expected up to the next valuation point. If sales exceed expected levels, the manager must either move to forward pricing or risk loss of money for the fund if there is an unfavourable price movement.
- On a forward pricing basis, the manager must create units at the valuation point sufficient to cover transactions since the last valuation point.

A manager using the historic pricing basis must move to a forward pricing basis if the value of the fund is believed to have changed by 2% or more since the last valuation and if the investor requests forward pricing.

## 2.5 Unit trust charges

The charges on a unit trust must be explicit in the trust deed and documentation. They should give details of the current charges and the extent to which managers can change them.

Charges need to be made to cover the following types of cost:

- Managing the fund
- General administration
- Administration of the fund
- Direct marketing costs
- Marketing
- Commissions for intermediaries
- Regulation and compliance

These charges can be taken in one or more ways, via an initial charge, an exit charge or through annual management charges.

The initial charge is added to the buying price. So, the buyer incurs the cost of both the difference (spread) between the buying and the eventual selling price, and the initial charge. Managers might make an initial charge of 3.0-6.5% on equities, and less on gilt and fixed interest funds (1-4%) because of their lower dealing charges. Other funds with lower charges include index tracker funds and cash/money market funds, where the lower price reflects the lower burden of management. Where an initial charge is small or non-existent, there may be a further charge on exit.

Fund managers may offer discounts on the usual initial charge, particularly for direct sales or sales through low cost 'fund supermarkets' which generally act via the internet.

Exit charges are typically invoked where the investor sells the investment within a set period of time, eg five years.

An annual management charge of around 0.5-1.5% of the underlying fund will generally be made to cover the on-going cost of the investment management of the trust. In some cases part of the annual management charge is paid to intermediaries as renewal commission, typically at a rate of 0.5% per annum. The cost will vary with the level of management required on a fund. Offshore funds require more management and costs are likely to be higher. Tracker funds require less management and costs will generally be lower. Certain funds will have several tiers of management and will allow access to a wide range of investment managers via a single management company. In this case, each tier of management will need to recoup its costs and, in these cases, annual costs will be higher.

## 2.6 Unit trust taxation

Authorised unit trusts are exempt from tax on gains made within the fund, giving them an advantage, for instance, over life funds. Any income (other than dividend income from UK companies, which is not taxable) is taxed to corporation tax. Foreign withholding tax on dividends will be offset against the tax charge, subject to double taxation treaties.

Management expenses can be offset against income from non-UK equities.

Unit trusts do not pay tax on gains from options or futures.

The tax treatment of distributions parallels the tax treatment of direct holdings of equities and interest. If the trust holds more than 60% of its investments in interest bearing securities, the income is deemed to be interest then the distribution is made net of 20% tax, which can be reclaimed by non taxpayers. 10% starting rate taxpayers can reclaim 10%, while basic rate taxpayers have no further liability. Higher rate taxpayers must pay 20% more in tax.

For equity unit trusts, the distribution is made with a 10% tax credit. The tax treatment for different types of taxpayer is then as for dividends from shares held directly. The tax credit cannot be reclaimed by non-taxpayers. The tax credit satisfies the tax liability for a basic or savings starting (10%) rate taxpayer, but higher rate taxpayers will be liable to an additional 22.5% (or 32.5% for additional taxpayer). Non-taxpayers cannot reclaim the tax credit.

The individual is liable to capital gains tax on disposals of unit trust investments.

There is no stamp duty to pay on purchases of UK unit trusts.

# 3 Investment Trusts

earning objective

**6.1.4 Analyse** the key features, accessibility, risks, tax treatment, charges and valuation and yield characteristics of Investment Trusts.

### The nature of an investment trust company

The name investment trust is, to an extent, misleading. Investment trusts are not trusts in law, rather they are **public limited companies** whose shares are listed on the Stock Exchange. Investment trusts initially raise money by issuing shares. If an individual wishes to liquidate his investment, or make a new investment, he needs to either sell the shares to or buy some shares from someone else. Unlike pension funds and life assurance funds, investment trusts do not have liabilities to be met, hence the money is invested by the fund manager on behalf of the shareholders to generate a combination of capital growth and income in accordance with the investment trust's objectives. Other than to pay income distributions, money will not be repaid from the fund unless it is terminated. As a result, investment trusts are not faced by inflows and outflows of funds as pension funds and life assurance funds are. Investment trusts are, therefore, referred to as **closed-end funds**, since the size of the fund itself is independent of the buying or selling of shares. It is a function of the initial capital subscribed and the gains generated on that capital. Furthermore investment trusts are able to gear up the portfolio by borrowing money. This has the potential to increase the risk of the fund, as well as increasing the potential for returns. As a result of its closed-ended nature, the price of an investment trust's shares will be influenced by the value of the assets held, but not directly related (as is the case for unit trusts and OEICs).

## 3.1 The market in investment trusts

Unlike unit trusts, there is a full secondary market operating in investment trust shares. They are, after all, merely shares that trade on the LSE in the same way that the shares of any other company would trade. Pricing is set by **supply and demand** and is normally at a **discount** to the underlying asset value of the assets in the company itself. This is different to unit trusts and OEICs, where prices are set according to NAV.

A net asset value can be calculated by looking at the value of each of the underlying shares in the investment trust and its relative weighting in the fund. In a simplified example, an investment trust comprises the following securities.

| Security | Weighting | Net Asset Value (Price × Weighting) |
|---|---|---|
| Company A shares worth £5 | 10% of fund | 50p |
| Company B shares worth £8 | 20% of fund | 160p |
| Company C shares worth £1 | 25% of fund | 25p |
| Company D shares worth £2 | 25% of fund | 50p |
| Company E shares worth £10 | 20% of fund | 200p |
| | Net Asset Value | 485p |

If the market price of the share is 436.50p, we would describe this as a 10% discount to net asset value (485p – 436.50p = 48.50p = 10% of 485p). The level of this discount can vary in line with the following factors.

- The market's view on the quality of the management of the investment trust. If a star fund manager leaves, the value of the share may fall.
- Fluctuations in overall stock market levels, for example, giving a bigger discount if the stock market falls, as it is not possible to immediately re-weight the investment trust.

Of course, it is possible that the investment trust's shares trade at a premium to NAV. In other words, where the market attributes more to the shares than just their intrinsic value. This is possibly a reflection of positive market sentiment towards the fund and the manager's expertise.

The Financial Times publishes both the net asset value and the discount / premium in the Investment Trust section of its London Share Service.

## 3.2 Gearing

Investment trust companies usually have an element of gearing. That is, part of their finance comes from fixed interest issues such as debenture stocks, as there are no restrictions on borrowing. This gives the shareholder an advantage during periods of rising market prices. Conversely, in bear markets, the shareholder suffers from a fall in the value of their shares greater than the fall of prices generally. Unit trust borrowings are restricted and the price of units moves largely in line with the value of the underlying portfolio.

## 3.3 Income

Unit trusts generally distribute all of their income, except in the case of accumulation trusts. Investment trust companies, like other companies, declare dividends that may or may not exhaust the available income. Most of them reinvest part of their profits, which increases the invested capital for the benefit of the Ordinary shareholder.

## 3.4 Savings schemes

As with unit trusts and OEICs, it is possible to purchase shares in an investment trust through regular monthly savings. The investment manager will aggregate all the amounts received each month by individual savers and use the total to purchase shares in the investment trust in the market. The large deal size saves on dealing costs. The shares may be held by a nominee company or issued to the individual savers monthly or annually. It is also possible to make one-off additional payments.

## 3.5 Tax treatment

**Dividend payments** from direct equities or from collective investment which are equity based are paid **net of a 10% tax credit** which discharges the liability of basic and starting rate taxpayers. Non-taxpayers cannot reclaim the tax credit.

**Higher rate taxpayers pay a further 22.5%** to bring their **total liability up to 32.5%** of the grossed up dividend (i.e. the net dividend plus tax credit). Additional taxpayers must pay 32.5% extra up to their liability of 42.5%.

## Example: Dividend taxation

Rose receives a net dividend from an equity unit trust of £360. If she is a non-taxpayer, starting rate taxpayer or basic rate taxpayer, no further action is necessary. There is no further liability, nor ability to reclaim.

If she is a higher rate taxpayer, she will have a further liability. The £360 is net of a 10% tax credit, so the grossed up dividend is £400 (£360/0.9) and the tax credit is £40 (10% of £400).

Rose's total tax liability is 32.5% of £400 = £130, of which £40 is met by the tax credit.

The extra liability is 22.5% of £400 = £90.

**Gains on disposal** of direct equities or holdings in unit trusts, OEICs or investment trusts are **subject to CGT**. Indexation allowance, taper relief and the annual exemption are available in the normal way.

Investment trust shares may be bought from the manager or from their broker. It is likely to be cheaper to purchase from the manager. The purchase of shares in an investment trust will incur 0.5% stamp duty.

Note that the **managers** of unit trusts, OEICs and investment trusts are **not subject to tax on gains within the portfolio**, so they can deal without regard to any tax consequences. **Disposals within the portfolio do not affect the investor**, who is subject to CGT only on disposal of his own holding in the collective investment.

*Note: Investment bonds and endowments are not explicitly covered by the syllabus. We have included a brief discussion here of both for the purpose of giving additional background in this subject area.*

## 3.6 Investment Bonds

An **investment bond** (sometimes called a single premium bond) is a **life assurance policy** designed to take in a **lump sum** (or a series of lump sums). Generally the arrangement is written as a **non qualifying whole of life policy** and does not therefore have a fixed maturity date.

These arrangements are often **unit linked**, and offer a wide range of different **investment funds** with the advantage of professional management in much the same way as applied to the collective investments described in Section 4.

In some ways, investment bonds perform a similar task to the collective investments already discussed, but there are some significant differences, which are considered in this section.

## 3.7 Fund choice and switching

The range of funds available for an investment bond will generally include **equity funds** of various types and also funds investing in **fixed interest securities**, so the range of choice is similar to that which is available under collective investment vehicles. However in addition, the range of funds offered by the life assurance company will often include a **commercial property fund** (such funds are relatively rare within other structures) and a **with profits fund** (which can only be provided by a life assurance company).

**Switching** between funds within the investment bond is generally on a basis which is **free or at very low cost**. This compares with switching between unit trusts etc where new initial charges are likely to be incurred.

However, the **range** of funds available is **determined** not by the individual, but by the **life assurance company**, and this then limits the flexibility of the investor. In the past, many life assurance companies have provided only a **modest range of funds**, perhaps 6 or 8 in number, most or all of which have been managed internally. This clearly reduces flexibility, and recent years have seen more and more providers **increase the range of funds** available by offering funds managed by various **external investment houses**.

If the range within the bond is **not sufficiently wide**, it would be possible to **encash** the bond and **move the money elsewhere**, either into an investment bond with another provider, or into another investment medium entirely, but if this is done there will be **tax consequences** as described in the next section as well as costs. It is important therefore that the investor ensures that the investment bond chosen offers a sufficiently wide range of funds to satisfy his needs.

## 3.8 Tax treatment of collective investments

The **investment funds** operated by the life assurance company are subject to **tax both on income and capital gains**, broadly in line with the basis which would apply to a basic rate taxpayer. There is therefore **no particular advantage** from a tax point of view for a **basic rate taxpayer** to invest in an investment bond. Indeed, if the individual is not subject to personal capital gains tax, because he has not used his annual exemption, the fact that the life fund does pay tax on capital gains could be a **disadvantage**.

However, for a **higher rate taxpayer**, it can be useful to **shelter investment returns** from higher rate tax during the investment term, and so generate a higher rate of growth. When the bond is eventually encashed, the tax treatment of any gain will depend on the **tax position of the investor in the tax year of encashment**, and if he is still a higher rate taxpayer, the liability will be calculated at **20% on the gain** (40% less the 20% regarded as discharged by the tax paid by the life fund).

If the individual is a **basic rate taxpayer**, and assuming that the gain does not take him into higher rate tax, there will be **no personal tax charge** on the individual at the time of encashment. One of the **most tax efficient uses** of an investment bond is therefore for the **higher rate taxpayer** who expects later to become a **basic rate taxpayer**, perhaps in retirement. Investment growth is achieved within the life fund with any potential higher rate tax liability deferred, and then on encashment in these circumstances the higher rate tax liability is **avoided entirely**.

If the gain would take a basic rate taxpayer into higher rate tax, the normal rules of **top slicing** apply and this may **minimise** the effect of **higher rate tax**, or **eliminate** it entirely.

Note that switching funds within a bond has no tax consequence (unlike switching from one unit trust to another, which is a disposal for CGT purposes).

In addition, **withdrawals are available** from the bond on a **tax deferred** basis, subject to the **normal 5% allowance** provisions and this can provide **access** to part of the investment during the investment term. However, if these **allowances are exceeded** or the bond is **cashed in entirely**, a **higher rate tax liability could arise**. The investment bond is therefore likely to work **most effectively** where an individual is able to accurately **predict** his future tax circumstances.

Note that the **tax charge** on the investor is to **income tax**, not CGT. It therefore follows that the CGT annual exemption are not available to reduce the liability.

Also, the investor should be aware that the **tax charge** arises in the same way if the bond is **encashed on death**, and the gain for tax purposes is based on the surrender value at the time, less the investments made, but not any additional insured death benefit. The **liability**, if any, falls on the **estate**.

3.8.1 Endowments are investments which generally aim to maintain the capital value to fund some form of charitable foundation. These are generally aimed at charitable causes or non-profit activities such as educational foundations and scholarships, museums or medical facilities. Endowments are very widely used in the US where they frequently part fund educational or health facilities together with government expenditure.

## 3.9 Qualifying rules

Endowment policies allow for certain tax advantages when they are qualifying.

**Qualifying policies** have been used for many years as a means of building **capital** from **regular savings**, generally on a monthly or sometimes annual basis. The **tax advantages** are now relatively **modest** compared to other investment vehicles and the **restrictions** imposed by the qualifying rules limit flexibility.

The **tax advantage** which is available for qualifying policies is that the **maturity proceeds are free of personal tax**. However, as with investment bonds, the fund is subject to **tax on both income and capital gains**, at a rate broadly equivalent to the liability of a **basic rate taxpayer**. This means that qualifying policies hold **little attraction** for a **basic rate taxpayer**, but the tax advantages can be useful for a **higher rate taxpayer**.

In order to be regarded as qualifying, an endowment policy must meet a number of HMRC requirements generally referred to as the **qualifying rules**. Endowment policies have a minimum term of 10 years if they are to avoid tax liabilities.

## 3.10 Endowment policy make up

### The investment policy

The investment policy is agreed with the fund manager and dictates the nature of investments that may be made.

### The withdrawal policy

The withdrawal policy states the way in which withdrawals may be made from the fund.

### The fund usage policy

The fund usage policy aims to ensure that the fund is being used to satisfy its original aims.

Non qualifying policies may result in income tax liabilities on proceeds for higher rate income tax payers, if not carefully structured.

## 3.11 Endowment life assurance policies

Life assurance policies provide payments of an assured sum on the death of the insured individual. Endowment policies may be created which have a substantial savings or investment element. On taking out a policy, the customer knows for certain the minimum sum payable should they die before the end of the term and they will also be notified of the anticipated maturity value of the policy on his survival.

### 3.12 Endowment mortgages

Endowment mortgage contracts were very popular in the UK especially in the 1980s. The mortgage, unlike repayment mortgages does not make regular payments towards repaying the capital balance. Instead they pay into an endowment fund which invests in assets which aim to pay off the loan and perhaps have an excess at the end of the life of the mortgage. It was suggested that a number of these mortgages were miss sold with investors not being fully clear that there was no guarantee that the value of the endowment would be sufficient to repay the loan value.

## 4 Real Estate Investment Trusts

Learning objective

**6.1.5 Analyse** the key features, accessibility, risks, tax treatment, charges and valuation and yield characteristics of Real Estate Investment Trusts (REITs).

**Real Estate Investment Trusts (REITs)** are '**tax-transparent**' **property investment vehicles** which were first formed in the USA, where the name 'REITs' originated. Other countries, including Japan, the Netherlands and France, now have their own versions of **REITs**. The UK introduced its own version of REITs from **1 January 2007**. **Tax-transparent property investment vehicles**, such as REITs, distribute nearly all of their taxable income to investors. Provided they do this, the vehicles are granted exemption from capital gains tax and from corporate taxes. Investors pay tax on the dividends and capital growth at their own marginal tax rates, thus avoiding the double taxation that would otherwise affect investors in UK property companies. In order to qualify as a REIT a company will need to meet certain conditions. The key features are:

- The company must be a UK resident, closed-ended company listed on a recognised stock exchange (which means the main market and does not include AIM).
- The shares in the company must not be closely held, which means that no one person (individual or corporate) should hold more than 10% of the shares.
- The property letting business, which will be tax-exempt, must be effectively ring-fenced from any other activities and should comprise of at least 75% of the overall company, with regard to both is assets and its total income.
- A minimum of 90% of the UK-REIT's profits from the ring-fenced letting business must be distributed to investors within 12 months of the end of the accounting period.
- The UK-REIT will be required to withhold basic rate tax on the distribution of profits paid to investors.
- The distributions are taxed as property income at the holder's marginal rate.
- The company will be subject to an interest-cover test on the ring-fenced part of its business, a measure of the affordability of any loans.
- Other distributions will be taxed in the same way as normal dividends.
- The ratio of interest on loans to fund the tax-exempt property business to rental income must be less than 1.25 : 1.
- If property is developed any gains will usually be taxable at 30% unless the property is held for at least three years from completion. It is possible to hold REITs within **ISAs** and **Child Trust Funds**. UK **property companies** are able to choose to **convert** to become REITs. The conversion charge for companies wishing to become REITs in the UK is 2% of the market value of the properties concerned. The charge can be spread in instalments (0.5%; 0.53%; 0.56%; 0.6%) over four years.

## 4.1 Tax implications of REITs

Distributions from REIT consist of two elements:

- A payment from the tax-exempt element. For individual investors this is classed as property income and paid net of 20% tax. Non-taxpayers may reclaim the excess tax deducted and ISA investors receive payments gross.
- A dividend payment from the non-exempt element which is taxed as any other UK dividend, i.e. it is paid with a non-reclaimable 10% tax credit. Gains on REIT shares are subject to capital gains tax in the normal way for investors.

So called 'enterprise zones', in the UK were so designated in the 1980s due largely to their dereliction and neglect. The idea was to give tax advantages to investors prepared to invest in Enterprise Zone Property Trusts (EZTs). There were also certain relaxations of the planning restrictions. Investors can make direct investments or do so via unit trusts.

# 5 Exchange Traded Products (ETPs)

The expression 'exchange traded products' covers a group of financial products, which includes: Exchange traded funds (ETFs), Exchange traded commodities (ETCs) and Exchange traded notes (ECNs)

earning objective

**6.2.1 Analyse** the key features, accessibility, risks, tax treatment, charges and valuation and yield characteristics of Exchange Traded Products (ETPs).

Exchange Traded Funds (ETFs) are open-ended collective investment vehicles that are UCITS compliant and represent a type of tracker fund. They allow exposure to an index through the purchase of shares which must be listed and tradable on a stock exchange. ETFs are most commonly available for various international equity and bond indices. In the UK, ETFs are listed on the LSE and their shares are traded through the SETS order book and settle through CREST. ETFs are shares that afford the legal right of ownership over part of a basket of individual assets held by the fund. These ETF shares trade at prices that very closely match their underlying assets, hence very closely match the index.

To create an ETF a fund manager first needs to describe precisely the composition of the ETF, usually an index whose constituents change infrequently. They then assemble the appropriate basket of stocks and send them to a custodian bank for safekeeping. This basket of securities may have been purchased by the fund manager for the purposes of establishing the ETF, alternatively they may have been borrowed from other investors such as pension funds. On receipt of the appropriate stocks, the custodian issues the appropriate number of ETF shares. The ETFs can then be freely sold into the open market and from then on they can be freely traded between investors. (Whilst it is common for ETFs to purchase pools of assets to create the ETF, some ETFs may employ derivative products such as swaps to create synthetic positions and as such may bear a degree of counterparty risk).

Redemption of ETFs is simply the reverse of the above creation process. The manager buys a large block of ETFs on the open market and sends it to the custodian bank and in return receives back an equivalent basket of individual stocks which are then sold on the open market or returned to their lenders. In practice, only the very biggest institutional money management firms with experience in indexing tend to play the role of managing an ETF. They direct pension funds with enormous baskets of stocks in markets all over the world to loan stocks necessary for the creation process. They also create demand by lining up customers, either institutional or retail, to buy a newly introduced ETF. Because ETFs are based on indices that tend to be quite stable, the fund management costs tend to be very low. The manager looks to make money on the bid-offer spread and from any price anomalies between the ETF and the underlying shares. Whenever there is an opportunity to earn a little by buying one and selling the other, yielding an arbitrage gain, the manager will do so. This activity will have the effect of keeping the price of the ETF in line with the price of the underlying shares since it will involve buying the relatively under-priced asset (driving its price up) and selling the relatively overpriced asset (driving its price down).

Though a little cumbersome, this process achieves transparency and liquidity at modest cost. Everyone can see what goes into an ETF, investor fees are clearly laid out, investors can be confident that they can exit at any time, and the manager's fees are guaranteed to be modest. ETFs are available in the UK over a wide variety of indices providing an easy and low cost route to investing in the main index, in high yield stocks, in growth stocks, in value stocks etc. They allow investors to adopt an investment style even with low levels of investment. In March 2008, actively managed ETFs were launched in the US. These funds are not based on an index; rather (to date) they are fully transparent, publishing their portfolios on their web sites. These funds have not, as yet, proved to be very popular with investors.

The market in ETFs has grown rapidly and there are a wide variety of forms of ETF now available.

Other recent innovations include products such as short ETFs such as 'Short ProShares' which are offered by the ProFunds Group. They are designed to go up in value, when the index upon which they are based go down in value – these may be known as inverse ETFs. They may be used by investors to hedge risk or to take advantage of a downturn in the market. Other forms of shares are also available such as the 'Alpha ProShares' which magnify the returns from an index to some multiple of the index return.

## 5.1 Charges / Taxation

Fees and charges for investors in ETFs are competitive and relatively low when compared to unit trusts and other more conventional funds.

Stamp duty is not paid when purchasing ETFs.

## 5.2 Exchange traded commodities (ETCs)

Exchange Traded Commodity ETCs are similar in nature to ETFs, and may be divided into two broad categories:

- Index tracking ETCs: These give exposure to commodity indices such as energy indices, all commodity indices or livestock indices
- Single commodity iniceies: The single commodities covered include live cattle, lean hogs, gold and crude oil.

Returns arising from ETCs will generally come from one or other of changes in spot prices, roll return and interest earned on collateral. Similar to ETFs ETCs are open ended, have market makers creating liquidity, trade like shares on exchange during market hours and have no stamp duty to pay. Because ETCs will generally achieve their returns by using derivatives such as swaps, counterparty risk should be considered by investors.

## 5.3 Exchange Traded Notes (ETNs)

Exchange traded notes like ETFs will generally track benchmarks and trade and settle on an exchange, allowing investors to take a long or short position. ETNs are a little like a bond issued by a bank (such as Barclays Bank issued ipath exchange traded notes), but rather than paying interest and a known par value on maturity, they pay no interest and the payment made on maturity will be based upon the value of an underlying index. ETNs are typically senior, unsecured debt securities compared with ETFs which are registered open ended investment companies. This gives the investor a return exposure which is linked to that of an index less fees.

# 6 Structured Products

earning objective

6.3.1 **Analyse** the key features, accessibility, risks, tax treatment, charges, valuation and yield characteristics of retail structured products and investment notes, compared with other forms of direct and indirect investment: structure, income and capital growth, investment risk and return, counterparty risk, expenses, capital protection and tax efficiency.

**Structured products** are securities that provide investors with an amount on redemption, which may provide either full or partial capital protection, plus a certain type of return. The return depends on underlying performance, and may be promoted through the buying and selling of embedded options or other **derivatives**. Structured products are investment vehicles designed to offer tailored combinations of risk and return. There is no water-tight definition of a structured product, as various types of pre-packaged products could be so described, including products based on a single security, a basket of securities, options, indices, commodities, debt issuances, foreign currencies or swaps. A structured product is a wrapper designed to meet a specific set of investment objectives with a specific risk/reward profile. It achieves this by offering a degree of participation in the return from a higher-performing but riskier underlying asset combined with an element of capital protection. SEC Rule 434 defines structures securities as 'securities whose cash flow characteristics depend upon one or more indices or that have embedded forwards or options or securities where an investor's investment return and the issuer's payment obligations are contingent on, or highly sensitive to, changes in the value of underlying assets, indices, interest rates or cash flows.' Structured products are usually constituted as a form of **offshore fund**.

## 6.1 Index-based structured products

Structured products are available that link repayment of capital to the investor by a pre-determined formula to the performance on an index such as the FTSE-100 Index (most commonly), or to other factors or combinations of factors.

- Some funds make use of derivatives in order to make a guarantee of a return of capital to the investor (which might be in the range of 85 to 100% of the original investment, for example).
- A **fixed period** often applies to the investment. There may or may not be a secondary market in the instrument, enabling the investor to sell before redemption.

## 6.2 Fixed interest structured products

There are **fixed interest structured products (FISPs)** which generally have debt instruments as their underlying. The capital protection they offer, which protects against the credit risk that bondholders usually bear, comes at a cost. FISPs encompass **inflation-linked notes**, which provide protection against rising **inflation**, having an inflation index as their underlying.

## 6.3 Constant proportion portfolio insurance

Constant proportion portfolio insurance (CPPI) products are distinct from FISPs, and do not use derivatives. The product comprises two categories of asset: the underlying fund of risky assets, and the reverse account, which comprises risk-free assets – usually cash, which may be consumed over the life cycle of the product, which is typically five or six years. The underlying principle of CPPI products is that the total asset value must never fall below the floor – the present value of the protected amount paid back on the maturity. In managing the assets, the proportion of risky assets is increased when the portfolio value moves away from the floor, and reduced when it moves towards the floor.

## 6.4 Investment notes

Investment notes are very similar to structured products, the main difference is that they're listed and tradable on the London Stock Exchange. This means they are more accessible than traditional structured products.

## 6.5 Advantages of structured products

These are:

- The amount of potential gain/loss is known at the outset
- Wide range of underlying asset combinations is available
- There is no exposure to a particular manager's style or ability
- Degree of participation is explicitly stated
- There is usually a degree of capital protection included in the product
- The risk/return characteristics are fixed and transparent
- The product can be matched to the investor's individual aims and objectives taking account of the investor's attitude towards risk
- Structured products are generally constructed so as to ensure that the proceeds are treated as capital gains (and not income). They may also be held within a Self Invested Pension Plan (SIPP) with the associated tax advantages

## 6.6 Disadvantages of structured products

These are:

- Returns earned in a strongly rising market will be lower due to the cap on the level of participation
- If the structured product cannot be sold on a secondary market then the product may mature in a falling market (i.e. lack of liquidity)
- There may be penalties for early encashment; thus not suitable if the investor needs access to funds at short notice
- Falls in the financial markets could be significant enough for the product to lose its capital protection
- Lack of daily pricing due to structured products being priced on a matrix, rather than by net asset value.
- Credit risk (see below)

## 6.7 Risk and returns

It is vital that the investor understands the risk and characteristics of any structured product. In particular, this would include consideration of the following:

- **Return**

  The precise details of how the return will be calculated and what factors may cause changes in the initial estimated returns.

- **Risk**

  The profile of the assets making up the product and the risk to the principal amount invested including the extent of any capital guarantees.

- **Costs**

  The cost and fees associated with the product as well as any tax implications for the investor.

- **Encashment**

  This would include any penalties for early encashment. In addition, the investor should consider the liquidity of the product in the secondary market. The transparency of the pricing of the product if it can be sold on the secondary market and the costs associated with any sale.

- **Credit risk**

  This involves consideration of the creditworthiness of the issuer and any counterparties involved in the underlying derivatives. The investments will not be covered under the Financial Services Compensation Scheme (FSCS).

# 7 Considerations when Selecting Collective Investments

earning objective

**6.4.1 Analyse** the factors to take into account when selecting collective investments: Quality of firm, management team, product track record and administration, Investment mandate – scope, controls, restrictions and review process, Investment strategy, Exposure, allocation, valuation and quality of holdings, Prospects for capital growth and income, Asset cover and redemption yield, Track record compared with appropriate peer universe and market indices, Location/ domicile/ Passporting arrangements, Tax treatment, Key man risk (KMR) and how this is managed by a firm, Shareholder base, Measures to prevent price exploitation by dominant investors, Total expense and turnover ratios and Liquidity, trading access and price stability.

## 7.1 Fund structure

Investors should consider the tax implications of each form of fund, its liquidity, and the charges, both initial and on-going (i.e. OEIC, unit trust...etc).

## 7.2 Fund classification

The IMA is a trade organisation for the £3 trillion investment UK fund industry, with a membership of over 90% of the UK industry (as defined by the Investment Management Association (IMA).

Funds are classified by the IMA in a number of ways such as:

- **Income funds** – which generally invest in either fixed income investments, or high dividend paying equities, such as large oil companies or utility firms, or often, a combination of both shares and bonds.
- **Growth funds** – which might invest in either regional (e.g. Asia Pacific) equities, equities from developing regions (for high expected growth) or from sectors such as small company equities,

which have historically delivered higher than average growth. They can also make use of fixed income where zero coupon bonds provide capital growth.

- **Capital protection funds** – which include money market funds, which have at least 95% of their assets in money market instruments, and protected funds which have the stated aim of returning a given sum to the investor with some form of capital protection.
- **Specialist funds** – which includes personal pension funds, property funds, technology and telecommunications, and absolute return funds.
- **Unclassified funds** – these funds have elected not to be classified by the IMA into sectors. (Also funds which have been removed due to non-compliance).

Each sector of fund type however will have very many specific fund types, which focus in on particular areas of the market, these would include ethical companies, or those only investing in environmentally progressive firms, or so called 'blue chip' companies.

## 7.3 Fund size and track record

While a large fund size probably indicates a long lived firm with successful marketing and track record, there is of course no guarantee that this past success will be replicated in the future. A fund which has an effective administration team will often be able to offer more satisfaction to clients with improved communication and more efficient service.

Track record may well be measured as the returns achieved against a particular index such as one or the MSCI indices or against the FTSE 100. **Survivorship bias** is however a significant bias which may give a highly distorting view of just how successful, firms are in outperforming indices. Those firms which are unsuccessful will at some point close down, so as such, by definition, the funds under consideration are those that have survived. (When looking at the universe of funds we tend to neglect the large proportion of failed firms).

## 7.4 Manager's experience

Fund managers with a successful record will be more attractive to investors and will tend to increase investments into a fund. Fund managers however may not remain for a very long period with a particular fund and can be poached by rivals.

### 7.4.1 Key man risk (KMR)

The nature of the fund management industry means that a particular fund manager will often play a key role in the operation and marketing of the fund. The risk posed by the possibility of this individual leaving the fund is such that it can cause a fund to be downgraded. This risk may be managed by ensuring that a fund is managed by a team rather than uniquely by an individual, or by tying the manager in with remuneration rewards.

## 7.5 Charges and taxation

As described in the previous discussions of the unique characteristics of each form of fund, charges can amount to a high proportion of the return of any fund. They should as such be considered to be among the most important factors considered by an investor.

The tax treatment of the various investment funds can be significant, more particularly in so much as the fund aims for growth or income. Offshore funds offer a degree of tax benefit. UK ISAs (Individual Savings Accounts) allow funds to be held free of capital gains and income tax up to the current limits. It is also possible to include most funds within a Self Invested Personal Pension or SIPP with the associated tax benefits.

### 7.5.1 The total expense ratio (TER)

Another way to consider the impact of fees is using the TER:

The total expense ratio is calculated as:

$$\frac{\text{A fund's total cost (i.e. auditors fees, custodian fees, purchase fees, redemption fees etc)}}{\text{Total fund assets}}$$

The TER is calculated by Fitzrovia International plc.

It should be considered however that there are a number of costs such as performance relate fees for managers which are not included in the TER.

## 7.6 Independence of trustees

Funds which are well run follow strong corporate governance principals and factors such as the independence of the trustees from the influence of the fund managers will lead to better investor protection.

# 8 'Passporting'

### EU provisions on collective investment schemes

The EU has enacted a number of directives relevant to collective investment schemes (CISs). These are known as the **UCITS Directives**. **UCITS** stands for **Undertakings for Collective Investment in Transferable Securities**.

The aim of UCITS was to create a type of passport throughout the EEA for collective investment schemes that meet the UCITS criteria. The idea was to promote the free movement of services in the same way as investment firms can passport their services throughout the EEA.

The CIS must be authorised in its home State and receive confirmation from its home State regulator that the CIS complies with UCITS criteria. That confirmation is then provided to the host State regulator, who the fund manager notifies that they wish to market the fund in that EEA state. Although UCITS aims to make cross-border sales of CIS easier, the CIS must comply with the marketing rules of the host state and the documentation requirements of the directive.

The first **UCITS Directive** contained a number of limitations. The main limitation was that the definition of **permitted investments** was very narrow. This meant that generally schemes wanting to use UCITS to sell cross-border could only invest in transferable securities. Initially the permitted investments included securities funds (containing for example shares and bonds), warrant funds and umbrella funds, where each sub-fund is either a securities fund or a warrant fund. In addition, the first UCITS Directive contained various categories of scheme, e.g. a securities fund and an umbrella fund, with separate investment rules for each category.

UCITS was updated in 2002 by the **UCITS III Product Directive,** which expanded the range of assets which UCITS funds are able to invest in. It also made provision for a single UCITS scheme to replace all of the previous categories of fund which had separate rules.

### UCITS schemes

As a result of the **UCITS Product Directive**, UCITS schemes are now able to invest in the following types of **permitted investment**.

- Transferable securities (see below)
- Money market instruments
- Forward contracts and financial derivatives
- Deposits
- Units in other Collective Investment Schemes

**Transferable securities** comprise shares, instruments creating or acknowledging indebtedness (e.g. debentures, loan stock, bonds, government and public securities) and certificates representing certain securities.

Although **commodity derivatives** are excluded, it would appear that derivatives based on commodity indices could be eligible as financial derivatives.

### UCITS and non-UCITS schemes

Under FSA Handbook (COLL) rules, both UCITS and non-UCITS retail schemes can invest in a variety of types of instrument, including warrants and financial derivatives, within their overall investment objectives, provided that they apply a risk management procedure. A non-UCITS retail scheme can invest in an even wider range of assets, including gold or 100% investment in immovable property.

Non-UCITS schemes may also **borrow** up to 25% of the fund value on a **permanent** basis, while UCITS retail schemes are only permitted to borrow on a **temporary** basis, up to 10% of the fund value.

As outlined in the FSA handbook: 'An EEA UCITS management company providing collective portfolio management services for a UCITS scheme from a branch in the United Kingdom or under the freedom to provide cross border services, is a relevant person ([Sic] for compensation) to the extent that it carries on those services.'

This means that those collective investment schemes such as authorised unit trusts and OEICS will be covered by the financial services compensation scheme.

## 8.1 Offshore funds

The term 'offshore fund' refers to funds run from low tax areas. These areas cover the significant areas of the Channel Islands, the Isle of Man, the Cayman Islands, Hong Kong and Bermuda. Luxembourg and Dublin have become more significant also, as 'tax havens' within the European Union.

Many offshore funds are run by companies associated with large UK unit trust groups and most of the countries involved now have their own regulatory framework.

Since 1979 when currency exchange controls were abolished, it has become relatively easy for the UK resident to invest his money abroad in equities, bonds or pooled investments such as bonds, UCITS and OEICS.

There may be income and capital gains tax advantages for UK expatriates who are non-UK resident and for non UK domiciled UK residents. For non-UK domiciled persons, there may be inheritance tax advantages. However investment in offshore funds may not be as advantageous for UK residents as they think, particularly from a tax point of view. Offshore funds require more management and their costs are likely to be higher.

In most cases, the tax benefit is limited to a possible deferral of tax payments resulting from income being paid gross.

# Chapter Roundup

## Collective Investments

- Return maximising funds
  - Investment trusts (closed ended).
  - Unit trusts, OEICs, ETFs (open ended).
  - Offshore funds (hedge funds, structured products).
- Open-ended funds – investing/divesting increases/decreases the fund value and funds trade at or close to for value.
- Closed-ended funds – investing/divesting is achieved by buying/selling an existing share. Fund values are heavily influenced by supply and demand and may trade at a notable premium or discount to fair values.
- Pooling investments into collective schemes offers diversification to the small investor.
- Collective investments include unit trusts, OEICs, investment trusts ETFs and REITs.
- Unit trusts are open-ended: if more investors wish to buy into the trust, new units are created.
- Units in a unit trust are priced in line with the daily prices of underlying investments. There is typically a spread between bid and offer prices, and the manager also makes money from the annual management charges.
- Open Ended Investment Companies (OEICs) are alternatively called Investment Companies with Variable Capital (ICVCs).
- An OEIC is open-ended, like a unit trust, with pricing in line with underlying asset values. An OEIC is a company, with shares, like an investment trust.
- An investment trust is a Stock Exchange-listed company whose business is to make investments.
- An investment trust is closed-ended, meaning that the number shares is limited. When an investor wants to buy the shares, he or she buys from another investor who already holds the shares.
- The price of shares in the investment trust is established by supply and demand for the shares, which can result in either a discount or premium relative to the value of the underlying assets.
- Exchange-Traded Funds are vehicles comprising baskets of shares reflecting particular indices which they are designed to track.
- Unlike unit trusts and OEICs, the prices of ETFs are adjusted in real time for trading throughout the day.
- REITs are listed companies that specifically invest in income-producing property.

# TEST YOUR KNOWLEDGE

*Check your knowledge of the chapter here, without referring back to the text.*

1. OEICs and ETFs are both open-ended investment companies. What is the difference in their pricing?

2. Can open-ended funds trade at a premium or discount?

3. What are structured products?

4. Outline the respective roles of the unit trust manager and the trustee.

5. What is indicated by an 'E' against a fund's name in the *Financial Times*?

6. Which types of collective investment are 'open-ended'?

   A Unit trusts and investment trusts

   B Investment trust and OEICs

   C Unit trusts and OEICs

   D Unit trusts, OEICs and investment trusts

7. Outline the respective roles of the Authorised Corporate Director and the Depositary of an Open Ended Investment Company.

8. The price of shares in an investment trust are a determined primarily by:

   A Supply and demand for the shares in the market

   B An FSA formula, reflecting the Net Asset Value

   C The discount specified by the investment trust company

   D The ability of the fund manager to create or cancel shares

9. Which one of the following is *not* correct in respect of Exchange Traded Funds (ETFs)?

   A The funds are listed on the Stock Exchange

   B ETFs may be included in an Individual Savings Account

   C Prices are determined daily, by reference to the previous day's valuation

   D No Stamp Duty Reserve Tax is payable on purchases

# Test Your Knowledge: Answers

1. OEICs are priced at valuation points, ETFs are continuously priced.

   **(See Section 7 and 1.2)**

2. Open-ended funds are always priced on the basis of the value of the underlying fund, hence they cannot trade at a premium or discount.

   **(See Section 1.2)**

3. Funds offering a return with full or partial guarantee of capital value.

   **(See Section 8)**

4. The **fund manager** runs the fund and makes the day-to-day investment management decisions, and appoints the trustee. The job of the trustee is to protect the investor's interests by ensuring that the manager adheres to the rules and regulations that are stipulated in the trust deed. The manager and the trustee are independent of each other.

   **See Section 2**

5. That an exit charge may be payable.

   **See Section 2.3**

6. C is the correct answer. When investors buy unit trusts or OEIC shares, new units are created.

   **See Sections 1, 2 and 3**

7. The ACD's responsibilities include managing the company's investments, buying and selling its own shares on demand and ensuring the accurate pricing of shares at net asset value. The Depositary's role is to safeguard the assets of the OEIC.

   **See Section 1.1**

8. A is the correct option. Investment trust shares are listed on the Stock Exchange, and freely traded.

   **See Section 3.1**

9. C is the correct answer. As with other Stock Exchange listed shares, prices are determined in real time, second-by-second, through the trading day.

   **See Section 7**

# 7 Portfolio Construction

## INTRODUCTION

While an individual investor may choose to manage their own money, the majority of investors will opt to use institutional fund managers to handle their investments.

It is important for investors to be invested in a suitable range of assets. It will often therefore make sense for investors to pool their money into large funds, these can then be invested on their behalf by professional fund managers.

This chapter discusses how to construct a portfolio, covering all of the important considerations which must be made.

### CHAPTER CONTENTS

# Chapter Learning Objectives

## Portfolio Construction

### 7.1 Market Information and Research

**7.1.1** **Understand** how to access and use regulatory, economic and financial communications:

- News services
- Government resources and statistics
- Broker research and distributor information
- Regulatory resources where relevant

**7.1.2** **Understand** the different types, uses and availability of research and reports:

- Fundamental analysis
- Technical analysis
- Fund analysis
- Fund rating agencies and screening software
- Broker and distributor reports
- Sector-specific reports

**7.1.3** **Assess** key factors that influence markets and sectors:

- Responses to change and uncertainty
- Volume, liquidity, and nature of trading activity in domestic and overseas markets
- Market abuse regime – enforcement and effectiveness
- Publication of announcements, research and ratings

**7.1.4** **Assess** the interactive relationship between the securities and derivatives markets, and the impact of related events on markets.

**7.1.5** **Assess** the interactive relationship between different forms of fixed interest securities and the impact of related events on markets.

### 7.2 Portfolio Construction

**7.2.1** **Understand** the main types of portfolio risk and their implications for investors:

- Systemic risk
- Market risk – asset price volatility, currency, interest rates and commodity price volatility
- Investment horizon
- Liquidity, credit risk and default
- Counterparty risk

**7.2.2** **Understand** the core principles used to mitigate portfolio risk:

- Correlation
- Diversification
- Active and passive strategies
- Hedging and immunization

**7.2.3 Understand** the key approaches to investment allocation for bond, equity and balanced portfolios:

- Asset class
- Geographical area
- Currency
- Issuer
- Sector
- Maturity

**7.2.4 Understand** the main aims and investment characteristics of the main cash, bond and equity portfolio management strategies and styles:

- Indexing/ passive management
- Active/ market timing
- Passive-active combinations
- Growth versus Income
- Market capitalization
- Liability driven (LDI)
- Immunization
- Long, short and leveraged
- Issuer and sector-specific
- Contrarian
- Quantitative

**7.2.5 Understand** how portfolio risk and return are evaluated using the following measures:

- Holding period return
- Total return and its components
- Standard deviation
- Volatility
- Covariance and correlation
- Risk- adjusted returns
- Benchmarking

# 1 Market Information and Research

## 1.1 Regulatory, economic and financial communications

Learning objective

**7.1.1 Understand** how to access and use regulatory, economic and financial communications: News services, Government resources and statistics, Broker research and distributor information and Regulatory resources where relevant.

Information may be sought from investment advisors themselves.

There are a large number of UK companies that provide investment advice to private customers. The provision of investment advice is investment business as defined by the Financial Services and Markets Act 2000 and consequently investment advisors must seek authorisation.

In addition to the investment advisory firms, members of the public are able to access various sources of investment information.

- **Newspapers** – almost all newspapers give some level of investment advice.
- **Specific journals**- there are a number of journals such as *investors Chronicle* that provide a detailed summary of investments and a summary of investment advice given by the main broking houses.
- **Screen based information services and quote vendors** – the public has access, albeit at a high cost, to many screens such as Bloomberg and Reuters.
- **Company accounts** – all companies are obliged to provide annual financial accounts. These statements are readily available to members of the public should they require a copy.
- **Regulatory Information Services** - Investors can follow public statements made by the company via a Regulatory Information Service such as the LSE's Regulatory News Service (RNS)
- **Secondary Information Providers** – bundle together information from companies into a single source of regulatory information, such as Reuters and Bloomberg for institutional investors and Financial Express-UK Wire or Hemscott.net for retail investors.

## 1.2 Examples of News providers:

### 1.2.1 The Financial Times

The Financial Times offers in its own words 'news, comment, data and analysis for the global business community'. According to figures on its website, ABC figures September 2010 give it a daily circulation of 390,228, with over 2.7 million registered users of FT.com and 149,000 digital users.

In conjunction with the London stock Exchange (LSE) they jointly own the FTSE International Limited, which is responsible for producing the FTSE indices which are widely used by the investment industry.

### 1.2.2 The Wall Street Journal

The Wall Street Journal is now a part of News Corporation, and offers daily business news and comment widely read around the world. It owns and prepares the Dow Jones family of indices, including the DJ30 industrial average.

### 1.2.3 Bloomberg

Founded in 1981 by New York mayor Michael Bloomberg, Bloomberg offers business information to the market. It now offers a global news service with TV, radio, the internet and print news. It offers a wide variety of news and analytical services to banks and businesses through its 'Bloomberg terminal' service.

### 1.2.4 Thomson Reuters

The Reuters organisation began life in London in the mid-19th century and the advent of technology such as the telegraph allowed the company to develop into a major information provider. Following its takeover by Thomson Corporation it is now a leading provider of business information, advice and solutions under its name of Thomson Reuters.

## 1.3 Government provided statistics and information

### 1.3.1 The UK Office for National Statistics (ONS)

The UK ONS is the key provider of statistics for and on behalf of the UK government. Statistics provided range in content from fisheries, to education, to the economy. Their websites states that economic accounts provided, offer an overall view of the economy following the 'sequence of accounts laid out in the System of National Accounts 1993 and the European System of Accounts 1995.'

It goes on to state that 'There are also short term indicators such as the Gross Domestic Product [GDP], Retail Sales Index [RSI], Index of Production and Index of Services. There are also statistics produced on the Balance of Payments and Trade in Goods and Services'.

The ONS websites suggests that key users of its data will include:

- The Bank of England (when making decisions on the base rate)
- The City of London for investing and forecasting decisions
- Businesses, for planning and benchmarks
- Academia for research modelling and teaching
- The public for judging the government
- International bodies for comparing the UK with other countries

A further set of key economic measures produced by the ONS are the measures of inflation in the UK economy, including the consumer price index (CPI), and the Retail Price index (RPI).

## 1.4 Central Bank Information

### 1.4.1 The Bank of England

The Bank of England provides a range of monetary and financial statistical data in line with its role of maintaining economic stability and controlling inflation. The statistics include domestic banking statistics, external finance statistics and international statistics. The bank will also provide a survey of Inflation Expectations.

In line with its statutory objective of contributing 'to protecting and enhancing the stability of the financial systems of the United Kingdom', the BOE publishes a half yearly report providing an assessment of the financial stability of the UK financial system. This has been known since July 2006 as the 'Financial Stability Report'. In addition to its introductory over view of the UK financial system, the report has four sections:

- Shocks to the UK financial system
- Structure of the UK financial system
- Prospects for the UK financial system
- Mitigating risks to the UK financial system

The Monetary Policy Committee (MPC) which is responsible for setting interest rates in the UK will also make a report of the meetings which occur each month.

### 1.4.2 The US Federal Reserve

The US Fed provides a wide range of statistical data including historical data, statistical releases and surveys and reports. These include banking data, flow of funds accounts and exchange rates and international data. Their surveys include such topics as the terms of business lending.

The Federal Open Markets Committee (FOMC) which consists of twelve members, holds meetings eight times per year. At these meetings, they discuss and review the position of US monetary policy, and what risks exist to US economic growth and stability. The reports by FOMC are of great interest to market observers and are keenly read.

### 1.4.3 The European Central Bank

The ECB publishes a wide range of statistical data primarily with regard to economic activities within the Eurozone. The ECB recently played its part in the UN orchestrated 'World Statistics Day', the first of which was on Oct 10 2010. In line with this initiative, the ECB stated that: 'most statistics used by the ESCB (European System of Central Banks), are European statistics provided either by the ECB in cooperation with the EU national central banks or by the European Statistical System (ESS)'

### 1.4.4 The regulators

In line with their role of regulating the financial services industries of their respective countries, regulators will be required to inform the market of regulatory requirements. The FSA website is a rich source of information on regulatory issues as well as providing consumer information on such matters as investments and pensions, in line with its' regulatory objective of Informing the public'.

### 1.4.5 Political announcements

Political decisions will at times have a profound impact on financial markets. Changes in fiscal policy have been at times dramatic in recent times with the UK and a number of countries cutting back on public spending to reduce their deficits. The European Union's declarations regarding support for member countries such as Greece has also had a major effect on securities prices particularly in the bond markets.

## 1.5 Uses and availability of research and reports

| Learning objective | |
|---|---|
| | **7.1.2** **Understand** the different types, uses and availability of research and reports: Fundamental analysis, Technical analysis, Fund analysis, Fund rating agencies and screening software and Broker and distributor reports Sector-specific reports. |

In theory, all investment managers should have undertaken a complete analysis of all available investment assets to be in a position to assess them in relation to a client's portfolio. Two key approaches to this are Fundamental analysis and Technical analysis.

### 1.5.1 Fundamental analysis

Fundamental analysis concentrates on the economic strengths or weaknesses of the market in question and the individual features of the stock within that market. Fundamental analysis will give indications of longer term investment decisions. The basic idea behind this approach is that every security has an **intrinsic value** that can be determined from a consideration of these factors.

With government bonds, this form of analysis entails reviewing the economic outlook for the economy and the funding requirement.

With corporate securities, in addition to assessing the economic environment and interest rate profile, it involves assessing the individual credit and operational risk, along with details of its dividend yield and P/E ratio.

### 1.5.2 Technical analysis

Technical analysts, rather than looking at the fundamentals of the economy, look to the pattern and trading history to determine the appropriate strategy to adopt. Technical analysis will give indications of shorter term trading decisions.

Frequently, through the use of charts, technical analysts develop patterns of market behaviour that they expect to be repeated time and time again. By charting the daily price movement in a stock, they believe they can predict the eventual out-turn of the market. To an extent these predictions will be self-fulfilling because, for example, if the charts predict the price will fall and investment managers react to this sell signal, then undoubtedly the supply and demand factors will force the price down.

The intellectual justification for the use of technical analysis is based on behavioural finance and the theories of crowd behaviour. Basically, the same group of people exposed to the same circumstances will react in the same way: 'history repeats itself.' From this we make the statement that prices will move in trends.

Trends may be defined as being either 'downtrends', 'uptrends' or sideways movements'.

#### Trend lines

Technical analysts will plot trend lines to show movements of share prices over time.

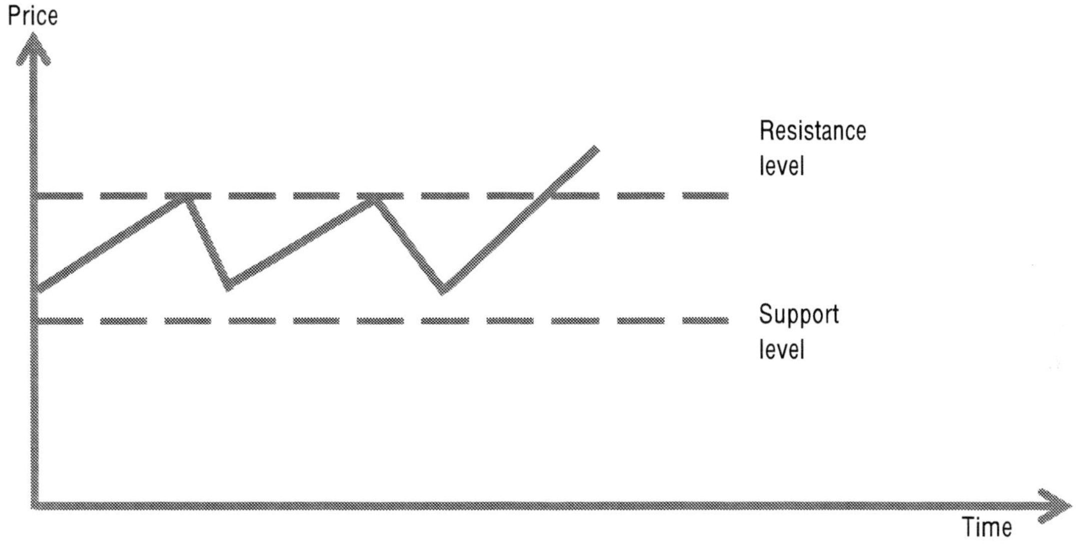


In the above example, the trend is neither up nor down but sideways at this time.

The channel between the support level and resistance level represents a psychological position for investors and the technical analyst will look for 'break outs' which when they occur will cause what are at times extreme and long lasting changes in the support and resistance levels to a new channel. These changes when identified will be indications to the technical analyst that they should sell or as in the breakout in the above diagram, to buy.

## 1.6 Fund analysis

When looking at funds the research available to the investor is fairly widespread in its availability given that many funds are aimed at the retail investor. The UK trade body for the investment management industry (IMA) offers background information for fund investors, while companies such as Trustnet and the Financial Times offer information largely provided by the funds for retail investors who are thinking of investing. Additional key factors to consider include:

- Fund structure
- Management style
- Fund size
- Managers experience
- Charges
- Administration quality
- Financial stability
- Independence of trustees

## 1.7 Fund rating

Fund rating provides an assessment of the performance of funds based upon measures such as the management, the portfolio makeup and ratio analysis on the portfolio. Standard and Poor's rates fixed income funds and bond funds using:

- Credit Quality Ratings ranging from AAAf down to CCCf for funds which are 'extremely vulnerable to losses from credit default'
- Volatility ratings which range from S1 which is the lowest volatility to S6 which is the highest volatility.

## 1.8 Broker reports

**Brokers' circulars and research** – brokers provide research material to their customers and will potentially make this information available to the public.

**Learning objective**

**7.1.3 Assess** key factors that influence markets and sectors: Responses to change and uncertainty, Volume, liquidity, and nature of trading activity in domestic and overseas markets, Market abuse regime – enforcement and effectiveness and Publication of announcements, research and ratings.

Analysis of portfolio risk and return based on individual security returns, risks and correlations assumes that investments can be bought at their fair value, ignoring completely any dealing costs and spreads. For large cap stocks or gilts this is probably a reasonable assumption under normal circumstances as they are usually highly liquid. The liquidity of smaller cap stocks may be much lower and the liquidity of property is very low even in normal circumstances. In more extreme circumstances, however, liquidity in all markets may dry up altogether, making it difficult, if not impossible, to deal at a fair value. In conclusion, more liquid investments are more likely to trade close to fair value, less liquid investments and more difficult market circumstances are likely to result in assets trading some way from their fair values.

## 1.9 Market abuse

### Overview

**Market abuse** is a **civil offence** under **S118 FSMA 2000,** which provides an alternative civil regime for enforcing the criminal prohibitions on insider dealing and misleading statements/practices.

The UK market abuse rules conform with the **EU Market Abuse Directive**.

The **territorial scope** of market abuse is very wide. It covers everyone, not just authorised firms and approved persons. Firms or persons outside the UK are also covered by the offence.

As market abuse is a **civil offence**, the FSA must prove, on the balance of probabilities, that a person:

- Engaged in market abuse, or
- By taking or refraining from action, required or encouraged another person to engage in market abuse

As shown in the following diagram, there are seven types of behaviour that can amount to market abuse.

Behaviour

↓

In relation to qualifying investments trading or to be traded on a prescribed market

↓

Which falls into one or more of the types of behaviour

- Insider Dealing
- Improper Disclosure
- Misuse of Information
- Manipulating Transactions
- Manipulating Devices
- Dissemination
- Misleading Behaviour and Distortion

### Requiring and encouraging

**Section 123(1)(b) FSMA 2000** allows the FSA to impose penalties on a person who, by taking or refraining from taking any action, has required or encouraged another person or persons to engage in behaviour, which if engaged in by A, would amount to market abuse.

The following are **examples** of behaviour that might fall within the scope of section 123(1)(b).

- A director of a company, while in possession of inside information, instructs an employee of that company to deal in qualifying investments or related investments in respect of which the information is inside information. (This could amount to **requiring**.)
- A person recommends or advises a friend to engage in behaviour which, if he himself engaged in it, would amount to market abuse. (This could be **encouraging** market abuse.)

### The regular market user test

A regular user is a **hypothetical reasonable person** who regularly deals on that market in investments of the kind in question. The **regular market user test** then determines in light of the circumstances whether an offence has been committed.

Since the implementation of the Market Abuse Directive, the regular market user is only used to determine whether market abuse has occurred in relation to the behaviours 'Misuse of Information', 'Misleading Behaviour' and 'Distortion'.

Therefore, the regular market user decides:

- Whether information that is not generally available would be relevant when deciding which transactions in qualifying investments or related investments should be undertaken, and

- Whether behaviour is below the expected standard, or creates a false or misleading impression or distorts the market

### Qualifying investments and prescribed markets

Behaviour will only constitute market abuse if it occurs **in the UK or in relation to qualifying investments traded on a prescribed market**. The term 'behaviour' is specifically mentioned as the offence of market abuse can cover both action and inaction.

A **prescribed market** means any UK RIE, and any regulated market. **Qualifying investment** thus means any investment traded on a UK RIE or a regulated market. **Regulated markets** comprise the main EEA exchanges.

The definition of prescribed market and qualifying investment are amended slightly with reference to the offences of '**Misuse of Information**', '**Misleading Behaviour**' and '**Distortion**'. Here, a prescribed market means any UK RIE. Qualifying investment thus means any investment traded on a UK RIE. Therefore, these offences are only relevant to the UK markets.

In addition, the rules confirm that a prescribed market accessible electronically in the UK would be treated as operating in the UK.

As behaviour must be **in relation to** qualifying investments, the regime is not limited to on-market dealings. A transaction in an OTC (Over The Counter) derivative contract on a traded security or commodity would be covered by the regime. In addition, abusive trades on foreign exchanges could constitute market abuse if the underlying instrument also trades on a prescribed market. This makes the regime much wider than the criminal law offences.

### The definition of market abuse

**Market abuse** is behaviour, whether by one person alone or by two or more persons jointly or in concert, which occurs in relation to:

- Qualifying investments admitted to trading on a prescribed market, or
- Qualifying investments in respect of which a request for admission to trading on a prescribed market has been made, or
- Related investments of a qualifying investment (strictly, this is only relevant to the offences of 'Insider Dealing' and 'Improper Disclosure' – see below)

and falls within one or more of the offences below.

### The seven types of market abuse offence

The seven types of behaviour that can constitute market abuse are as follows:

1. **Insider Dealing**. This is where an insider deals, or attempts to deal, in a qualifying investment or related investment on the basis of **inside information**.
2. **Improper Disclosure**. This is where an insider discloses **inside information** to another person otherwise than in the proper course of the exercise of his employment, profession or duties.
3. **Misuse of Information**. This fills gaps in '1' or '2' above and is where the behaviour is
   - Based on information which is not generally available to those using the market but which, if available to a regular user of the market, would be regarded by him as relevant when deciding the terms on which transactions in qualifying investments should be effected, and
   - Likely to be regarded by a regular user of the market as a failure on the part of the person concerned to observe the standard of behaviour reasonably expected of a person in his position.

4. **Manipulating Transactions**. This consists of effecting transactions or orders to trade (otherwise than for legitimate reasons and in conformity with accepted market practices) which

   – Give, or are likely to give a false or misleading impression as to the supply, demand or price of one or more qualifying investments, or

   – Secure the price of one or more such investments at an abnormal or artificial level.

5. **Manipulating Devices**. This consists of effecting transactions or orders to trade which employ fictitious devices or any other form of deception.

6. **Dissemination**. This consists of the dissemination of information by any means which gives, or is likely to give, a false or misleading impression as to a qualifying investment by a person who knew or could reasonably be expected to have known that the information was false or misleading.

7. **Misleading Behaviour** and **Distortion**. This fills any gaps in '4', '5' and '6' above and is where the behaviour

   – Is likely to give a regular user of the market a false or misleading impression as to the supply of, demand for, or price or value of, qualifying investments, or

   – Would be regarded by a regular user of the market as behaviour that would distort the market in such an investment and is likely to be regarded by a regular user of the market as a failure on the part of the person concerned to observe the standard of behaviour reasonably expected of a person in his position.

### Intention

The market abuse regime is **effects based** rather than 'intent based'. Thus, whether the perpetrator intended to abuse the market is largely irrelevant – the key question is whether the action **did** abuse the market.

### Code of Market Conduct

While the law is set out in FSMA, the FSA also has a duty to draft a **Code of Market Conduct**.

The main provisions of the Code of Market Conduct are that it sets out:

- Descriptions of behaviour that, in the opinion of the FSA, do or do not amount to market abuse. Descriptions of behaviour which do not amount to market abuse are called '**safe harbours**'
- Descriptions of behaviour that are or are not **accepted market practices** in relation to one or more identified markets
- Factors that, in the opinion of the FSA, are to be taken into account in determining whether or not behaviour amounts to market abuse

The Code does not exhaustively describe all types of behaviour that may or may not amount to market abuse.

### Enforcement and penalties

The FSA may impose one or more of the following **penalties** on those found to have committed market abuse.

- An unlimited **fine**
- Issue a **public statement**
- Apply to the court to seek an **injunction** or **restitution order**

- Where an authorised/approved person is guilty of market abuse, they will also be guilty of a breach of the FSA's Principles and they could, in addition to the above penalties, have disciplinary proceedings brought against them, which may result in withdrawal of authorisation/approval.

The case of Paul Davidson ('The Plumber') has led to change in perceptions about how market abuse may be treated. The current position is that a **civil standard of proof** (on the balance of probabilities) of the appropriate degree can still be used by the FSA in market abuse cases. However, even when the punishment (in accordance with S123 FSMA 2000) is treated as **civil** for domestic law purposes, market abuse is a **criminal** charge (with a standard of proof 'beyond reasonable doubt') for the purposes of the European Convention on Human Rights, and someone committing it is subject to possible criminal prosecution.

In addition to being able to impose penalties for market abuse, the FSA is given criminal prosecution powers to enforce insider dealing and S397. The FSA has indicated that it will not pursue both the civil and criminal regime. In terms of the enforcement process for market abuse, this is the same as FSA's disciplinary process.

## 1.10 The Panel for Takeovers and Mergers

The **Panel on Takeovers and Mergers** (the **Takeover Panel**) is an independent body established in 1968, whose main functions are to issue and administer the **City Code on Takeovers and Mergers** and to supervise and regulate takeovers and other matters to which the Code applies. Its central objective is to ensure fair treatment for shareholders in takeover bids.

The regulation of takeovers and mergers was the last aspect of the UK regulatory environment left almost exclusively to practitioner self-regulation. However, there was change when the **Takeover Directive (Interim Implementation) Regulations 2006** were implemented as Part 28 of the Companies Act 2006 (CA 2006).

Before the implementation of the Takeover Directive on 20 May 2006, the Panel did not have, nor did it seek to have, the force of law. Its only direct disciplinary powers were censures and withdrawing the facilities of the market from anybody who broke its rules.

The **Takeover Panel** was given **statutory authority** in the **Companies Act 2006**, with effect from January 2007. CA 2006 gives the Panel this authority in respect of all bids subject to the Takeover Code and not only those to which the Takeover Directive applies. The Panel has statutory powers under CA 2006 to make rules on takeover regulation, to require disclosure of information and to impose sanctions on those who breach its rules. In practical terms however, these changes are likely to make little difference to how the Panel operates.

The **City Code on Takeovers and Mergers** may be variously referred to as the City Code, the Blue Book, the Takeover Code or simply the Code. The **Code** has been developed since 1968 to reflect the collective opinion of those professionally involved in the field of takeovers as to appropriate business standards and as to how fairness to shareholders and an orderly framework for takeovers can be achieved. The rules set out in the Code, which are derived from the Takeover Directive, now have a statutory basis.

The **Takeover Panel** comprises up to 34 members which include a Chairman, up to two Deputy Chairmen, and up to twenty members and other individuals appointed by various industry bodies.

The Takeover Panel assumes overall responsibility for the policy, financing and administration of the Panel's functions and for the functioning and operation of the Code. The Panel operates through a number of committees and is directly responsible for those matters which are not dealt with through one of its committees.

- The day-to-day work of takeover supervision and regulation is carried out by the **Executive**. In carrying out these functions, the Executive operates independently of the Panel. The Executive may be approached for general guidance on the interpretation or effect of the Code, or in relation to a specific issue on a 'no names' basis.

- The **Code Committee** carries out the rule-making functions of the Panel and is responsible for keeping the Code under review and for proposing, consulting on, making and issuing amendments to the Code.
- The **Hearings Committee** reviews rulings of the Executive and hears disciplinary proceedings instituted by the Executive when the Executive considers that there has been a breach of the Code.
- The **Takeover Appeals Board** is an independent body which hears appeals against rulings of the Hearings Committee. The Board may confirm, vary, set aside, annul or replace the contested ruling of the Hearings Committee.

The **Panel** is **financed** by:

- A £1 levy on the buyers and sellers of share transactions in certain securities over £10,000 (the 'PTM levy')
- Document charges (payable on offer documents), and
- Exemption charges (£5,000 per review, payable by groups enjoying exempt status)

# 2 Portfolio Risk

earning objective

7.2.1 **Understand** the main types of portfolio risk and their implications for investors: systematic risk, market risk – asset price volatility, currency, interest rates, commodity price volatility, investment horizon, liquidity, credit risk and default and counterparty risk.

## 2.1 Market or systematic risk

Holding **equities** presents a **capital risk** even in a well-diversified portfolio. General market falls will reduce capital values and this risk may be referred to as **market risk**.

Systemic risk is the risk of the failure or collapse of the entire financial system. This could be caused by extraneous events such as natural disasters or failures in a part of the system that could cause a cascading effect on other parts of the system.

Systemic risk is a function of:

- **Events risk** – the risk that a security may default due to unexpected events such as natural disasters, takeovers or regulatory change.
- **Settlement or counterparty risk** – the risk that a counterparty may default on a transaction.

## 2.2 Liquidity risk

An investor in **property** suffers from the risk associated with **illiquidity**. A sale can only be made if a buyer can be found and this can prove a great problem. During the early 1990s, with a stagnant housing and property market few buyers of residential property could be found and prices fell. Many homeowners had negative equity: the value of their house fell to below the value of their debt (mortgage). If a client invests in property via the medium of a property unit trust or investment bond he may suffer similar, although not such acute, illiquidity. Under the terms of these investments the proceeds of a sale may be delayed for up to six months to allow the managers to realise assets to pay the investor.

## 2.3 Counterparty risk

This describes the risk that counterparty may default on a transaction.

## 2.4 Exchange rate risk

Investors in overseas investments will face the danger that the exchange rate between their home country and that of the investment will alter. If for example the investment currency depreciates, this will reduce the value of any cash flows. Interest rate hedges may be used such as currency swaps, or forward exchange agreements to reduce the risk.

## 2.5 Inflation risk

The cash flows from an investment will have lower spending power when inflation is unexpectedly high. Fixed income investments are particularly susceptible to inflation risk. Investments such as index linked gilts may be used as an inflation hedge.

## 2.6 Diversifiable and systemic risk

When we suffer a stock market crash. In these circumstances, even the most highly diversified portfolios suffer a loss in value – the market as a whole collapses.

Thus, it would appear that we can analyse the total risk of an investment into two subcategories as follows.

**Total Risk of Investment**

$\sigma_i$

| **Systematic/Market Risk** | **Unsystematic/Idiosyncratic/ Specific Risk** |
|---|---|
| $\sigma_s$ | $\sigma_u$ |
| Potential variability in the returns offered by a security caused by general market influences, e.g. | Potential variability in the returns offered by a security as a result of factors specific to the company, e.g. |
| ■ Interest rate changes.<br>■ Inflation rate changes.<br>■ Tax rate changes.<br>■ State of the economy. | ■ Quality of management.<br>■ Susceptibility to demands of suppliers and customers.<br>■ Profitability margins and levels. |
| **Cannot be eliminated through diversification** | **Can be eliminated through diversification** |



BPP LEARNING MEDIA

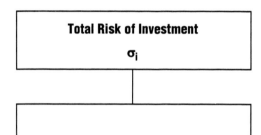

As we note, the unsystematic risk can be eliminated through diversification. This arises as a result of the trade between companies. If one company makes a mistake and undertakes a bad deal (loses money), then its trading partner will be making a corresponding amount of money. Hence, by investing in both companies, we can eliminate this variability from our overall portfolio returns. We get the combined return regardless of which company generates it.

The systematic or market risk is something that impacts on the economy in general, which all companies are parts of; hence this is the type of risk that cannot be eliminated.

### 2.6.1 Consequences

An **undiversified investor**, i.e. one who has most/all of his money invested in the shares of one company, will **face the full risk** of that investment, $\sigma_i$. He will therefore look for a return commensurate with this full level.

A **diversified investor** will have eliminated, through diversification, the unsystematic risk inherent in the individual securities in his portfolio and **face just the systematic risk**, $\sigma_S$. Hence, he will seek a return commensurate with the level of systematic risk only.

## 3 Principles to Mitigate Portfolio Risk

earning objective

**7.2.2 Understand** the core principles used to mitigate portfolio risk: correlation, diversification, active and passive strategies and hedging and immunization.

### 3.1 Correlation

The effectiveness of this cancellation will depend on the degree of correlation between the movements of the returns. Correlation is a measure of how two variable factors move in relation to each other. A correlation coefficient will have any value between +1 and –1. The meaning of the correlation coefficient can best be understood by considering the extremes.

#### 3.1.1 Perfect positive correlation – (correlation coefficient = +1)

If the returns from two securities are perfectly positively correlated, then they move up and down together in proportion. The consequence of this is that if they were combined in a portfolio, we would not get the cancelling effect that we were looking for.

#### 3.1.2 Perfect negative correlation – (correlation coefficient = –1)

If the returns from two securities are perfectly negatively correlated, then they move up and down in exact opposition and in proportion. As a result, if we were to combine two such securities in a portfolio, we could achieve an exact offset of profits from one against losses from the other.

#### 3.1.3 Uncorrelated – (correlation coefficient = 0)

If the returns from two securities are uncorrelated, then they move independently of each other, i.e. if one goes up, the other may go up or down or not move at all. As a result, if we were to combine two such securities in a portfolio, we would expect to see cancellation of profits and losses on some occasions, but not on others. However, this is still a better position than investing in just one share where there is no cancellation of gains and losses at all.

### 3.1.4 Limitations of correlation coefficient

Correlation coefficients may not always be a reliable measure when outliers are present. These are small numbers of observations at the extremes of a sample of data. The analyst must decide whether it is better to include or exclude outliers on a case-by-case basis. Furthermore, a correlation between two variables may reflect a chance relationship in a particular set of data, or may arise because the two variables are themselves correlated to a third variable. For example bee stings may be positively correlated to ice cream consumption, but the underlying relationships are between sunshine and bee stings, and sunshine and ice cream consumption. Finally, correlation coefficients are susceptible to change in times of market turbulence. A portfolio may be thought of as risk averse with a basket of uncorrelated equities, only to find the correlation between the securities becomes increasingly positive in times of market turmoil, removing many of the diversification benefits which previously existed.

### 3.1.5 Conclusion

The sign of the correlation coefficient tells us the relative direction of movement. A positive correlation implies that returns move up and down together, negative correlation means that they move in opposition. The value of the figure, ignoring the sign, gives an indication of the strength of the relationship. The closer to a value of 1, the stronger the relationship. The effectiveness of the diversification will depend on the degree of correlation between the returns on the securities. In practice, we are unlikely to encounter perfect positive or perfect negative correlation (though we may get close with certain derivative instruments). Most shares show a small degree of correlation in practice, and hence we see some benefit from diversification.

### 3.1.6 Portfolio standard deviation

A rather complicated equation is needed to calculate the variance of a portfolio where two assets have been combined.

Variance of Portfolio = $p_a^2.\sigma_a^2 + p_b^2.\sigma_b^2 + 2\ p_a.p_b.\sigma_a.\sigma_b Corr(ab)$

Where:

- $P_a$ = Proportion of security a
- $P_b$ = Proportion of security b
- $\sigma_a^2$ = Variance of security a
- $\sigma_b^2$ = Variance of security b
- $\sigma_{a.}$ = Standard deviation of a
- $\sigma_{b.}$ = Standard deviation of b
- Corr(ab) = Correlation of securities a and b

When we look at the formula it is apparent that securities with the greatest degree of negative correlation, will reduce the overall variance (and of course hence the risk) of the portfolio by the greatest degree. This shows that the greater the degree of negative correlation, the greater the diversification effect.

## 3.2 Diversification

Due to the large number of investments that are liable to be held within any portfolio and the complex interrelationships between them, the economy, etc. computerised portfolio optimisation techniques are frequently used to establish measures such as portfolio yield, total risk (both systematic and unsystematic components), maximum and minimum stock numbers, maximum levels in any one stock, etc. These techniques all tend to be based on diversification ideas, requiring the calculation and input of appropriate measures such as standard deviations and correlation.

### Types of diversification

Two types of diversification can be distinguished:

- **Diversification by asset class**. This is achieved by holding a combination of different kinds of asset within a portfolio, possibly spread across: cash, fixed interest securities, equity investments, property-based investments, and other assets.
- **Diversification within asset classes**. An investor can diversify a portfolio by holding a variety of investments within the particular asset types that he holds. This may be achieved by holding various fixed interest securities, by spreading investments across different industry sectors and geographical markets, by holding equities in a number of different companies, and by holding a number of different properties or property-based investments.

### Diversification by asset class

As we saw earlier in this Study Text, the greatest diversification benefits arise when we combine securities with low or negative correlations. As a result, diversification between asset classes is the primary route to portfolio risk reduction.

The average correlation coefficients experienced between the major classes of assets over the last ten years are given below.

| | | Equities | | | Bonds | | | Property | Commodity |
|---|---|---|---|---|---|---|---|---|---|
| | | Large cap | Mid cap | Small cap | Corp | Gilt | ILG | | |
| **Equities** | Large cap | 1.00 | 0.78 | 0.62 | 0.32 | 0.21 | –0.30 | 0.84 | –0.58 |
| | Mid cap | 0.78 | 1.00 | 0.90 | 0.33 | 0.25 | 0.11 | 0.68 | –0.40 |
| | Small cap | 0.62 | 0.90 | 1.00 | 0.27 | 0.17 | –0.06 | 0.58 | –0.47 |
| **Bonds** | Corporate bonds | 0.32 | 0.33 | 0.27 | 1.00 | 0.95 | –0.41 | 0.11 | –0.26 |
| | Gilts | 0.21 | 0.25 | 0.17 | 0.95 | 1.00 | –0.29 | 0.10 | –0.15 |
| | ILGs | –0.30 | –0.11 | –0.06 | –0.41 | –0.29 | 1.00 | –0.24 | 0.67 |
| **Property** | | 0.84 | 0.68 | 0.58 | 0.22 | 0.10 | –0.24 | 1.00 | –0.29 |
| **Commodities** | | –0.58 | –0.40 | –0.47 | –0.26 | –0.15 | 0.67 | –0.29 | 1.00 |

A broadly spread portfolio of equities and bonds should, therefore, be reasonably well diversified and achieve strong risk reduction under normal circumstances.

One limitation of this correlation analysis in determining portfolio risk is that these correlation figures are not static, rather they vary over time. In the extreme market circumstances experienced in the 2008 credit crunch, all of these correlations became more extreme, moving strongly towards either +1 or –1. As a consequence, much of the hoped for risk reduction in many portfolios was not realised and even quite broadly diversified portfolios suffered significant losses.

Another limitation of this analysis is that it takes no account of the liquidity of stocks held. Analysis of portfolio risk and return based on individual security returns, risks and correlations assumes that investments can be bought at their fair value, ignoring completely any dealing costs and spreads. For large cap stocks or gilts this is probably a reasonable assumption under normal circumstances as they are usually highly liquid. The liquidity of smaller cap stocks may be much lower and the liquidity of property is very low even in normal circumstances. In more extreme circumstances, however, liquidity in all markets may dry up altogether, making it difficult, if not impossible, to deal at a fair value. In conclusion, more liquid investments are more likely to trade close to fair value, less liquid investments and more difficult market circumstances are likely to result in assets trading some way from their fair values.

#### Diversification within asset classes

A portfolio that includes a collection of securities will be less exposed to any loss arising from one of the securities.

Using a **spread of shares** across different **sectors** of the market can also reduce risk. In this way there is a reduced concentration of capital in any one sector.

Diversification across different **markets** can also be achieved within an asset class. For example, a portfolio of shares or equity-based collective investments may be spread across different national markets and regions, perhaps with holdings in Asia as well as North America, Europe and the UK. Gaining exposure to particular markets can be relatively difficult – for example, there are currently relatively few investment vehicles providing exposure to China, although new collective investments (such as **exchange-traded funds** or **ETFs**, based on the shares in an index) covering China are now becoming available.

Sometimes a client will have a large holding in one share, perhaps because of an inheritance or as the result of a share option scheme. Such a client should be made aware of the potential risk of such a large holding.

Although different economies and stock markets influence each other, there are differences in how well different regions and national markets perform. Different economies will be at different stages of the **business cycle** than others at any particular time. On the same principle as that of different companies' shares, a **portfolio spread across different markets or regions of the world** will be less exposed to poor performance of a particular economy such as the UK.

#### Diversification by manager

A number of fund of funds have sprung up in recent years which allows an investor to spread their investments across a number of funds and in doing so avoid committing their whole investment to a single fund manager.

## 3.3 Active versus passive strategies

#### Introduction

There are two alternative investment management styles that may be adopted.

- Active investment management.
- Passive investment management

### 3.3.1 Active

An active investment manager is one who intervenes in the portfolio on a regular basis, attempting to use individual expertise in order to enhance the overall return of the fund. This means the fund manager constantly takes decisions and appraises the value of investments within the portfolio.

Whilst, to many, this may seem the only thing a fund manager could do, it has to be appreciated that in practice there are costs involved with all transactions and hence, a limit on the number of active interventions taking place that is likely to be to the advantage of the fund holder.

Moreover, from a more theoretical point of view, there are a number of theories that indicate that the market itself is efficient and therefore, the prices currently quoted in the market contain within them all available information. If this is so, then the only reason that a price will move is because of information that is not already known to the market and, as such, fund managers buying and selling (switching between stocks) will only make money if they are 'lucky' and switch to the right stock at the right time.

Active fund managers do not believe that the securities markets are continuously efficient. Instead, they believe that markets and securities can be misvalued and that at times, **winners** can be found. They also attempt to correctly **time** their purchase or sale on the basis of specific stock information, market information, economic factors, etc.

Active fund managers may obtain research from external sources such as investment banks. In this instance analysts are referred to as 'sell-side' analysts. Alternatively they may establish an in-house research department, made up of 'buy-side' analysts. The benefit of generating unbiased internal research needs to be weighed against the costs of setting up the department.

### 3.3.1 Passive

Passive management involves establishing a strategy with the intention of achieving the overall objectives of the fund. Once established, this strategy should require little active intervention, being largely self-maintaining.

There are, however, few perfectly passive strategies. Most such strategies require some intervention in response to the occurrence of events, the publication of information, or market/stock movements that have occurred. Passive management does not attempt to beat the market, it follows the market.

Passive portfolio management is consistent with two conditions being satisfied in the securities market: efficiency and homogeneity of expectations. If securities markets are efficient, then securities will be fairly priced at all times. There will be no mispriced securities and hence, no incentive to actively trade. Similarly, if securities markets are characterised by investors who have homogeneous expectations of risks and returns then, again, there is no incentive to trade actively.

### 3.3.2 Hybrids

Increasingly, fund managers are being requested to outperform indexes, rather than merely track them, and this inevitably requires a less passive, more interventionist approach, potentially with an **indexed core fund** and a **peripheral** or **satellite fund** (which is more actively managed and potentially involves the use of derivatives in order to establish larger trading positions than the fund itself can obtain). The regulator of collective investment schemes such as unit trusts, the FSA, has established a number of important rules limiting the extent to which a fund can invest in futures and options.

Alternatively, the fund manager may combine both active and passive fund management methods by **tilting** the fund. That is holding all/a representative sample of the constituents of an index (like a passive tracker fund), but with larger proportions in some areas that he favours and smaller proportions in others, this asset allocation decision constituting the active management component.

## 3.4 Passive approach to bond selection (immunisation)

Using immunisation (bond duration matching), it is possible to create a portfolio to have an assured return over a specific time horizon, irrespective of any changes in the interest rate. Hence, if we need to match a liability, we should select a bond portfolio with the same duration as the liability it is intended to meet.

### 3.4.1 The concept of immunisation

A bond is purchased with a yield of 10%. Interest rates fall to 8%. Consequently, the price of the bond will rise. However, the reinvestment return on the bond will fall, as it is now only possible to reinvest the coupons received at the rate of 8%. As the bond approaches maturity, this fall in the return will become greater as the reinvestment loss outweighs the gain (which will fall as the bond moves to redemption and the price pulls to redemption at par). Overall, the investor will not receive a return of 10% (the yield).

The same is true of the opposite situation where interest rates rise and bond prices fall. Again, the fall in the bond's price will gradually be repaired as the bond approaches maturity and the bond pulls to redemption. The coupons, however, will have been reinvested at a higher rate, therefore generating greater returns. Under this scenario, the overall return from the investment will have outperformed the quoted yield of 10%.

As we saw earlier, the yield is not an effective measure of the anticipated return on a bond if it is held to maturity precisely because it assumes reinvestment at the same rate as the yield.

The concept of **immunisation** relies on the fact that these two effects (price and reinvestment) are balanced at the point of duration, the **weighted average life** of the bond. Therefore, by holding a bond to its duration and not its maturity, the return can be guaranteed.

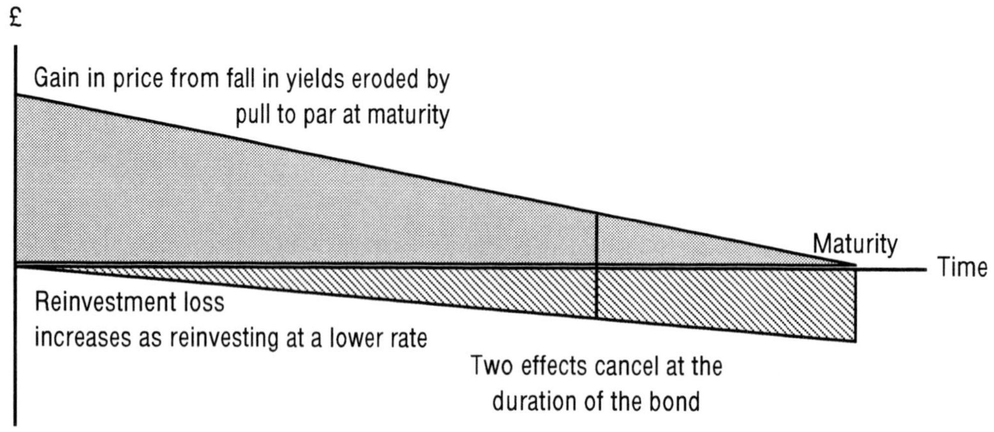


Immunisation is a process whereby the fund manager purchases a bond or portfolio of bonds with a duration equal to the liability. If the manager is able to do this, then it is likely the fund's asset will be close to the liability at the date the liability falls due.

### 3.4.2 Immunisation risk

Immunisation risk arises whenever there is a **non-parallel shift in the yield curve**. The above example of immunisation showed that it works for parallel shifts in the yield curve, i.e. the reinvestment rate fell from 10% to 9% for each coupon. If this does not happen, then matching the duration of the investment to the liability horizon no longer guarantees immunisation. Non-parallel shifts in the yield curve will lead to the income component and the capital component changing in value by differing amounts.

Immunisation will also only avoid risk completely if there is a flat yield curve, as the example above illustrates.

This risk is reduced if the durations of the individual bonds in the immunising portfolio are close to that of the liability, i.e. a bullet portfolio. In this case, the non-parallel yield curve shift will affect the individual bonds and the liability in similar ways. This is unlikely to be the case if a barbell portfolio had been constructed, since the individual bonds within the portfolio would be affected in different ways.

### 3.4.3 Rebalancing

Immunisation is not a completely passive approach to investment management because the portfolio will require a continual **rebalancing**. The initial bonds are selected on the grounds of their portfolios' duration, but because duration erodes over time and due to the effects of immunisation risk, new bonds will have to be purchased in order to match the liability.

One possible way around this is to immunise the portfolio using **zero-coupon bonds, as they have a duration equal to their time to maturity**. The advantage of zero-coupon bonds would be that their duration will change in line with time and, therefore, the portfolio will not require a constant rebalancing. However, without the existence of a strips market, there are unlikely to be the stocks that are required as straight zeros.

### 3.4.4 Contingent immunisation

With **contingent immunisation**, the fund manager actively manages the portfolio attempting to enhance returns subject to an absolute **floor rate of return** which the fund must generate. If active management fails to generate the floor level of return, at that stage, the portfolio is immunised, locking in the minimum rate of return. In this way, the liabilities of the fund are insured against risk, guaranteeing that the rate of return will be sufficient to meet the liabilities as and when they mature.

### 3.4.5 Other problems

Any uncertainty surrounding a bond's cash flows will present a **problem** to the manager wishing to employ immunisation. For instance, **the existence of callable bonds** in the portfolio will render the duration calculation partly dependent on an estimate of when the issuer might call for redemption.

## 3.5 Cash flow matching or dedication

#### Introduction

Cash flow matching (also referred to as dedication) is a more straightforward approach to investment management. The approach is simply to purchase bonds whose redemption proceeds will meet a liability of the fund as they fall due.

Under the concept of matching, bonds are purchased to exactly match the liabilities of the fund. Starting with the final liability, a bond (Bond 1) is purchased whose final coupon redemption proceeds will extinguish the liability.

Turning next to the penultimate liability, this may be satisfied in part by the coupon flows arising from Bond 1. Any remaining liability can be matched against the redemption value of a second bond (Bond 2).

This process is continued for each liability, ensuring that bonds are purchased whose final coupon redemption values extinguish the net liabilities of the fund as and when they occur.

If we assume that the bonds are held to maturity, then there is no reinvestment risk and also no interest rate risk, and any changes in the yield curve will not have any effect on the cash flow matching process.

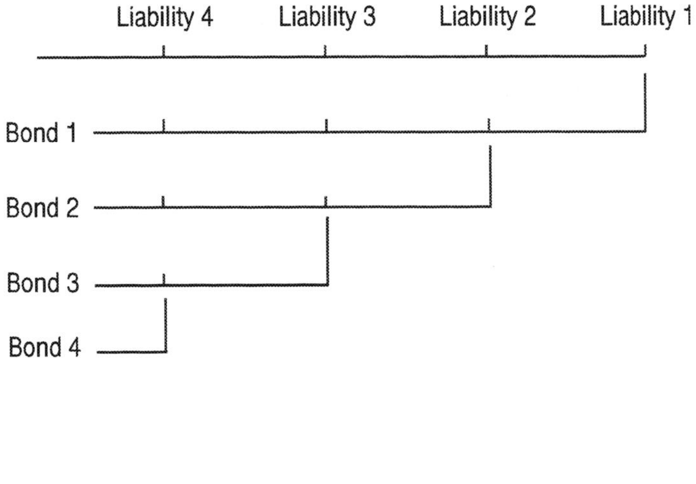


## Example

A fund has to meet liabilities of £1,000 arising at the end of each of the next three years. There are three bonds available.

| Maturity Years | Coupon % | Redemption Payment, Capital and Coupon £ |
|---|---|---|
| 1 | 14.29 | 114.29 |
| 2 | 12.50 | 112.50 |
| 3 | 11.11 | 111.11 |

Construct a portfolio to achieve cash matching.

## Solution

| Number of Bonds | Coupon £ | Maturity (Years) | Cash Flows Year 1 £ | Year 2 £ | Year 3 £ |
|---|---|---|---|---|---|
| 9 | 11.11 | 3 | 100 | 100 | 1,000 |
| 8 | 12.50 | 2 | 100 | 900 | – |
| 7 | 14.29 | 1 | 800 | – | – |
| | | | £1,000 | £1,000 | £1,000 |

In effect, this policy is a simple buy and hold strategy and as such does not require a regular rebalancing. Technically, it is inferior to immunisation since, in practice, it is unlikely that bonds exist with appropriate maturity dates and coupons. It involves a greater initial capital outlay but, intuitively, it is easier to understand.

#### Combination matching or horizon matching

Combination matching is a mixture of the above two approaches to investment management. For example, we could construct a portfolio that cash flow matches the liabilities for the next four quarters but is immunised for the remaining investment horizon. At the end of the four quarters, the portfolio is rebalanced to match cash flow over the subsequent four quarters and is again immunised for the remaining period.

# 4 Approaches to Portfolio Construction

**Learning objective**

7.2.3 **Understand** the key approaches to investment allocation for bond, equity and balanced portfolios: Asset class, Geographical area, Currency, Issuer Sector and Maturity.

## 4.1 Asset classes

Assuming that a top-down approach has been applied, the first stage in the investment management process will be the strategic asset allocation decision.

Strategic asset allocation is the allocation of the funds available between these various instruments or financial markets. At the asset allocation stage, the fund manager decides what proportion of the total portfolio to invest in broad asset categories such as shares, bonds, property, etc. Where a technical or quantitative analysis system has been used, this system may suggest the appropriate asset allocation.

Despite the existence of these techniques, all fund managers require knowledge of asset allocation according to more fundamental principles. This is perhaps the most subjective area of fund management, and one where there will never be a single correct answer. Given the same fund and client, it is unlikely that any two fund managers would produce exactly the same asset allocation and make exactly the same investment decisions. However, it would be reasonable to assume that any allocations would have a broadly similar effect. The justification for this last statement is that the fund manager has a legal and professional duty to base the asset allocation on the client's wishes with particular regard to the criteria discussed above, when identifying the client's objectives, specifically

- Matching liabilities
- Meeting any ethical considerations
- Remaining within risk tolerances
- Maximising fund performance

There are three basic rules the fund manager should bear in mind when trying to satisfy the client's investment objectives.

- The fund manager should take every step to **diversify risk**, a process requiring an understanding of the different risk factors affecting all the investments in which he may be investing as well as the impact of foreign exchange.
- The fund manager should be aware that the best way to match the client's liabilities if they are fixed in money terms is by investing in bonds (or similar nominal returning assets), since this will generate cash flows from interest and redemption proceeds, which will allow the liabilities to be met as they arise.
- Asset allocation is effectively a compromise between matching investments to client liabilities and investing assets in more attractive markets in order to maximise fund performance.

## 4.2 Asset allocation approach

The optimal asset allocation should be based on the objectives and constraints of the fund and the fund manager's estimate of the risks and returns offered by the various securities.

The idea is that the objectives and constraints of a fund direct the investment manager towards certain asset classes and away from others, leading towards the asset allocation decision. For example, if real liabilities are to be met, these must be matched by real assets (equities/property/index-linked bonds), or if high liquidity is needed, then property is inappropriate.

The asset allocation decision is extremely important, since it dominates the performance of most portfolios. As we have already noted, this is because returns on securities within each asset category are usually highly correlated, i.e. they generally rise or fall together. This implies that selecting the best performing asset category is more important for performance than selecting the best performing securities within each asset category.

A fund manager should also be aware of the restrictions placed on them by the trustees, as these may mean that they are not completely free in making their asset allocation decisions.

## 4.3 Geographical area

Investors may choose to invest in international investments to increase portfolio diversification. International stocks have been shown to have low correlation with domestic investments.

Particular regions such as the emerging BRIC economies may also add high growth potential to a portfolio. These regions have recently seen periods of growth while regions such as North America and Europe have seen slow or even negative growth during the 2007-2010 period. This 'de-coupling' of regions is useful for investors, as it allows them to experience growth within their portfolios even while domestic investments may be performing poorly.

Regions may also have specific attributes which may be attractive to an investor, such as the Russian, South Africa, China and Australian markets who produce much of the worlds minerals.

## 4.4 Currency

While many investors are exposed to foreign currencies and the associated foreign exchange risk by their investments in international securities, foreign currencies themselves are a class of investment available to the speculator. Rather than simply selling one currency to purchase another however, it is probably more common for the investor to gain exposure and gain from foreign exchange movements by investing in investments in a particular currency.

The risk associated with investing in foreign currencies may be hedged to some degree by using over the counter instruments such as forward contracts as described in an earlier chapter, and currency swaps. Alternatively the more liquid exchange traded contracts such as foreign exchange options or futures may be used.

## 4.5 Currency swaps

### Definition

A short-term currency swap is a contract which commits two parties to exchange pre-agreed foreign currency amounts now and re-exchange them back at a given future date (the maturity date). The flows include both capital payment and interest.

### Primary and secondary currencies

**Primary currency**

One currency is defined as the primary currency and most deals are structured such that the nominal value of the primary currency exchanged on the two dates is equal.

**Secondary currency**

The other currency is the secondary currency and the nominal value of this exchanged on the two dates is a function of the spot rate and the swap market forward rate.

### Buyer and seller

**Terms**

The terms buyer and seller are a little awkward in relation to currency dealing since each party is giving (selling) one currency and receiving (buying) the other.

The terms buyer and seller relate to these swap arrangements from the point of view of the primary currency cash flows at inception. The **buyer** is the person who, at inception, purchases the primary currency (selling the secondary currency), the **seller** is the individual who, at inception, sells the primary currency (buying the secondary currency).

### Cash flows

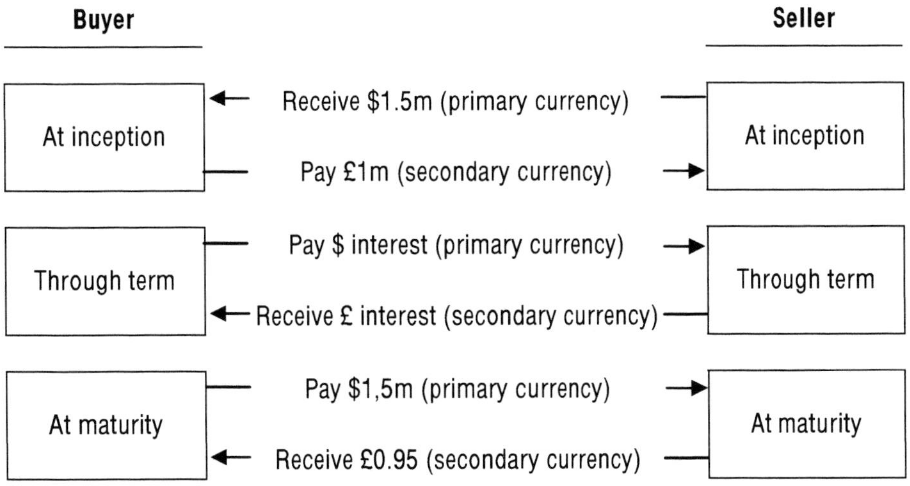


### Dealing

The market in short-term currency swaps, as for interest rate swaps, is an OTC market. Trading is conducted over the telephone and price information is disseminated through quote vendor systems.

### Issuer

When investing in fixed income it is common to refer to credit ratings when considering the issuer and the specific issue in question. For equities, ratio analysis to compare the issuer in question with similar firms in the same sector together with fundamental analysis of the corporate structure.

### Sector

Portfolios constructed top down will begin by focusing upon the question of asset allocation and will then proceed to consider the sector of the market to invest in. The decision to invest in a particular sector is often heavily governed by the economic cycle. Sectors such as utilities are good defensive positions to take as an economy enters a down turn while commodities tend to perform well as the economy improves.

### Maturity

The use of immunisation techniques are widely used to overcome the problem of interest rate risk and reinvestment risk when constructing a portfolio, particularly one aimed at matching a specific liability. The maturity of investments such as bonds will have a close link to the duration of the investment and hence their use immunisation.

Duration matching can be achieved with a wide range of portfolios, as it the duration of a portfolio arises as the weighted average of the durations of its constituent bonds. This means that if say a liability were being met after three years, three year maturity bonds might be used but so might a range of bonds whose average duration was three years.

# 5 Portfolio Management, Strategies and Styles

Learning objective

**7.2.4 Understand** the main aims and investment characteristics of the main cash, bond and equity portfolio management strategies and styles: index/passive management, active / market timing, passive-active combinations, growth versus income, market capitalization, liability driven (LDI), immunization, long, short and leveraged, issuer and sector specific, contrarian and quantitative.

## 5.1 Management style

Management style relates to the idea that investors have different views about key determinants of stock price movements, resulting in different fund managers holding different portfolios in terms of investment characteristics. The various views can be categorised into distinct classes and portfolios can be grouped in the same way. There are two major classes of style that illustrate the above idea.

- Growth investors
- Value investors

There are also two other management styles, market orientation and small capitalisation, that are discussed below.

## 5.2 Growth investors

When looking at a price to earnings ratio, the growth investor is primarily concerned with the earnings. If he believes that the earnings will grow substantially, then he will buy the stock. Assuming that the P/E ratio stays constant, this will give rise to growth in the stock price.

### 5.2.1 Growth styles

As noted above, growth investors focus on companies with higher growth prospects for earnings. As a result, they often will have to buy a stock on a relatively high P/E multiple, reflecting the company's strong fundamentals. However, they are trying to identify companies where the growth prospects are not fully reflected in the price so far. Other characteristics of growth investors are as follows.

- Invest in high quality companieș Focus on consumer, service, healthcare and technology
- Little interest in cyclical and defensive stocks

The growth style can be sub analysed into two sub styles.

### 5.2.2 Consistent growth

- Where the investor concentrates on high quality companies with a consistent record of growth.

### 5.2.3 Earnings momentum

- Where the investor concentrates on companies with more volatile but above average growth rates.

## 5.3 Value investors

In contrast, value investors are less concerned with future growth in earnings. Instead, they focus on whether the existing price of the company looks cheap on the basis of some comparison, such as price to book or price to earnings. The value investor will buy the cheap stock, in the expectation that the price will move to a more normal level in the future. In other words, the value investor expects the P/E ratio to increase even if the earnings stay the same, resulting in growth in the stock price.

### 5.3.1 Value styles

Value styles are based around analysing the price of a company. When looking at price, different investors may focus on different comparisons, as follows.

- Low P/E ratios
- High dividend yield
- Low price to book ratio
- Low price to sales ratio

Three sub styles of the value style can be identified.

### 5.3.2 Low P/E

Where investors concentrate on companies with low prices compared to earnings. Such companies are often cyclical or defensive and may be in an unfashionable industry.

### 5.3.3 Contrarian

Where investors concentrate on companies with low price to book values. They will often select cyclical companies with low profits or dividends relative to their asset base. The hope is that the assets will provide a base from which price can rebound. This rebound may be due to cyclical factors or be company specific.

### 5.3.4 High yield

Where investors focus on companies with high (dividend) yields, since they believe that the companies can maintain or increase their dividend payments.

This sub style is the most conservative, since it is focusing on the ability to maintain dividends.

## 5.4 Growth at a reasonable price [GARP]

### PEG ratio

The PEG ratio of a security is calculated by dividing the P/E ratio by the growth of the share. A PEG ratio of one or less is considered acceptable to both value investors looking for a relatively low P/E ratio and growth investors who tend to look for higher P/E ratios.

## 5.5 Passive equity selection strategies

### 5.5.1 Buy and hold

A buy and hold strategy involves buying a portfolio of securities and holding them for a long period of time, with only minor and infrequent adjustments to the portfolio over time. Under this strategy, investments bought now are held indefinitely, or if they have fixed maturities, held until maturity and then replaced with similar ones. The returns from a buy and hold strategy will be dominated by income flows, i.e. dividends and coupons and, for shares, long-term capital growth. Short-term capital movements are irrelevant for this strategy. Since there is a consensus view when adopting a passive strategy that all securities are fairly priced at all times, it does not really matter which securities are bought and held. However, by buying and holding only a few securities, a substantial amount of diversifiable risk may remain in the portfolio. Hence, a reasonable number of securities must be held within the portfolio.

## 5.6 Indexation

A version of buy and hold that eliminates diversifiable risk is **index matching** or **indexation**. Indexation involves the construction of an index fund that is designed to replicate the performance of a market index. With indexation, the fund manager selects an appropriate index quoted in the market place. Having established the index, the fund manager builds a portfolio that mimics the index, the belief being that this portfolio will then perform in line with the index numbers.

### 5.6.1 Approaches to indexation

Indexation can be achieved in a number of ways, including:

- **Full index replication** – where all of the securities in an index are held in proportion to their index weighting. This should perfectly match index performance (ignoring management fees) but will need rebalancing every time the index changes which may be costly (adversely affecting performance). This approach may be suitable for an index with few shares but would be problematic for larger indices such as the FTSE All-share index.
- **Stratified sampling/optimisation** – as an alternative, a stratified sampling approach may be adopted where a range of shares are selected that closely mirror the performance of the index. This approach will reduce the need for rebalancing when the index changes, but is unlikely to exactly mirror the index performance. Optimisation is a sampling approach designed to minimise intervention (buying and selling) and management fees.
- **Factor matching** – selecting a portfolio of shares that have the same exposure to various economic factors as that of the index, perhaps based on Arbitrage Pricing Theory ideas.
- **Co-mingling** – involves the use of co-mingled funds, such as unit trusts or investment trusts, rather than the explicit formation of an index fund. Co-mingling may be especially suitable for clients with relatively small portfolios and may provide an acceptable compromise between the transaction costs of complete indexation and the tracking error of stratified sampling.
- **Synthetic index fund** – one where, rather than investing in securities contained within the index, the fund is synthesised through the use of derivatives such as futures or equity swaps. For a futures based fund the approach would be to invest the fund's resources in a secure risk-free asset and gain exposure to the market through a long futures position in the relevant index to be tracked. For a swaps based fund the approach would be very similar. An equity swap exchanges the returns from a cash asset for those of a specific index. Once again we can, therefore, invest the fund's resources in a secure risk-free asset and gain exposure to the market, this time through an equity swap based on the relevant index to be tracked. The advantages of this approach are that there are no rebalancing, transaction costs or tracking error as we are effectively investing directly in the index. The disadvantage of this approach is that we do not receive any dividends from the future or swap.

### 5.6.2 Results of indexation

Apart from the transaction costs involved in setting up and rebalancing, there are other problems associated with running an index fund. The most important of these concerns management fees and the treatment of income payments on the securities. Indexation is, however, a popular form of fund management. It attempts to avoid, as far as possible, decisions about selection and timing of investment. However, it is not purely passive. At the very least, the choice of index and the reinvestment of income involve active intervention.

Indexation is normally used in conjunction with other active methods whereby there is an indexed core fund with actively managed peripheral funds, again with the objective of enhancing the overall return of the fund.

### 5.6.3 Arguments supporting index tracking

Following on from our discussion of EMH earlier, if an investor believes that markets are efficient then active fund management will simply incur fees with no superior performance benefit. In this situation it would be better to establish an index fund that, through its nature, will incur lower dealing and management charges and therefore maximise the return to the investor.

### 5.6.4 Arguments against index tracking

Despite the theoretical support for indexation, the approach is not universally accepted. Supporters of active management would counter that:

- Active funds can be customised to the needs of clients whereas trackers simply follow an index.
- Active funds may outperform the index, tracker funds cannot.
- Tracker funds will always underperform the index, if only because of management fees.
- Mergers of major companies may create an overexposure to a few large businesses. For example the seven largest UK companies represent over 40% of the FTSE 100 index by value.
- Index tracking ensures mediocrity of fund management.

Tracker funds will always fall when the index falls, active funds may reduce their exposure.

### 5.6.5 Selecting a tracker fund

If we have decided that it would be most appropriate to use a tracker fund then what factors do we need to consider in order to make our fund selection? The following factors are relevant.

- **Choice of index** – The first stage in the process must be the selection of the index we wish to track
- **Cost structure** – Once the appropriate index has been established, the issue to consider is the cost structure of alternative managers. Generally speaking, we should look for the lowest costs since before costs the returns should be identical.
- **Tracking error** – In additional to costs, however, we also need to consider tracking error, i.e. how far the performance of the fund varies from that of the index being tracked.
- **Tax** – The tax status of the fund and its tax implications for the investor will clearly be relevant to any investment decision.
- **Alternative structured products** – Any structured alternatives should also be assessed. Some of these offer index based returns whilst also providing capital guarantees that may appeal to certain investors.

## 5.7 Active bond selection strategies

As with shares, a bond portfolio will be actively managed whenever there are misvalued bonds around. Similarly, with asset allocation decisions having been made, active bond portfolio management operates around the activities of security selection and market timing. However, there is a difference between share and bond portfolio managers. Most share managers engage in security selection, whereas most bond managers engage in market timing. A bond picker will construct a portfolio of bonds that, in comparison with the market portfolio, has less than proportionate weightings in the overpriced bonds and more than proportionate weightings in the under-priced bonds. A market timer engages in active management when he does not accept the consensus market portfolio and is either more bullish or more bearish than the market. Expectations of interest rate changes are therefore a crucial input into successful market timing. A bond market timer is interested in **adjusting the relative duration** of his portfolio over time. Market timing with bonds is sometimes called duration switching. If the fund manager is expecting a bull market because he anticipates a fall in the general level of interest rates, he will want to increase the duration of his portfolio by replacing low-duration bonds with high-duration bonds. If the fund manager is expecting a bear market because he is anticipates a rise in the level of interest rates, he will want to reduce the duration of his portfolio. Active bond portfolio management is generally not as profitable as active share portfolio management. There are several reasons for this.

- There are more shares traded than bonds in the UK.
- The most liquid bonds are UK government bonds that have only certain maturities.
- The volatility of bond prices is generally much lower than that of shares, hence fewer opportunities for substantial mispricing of bonds exist.
- With only a few bonds suitable for active trading, the portfolio consisting of these bonds will be relatively undiversified. The cost of active bond portfolio management can be reduced using futures and options.

### 5.7.1 Riding the yield curve

Riding the yield curve is a valid strategy when the yield curve is upward sloping. If this is the case, then an investment manager can buy bonds with maturities in excess of his investment horizon. He proceeds to hold the bonds until the end of his investment period and then sells them. **If the yield curve has not shifted during that period**, the investment manager will have generated higher returns than if he had bought bonds with the same maturity as his investment horizon. This follows because as the time to maturity declines, the yield to maturity falls and the price of the bond rises, thereby generating a capital gain (hence, the term yield curve ride). These gains will be higher than those available if bonds with the same maturity as the investment horizon are used because the maturity value of the latter bonds is fixed.

### 5.7.2 Bond switching

Bond portfolio adjustments involve the purchase and sale of bonds, i.e. switching or swapping of bonds. There are two main classes of bond switches:

- Anomaly switches
- Policy switches

### 5.7.3 Anomaly switching

An anomaly switch is a switch between two bonds with very similar characteristics, but whose prices or yields are out of line with each other.

### 5.7.4 Substitution switching

The simplest example of an anomaly switch is a substitution switch. This involves the temporary exchange of two bonds that are similar in terms of maturity, coupon, quality rating and every other characteristic, but which differ in terms of price and yield. Since two similar bonds should trade at the same price and yield, this circumstance results in an arbitrage profit opportunity with the expensive bond being sold and the cheap bond purchased initially. If the coupon and maturity of the two bonds are similar, then a substitution swap involves a one-for-one exchange of bonds. However, if there are substantial differences in coupon or maturity, then the duration of the two bonds will differ. This will lead to different responses if the general level of interest rates changes during the life of the switch. It will, therefore, be necessary to weight the switch in such a way that it is hedged from changes in the level of interest rates but is still exposed to changes in the anomalous yield differential between the bonds.

### 5.7.5 Pure yield pickup switch

Another type of anomaly switch is a pure yield pickup switch. This involves the sale of a bond that has a given yield to maturity and the purchase of a similar bond with a high yield to maturity. With this switch, there is no expectation of any yield or price correction, so no reverse transaction will need to take place at a later date, which may be the case with a substitution switch.

### 5.7.6 Policy switching

A policy switch is a switch between two dissimilar bonds, which is designed to take advantage of an anticipated change in:

- Interest rates
- Structure of the yield curve
- Bond quality rating
- Sector relationships

Such changes can be expected to lead to a change in the relative prices and yields of the two bonds. Policy switches involve greater expected returns, but also greater potential risks than anomaly switches.

### 5.7.7 Changes in interest rates

A market timer will always be on the lookout for changes in interest rates. Switching from low-duration to high-duration bonds if interest rates are expected to fall is an example of a policy switch.

### 5.7.8 Changes in bond quality ratings

A bond whose quality rating is expected to fall will fall in price. To prevent a capital loss, it can be switched for a bond whose quality rating is expected to rise or remain unchanged.

### 5.7.9 Changes in sector relationships

An example of a change in sector relationships is a change in taxes between two sectors. For example, one sector may have withholding taxes on coupon payments, e.g. domestic bonds, whereas another, e.g. Eurobonds, may not. If it is anticipated that withholding tax will either be applied to all sectors or will be withdrawn from all sectors, then another switch is possible.

# 6 Measurement of Returns

earning objective

**7.2.5** **Understand** how portfolio risk and return are evaluated using the following measures: Holding period return, Total return and its components, Standard deviation, Volatility, Covariance and correlation, Risk- adjusted returns and Benchmarking

In order to reflect the full return of a portfolio, any performance measures must include both income (dividends or coupons) and capital growth. As such, we must always be looking at the market values of any securities held in the fund, as opposed to their historical costs.

## 6.1 Holding period return

Each investment is characterised by a cost and a pattern of cash flows. We could describe a fund's total performance by stating the dividends or coupons plus capital growth (final market value less initial value) as a percentage of the initial amount invested. Alternatively, we could assess the income (dividends/coupon) above as a percentage and the gain as a percentage, decomposing the total return into income and gain.

## Example

Suppose Investment A costs £100 and at the end of six months, returns £10, before being sold for £110. How can it be compared with Investment B, bought at £50, held for one year and then sold for £70 with no income paid out? Obviously, the different costs must be taken into account, as well as the different returns and time periods involved.

### Basic calculation

Calculating the percentage holding period return for each investment avoids the problem of comparing different size investments. This return is simply the total return during the period held (money received less cost) divided by the initial cost, i.e.

$$r_p = \frac{D_1 + V_1 - V_0}{V_0}$$

where

$r_p$ = holding period return

$D_1$ = any returns paid out from the investment/fund at the end of the period

$V_0$ = is the initial cost at the start of the holding period

$V_1$ = the value of the investment at the end of the holding period

## Solution

Using this equation, the holding period returns for Investments A and B along with the income and gain sub-components of that holding period return can be calculated as

#### Investment A

| Total return | Income | Gain |
|---|---|---|
| $r_a = \frac{D_1 + V_1 - V_0}{V_0}$ | $r_a = \frac{D_1}{V_0}$ | $r_a = \frac{V_1 - V_0}{V_0}$ |
| $r_a = \frac{£10 + £110 - £100}{£100} = 0.20$<br>i.e. 20% in six months | $r_a = \frac{£10}{£100} = 0.10$<br>i.e. 10% income in six months | $r_a = \frac{£110 - 100}{£100} = 0.10$<br>i.e. 10% gain in six months |

#### Investment B

| Total return | Income | Gain |
|---|---|---|
| $r_b = \frac{D_1 + V_1 - V_0}{V_0}$ | $r_b = \frac{D_1}{V_0}$ | $r_b = \frac{V_1 - V_0}{V_0}$ |
| $r_b = \frac{0 + £70 - £50}{£50} = 0.40$<br>i.e. 40% in a year | $r_b = \frac{£0}{£50} = 0.00$<br>i.e. 0% income | $r_b = \frac{£70 - £50}{£50} = 0.40$<br>i.e. 40% gain |

### 6.1.1 Using the results – annualising

The holding period returns of A and B are not directly comparable, since B was invested for twice as long as A. When A was sold, the proceeds could have been reinvested for another six months, but we do not know what return would have been available to the investor at that time. To compare the returns, they must be for a standard period. This is achieved by using the equivalent period interest rate formula to annualise the returns as follows.

#### Solution

##### Investment A

$r_a = 20\%$ in six months

Hence, annualising this return, we get

$1 + r = (1+R)^n$

$1 + r = 1.2^2 = 1.44$

$r = 0.44$ or 44% p.a.

##### Investment B

$r_b = 40\%$ p.a.

We have now got a standardised measure of return and the annualised holding period return.

## 6.2 Risk

### 6.2.1 Standard deviation and variance

#### Calculation

The standard deviation is a dispersion measure that is related to the arithmetic mean. The idea behind the calculation is to establish how far each observed value falls from the mean, the standard deviation being a function of this divergence, and the variance being the square of the standard deviation.

The greater the divergence of the observed values from the mean, the greater the standard deviation (or risk).

When we are considering the total population of values with no omissions, the approach, as for location measures, varies slightly depending on how the data is presented, though in outline the calculation of the standard deviation is

- Calculate the arithmetic mean $\bar{x}$.
- Calculate the difference between each observed value and the arithmetic mean $(x - \bar{x})$, the sum of which must be zero since some items lie above the mean and have positive values and some below the mean and have negative values.
- Square the differences to remove the negative signs from those lying below the mean, i.e. we are now considering just the absolute value (or square of the value) of the differences, ignoring whether they lie above or below the mean.
- Sum these squared differences.

- Calculate the average of these squared differences by dividing by the number of observed values.
- Take the square root of this average to cancel the effects of our earlier squaring up.

Since we square the differences up, then later take the square root, the units of the standard deviation will be the same as those for the mean, i.e. if the mean is the average number of miles travelled in several journeys, the standard deviation will also be in miles.

$$\text{Standard deviation} = \sigma = \sqrt{\frac{\sum(x-\overline{x})^2}{n}}$$

The value of variation is simply standard deviation squared.

In summary, the standard deviation and also variance give an indication of the average movement of an investment around the mean and as such indicates the risk of the investment.

## 6.3 Correlation

The purpose of the correlation measure is to measure the strength of the relationship between two variables. In the context of regression analysis with only one independent variable, the correlation coefficient will give an indication of how accurately the regression line matches the observed values.

### 6.3.1 Correlation coefficient

The correlation coefficient is a relative measure indicating how two variables move with respect to each other. It is also referred to as Pearson's correlation coefficient. When a correlation coefficient is calculated by reference to a sample of data, it is referred to by the symbol r. When it is calculated by reference to the whole population, it is referred to as $\rho$ (pronounced **rho**).

The correlation coefficient measures the direction and degree of linear association between the two variables.

A correlation coefficient will have any value between +1 and –1 and the meaning of the correlation coefficient can best be understood by considering the extremes.

### 6.3.2 Perfect positive correlation (correlation coefficient = +1)

If two variables are perfectly positively correlated then they move up and down together and in proportion.

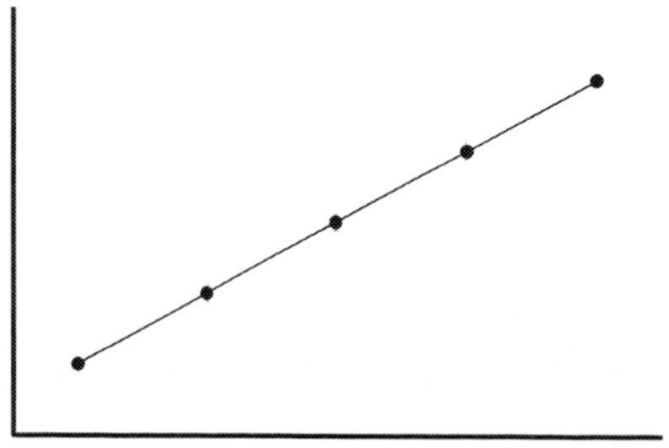

Here, it can be seen that the line is upward sloping and all the actual values of y are exactly the same as the predicted value given the regression line.

### 6.3.3 Non-perfect positive correlation (0< correlation coefficient < 1)

If two variables are positively correlated, but not perfectly positively correlated, we will have something like this.

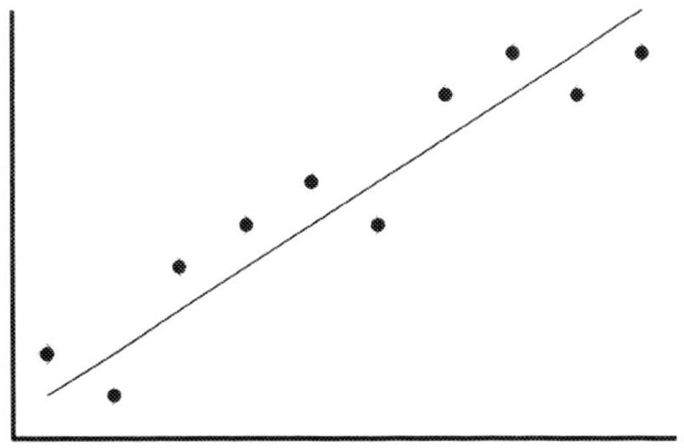

Here, it can be seen that there is a positive relationship between the two variables – as the value of x increases, so does the value of y. However, the relationship is not exact and so this is not perfect correlation. The correlation coefficient here may be +0.8, for example.

### 6.3.4 Perfect negative correlation (correlation coefficient = –1)

If two variables are perfectly negatively correlated then they move up and down in exact opposition and in proportion.

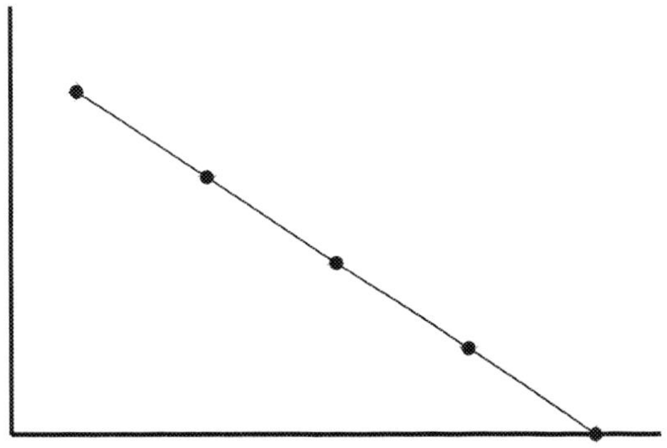

Once again, all the actual values of y are as predicted by the regression line, meaning that the relationship is perfect. However, the slope is downward, indicating a negative relationship.

### 6.3.5 Uncorrelated (correlation coefficient = 0)

If two variables are uncorrelated then they move independently of each other, i.e. if one goes up, the other may go up or down or not move at all.

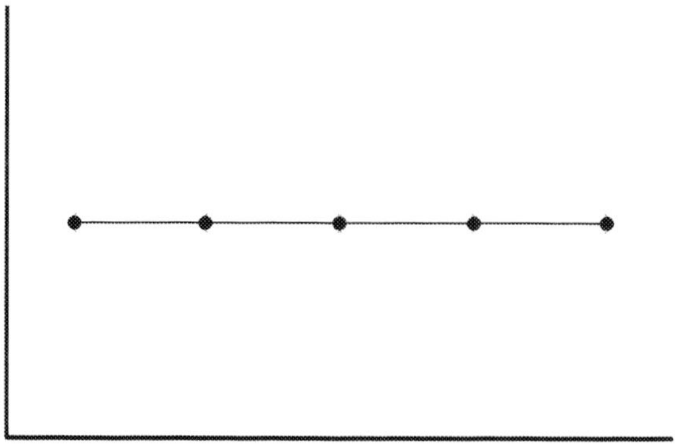

In this case, it can be seen that the value of y is independent from the value of x – it does not change regardless of the value of x. An alternative presentation of zero correlation would be to have points randomly scattered across the whole of the diagram.

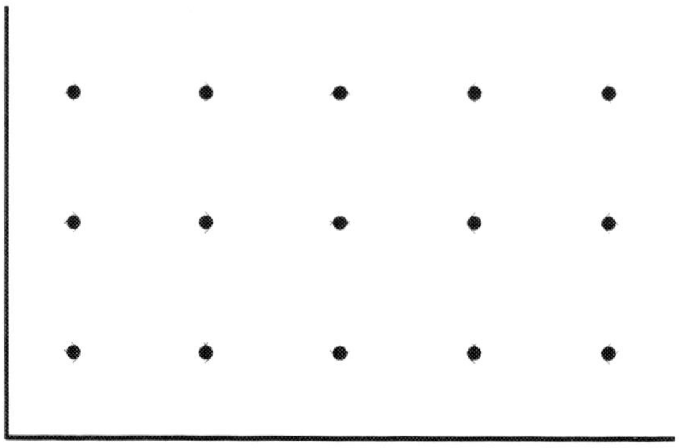

In between perfect correlation and no correlation, there are relationships between variables of varying strength. Generally, a correlation coefficient of 0.5 would be viewed as moderate correlation. Values of less than this would be viewed as weak correlation while values above this would be viewed as strong correlation.

### 6.3.6 Calculating the correlation coefficient

The formula for calculating the correlation coefficient of x and y is as follows.

$$cor_{x,y} = \frac{\text{Covariance}(x,y)}{\sigma_x \sigma_y}$$

The **covariance** is a number related to the correlation coefficient. It is calculated as follows, given a sample of data.

$$cov_{x,y} = \frac{\sum(x-\bar{x})(y-\bar{y})}{n-1}$$

### 6.3.7 Conclusion

There are two relevant factors in a correlation coefficient, the sign (+ or –) and the value. Their effects are

- Positive correlation implies that variables move up and down together, negative correlation means that they move in opposition.
- The value of the figure, ignoring the sign, gives an indication of the strength of the relationship, the closer to a value of 1 the stronger the relationship.

## 6.4 Risk adjusted returns

An absolute measure of return does not tell the full story of the performance of a portfolio. When comparing portfolios it is often more appropriate to measure the return relative to the risk.

### 6.4.1 Sharpe measure

The Sharpe measure uses as its measure of risk, the total portfolio risk or standard deviation.

The Sharpe measure is calculated as

$$\text{Sharpe measure} = \frac{r_p - r_f}{\sigma_p}$$

where

$r_p$ = portfolio return

$r_f$ = risk-free return over the same interval

$\sigma_p$ = portfolio risk (standard deviation of the portfolio returns)

As noted above, this measure is appropriate where this portfolio represents the full set of investments of the client (**an undiversified investor**). The higher the measure, the better the performance, which can be achieved by either **better stock selection** or **greater diversification**.

## 6.5 Comparison to a benchmark index

In order to assess how well a fund manager is performing, we need a yardstick for comparison. One such suitable yardstick may be a benchmark index. Once we have determined an appropriate benchmark, we can then compare whether the fund manager outperformed, matched, or underperformed.

The appropriate benchmark is one that is consistent with the preferences of the fund's trustees and the fund's tax status. For example, a different benchmark is appropriate if the fund is a gross fund and does not pay taxes (e.g. a pension fund), than if it is a net fund and does pay taxes (e.g. a general insurance fund).

Similarly, a general market index will not be appropriate as a benchmark if the trustee has a preference for high-income securities or an aversion to certain securities, e.g. rival companies. The FTSE All Share Index would not be an appropriate benchmark if half the securities were held overseas.

There will therefore be different benchmarks for different funds and different fund managers. The benchmark is likely to be an index of one kind or another, hence it is important to understand the structure of the relevant index. The structure of indices has been discussed in an earlier chapter.

The characteristics that are required to render an index suitable as a benchmark are that it is

- Specified and unambiguous.
- Appropriate to the preferences of the fund (e.g. a UK blue chip fund may utilise the FTSE 100 Index).
- Appropriate to the currency of the fund.
- Investable, i.e. composed of investments that could conceivably be held in the fund.
- Measurable, i.e. the return can be calculated on a frequent basis as required.
- Representative of achievable performance, i.e. it has an arithmetic weighted composition (remember that the return of a portfolio is an arithmetic weighted average of the individual stock returns).
- Measures the relevant component of performance, i.e. total return indices for total return performance and capital value indices for capital growth.

# 7 Use of Derivatives

| Learning objective | 7.1.4 **Assess** the interactive relationship between the securities and derivatives markets, and the impact of related events on markets. |
|---|---|

## 7.1 Introduction

In the minds of the general public, and indeed those of many people involved in the financial services industry, derivative products such as futures and options, warrants and swaps are thought of as very complicated. They are also thought of as having little to do with the real world. Television coverage, showing pictures of young traders in brightly coloured jackets shouting at each other in an apparent frenzy, makes it difficult to imagine that what they are engaged in may be of enormous value to the smooth functioning of the economy.

At the heart of these products is the concept of deferred delivery. The instruments allow you, albeit in slightly different ways, to agree **today** the price at which you will buy or sell an asset at some time in the future. This is unlike normal everyday transactions. When we go to a supermarket, we pay our money and take immediate delivery of our goods. Why would someone wish to agree today a price for delivery at some time in the future? The answer is **certainty**.

Imagine a farmer growing a crop of wheat. To grow such a crop costs money; money for seed, labour, fertiliser and so on. All this expenditure takes place with no certainty that, when the crop is eventually harvested, the price at which the wheat is sold will cover these costs. This is obviously a risky thing to do and many farmers are unwilling to take on this burden. How can this uncertainty be avoided?

By using derivatives, the farmer is able to agree **today** a price at which the crop will ultimately be sold, in maybe four or six months' time. This enables the farmer to achieve a minimum sale price for his crop. He is no longer subject to fluctuations in wheat prices. He knows what price his wheat will bring and can thus plan his business accordingly.

From their origins in the agricultural world, derivative products have become available on a wide range of other assets, from metals and crude oil to bonds and equities. To understand these instruments properly requires some application. There is much terminology to master, and definitions to be understood but, essentially, they are really quite simple. They are products that allow you to fix today the price at which assets may be bought or sold at a future date.

## 7.2 Futures

### 7.2.1 Definition of a future

> A future is an agreement to buy or sell a standard quantity of a specified asset on a fixed future date at a price agreed today.

There are two parties to a futures contract, a buyer and a seller whose obligations are as follows.

- The buyer of a future enters into an **obligation** to buy on a specified date.
- The seller of a future is under an **obligation** to sell on a future date.

These obligations relate to a standard quantity of a specified asset on a fixed future date at a price agreed today.

### 7.2.2 Standard quantity

Exchange-traded futures are traded in standardised parcels known as **contracts**.

For example, a futures contract on a gilt is to be for **£100,000 nominal of a 6% gilt**, or an interest rate future might be for £0.5m nominal value. The purpose of this standardisation is that buyers and sellers are clear about the quantity that will be delivered. If you sold one gilt future, you would know that you were obligated to sell £100,000 nominal of gilts.

Futures are only traded in whole numbers of contracts. So, if you wished to buy £200,000 nominal of gilts, you would buy two gilt futures.

### 7.2.3 Specified asset

Imagine that you entered into a futures contract on a car. Let us say you buy a car futures contract that gives you the obligation to buy a car at a fixed price of £15,000, with delivery taking place in December.

It is obvious that something very important is missing from the contract – namely any detail about what type of car you are to buy. Most of us would be happy to pay £15,000 for a Porsche, but would be rather less happy if all our £15,000 bought was a Ford Escort.

All futures contracts are governed by their **contract specifications**. These legal documents set out in great detail the size of each contract, when delivery is to take place and what exactly is to be delivered.

### 7.2.4 Fixed futures date

The delivery of futures contracts takes place on a specified date(s) known as **delivery day(s)**. This is when buyers exchange money for goods with sellers. Futures have finite lifespans so that, once the **last trading day** is past, it is impossible to trade the futures for that date.

At any one time, a range of delivery months may be traded (for example most NYSE Liffe contracts have **March**, **June**, **September** and **December** delivery months) and as one delivery day passes, a new date is introduced.

In many cases, a physical delivery does not actually occur on the delivery day. Rather, the exchange calculates how much has been lost, or gained, by the parties to a futures contract. It is only this monetary gain or loss that changes hands, not the underlying asset. The **NYSE Liffe gilt future** is an example of a **physically settled contract**, whereas the FTSE 100 Index future is **cash settled** and may be described as an example of a 'contract for difference' or CFD.

### 7.2.5 Price agreed today

The final phrase in the definition is the most important of all. The reason why so many people, from farmers to fund managers, like using futures is, as was explained in the introduction to this chapter, that they introduce certainty.

Imagine a farmer growing a crop of wheat. In the absence of a futures market, he has no idea whether he will make a profit or a loss when he plants the seeds in the ground. By the time he harvests his crop, the price of wheat may be so low that he will not be able to cover his costs. However, with a futures contract, he can fix a price for his wheat many months before harvest. If, six months before the harvest, he sells a wheat future, he enters into an obligation to sell wheat at that price on the stipulated delivery day. In other words, he knows what price his goods will fetch.

You might think that this is all well and good, but what happens if there is a drought or a frost that makes it impossible for the farmer to deliver his wheat?

Futures can be traded, so although the contract obligates the buyer to buy and the seller to sell, these obligations can be **offset** (closed out) by undertaking an equal and opposite trade in the market.

## Example

Let us suppose a farmer has sold 1 September wheat future at £120 per tonne. If, subsequently, the farmer decides he does not wish to sell his wheat, but would prefer to use the grain to feed his cattle, he simply buys 1 September future at the then prevailing price. His original sold position is now offset by a bought position, leaving him with no outstanding delivery obligations.

This offsetting is common in future markets; very few contracts run through to delivery.

### 7.2.6 Futures v Forwards

A **forward** is an agreement to buy or sell a specified quantity of a specified asset on a specified future date at a price agreed today.

From the above definition you can see they have many of the same characteristics as futures. However, there are some key differences that can best be summarised in the following table.

| Attribute | Futures | Forward Contracts |
|---|---|---|
| Traded | Exchange traded | OTC |
| Quality and Quantity | Standardised by the exchange for all products | Specified in the contract |
| Delivery Dates | Standard fixed dates | Specified in the contract |
| Liquidity/Ability to Close Out | Generally good liquidity/easy to close out | May be limited |
| Counterparty Risk | None due to the workings of the clearing and settlement system | Default risk exists |
| Costs/Margin | Relatively low initial costs (margin) | Costs specifically agreed, may be high. Margin not normally required |
| Regulation | Significant regulation and investor protection | Less regulated |

### 7.2.7 Using futures

All sorts of people use futures. Some may use them to reduce risk, others to seek high returns – and for this, they must be willing to take high risks. Futures markets are, in fact, wholesale markets in risk – markets in which risks are transferred from the cautious to those with more adventurous (or reckless) spirits. The users fall into one of three categories; the **hedger**, the **speculator** and the **arbitrageur** whose motivations are as follows.

- **Hedger** – someone seeking to reduce risk.
- **Speculator** – a risk-taker seeking large profits.
- **Arbitrageur** – seeks riskless profits from exploiting market inefficiencies (mispricing).

In this section, we will look at the first two types of user, starting with the speculator.

### 7.2.8 The speculator – Buying a future or forward

A transaction in which a future is purchased to open a position is known as a **long futures position**. Thus, the purchase of the oil future would be described as **going long of the future** or simply **long**.

The purpose of undertaking such a transaction is to open the investor to the risks and rewards of ownership of the underlying asset by an alternative route.

### 7.2.9 The hedger – Protecting against a rise

The scenario that we are considering here is that an investor wishes to acquire an asset at some time in the future when cash is available, but is concerned that the current price may rise making the asset unaffordable. He therefore wishes to protect against this price rise.

### 7.2.10 Summary

In short hedges, you sell futures to protect an existing holding.

In long hedges, you buy futures to protect an anticipated holding.

### 7.2.11 Specific contracts and their uses

In order to understand the use of futures to a fund manager we need to be familiar with contracts that he may wish to use, how he may use them and why. We consider three futures contracts, in particular

- FTSE 100 Index Future.
- Three-Month Sterling Future.
- UK Gilt Future.

One bit of terminology we will introduce here in relation to futures is the **tick**. There are two aspects to this.

- The **tick size** is the smallest permitted quote movement on one contract.
- The **tick value** is the change in the value of one contract if there is a one-tick change in the quote.

These two factors enable us to calculate our futures dealing profit or loss by using

**Formula to learn**

Profit = Quote change in ticks × Tick value × Number of contracts

When we look at the Three-Month Sterling Futures contract in particular, it will be most convenient to calculate the profit this way.

### 7.2.12 FTSE 100 Index Future

#### Purpose and characteristics

The FTSE 100 Index future fixes the price at which the underlying index may be bought or sold at a specific future date.

The general characteristics of the contract are as follows.

##### Unit of trade

**Formula to learn**

Unit of trade = Index value × £10

That is, a contract can be valued by multiplying the index value by £10. If, for example, the index stood at 6,000, then one contract would have a value of 6,000 × £10 = £60,000.

What this means is that

- A speculator may gain £60,000 of exposure to the market by buying a contract.
- A hedger who already holds shares could use the contract to hedge his exposure to £60,000 of those shares.

### Delivery

This contract is **cash settled**. That is, rather than the two parties exchanging the underlying asset and the pre-agreed price at the delivery date, they simply settle up by the payment from one to the other of the difference in value.

### Quotation

The quote given is in index points.

### Tick

The tick size, the smallest permitted quote movement, is 0.5 index points, which corresponds to a tick value of £5.00 (0.5 × £10).

### Uses

As we indicated above, we may use this contract to gain exposure to, or hedge exposure against, the index, i.e. the stock market in general.

## Example

We are managing a £20m pension fund portfolio and we believe that the market is about to fall. The index and the future currently stand at 6,000.

The alternatives that we have are as follows.

- Sell the portfolio and move into cash/bonds – this will avoid the market fall, but will clearly incur massive dealing costs.
- Set up a short hedge using the futures contract.

### Short hedge

The future is quoted at 6,000, hence each contract will hedge £60,000 (6,000 × £10) of our exposure. To hedge the full portfolio, we will therefore need $333^1/3$ contracts (£20m ÷ £60,000). However, we can only deal in whole contracts, therefore we will sell 333 contracts (the closest whole number).

Let us now consider what our position is if the market (and the futures contract) fall 200 points.

*Cash position*

| | (£) |
|---|---|
| Old portfolio value | 20,000,000 |
| New portfolio value = £20m × $\frac{5,800}{6,000}$ | 19,333,333 |
| Loss | (666,667) |

*Futures position*

| | Points |
|---|---|
| Sold index at | 6,000 |
| Bought index to close position at | 5,800 |
| Gain | 200 = 400 ticks |

Hence, the total profit on our 333 contracts will be

Profit = Ticks × Tick value × Number of contracts
= 400 × £5.00 × 333 = £666,000

As we can see, our futures profit almost exactly cancels the loss on the portfolio and hence represents a good hedging strategy.

### 7.2.13 Hedge ratio

One assumption we have made here is that our portfolio is as volatile as the index, i.e. it has $\beta = 1$. If this is not the case, then we may need to sell more or less contracts to achieve the hedge. The important determinant is the relative volatility.

By definition, the futures contract has a $\beta = 1$. If the portfolio has a $\beta = 1.2$, then a 1% change in the index will cause a 1% change in the value of a future but a 1.2% change in the portfolio value. We will therefore need 1.2 times as many futures contracts to provide sufficient profit to cancel any losses suffered in the portfolio. When we hedge with futures, we should use

Formula to learn

$$\text{Number of contracts} = \frac{\text{Portfolio value}}{\text{Futures value}} \times \beta$$

## Example

A fund manager wishes to hedge a portfolio with a value of £30m and a beta of 1.27. How many FTSE 100 futures contracts will be required to hedge (assuming the future is at 4050)?

$$\frac{£30\text{m}}{(4050 \times £10)} \times 1.27 = 940.74$$

To hedge, sell 941 contracts.

Note that beta hedging applies equally to hedging a portfolio with index options.

### 7.2.14 Hedge efficiency

The futures contracts utilised in a hedge will not necessarily move exactly in parallel with the portfolio being hedged.

The following ratio could be utilised to assess the efficiency of a futures hedge.

Formula to learn

$$\%\ \text{Hedge efficiency} = \frac{\text{Absolute loss/gain on futures}}{\text{Absolute gain/loss on cash market}}$$

A value of 100% indicates a perfect hedge. A value of less than or greater than 100% indicates that a level of residual exposure remains.

## 7.3 Options

### Definition

An **option** is a contract that confers the right, but not the obligation, to buy or sell an asset at a given price on or before a given date.

All the comments relating to standard quantities, specified assets, fixed future dates and price agreed today that we noted above for futures still apply.

### 7.3.1 The speculator – buying an option

Conventionally, a speculator anticipating a rise in the price of shares would simply buy the shares for immediate delivery and then hold them, hoping to sell them for a profit once the price rose. If we imagine that the price of a share is £6.00 and that the speculator buys just one share, the expenditure would be £6.00.

Another way of representing the hope of a rise in share prices would be to buy an option on a share – specifically, an option that would give the right, but not the obligation, to buy a share at a price of £6.00 for a period of three months. The purchase of this option would cost, say, 50p.

Remember that an option is a contract for a future delivery, so it would not be necessary to pay £6.00 in the first instance; the only money to be invested at this point is the 50p.

One advantage is immediately apparent. Options are cheaper than purchasing the underlying asset.

## Example

If three months later, as expected, the price of the share has risen from £6.00 to £7.00, what will be the position of

- The speculator who bought the physical share?
- The speculator who bought the option on the share?

## Solution

*Physical Share*

| | £ |
|---|---|
| Sale Price | 7 |
| Purchase Price | (6) |
| Profit | 1 |

On an investment of £6.00, the investor has made a profit of £1.00 in just three months.

*Option on Share*

Now let us look at the profit for the options buyer. Three months ago, he entered into a contract that gave him the right, but not the obligation, to buy a share at £6.00. When purchased, that right cost just 50p per share. With the share now trading at £7.00, the right to buy at £6.00 must be worth at least £1.00 – the difference between the current price and the stated price in the contract.

This right to buy at £6.00 was purchased for 50p. With the market price at £7.00 at the end of the option's life, the option will now be worth £1.00, hence

| | £ |
|---|---|
| Sale Price | 1 |
| Purchase Price | (0.5) |
| Profit | 0.5 |

On an investment of 50p, a 50p profit has been achieved. In percentage terms, this profit is spectacularly greater than on the conventional purchase and sale of the physical share.

One important thing to note is that options can be traded. It is not necessary for the underlying asset to be bought or sold. What more commonly occurs is that **options** are bought and sold. Thus, an option bought at 50p could be sold to the market at £1.00, realising a 100% profit with the investor never having an intention of buying the underlying asset.

At this stage, it is necessary to introduce some of the vocabulary used in the options market.

### 7.3.2 Terminology

In the definition of an option given earlier, an option was described as being the right, but not the obligation, to buy or sell. The right to buy and the right to sell are given different names.

- The right to buy is known as a **call option**.
- The right to sell is known as a **put option**.

The rights to buy (call) or sell (put) are held by the person buying the option who is known as the **holder**.

The person selling an option is known as a **writer** and is obliged to make (call) or take (put) delivery on or before the date on which an option comes to the end of its life. This date is known as its **expiry date**.

Options can also be differentiated by their exercise style. Most options are known as **American style**, which means that the holders can exercise at any time until the expiry date. A less common type of exercise is the **European style** exercise. In these types of options, the holder can only exercise on the expiry date. The exchange stipulates the type of exercise style in its contract specifications. Most option contracts traded on NYSE Liffe are American style.

The following diagram shows the relationship between holders and writers.

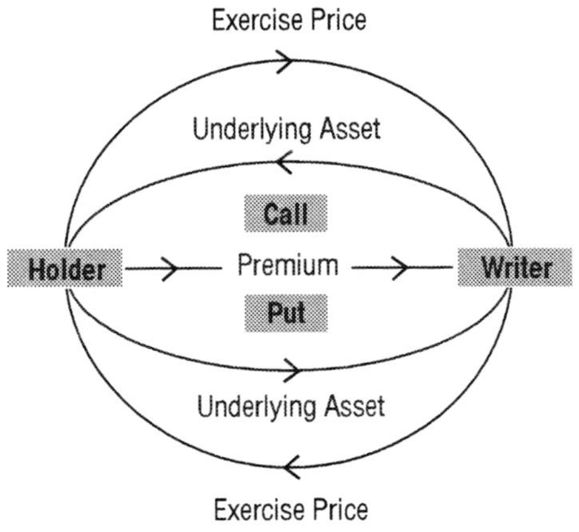


The first thing to understand is the flow of **premium**. Premium is the cost of an option. In our share example, the premium was 50p and this is paid by the holder and received by the writer.

In return for receiving premium, the writer agrees to fulfil the terms of the contract, which of course are different for calls and puts.

### 7.3.3 Call options

Call writers agree to deliver the asset underlying the contract if **called** upon to do so. When options holders wish to take up their rights under the contract, they are said to **exercise** the contract. For a call, this means that the writer must deliver the underlying asset for which he will receive the fixed amount of cash stipulated in the original contract.

Thus, for a share call option that gives the holder the right, but not the obligation, to buy at £6.00, this would mean that the writer would be required to deliver the share to the holder at £6.00. The option holder will only want to buy at £6.00 when it would be advantageous for him to do so, i.e. only when the real or market price is somewhat higher than £6.00. If the market price were less than £6.00, there would be no sense in paying more than the market price for the asset.

Call options writers run very considerable risks. In return for receiving the option's premium, they are committed to delivering the underlying asset at a fixed price. As the price of the asset could, in theory, rise infinitely, they could be forced to buy the underlying asset at a high price and to deliver it to the option holder at a much lower value. The price at which an options contract gives the right to buy (call) or sell (put) is known as the **exercise price** or **strike price**.

### 7.3.4 Put options

The dangers for put options writers are also substantial. The writer of a put is obligated to pay the exercise price for assets that are delivered to him. Put options are only exercised when it is advantageous for the holders to do so. This will be when they can use the option to sell their assets at a higher price than would be otherwise available in the market.

### 7.3.5 Summary

To summarise, options writers, in return for receiving a premium, run very large risks. This is similar to the role undertaken by insurance companies. For a relatively modest premium, they are willing to insure your house against fire, but if your house burns down, they will be faced with a claim for many thousands of pounds. The reasons why insurers and options writers enter into such contracts are that houses do not often burn down, and markets do not often rise or fall substantially.

If writers price options properly, they hope to make money in most instances. Options writing is not for the faint hearted, nor for those without substantial resources. This said, many conservative users do write options as part of strategies involving the holding of the underlying asset. Such strategies are **covered** (as opposed to **naked**) and much less risky. We discuss these later.

When investors buy or hold options, the risk is limited to the option's premium. If the market moves against them, they can simply decide not to exercise their options and sacrifice the premium. Remember, options holders have the right, **but not the obligation** to buy (call) or sell (put). If it does not make sense to buy or sell at the exercise price, the holder can decide to **abandon** the option.

### 7.3.6 The simple uses of options

#### Buying a call

##### Introduction

This strategy is motivated by a view that an asset's price will rise.

**Risk** – The investor's risks are limited to the premium he pays for the options. So, if the 80 call could be bought for a premium of 5, this 5 is all he risks. The premium of the call option will only be a fraction of the cost of the underlying asset, so the option can be considered less risky than buying the asset itself.

Whilst this is true, remember that the whole premium is at risk and it is easy to lose 100% of your investment, albeit a relatively small amount of money.

**Reward** – The rewards from buying a call are unlimited. As the contract gives the holder the right to buy at a fixed price, this right will become increasingly valuable as the asset price rises above the exercise price.

Imagine an investor who buys one XYZ call option which gives him the right, but not the obligation, to buy the XYZ asset at a fixed price of 80 between now and the option's expiry date in January. The cost of this option is 5.

If the asset price rises to 120, the right to buy at 80, i.e. the premium of the 80 call, must be worth at least 40. The net profit for the call would be 35 (40 – 5). Of course, if the price of XYZ falls below 80 at the option's expiry date, the 80 call will be worthless and 100% of the initial 5 invested will be lost. This loss occurs because no sensible person would want the right to buy at 80 if they could buy the asset more cheaply elsewhere.

### Graphically

By using graphs, we can show how much an option will be worth at expiry.

On the vertical axis of the graph is profit/loss and on the horizontal axis is the asset price.

**Holder of 1 XYZ January 80p Call – Premium 5p**

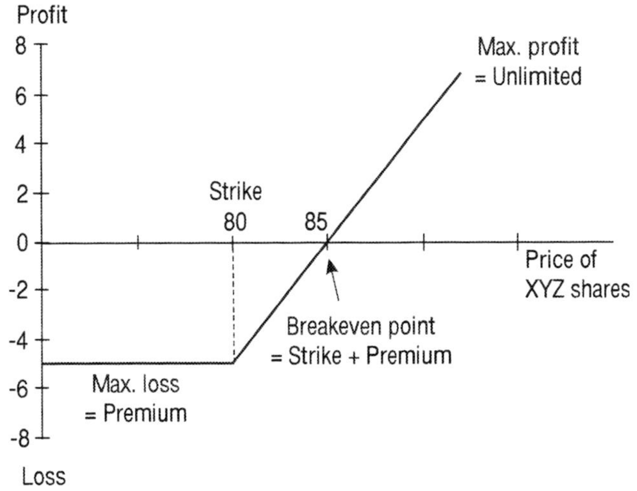


What the graph shows is that losses of 5 are made anywhere below 80, whilst profits emerge above 85. 85 which represents the **breakeven** point. This is the point at which the original investment is recouped and it is calculated by simply adding the premium to the exercise price, e.g. 80 + 5 = 85. The buying of a call to open a position is known as a 'long call'.

## Selling a call

### Introduction

**Risk** – The selling or writing of a call without, at the same time, being in possession of the underlying asset, is extremely risky. The risk is unlimited because the writer has a duty to deliver the asset at a fixed price regardless of the prevailing asset price. As the share price could, in theory, rise to infinity, the call writer assumes an unlimited risk. This strategy is sometimes called naked call writing and as it suggests, can leave you feeling very exposed.

**Reward** – You might ask why someone would assume such an unlimited risk. The answer, of course, is the hope of a profit. The maximum profit the writer can make is the premium he receives. Let us look again at an 80 call with a premium of 5. The seller of this call will receive the 5 premium, and providing the asset price at expiry is less than 80, no-one will rationally want to exercise the right to buy. The graph for selling a call is set out below. You will see that it is the equal and opposite of buying a call.

#### Graphically

**Writer of 1 XYZ January 80p Call – Premium 5p**

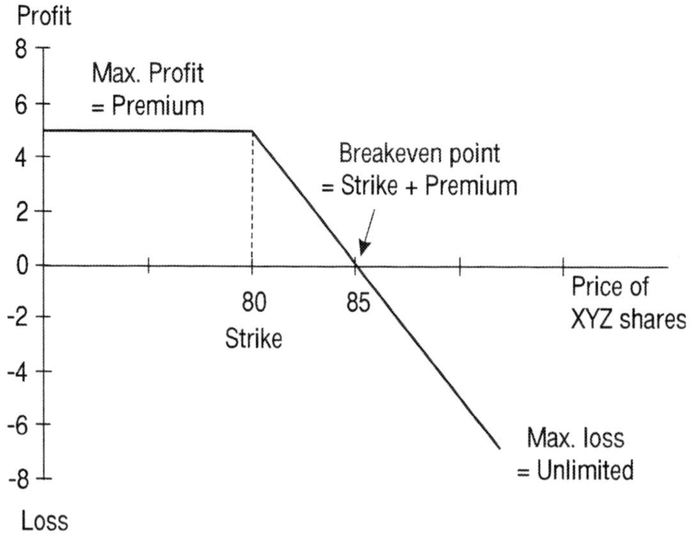


As the graph demonstrates, the call writer believes that the asset price is likely either to stay the same or fall. If this happens, the writer simply pockets the premium received and will not have to deliver the asset. The selling of a call to open a position is known as a 'short call'.

### Buying a put

#### Introduction

**Risk** – As when buying a call, the risk is limited to the premium paid. The motivation behind buying a put will be to profit from a fall in the asset's price. The holder of a put obtains the right, but not the obligation, to sell at a fixed price. The value of this right will become increasingly valuable as the asset price falls.

**Reward** – The greatest profit that will arise from buying a put will be achieved if the asset price falls to zero.

#### Graphically

**Holder of 1 XYZ July 80p Put–Premium 8p**

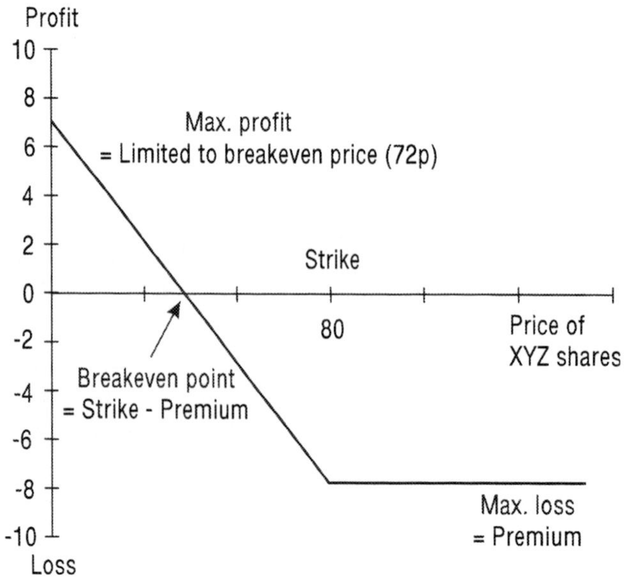

The breakeven point, and maximum profit, is calculated by deducting the premium from the exercise price, e.g. 80 – 8 = 72. Like the purchase of a call, the premium needs to be recovered before profits are made. The buying of a put to open a position is known as a 'long put'.

### Selling a put

#### Introduction

**Risk** – The selling of a put is dangerous, as the writer enters into an obligation to purchase an asset at a fixed price. If the market price of that asset falls, the put writer will end up paying a large amount of money for what could be a valueless asset. The worst case will arise when the asset price falls to zero. If this happens, the loss will be the exercise price less the premium received.

**Reward** – What the put option writer hopes for is that the put will not be exercised. This will occur if the asset has a price above the exercise price at expiry. The maximum reward is the premium received. The selling of a put to open a position is known as a 'short put'.

#### Graphically

**Writer of 1 XYZ July 80p Put -Premium 8p**

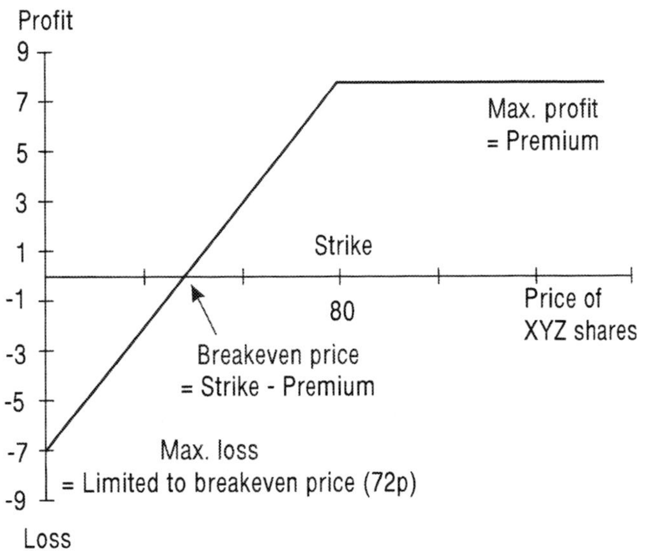


The four basic strategies outlined above form the building blocks of the more complicated option techniques. You should ensure that you are clear about three things.

- What is the motivation behind each trade?
- What are the risks associated with them?
- What are the rewards?

## 7.4 Credit default swaps

The credit default swap is the core credit default instrument. If a bank was to make a loan to a borrower the bank would be able to collect interest on the loan in return for taking on the counterparty credit risk. However, the bank may not want to take on board this credit risk and want to offset it in some way. This is where the credit default swap (CDS) comes into play.

The CDS allows the bank to find someone who is willing to take on this risk and enter into a transaction with them. Under the CDS the bank pays the investor a fee. In return the investor agrees to indemnify the bank against losses if the company fails to pay the interest on its loan or goes into bankruptcy.

The CDS is therefore enabling the transfer of default risk. The buyer of the protection (the bank) pays a fee (the premium) which is normally expressed as a number of basis points per annum. In the example above the asset was a loan, but it could have been a bond or even a swap. In effect a CDS acts like a put option.

Various default indices have been created to track the performance of credit default swaps. These include the CDX US investment-grade index which tracks the cost of debt insurance for a portfolio of investment grade companies in the US. There is also a CDX.EM Diversified index, which was launched in 2005, and monitors 40 equally weighted sovereign and high quality emerging market corporates. In Europe there is an iTraxx Crossover index tracking 50 European corporates, many of which are junk rated. All of these help investors gauge the relative risk within their respective markets.

Over the last decade, credit derivatives have boomed, in part because of the benefits they offer to lenders and investors. They enable lenders and investors to take the credit risks they want and largely eliminate the risks they do not want. Furthermore, they diffuse credit risks across markets and reduce risk concentration by putting such risks in the hands of those who want (and are better equipped) to take it on.

However, with the benefits come risks. In particular, a credit derivative's ability to manage risk depends on markets staying relatively liquid, even in periods of stress. Events throughout 2007 showed this will not always be the case.

## 7.5 Basis

**Basis** is the term used to describe the numerical difference between a cash price and a futures price. Basis is normally quoted as the futures price minus the cash price.

**Formula to learn**

Basis = Futures Price – Cash Price

Let us look at the following example.

Cash price = £120

Price of July future = £125

The basis is therefore

£125 – £120 = £5

Although cash and futures prices generally move broadly in line with one another, the basis is not constant. During some periods, cash prices move faster than futures. At other times, futures outpace the cash market. For this reason, futures hedges are sometimes less than perfect.

This movement in basis is brought about by a variety of factors. Most important is the relationship between supply and demand. Under normal conditions, futures prices, at least those of physical commodities, are higher than cash prices. Where this occurs, the market is said to be in **contango**.

However, this normal or contango situation in which futures prices are higher than cash prices can be radically altered if there is some short-term lack of supply. If, for example, there is very little zinc available for delivery, the price demanded for what little is available can be very high indeed. Markets in which futures prices are lower than cash prices are said to be in **backwardation**. The terms 'contango' and 'backwardation' are not used in all markets. Sometimes, when futures are higher than cash prices, the market is said to be at a **premium**; when futures are lower than cash, it is said to be at a **discount**.

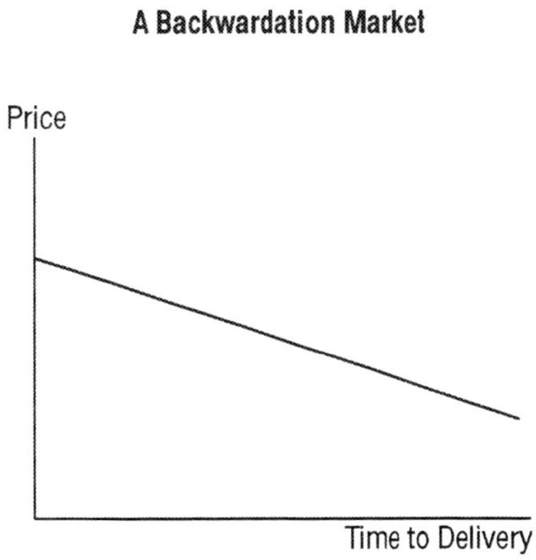


## 7.6 Interaction between debt securities

Learning objective

**7.1.5 Assess** the interactive relationship between different forms of fixed interest securities and the impact of related events on markets.

The US house price boom of the early part of the 21st century stopped around 2006-07 and prices began to fall. One knock on consequence of this was a rise in the number of house owners who had taken out 'subprime' mortgages who began to default on their repayment obligations. As these mortgages began to default a knock on consequence was that concerns rose as to the true value of collateralised mortgage obligations (CMOs) which relied on mortgage payments being made. As confidence in the market in mortgage backed securities fell, so confidence in those banks who held large quantities of such bonds likewise fell, leading to a credit crisis in western banking.

The market in fixed interest securities is one which relies on confidence that repayment will be made as predicted. Credit rating agencies offer the service of rating debt securities to predict the probability that a default may occur. The pricing of debt securities and their consequent bond yields are a factor of the perceived risks of the bonds so where the uncertainty increases in future risk of default increases, bond yields increase and the cost to borrowers rises.

The European debt problems of 2011- have arisen as a consequence of market uncertainty as to the ability of a number of a number of Euro zone countries to repay their borrowings. This has led to the yields demanded by lenders to certain Euro zone members rising steeply. The resulting market concerns about banks in the member countries holding sovereign debt which may default together with the structural links between Euro zone countries requiring potentially large payments to cover losses made in the default of other member countries have threatened the continued existence of the Euro currency and the uncertainty in the market has continued to make future borrowings difficult. The Euro debt crisis which has its roots in fixed interest sovereign borrowing has an on-going effect on the real economy and threatens the economic growth of the majority of European economies.

# Chapter Roundup

## Fund Management

- Fundamental analysis focuses on identifying the intrinsic value of stock using techniques such as discounting future cash flows.
- Technical analysis, also known as Chartism, looks at past price movements in trying to establish future performance.
- Strategic asset allocation is the first step in the asset allocation process and is the allocation of funds between various financial markets based on their returns, risks and correlations.
- Market timing involves the short-term variation of the asset allocation in order to take advantage of market changes or fluctuations.
- Stock selection strategies may take a passive approach or an active approach. Passive approaches include buy and take hold strategies and indexation.
- Top down = Strategic asset allocation then stock selection.
- Bottom up = Select stocks first, asset allocation results.
- Active management = Regularly trading within the fund in order to enhance returns.
- Passive = Establish and maintain a policy (assumes market are efficient and hence active trading incurs dealing costs at no benefit).
- Mixed (active + passive) = Core and satellite or portfolio tilting.
- SRI
  - Negative screening = avoiding certain activities.
  - Positive screening = supporting certain activities.
  - Engagement – enter into dialogue with companies in order to encourage certain behaviour.

## Fixed Income Techniques

- Riding the yield curve = invest in a bond whose term exceeds the term of the liability when there is an upward sloping yield curve in order to enhance returns.
- Anomaly switch = Switching between bonds with similar characteristics in order to take advantage of price anomalies.
- Policy switch = Switching between dissimilar bonds to take advantage of anticipated changes.
- Immunisation = Invest in a bond whose duration matches the term of the liability to guarantee the portfolio terminal value irrespective of interest rate movements.
- Contingent Immunisation = actively manage a fund to enhance returns but immune to guarantee the financial value if the return falls below a floor level.
- Cash flow matching = Invest in a bond/bond portfolio whose cash flows exactly match the scale and timing of fund liabilities.
- Immunisation and cash flow matching are both ways of matching future liabilities.
- Credit risk management = Analysing a portfolio's credit exposure and altering holdings/using CDSs to achieve on acceptable level of risk.


BPP LEARNING MEDIA

### Return measures

- Holding period return

  $$r_p = \frac{D + V_e - V_s}{V_s} \times 100\%$$

  and this total return can be decomposed into an income and a gain component.

# Test Your Knowledge

*Check your knowledge of the chapter here, without referring back to the text.*

1. What is a weakness of the holding period return?

2. An analyst believes that a firm's dividends will grow at 8% p.a. indefinitely. If the current share price is £4.60, and last year's dividend, which has just been paid, was 20 pence per share, what is the expected annual net holding period return?

3. A US investor buys €1 million at an exchange rate of $1.50: €1 to the dollar to hold for six months in an account yielding 3% p.a. If the euro are sold at the end of the period at an exchange rate of $1.40:€1, what is the dollar holding period return?

4. A firm has just paid a dividend (net of tax) of 20 pence per share. An analyst believes that the firm's dividends will grow at 6% per annum forever. If the current share price is 300 pence, what is the expected annual net holding period return?

5. What is the aim in riding the yield curve?

6. A liability is due in five years. Using immunisation, what duration bond, or weighted duration for a bond portfolio, is required to try and meet this liability?

7. What is a risk when immunising?

8. Name two approaches that combine active and passive management.

9. Describe the nature of technical analysis.

# TEST YOUR KNOWLEDGE: ANSWERS

1. It does not allow for cash flows made between the start and end dates of the calculation.

   **(See Section 6.1.2)**

2. Holding period return = $\frac{(460+20)\times 1.08-460}{460}$ = 0.1270 ie 12.70%

   **(See Section 6.1.1)**

3. Cost at the start at \$1.50:€1.00 = \$1,500,000

   Value at end

   | | |
   |---|---|
   | – € Capital | 1,000,000 |
   | – € 1 interest (1.5%) | 15,000 |
   | | €1,015,000 |
   | – Dollar value at \$1.40:€1.00 | \$1,421,000 |

   Holding period return = $\frac{1,421,000-1,500,000}{1,500,000}=-0.0527$

   **(See Section 6.1.1)**

4. Holding period return = $\frac{Ve-Vs}{Vs}$

   Current cum-div price = 300 + 20 = 320

   Cum-div price in one year = 320 × 1.06 = 339.2 (growth 6% p.a.)

   Holding period return = $\frac{339.2-300}{300}$ = 0.131 or 13.1%

   **(See Section 6.1.1)**

5. To obtain a higher return by buying longer dated bonds. This strategy only works with an upward sloping yield curve.

   **(See Section 5.6.1)**

6. Five-year duration.

   **(See Section 5.4)**

7. Non-parallel shifts in the yield curve.

   **(See Section 3.4.2)**

8. Core and Satellite funds and fund tilting.

   **(See Section 3.3.3)**

9. Technical analysts, rather than looking at the fundamentals of the economy, look to the pattern and trading history to determine the appropriate strategy to adopt.

   **(See Section 1.5.2)**

# 8

# Investment Selection and Administration

## INTRODUCTION

Investment management is the process of managing assets on behalf of institutional and private investors. Before investing it is important for the portfolio manager to identify the objectives and constraints of the client.

Asset allocation, market timing and stock selection all contribute to the overall performance of the portfolio. Stock selection approaches consist of both active and passive approaches.

The day to day requirements of managing a portfolio, involve constant monitoring plus an awareness of all changes occurring in the wider environment.

### CHAPTER CONTENTS



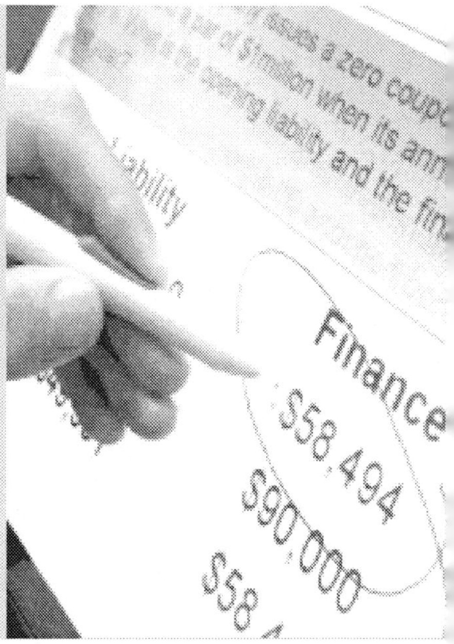

# Chapter Learning Objectives

## investment Selection and Administration

### 8.1 Investment Selection

**8.1.1 Apply** a range of essential information and factors to form the basis of appropriate financial planning and advice for clients:

- Financial needs, preferences and expectations
- Income and lifestyle – current and anticipated
- Attitude to risk
- Level of knowledge about investments
- Existing debts and investments

**8.1.2 Analyse** and select strategies suitable for the client's aims and objectives in terms of:

- Investment horizon
- Current and future potential for capital protection, growth and yield
- Protection against inflation
- Risk tolerance
- Liquidity, trading and ongoing management
- Mandatory or voluntary investment restrictions
- Impact of tax
- Impact of fees and charges

**8.1.3 Analyse** and select investments suitable for a particular portfolio strategy:

- Direct holdings, indirect holdings and combinations
- Role of derivatives
- Impact on client objectives and priorities
- Balance of investments

### 8.2 Administration and Maintenance

**8.1.1 Apply** key elements involved in managing a client portfolio:

- Systematic and compliant approach to client portfolio monitoring, review, reporting and management
- Selection of appropriate benchmarks to include market and specialist indices, total return and maximum drawdown
- Arrangements for client communication

**8.1.2 Apply** measures to address changes that can affect a client portfolio:

- Client circumstances
- Financial environment
- New products and services available
- Administrative changes or difficulties
- Investment-related changes (e.g. credit rating, corporate actions)
- Portfolio rebalancing
- Benchmark review

# 1 Financial Planning and Advice

Learning objective

**8.1.1 Apply** a range of essential information and factors to form the basis of appropriate financial planning and advice for clients: Financial needs, preferences and expectations, Income and lifestyle – current and anticipated, Attitude to risk, Level of knowledge about investments and Existing debts and investments.

Investment management involves the investment of a client's assets in order to meet a number of key objectives. The objectives will vary from investor to investor and, consequently, the process of investment management must start with a detailed consideration of the client's objectives.

## 1.1 Client objectives

Any individual is likely to have a number of **objectives**, for which some financial provision may be required. Having a particular view of risk does not imply that the same attitude to risk should be applied to all of the individual's objectives. An individual might have investments that they wish to use for specific purposes or objectives and which they cannot easily afford to bear a great degree of **shortfall risk**. In such cases, the individual may wish to choose low risk investments, so that they can be reasonably certain that their objective will be achievable by the desired date. Examples of such purposes or objectives could include:

- Saving for a deposit on a house
- Payment of a child's school fees
- Payment of university costs
- Provision to cover care of a baby
- Replacement of a car
- Increase net wealth

The same individual who has investment objectives such as those above might have other possibilities in mind for which the person would be prepared to tolerate a higher level of risk. The objective may be seen as less essential to the individual, and may be something that the person accepts that they will have to do without if investment returns are not sufficient. Examples of purposes or objectives for which an individual might typically be prepared to take on higher risk could include:

- Purchase of a vintage car
- A second home
- The possibility of an early retirement
- A 'dream' holiday

Of course, every individual is different, and the ways in which people rank their objectives and their risk tolerance in relation to different objectives vary. For one person, having enough money to spend on a comfortable home may take a higher priority than having the funds to travel widely. Another person may treat travelling as a higher priority than spending on a home. In general, the objectives that an individual sees as having the highest priority are those for which they will want to take the lowest risk if they are investing to achieve those objectives. Lower priority objectives can generally be more easily foregone if investments suffer losses.

## 1.2 The fact find process

Key to the assessment of the affordability, therefore, is the client's current personal and financial circumstances which may be determined through the fact find.

The fact find will seek to establish both personal and financial information. **Personal information** detailed in the fact find would, for a retail client, include family names and addresses, dates of birth, marital status, employment status and tax status. **Financial information** would include current income and expenditure levels, levels of savings and investments, the scale of any financial liabilities (usually mortgages, loans and credit cards), the existence of any life assurance policies and pensions etc.

The client will have much of this information easily to hand, however certain information may need to be obtained from third parties. For example, the current performance and value of any pension schemes or life policies such as endowments will probably need to be obtained from the relevant pension fund manager or life assurance fund manager. The overall financial plan will need to take account of any payments that are committed to such funds, any receipts that may be expected from them and whether it is worth considering changing providers. Other areas that may be considered at this stage are current mortgage terms and the terms of other loans as it may again be appropriate to refinance at better rates.

In order to obtain this information from a third party, the fund manager will require a **letter of authority** from the client that authorises the release of the information. Such enquiries typically take several weeks to get resolved and may cause a substantial delay in finalising the fund investment plan.

The objective information regarding the client's personal and financial situation may be referred to as **hard facts**. One final aim of the fact find will be to seek to understand the more subjective information that may be relevant, such as client aspirations, risk tolerances and any other subjective factors such as their attitude towards issues such as socially responsible investment. This subjective information may be referred to as **soft facts**. Understanding such soft facts requires face-to-face meeting with the client to discuss and consider the issues alongside them. Establishing a client's risk tolerance, for example, is far from straight forward as standard risk measures are far from familiar to most retail clients. The approaches are covered below.

## 1.3 Quantifying and prioritising client's objectives

The first stage is to determine all of the objectives that the client is looking to meet and to prioritise and quantify those objectives, especially quantifying any liability targets since they will invariably be the top priorities. From a priority viewpoint, this will clearly be specific to and determined by the client.

Factors that are liable to be relevant in here include:

Client personal facts

- Age and life expectancy
- Family situation and dependents
- UK residence and domicile status that are essential for the consideration of tax

Client financial information:

- Current net worth
- Holdings of cash reserves and other liquid investments
- Levels and types of insurance cover

Client views and opinions:

- Psychological make-up, especially from the point of view of risk
- Any beliefs (ethical or religious) that may impact on the management of the fund

For private individuals these return objectives may be classified under various headings such as:

- **Total return** – a long-term investor looking to maximise the total return, ie the combination of capital gains and reinvested income.

- **Capital growth** – a long-term fund aimed at maximising capital gains and the ultimate capital value. Such an approach would be sensible for a pension fund where no fund withdrawals will be required until the individual retires.
- **Income** – a fund designed to concentrate on the generation of income, though this should not be at the expense of the capital value.
- **Capital preservation** – a fund for a risk-averse investor who wishes to minimise the potential for any loss in the real value of his fund.

## 1.4 Affordability of client's objectives

Based on the quantification, the fund manager will be able to determine any lump sum or annual contributions that needs to be paid into the fund in order to establish the required pool and at this stage the issue of affordability needs to be considered. Affordability is the primary issue since if a client cannot afford a proposal then it is not suitable.

If the current assets and/or disposable income of the client are more than sufficient to meet the liability needs then the surplus funds are available for (return maximising) savings. If, on the other hand, there is a deficit or shortfall then the client's targets and, potentially, priorities will need to be reconsidered.

## 1.5 Client's risk tolerance

There are two approaches that a fund manager will utilise in order to get an understanding of the client's risk tolerance, specifically the fact find soft facts discussion and undertaking a review of any current investments. Since a full appreciation of risk is essential to how the fund is managed, the fund manager will investigate both.

The process will probably start with a review of the client's current investments and risks, which will clearly illustrate the client's historical attitude to risk. As we noted above, however, risk tolerance changes over time, so this historical information, while a very useful insight, is not of itself sufficient for a full understanding of the client's risk tolerance.

To augment this, the fund manager will also undertake the fact find soft facts review. The standard fact find approach is to ask the client to select a mix of, say, equities and bonds, to give an idea of the normal mix (and hence risk) that the client wishes to face. We noted above that as part of the fact find process the fund manager will illustrate various possible asset allocations and discuss in detail the potential returns and risks of each. Such targeted discussions should enable the manager to get an understanding of the client's general risk tolerance. The fund manager will also be looking to establish limits for each asset class, maximum and minimum holdings of the different assets available, representing investment risk limits.

Different firms have different descriptions for the risk levels that are appropriate for different investors. The scale of risk as appropriate to different investors could be divided up as:

- **Cautious** – The most appropriate investments are deposit based investments where capital is secure even if it means giving up potential growth.
- **Cautious/Medium** – A balance of investments is appropriate, offering some security with potential for long term growth/ income. The capital value can go up and down. • **Medium** – A balance of investments is appropriate, offering a wide spread of investment with potential for long-term growth/income. The capital value can go up and down.
- **Medium/Adventurous** – At this risk level, there is a narrower spread of investment in such areas as UK shares and international shares. The value of the funds can go up and down.

- **Adventurous** – This category of risk level involves investing in areas considered to be specialised, with a correspondingly high degree of volatility.

An adviser will assess the appropriate level of risk in discussion with the client, having ascertained by interview the client's various circumstances, level of experience as an investor, and attitudes.

### 1.6 Clients' ethical preferences

There may be a number of clients who have strongly held preferences for investments which satisfy certain strongly held ethical (or religious views).

Clients may aim to promote certain desirable attributes such as investing in environmentally friendly industries, or socially beneficial firms. There may be a screening process, either negative or positive which removes possible investments in companies considered undesirable (perhaps tobacco or armaments) or positively in favour of other companies such as renewable energy companies. Other funds invest only in companies which are in line with the investors' religious views.

## 2 Client Strategies

**Learning objective**

**8.1.2 Analyse** and select strategies suitable for the client's aims and objectives in terms of: Investment horizon, Current and future potential for capital protection, growth and yield, Protection against inflation, Risk tolerance, Liquidity, trading and on-going management, Mandatory or voluntary investment restrictions, Impact of tax and Impact of fees and charges.

### 2.1 Investment horizons

The time horizons for the attainment of the return, or the matching of the liabilities, will clearly influence the types of investments that will be worthwhile for the fund.

A fund whose purpose is to meet some liabilities in, say, two years' time, may find that the investment vehicle is low coupon gilts. This will especially be the case if the client is a high rate taxpayer as he will be able to benefit from a tax-free capital gain on these gilts at redemption.

For a fund that has liabilities to meet in 20 years' time, such investments would be inappropriate.

The time horizon will also influence the level of risk that can be taken in order to achieve the objectives. As we saw earlier, a fund with a long-term time horizon can probably stand a higher risk, as any poor returns in one year will be cancelled by high returns in subsequent years before the fund expires. Clearly, this sort of risk cannot be taken in a very short-term fund which may only span a couple of years and, therefore, may not have counterbalancing good and bad years.

Broadly speaking, the requirements of clients fall into one of two categories, those who seek:

- To maximise their returns, i.e. positive net worth individuals looking for a portfolio to match their risk/return preferences.
- To match liabilities, e.g. pension funds, where the aim is to match assets and liabilities or minimise any mismatch.

## 2.2 Return maximisation

Given the choice, most investors would elect to have a high performance fund with minimal risk. However, this is not achievable and some trade-off between the two will have to take place. Understanding this **risk/reward trade-off** is crucial to understanding the overall objectives of a return maximising fund and then to establishing the policy of a fund. Lower risk aversion or greater risk tolerance results in:

- Greater allowable portfolio risk.
- Greater potential gains (and losses).

The primary concern in this type of fund is, therefore, to fully understand the client's risk tolerance, be they private or institutional clients.

## 2.3 Liability matching

The only way to guarantee the matching of any liability is through investment in government bonds where the income and capital inflows exactly match those liabilities. If the return from bonds is insufficient to achieve this required return then we must use other assets. The result of the use of other assets is that we may achieve the higher return required. However, the risk associated with the use of these other assets means that the liabilities may not be exactly met – there may be a mismatch. Once again, a key requirement here will be to establish the clients attitude to risk, though here we have more specific financial objectives to meet, i.e. a future liability to satisfy.

## 2.4 Mixed requirements

For most institutional clients the primary requirement will be quite clear cut, for example collective investments are generally return maximising funds whereas pension funds are liability driven as we discuss later. For many private clients, however, the requirements may be more mixed. A wealthy private client may have certain liabilities to meet such as paying for children's/grandchildren's school and college fees, repaying loans/mortgages or providing financial protection for relatives/dependents, but may wish that any 'spare' resources be managed to maximise returns. There are, therefore, a number of stages that need to be undertaken when considering client objectives.

## 2.5 Liquidity needs

Within any fund there must be the ability to respond to changing circumstances and, consequently, there needs to be a degree of liquidity. Government fixed interest instruments can guarantee a tranche of the investment portfolio which will give easy access to cash should the fund need it. In general, exchange-traded investments (equities and bonds) tend to be highly liquid while investments that are not exchange-traded, such as property, have low liquidity.

Individual investors will generally keep a certain amount of their assets in the form of cash. This allows them to react to altering investment conditions or personal needs. Certain assets such as types of insurance policy have severe penalties imposed upon the early redemption of their assets, and in planning should be made to avoid the need to redeem such assets prior to term.

## 2.6 Risk/Return relationship

Fundamental to an understanding of investment management is an appreciation of the relationship between risk and reward, that is:

High risk = High expected return

Investments offer a range of risk and return that can be summarised as follows.

| Risk | Investments |
|---|---|
| Low Risk | National Savings Certificates |
| | Bank and Building Society Accounts (Including money market deposits) |
| | Gilts Held to Redemption |
| | Gilts Sold Before Redemption (Here, there is the risk of a fall in the value of the stock) |
| | Local Authority Issues |
| | Corporate Bonds |
| | (Dependent on the credit rating) |
| Medium Risk | Life Assurance Policies |
| | Unit and Investment Trusts (Obviously, certain schemes, carry greater risk than others) |
| | Shares and Property (Ranging from 'blue chips' to penny shares in small dynamic companies) |
| | Commodities and collectibles |
| High Risk | Warrants, Futures and Options |
| | (However, there is only a limited risk in purchasing an option or a warrant since, here, only the premium can be lost) |

Before offering any investment advice, it is vital to ensure that the risk and returns match the customer's criteria. These assets can be sub-categorised between:

- **Nominal** – those whose returns are fixed in value irrespective of future inflation, e.g. money market instruments and bonds.
- **Real** – those whose returns vary as we experience inflation, e.g. index linked gilts, shares, property, commodities, collectibles.

## 2.7 Mandatory or voluntary investment restrictions

Obviously, when constructing a portfolio for any investor, the manager should consider the preference and legal constraints that may exist. The regulatory framework adopted in the market needs to be adhered to. For collective investment schemes in the UK, there are certain investments into which the fund may not invest, such as derivatives.

Equally, a **trust deed** may exist which binds the investment manager to invest in certain securities and, consequently, the manager must abide by this trust document. Where there is no trust deed, the **Trustee Act 2000** provides guidance on the appropriate mix of investments. This places a duty of care on the trustees to exercise reasonable care in investments.

Investors may also have particular requirements in line with their ethical or religious views. Socially Responsible Investing (SRI) is a term used to describe an investment approach that integrates personal values and social concerns into the investment decision-making process.

Socially responsible investment allows the investor to bring together his values and beliefs with his financial requirements. This allows an investment to be made, for profit, but with principles.

The main approach of SRI is investment **screening**. This can involve either negative or positive screening, where certain investments can either be screened out or screened in, depending upon their social and environmental position.

Secondly, there is **active engagement**, where investors enter into a dialogue with a company with a view to understanding and potentially changing their behaviour. This form of **shareholder advocacy** will then assist the company in improving their social and environmental performance.

## 2.8 Impact of tax

Taxation is a consideration for all investment managers. The investment portfolio and the strategy adopted must be consistent with the fund's tax position. In some cases, such as pension funds, the fund does not suffer taxation. For these **gross funds** the manager should, normally, avoid those stocks which involve the deduction of tax at source. For, even though it may be possible to reclaim any tax suffered, the fund will have incurred the opportunity cost of the lost interest on the tax deducted. The use of tax free investment measures such as Individual Savings Accounts (ISAs) in the UK may well be employed by investors.

It might seem that, the answer to the question: 'who is liable to UK tax?' is simply UK citizens, and to a very large extent this is true. There are many different countries in the world, each with their own tax rules and regulations and chiefly the citizens of any one country pay tax in that country and no other.

However, complications arise when the citizens of one country work in, own assets in, or live in another country.

Depending on the exact circumstances, that citizen may be subject to tax in his 'home' country, in the foreign country, or even in both (though in this last situation the individual may be able to claim double tax relief as noted above with the result that they are only taxed once).

With respect to UK tax, whether an individual or whether a part of their revenue or capital is subject to UK taxes is determined by their:

- **Residence** – an individual may be non-resident, resident or ordinarily resident for tax purposes. In addition, residence is not unique and, as noted below, an individual may be resident in more than one country. The rules on residency are detailed, but the general idea in UK terms is that:

  An individual is resident in the UK for a tax year if:

  - He is present in the UK for 183 days (i.e. six months) or more
  - He makes substantial annual visits to the UK averaging 91 days (i.e. three months) or more a year, for each of four or more consecutive years, ignoring days spent in the UK due to circumstances beyond the individual's control (e.g. illness). He will be resident for each of these tax years. For someone leaving the UK, the four years are reduced to three.

- **Domicile** – an individual may be domiciled in just one country so will either be domicile or non-domicile for UK tax purposes. An individual's domicile is the country which they regard as being their permanent home. This will usually be the country in which the individual is a citizen or national, but this is not necessarily the case as domicile is distinct from nationality or residence. A person may be resident in more than one country, but can be domiciled in only one country at a time. The original domicile acquired by an individual is at birth and is usually that of his father's domicile (or that of his mother if his father died before he was born or his parents were unmarried at his birth) and therefore not necessarily the country where he was born. This is referred to as the individual's **domicile of origin**.

A person retains this domicile until he acquires a different **domicile of dependency** (if, while he is under 16, his father's domicile changes) or **domicile of choice**. A domicile of choice can be acquired only by individuals aged 16 or over.

## 2.9 Fees and charges

Different investments incorporate different levels of cost and inevitably this will be a factor that influences overall portfolio design. If an investment is intended only for the short term, any significant initial costs may seriously erode or even eliminate any potential returns. If on the other hand, longer term investments should have time to recoup initial charges and the level taken into account in any recommendations.

A look at the example of Unit Trust charges:

Charges made for the investment in a fund such as a unit trust would be taken to cover:

- Managing the fund
- General administration
- Administration of the fund
- Direct marketing costs
- Marketing
- Commissions for intermediaries
- Regulation and compliance costs

These charges are generally made in one of three ways, via an initial charge, an exit charge or through annual management charges.

The initial charge is added to the buying price. So the buyer incurs the cost of both the bid-offer spread and also the initial charge.

Exit charges may be applied where investors sell the investment within a set period of time e.g. within a five year period.

The annual charge is likely to be between around 0.5% - 1.5%. It may be that a part of the annual management charge will go towards paying a renewal commission to intermediaries.

Costs will vary from fund to fund no matter the general fund structure with funds such as offshore funds having higher charges and tracker funds requiring less management and costs having generally lower fees.

Potential additional costs in addition to those owed to a fund would include dealing charges paid to a broker. Stamp duty is paid on many investments. Payments made to financial advisors, which may be taken either upfront or in the form of a rebate on the commission paid. Where tax wrapper products such as ISAs are used, administration charges may be made.

## 2.10 Inflation

From a quantification viewpoint, the fund liabilities may include such factors as school/college fees, loans, dependent pensions etc, and a primary consideration here will be whether those liabilities are nominal or real. A **nominal liability** is one that is fixed in monetary terms irrespective of future inflation. An example of a nominal liability would be a bank loan or mortgage where the monetary sum borrowed must be paid off at the end of the term and does not alter with inflation over that time. In contrast, a **real liability** is one which changes in monetary terms as we experience inflation.

Real Interest rates are approximated as:

**Real Interest rate = Nominal interest rate - Inflation**

Where the real interest rate reflects the increase in spending power experienced by the investor and the nominal interest rate is the quoted return. Where the inflation rate is higher than the nominal rate, the investor experiences negative returns.

For example, in order to maintain a standard of living a pension needs to pay out the same amount each year in real terms, i.e. a rising monetary amount to cover the impacts of inflation, and this sum needs to be paid for the remaining life from retirement – an indeterminate term. Insurance companies however will see nominal liabilities not necessarily impacted by inflation, life insurance will have long term investment horizons, while general insurance with its higher liquidity needs will see the need for shorter term low risk investments. Whatever the liability, assessment will involve a **present value analysis** of the anticipated future liabilities that the fund is aiming to meet. For example, to pay a pension of £20,000 pa for a period of 20 years when real returns (asset returns in excess of inflation) are 3% will require a fund value at retirement of almost £300,000 and so we would be looking to achieve this fund value at the retirement date.

# 3 Portfolio Strategies

Learning objective

8.1.3 **Analyse** and select investments suitable for a particular portfolio strategy: Direct holdings, indirect holdings and combinations, Role of derivatives, Impact on client objectives and priorities, Balance of investments

## 3.1 Direct Investments

There are a great variety of possible investments which may be used to match up to the requirements of clients; a summary of those available is given below:

- **Variable interest cash deposits** – provide capital protection and a small return, however they tend to offer a poor long-term return, especially in times of high inflation.
- **Government fixed interest securities** – provide a safe nominal return and are therefore suitable for satisfying nominal liabilities. They perform well when interest rates are falling but poorly when they are rising. Volatility is low but increases with longer-dated issues.
- **Corporate fixed interest securities** – provide a nominal return, though the security of this return depends on the credit risk of the issuer. Again, they perform well when interest rates are falling but poorly when they are rising. Volatility is fairly low for high quality issues but can be high for poorer credit ratings.
- **Index-linked securities** – provide a safe real return, hence protect income and capital against the effects of inflation. The coupon level tends to be very low, reflecting the safety of the issues.
- **Equities** – provide a long-term real return, but offer little security. Both income and gains tend to grow over time with equities performing particularly well when the economy is booming. They can, however, perform poorly or even fail completely in harder economic circumstances so must be regarded as high risk.
- **Property** – like equities, property provides a long-term real return, but property slumps demonstrate that this return is not without risks. Property markets and equity markets tend to show little correlation so property offers some diversification benefits to a portfolio looking for a real return, its low liquidity and problems of management are its biggest drawbacks.
- **Commodities** – again provide a long-term real return, but offer little security. Commodities pay no income but gains tend to grow over time. Commodity markets also show little correlation to equity markets so, once again, offers some diversification benefits to a portfolio looking for a real return.

## 3.2 Asset classes and the business cycle

The first three of these asset classes are nominal returning assets which are of use for satisfying nominal liabilities. For example, if you wish to save to pay off a mortgage (a nominal liability) then investing in bonds may be appropriate. The maturity value of these investments will largely be immune to the effects of inflation or deflation unless it brings into question the potential of default. The interest paid on variable interest cash deposits will vary as interest rates vary in an effort by the Central Banks to control inflation, though it will not affect bond income. In times of inflation, then, an investment in a nominal asset will lose value in real terms. Conversely, in times of deflation these nominal returning assets will gain in real terms. Looking long term, however, all economies tend to experience positive inflation and hence an investment in these assets should be expected to lose real value in the long term. The last four categories are real returning assets that are suitable for matching real liabilities such as a pension. The values of, and returns from, real returning assets are very much affected by, and correlated to, inflation/deflation. An investment in real returning assets is optimal when the economy is improving or booming when corporate performance is maximised. The various assets perform differently at varying stages of the economic cycle and so any strategic asset allocation cannot be simply determined and set in stone.

## 3.3 Indirect investments

Indirect investment provides a low cost route to a professionally managed diversified fund for small investment levels with the advantage of there being no CGT liability to the investor until the fund is sold (irrespective of the trading within the fund).

### 3.3.1 Advantages and disadvantages of indirect investments

There are advantages and disadvantages of indirect investment, as compared with direct investment.

| Advantages of indirect investments | Disadvantages of indirect investments |
|---|---|
| An individual can invest relatively small amounts, perhaps on a regular basis. | The individual can only choose baskets of investments selected by fund managers, not by himself, and this will not suit all investors. |
| The pooling of investments enables the fund to make purchases of securities at lower cost than would be possible for an individual. | Although the individual does not have to pick individual securities, he still has to choose the fund manager, and different managers' performance can vary widely. |
| The time involved in directly managing one's own portfolio is saved. | Although 'star' fund managers can have a successful track record with a fund, such 'star' managers may switch jobs, making future management of the fund less certain. |
| The funds are managed by professional fund managers. A fund manager with a good past performance record may be able to repeat the performance in the future. | Larger collective funds find it more difficult to invest in shares of companies with a relatively small capitalization, because of the small quantities of stock available. |
| A wide diversification between different shares and sectors can be achieved: this can be impractical and costly in dealing charges for a small portfolio held by an individual. | Successful collective funds investing in smaller companies can become a victim of their own success if more funds are brought in, as a greater fund size can make it more difficult for such a fund to follow their successful strategy. |
| Risk is reduced by exposure to a widely diversified spread of investments in the underlying portfolio. | |

| Advantages of indirect investments | Disadvantages of indirect investments |
|---|---|
| Specialisation in particular sectors is possible. | |
| The investor can gain exposure to foreign stocks, which can be costly and inconvenient for an individual who holds shares directly. | |
| Different funds provide for different investment objectives, such as income or growth, or a combination of both. | |
| There is no capital gains tax payable when the fund trades in shares, (as would be the case with direct investment), CGT only arises for the investor when the fund is sold. | |

### 3.3.2 Combination of direct and indirect holdings

A combination of direct and indirect holdings may well be employed. This should be done with a view to maintaining appropriate diversification, and the levels of risk and return required by the investor.

## 3.4 Asset allocation

Asset allocation is generally considered to be the most significant decision made by an investment manager. It involves deciding which of the major asset classes to invest in and to what proportion of each the investment should be made. i.e. investment into bonds or shares

Portfolio managers tend to use either a top-down or a bottom-up approach to the investment process.

### 3.4.1 Top-down approach

The investment manager using a top-down approach first allocates his assets based on the objectives and constraints of the fund and then selects individual securities to satisfy that allocation. The most important decision in this approach is the choice of markets and currencies. Once these choices have been made, the manager then selects the best securities available.

### 3.4.2 Bottom-up approach

The manager using a bottom-up approach studies the fundamentals of many individual stocks and constructs a portfolio from the ones he considers best satisfy the fund's objectives and constraints. The product of this approach is a portfolio with a market and currency allocation that is more or less the random result of the securities selected. This approach is appropriate when the manager is more concerned with risk exposure in various sectors than with either market or currency risk exposure.

### 3.4.3 Consequences of the choice of approach

The approach adopted will have an impact upon the organisation of the department. A research department using a top-down approach focuses on country and currency analysis primarily. Such a department will therefore be specialised by country. Financial analysts using the bottom-up approach are specialised by worldwide industry sector.

Empirical evidence has shown that all securities within a single market tend to move together, but national markets and currencies do not. This appears to demonstrate that the major factor contributing to portfolio performance is the choice of markets and currencies (asset allocation), not the individual securities (stock selection). This, in turn, suggests that an investment organisation should be organised along primarily top-down lines with its analysts specialised by country, with possibly a few international sectors such as oil stocks.

Where a top-down approach is adopted, investment management involves three activities.

- Asset allocation.
- Market timing.
- Stock selection.

This top-down approach is the one we concentrate on below since it is drawn directly from a consideration of the clients' objectives and circumstances

### 3.4.4 Market timing – tactical asset allocation

Strategic asset allocation discussed above is the asset allocation that the fund should operate with in the long term (on average) in order to satisfy its objectives and constraints. The strategic asset allocation is based on long-run estimates of capital market conditions; it ignores short-term fluctuations on the premise that markets are efficient in the long term. As such, the strategic asset allocation is inherently based on the Efficient Market Hypothesis.

Market timing (or tactical asset allocation) involves the short-term variation of the asset allocation of the fund in order to take advantage of market changes or fluctuations. Market timing implies that asset classes are mispriced and looks to take advantage of this mispricing in order to enhance returns. As such, market timing assumes that markets are not efficient in the short term and may overreact to information.

Market timing is the variation of the asset allocation of the fund in anticipation of market movements. It involves adjusting the sensitivity of the portfolio to anticipated market changes. A fund manager engages in market timing when he does not agree with the consensus about the market, i.e. he is more bullish or more bearish than the market, and rebalances his portfolio to take advantage of this view.

In determining the strategic asset allocation it is normal to specify a range of values the fund can move from the strategic allocation, e.g. the tactical asset allocation limits my be that we can vary up or down by 4% from the strategic limits. The scale of any permitted variation is usually linked to the liquidity and transaction costs of the asset class, more liquid and lower transaction cost assets being allowed a greater degree of flexibility.

The approach to market timing is to adjust the $\beta$/duration of the portfolio over time. If the fund manager is relatively bullish, he wants to increase the $\beta$/duration of the portfolio, i.e. make it more aggressive. If, on the other hand, the fund manager is more bearish, he will want to reduce the $\beta$/duration of the portfolio, making it more defensive.

One way of achieving this result would be to buy high $\beta$ shares or high duration bonds in a bull market and sell them in a bear market. However, the transaction costs involved would make this an expensive strategy. An alternative is to keep the portfolio of risky assets constant and raise or lower the beta or duration through the use of derivative instruments, such as futures and options.

In summary, the action is

- **Falling market** – reduce the sensitivity to the market fall, through
  - Switching from sensitive (high $\beta$/duration) stocks to less sensitive (low $\beta$/duration) stocks.
  - A derivatives overlay, such as selling futures or buying put options.
- **Rising market** – increase the sensitivity to the market rise, through
  - Switching from insensitive (low $\beta$/duration) stocks to more sensitive (high $\beta$/duration) stocks.
  - A derivatives overlay, such as buying futures or buying call options (if these are permitted for the fund).

Many fund managers become involved in market timing. For example, pension funds have regular inflows from their clients that the investment manager may decide to

- Invest immediately, in which case the fund will benefit from pound cost averaging, i.e. the purchases are made at both the peaks and troughs throughout the year, hence the fund acquires the investments at the average cost for the year – a passive strategy; or
- Delay his investment (i.e. hold cash as an asset) and time his acquisitions in the hope that it will be the most favourable price – an active strategy.

### 3.4.5 Importance of market timing

As noted earlier, studies have shown that the asset allocation decision has a greater effect on performance than stock selection for most funds, especially international funds where the correlations between markets are low.

It follows that achieving the correct strategic allocation, and responding correctly to market movements with an appropriate tactical move should be the primary objective of most fund managers in order to maximise their funds' returns.

## 4 Use of Derivatives

Another approach is to develop a mixed active-passive strategy involving options and futures. Fund managers may have a passive portfolio of cash market securities that are not traded because of the high transaction costs involved. Instead, the fund managers trade individual stock options.

Portfolio insurance allows an investor to limit the maximum potential loss of a portfolio. Two basic approaches are the use of the covered call and the protective put.

### 4.1 Covered calls

| | |
|---|---|
| **Strategy 7** | Covered Call |
| **Motivation** | Normally Neutral Subject to Strike. |
| **Construction** | Long position in stock and sale of call. If call sold is out-of-the-money, the trade is bullish; if at-the-money, call is sold, trade is neutral; if in-the-money, call is sold, trade is bearish. |
| **Comments** | Very familiar investment strategy that can enhance returns in static markets, whilst also providing limited protection against falls. (Protection = Call premium). The trade is commonly used by fund managers who already hold a stock, but are neutral about the share's prospects in the short term. To enhance the returns over any dividend flows, they sell the call and thereby receive premium. In doing this, they effectively give up their opportunity to profit if the share unexpectedly rises above the exercise price. |
| **Example** | BUY ABC STOCK @ 99.07, SELL 100 CALL @ 0.98 |

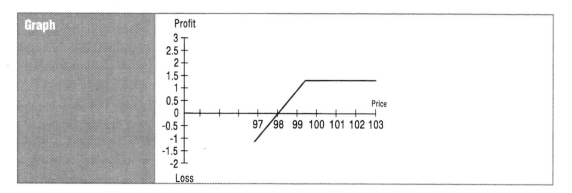

| | |
|---|---|
| Graph | 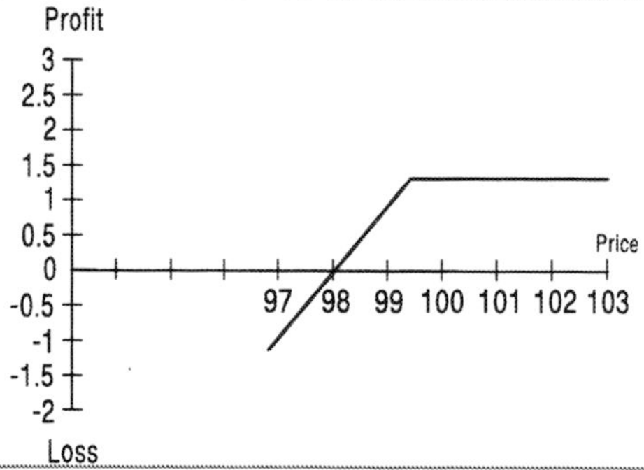 |



## 4.2 Protective puts

| | |
|---|---|
| Strategy 8 | **Protective Put** |
| Motivation | Directional, bullish, but with limited downside risk |
| Construction | Long position in stock/future and purchase of put. |
| Comments | Classic options hedge of long position in underlying; protects downside but allows profit if market advances. More flexible and thus more expensive than short hedge with futures. If we use an out-of-the-money put then losses will be incurred until the price falls to the strike price. Any further price falls on the asset will be offset by gains on the put, providing the desired hedge. |
| Example | BUY STOCK @ 99, BUY 100 PUT @ 6 |
| Graph | 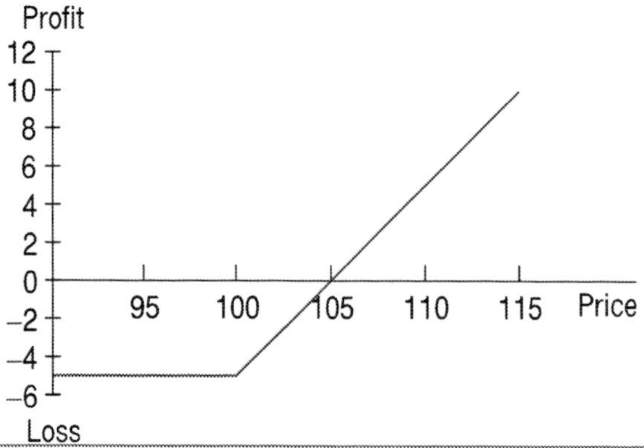 |



# 5 Administration and Maintenance of a Portfolio

**Learning objective**

**8.2.1 Apply** key elements involved in managing a client portfolio: Systematic and compliant approach to client portfolio monitoring, review, reporting and management, Selection of appropriate benchmarks to include market and specialist indices, total return and maximum drawdown, Arrangements for client communication

## 5.1 Monitoring review and reporting

### 5.1.1 Investment policy or investment strategy statement

The manager's responsibility is to ensure that she has fully understood the client's objectives and constraints and that she professionally manages the fund to achieve those objectives.

The objectives and constraints of the fund lead the fund manager to consider a variety of strategies or possible asset allocations, and within these to select specific stocks that meet the fund objectives. The fund manager will be judged by her performance with regard to the objectives of the fund and, in the highly competitive world of fund management, an under-performing manager will not be given many second chances.

Once the objectives and constraints of the particular fund have been established, the next stage is to develop the investment policy/strategies that will be used in order to achieve these objectives. All these considerations will be detailed as recommended investment policy/strategy options. These recommendations must then be submitted to the client for approval. In simple situations there may be one obvious approach for the manager to adopt, in more complex situations; several alternatives may be presented to the client forming the basis of a discussion leading to the finally agreed investment policy/strategy statement. The resultant investment policy/strategy statement forms the basis of the management approach. This strategy will detail the long-term strategic asset allocation options selected to achieve the client's objectives. Asset allocations should not, however, be set in stone. Different asset categories perform better in different economic situations and the fund manager must be ready to respond to such circumstances. Along with the long-term strategic asset allocation, the strategy may also detail market timing/tactical asset allocation options that may be adopted by the fund in those differing circumstances. The strategy details asset allocations and limits but will not detail stock or product recommendations.

### 5.1.2 Benchmarks and peer group benchmarking

Finally, the investment strategy will probably detail any performance benchmarks against which the fund performance is to be assessed. It is common to employ peer group benchmarking, which allows investors to compare the performance of a particular fund to that of a similar fund with similar asset allocation, to the one in question. The use of such peer benchmarks has at times been criticised, by such industry commentators as Paul Myners. (See below).

Comparison could either be with an index benchmark such as the FTSE 100 or with Private Investor Indices such as the FTSE APCIMS (Association of Private Client Investment Managers and Stockbrokers) indexes. The FTSE APCIMS indices were introduced as a result of the need for a guide as to how an individual investor should approach evaluating performance of their own portfolio. There are three indices, and they are based on the assumption of domestic investors with sterling denominated account.

- FTSE APCIMS **Stock market Growth Portfolio Index** – aiming for growth/capital appreciation from predominantly equity investments
- FTSE APCIMS **Stock Market Income Portfolio Index** – aiming for income from predominantly equity and fixed interest investments.
- FTSE APCIMS **Stock Market Balanced Portfolio Index** – aiming for a balance between growth and income.

The general aim of these indices is to allow investors to compare performance of their portfolio to industry averages, and as such to gauge the performance of their discretionary fund managers.

### The Myners Report

In 2001 the Myners review by Paul Myners, stated a degree of concern regarding the use of benchmarks. 'many objectives are set which give managers unnecessary and artificial incentives to **herd**. So called "peer group" benchmarks, directly incentivising funds to copy other funds, remain common. And risk controls for active managers are increasingly set in ways which give them little choice but to cling closely to stock market indices, making meaningful active management near-impossible'.

He made a number of recommendations amongst which were that: 'In consultation with their investment manager, funds should explicitly consider whether the index benchmarks that they have selected are appropriate. Where they believe active management to have the potential to achieve higher returns, they should set both targets and risk controls that reflect this, allowing sufficient freedom for genuinely active management to occur.'

### 5.1.3 Performance appraisal

Once we have established a suitable benchmark we can appraise the fund manager's performance by reference to it. The benchmark performance can be quite simply calculated as the weighted average of the holding period returns on the relevant benchmark indices.

## Example

A pension fund manager has a portfolio with an initial value of £100m. The company for whom the fund is run is internationally based with 80% of its employees in the UK and 20% in the US. As such, it requires a corresponding international investment strategy concentrating on a diversified spread of shares.

The company feels that the fund manager should be able to at least match the following two indices on the relevant portions of the fund.

- FTSE 100 Index on the UK portion.
- S&P 500 Index on the US portion.

The values on these indices at the start and end of the year were

| | FTSE 100 | S&P 500 |
|---|---|---|
| End of Year | 4520 | 1000 |
| Start of Year | 4000 | 920 |

The fund had a capital value of £113m at the end of the year, there having been no cash inflows and outflows during the year. What return has the fund manager achieved, what return has the benchmark portfolio achieved and has the fund manager achieved his target of at least matching the benchmark?

### Solution

#### Fund performance

Since there have been no cash inflows/outflows during the year, we can use the simple holding period return formula to assess the fund performance, giving

$$r = \frac{D + V_e - V_s}{V_s} \times 100$$

Gives

$$r = \frac{0 + £113m - £100m}{£100m} \times 100 \; = +13\%$$

#### Benchmark performance

FTSE 100 Index

$$r = \frac{4520 - 4000}{4000} = 0.13 \text{ or } 13\%$$

S&P 500 Index

$$r = \frac{1000 - 920}{920} = 0.087 \text{ or } 8.7\%$$

Weighted average

$r = (80\% \times 13\%) + (20\% \times 8.7\%)$

$r = (0.8 \times 13\%) + (0.2 \times 8.7\%) = 12.14\%$

### Appraisal

| | | | |
|---|---|---|---|
| **Portfolio Performance** | +13.00% | +0.86% | **Outperformance** |
| **Original Benchmark Performance** | +12.14% | | |

The fund manager has achieved a return of 13% against the benchmark portfolio return of 12.14%. Hence, the fund manager has achieved his target of outperforming the benchmark, his performance being 0.86%.

Note, however, that this conclusion is only truly valid so long as the total return achieved was at no higher a level of risk than that of the underlying index. If this actual return has been achieved at a significantly elevated level of risk, this conclusion would be invalid.

In addition, no account has been taken of currency effects in this example.

### Maximum drawdown

When considering the performance of a portfolio, measurement of the yield as described above is a significant consideration, but so also is the maximum difference between the highest and lowest value of investment in a given time period. This measure is often given as a percentage. A high level of drawdown will therefore be an indication of high risk for the investor.

## 5.1.4 Review

The final stage of the investment process is to evaluate whether the fund is achieving its objectives through a consideration of its performance. Fund performance should be reviewed no less than once a year, certainly more regularly for short-term funds, and will look to achieve a number of objectives.

- **Client circumstances** – we should look first to determine whether any client circumstances have altered as this may result in an alteration of the client's objectives. Any significant changes may require a modification to the investment strategy.
- **Performance review** – we need to monitor the performance of the fund against the selected benchmark to ensure that it is achieving its objectives.
- **Portfolio rebalancing** – following on from the performance review we should consider whether there is any need to update the agreed asset allocations. Care needs to be taken here in respect of the tax liabilities that may arise from the effects of any rebalancing.

The fund management process cannot, however, be thought of as a step-by-step process that finishes at this stage, rather it is an on-going process. This review will establish the strategy for the next period and the process will continue.

Throughout this process there are, however, a number of considerations that must be kept in mind in carrying out this fund management process. These include:

- Should the fund management be conducted on an active or a passive basis?
- Should fund management be conducted top-down or bottom-up?
- Should the fund manager be conducting a value or growth style of management?
- Should the fund be directly or indirectly invested?

## 5.1.5 Client communication arrangements

Depending upon the agreed requirements of the client the means and regularity of reporting will vary.

Regulators require that any communications with clients be fair, clear and not misleading, as is appropriate and proportionate considering the chosen means of communication and the information to be conveyed.

**Learning objective**

**8.2.2 Apply** measures to address changes that can affect a client portfolio: Client circumstances, Financial environment, New products and services available, Administrative changes or difficulties, Investment-related changes (e.g. credit rating, corporate actions), Portfolio rebalancing and Benchmark review.

## 5.2 Changes in circumstances

The portfolio should be regularly reviewed to ensure that it remains suitable for the investor.
Factors to consider include:

- Whether any loan stocks or gilts are coming up for redemption
- Whether the investor's tax position has changed and how this might affect the tax efficiency of the portfolio
- Whether the investor has any needs for cash in the short term
- Whether the balance of the portfolio has shifted and is still appropriate (e.g. is the portfolio now overweight in equities and in need of more gilts)
- Use of the benchmark indices may provide a comparison from which the investors can review the asset allocation and structure of their portfolio with their broker.

### 5.2.1 Changing client circumstances

All of the factors used in constructing a portfolio may each alter in time. This might be due to alterations in time horizons, changes to tax status, different liabilities to those originally thought of and so on. Any changes would require that the portfolio be adjusted accordingly, to match needs.

### 5.2.2 New products and changes in financial environment

The financial services sector has demonstrated its constant ability to innovate. Considerable numbers of original products are offered each year and investors will consider altering their portfolio to make use of these products. Alterations to the taxation environment will require investors to consider their portfolio and instruments allowing tax management such as any increase in the Individual Savings Account (ISA) rules should also be considered.

## 5.3 Portfolio re-balancing

A portfolio will require re-balancing periodically either due to changes in client requirements or because the economic conditions have altered. By constantly reviewing economic conditions and client objectives appropriate asset allocation can be maintained.

Where portfolio managers believe that an active policy can outperform a passive policy they may employ one of a number of tactics.

### 5.3.1 Bond switching

Bond portfolio adjustments involve the purchase and sale of bonds, i.e. switching or swapping of bonds. There are two main classes of bond switches.

- Anomaly switches

- Policy switches
- Inter-market spread switch

### 5.3.2 Anomaly switching

An anomaly switch is a switch between two bonds with very similar characteristics, but whose prices or yields are out of line with each other.

### 5.3.3 Substitution switching

The simplest example of an anomaly switch is a substitution switch. This involves the temporary exchange of two bonds that are similar in terms of maturity, coupon, quality rating and every other characteristic, but which differ in terms of price and yield. Since two similar bonds should trade at the same price and yield, this circumstance results in an arbitrage profit opportunity with the expensive bond being sold and the cheap bond purchased initially.

If the coupon and maturity of the two bonds are similar, then a substitution swap involves a one-for-one exchange of bonds. However, if there are substantial differences in coupon or maturity, then the duration of the two bonds will differ. This will lead to different responses if the general level of interest rates changes during the life of the switch. It will, therefore, be necessary to weight the switch in such a way that it is hedged from changes in the level of interest rates but is still exposed to changes in the anomalous yield differential between the bonds.

### 5.3.4 Pure yield pickup switch

Another type of anomaly switch is a pure yield pickup switch. This involves the sale of a bond that has a given yield to maturity and the purchase of a similar bond with a high yield to maturity. With this switch, there is no expectation of any yield or price correction, so no reverse transaction will need to take place at a later date, which may be the case with a substitution switch.

### 5.3.5 Policy switching

A policy switch is a switch between two dissimilar bonds, which is designed to take advantage of an anticipated change in

- Interest rates
- Structure of the yield curve
- Bond quality rating
- Sector relationships

Such changes can be expected to lead to a change in the relative prices and yields of the two bonds. Policy switches involve greater expected returns, but also greater potential risks than anomaly switches.

### 5.3.6 Changes in interest rates

A market timer will always be on the lookout for changes in interest rates. Switching from low-duration to high-duration bonds if interest rates are expected to fall is an example of a policy switch.

### 5.3.7 Changes in bond quality ratings

A bond whose quality rating is expected to fall will fall in price. To prevent a capital loss, it can be switched for a bond whose quality rating is expected to rise or remain unchanged.

### 5.3.8 Changes in sector relationships

An example of a change in sector relationships is a change in taxes between two sectors. For example, one sector may have withholding taxes on coupon payments, e.g. domestic bonds, whereas another, e.g. Eurobonds, may not. If it is anticipated that withholding tax will either be applied to all sectors or will be withdrawn from all sectors, then another switch is possible.

### 5.3.9 Inter-market spread switching

Investors may switch between gilts and comparable corporate bonds, where the spread between the two indicates that one or the other is under-priced. The yield curve may give an indication of future interest rate changes. From this an investor may take a view of the markets and attempt to anticipate moves to or away from the gilt markets and buy or sell accordingly.

## CHAPTER ROUNDUP

- For private individuals, their return objectives may be classified as:
  - Total return
  - Capital growth
  - Income
  - Capital preservation
- The Ethical preferences of clients may be accommodated by a fund which may:
  - Negatively screen out undesirable funds (e.g. arms funds)
  - Positively screening to select desirable investments (e.g. renewable energy funds)
  - Screen for firms with strong corporate government
- Client strategies for selecting investments should take account of:
  - Their required investment horizons
  - Risk tolerance
  - Liabilities to be paid by the investments
  - The need for liquidity
  - Any voluntary or mandatory restrictions imposed
  - The impact of taxes and charges
- A clients investment horizon indicates the length of time that an investment may be invested , it may be that a liability must be met on a particular date and the value of the investment on that date must be considered carefully.
- Return maximisation must be considered in terms of the risk of the investment.
- Where a client requires their investments to be liquid, it is important that they may be redeemed without significant loss at short notice.
- The term SRI refers to Socially Responsible Investing.
- Real Interest rates = nominal interest rate – Inflation rate.
- Direct investments may be made into investments such as cash deposits, fixed interest investments, equities, properties and commodities. It is important that investors consider the need to diversify appropriately. They will also require advice if not already expert, in the investment field.
- Indirect investments may be made via the various collective investment vehicles on the market such as Unit trusts and OEICs, which employ investment professionals to undertake investment decisions, charges may be costly however. Indirect investments may well be already diversified.
- Top down asset allocation involves an investment process in the following order:
  - Asset allocation
  - Market timing
  - Stock selection
- Market timing involves the short term variation of the asset allocation of the fund in order to take advantage of market changes (e.g. investing in higher beta stock in a rising market).
- Covered call option strategies, or protective puts, may allow a degree of to portfolio insurance.
- Benchmarks are widely used to measure the returns of a fund as compared to an index or their peers.

- Peer benchmarking compares the performance of a fund to that of a similar fund.
- The final stage of the investment process is to evaluate whether the fund is achieving its objectives.
- Fund review concerns looking at whether the fund has achieved a number of objectives an whether changes may need to be made:
  - **Client circumstances** –look first to determine whether any client circumstances have altered as this may result in an alteration of the client's objectives.
  - **Performance review** – we need to monitor the performance of the fund against the selected benchmark to ensure that it is achieving its objectives.
  - **Portfolio rebalancing** – following on from the performance review we should consider whether there is any need to update the agreed asset allocations.

# TEST YOUR KNOWLEDGE

*Check your knowledge of the chapter here, without referring back to the text.*

1. What are the advantages of indirect investment in terms of diversification and taxation?

2. List three examples of direct investments.

3. List the three stages of top-down approach to investment management, in order.

4. An investor in bonds would switch to (high or low) duration bonds if they believe that interest rates are about to rise?

5. Describe the nature of a protective put?

6. What does APCIMS stand for?

7. Give some of the of the processes which should be undertaken as a part of a fund review?

8. Describe the nature of anomaly switching?

9 Describe the nature of a policy switch?

# Test Your Knowledge: Answers

1. Indirect investment offers broad diversification potential even for small investment. With direct investment, CGT would be payable as a result of any trading within the fund, with an indirect investment CGT only arises when the fund is realised.

   **(See Section 3.2)**

2. Direct investments might include such assets as cash deposits, fixed income securities, equities, property, commodities.

   **(See Section 3.1)**

3. i Asset allocation.
   ii Market timing.
   iii Stock selection.

   **(See Section 3.3.2)**

4. Switching to low duration bonds would result in a less significant fall in the bond values when interest rates rise, which would be an example of market timing.

   **(See Section 3.5)**

5. A protective put involves the purchase of put options when holding the underlying stock. This will give a degree of insurance against falls in the stock value.

   **(See Section 4.2)**

6. APCIMS refers to the Association of Private Client Investment Managers and Stockbrokers.

   **(See Section 5.1.2)**

7. A fund review should consider:

   - Client circumstances and whether they have changed
   - Performance review of the fund and whether it is achieving its objectives
   - Whether the portfolio requires rebalancing

   **(See Section 5.1.4)**

8. An anomaly switch is a switch between two bonds with very similar characteristics, but whose prices or yields are out of line with each other.

   **(See Section 5.3.2)**

9. A policy switch is a switch between two dissimilar bonds, which is designed to take advantage of an anticipated change in

   - Interest rates
   - Structure of the yield curve
   - Bond quality rating
   - Sector relationships

   **(See Section 5.3.5)**

# INDEX